D1329229

Lucy Bland teaches Women's Studies at the University of North London and is on the Editorial Collective of *Feminist Review*. She is co-editor (with Laura Doan) of two historical books on sexology: *Sexology in Culture: Labelling Bodies and Desires* and *Sexology Uncensored: the Documents of Sexual Science*.

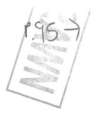

'Bland argues persuasively that feminist attitudes to sexual and re-productive issues in turn-of-the-century Britain were contradict-ory, ambiguous and unpredictable.' – *The Women's Review of Books*

'It provides readers with a great deal of important information, ranging from the character of the various Criminal Law Amend-ment Acts to the arguments of long-forgotten, important publicists. More impressively, it is accessible. Bland is witty with her pen.... As a thought-provoking, informative contribution to debates about feminism and morality, it deserves a wide audience.' – *Women: A Cultural Review*

'Providing such a precisely constructed map of the debates enables Bland to fulfil her intention of eliciting for her readers the convol-uted reality and complexity of the varied feminist positions taken with regard to questions on which we still ponder. What is the nat-ure of sexual morality? Are there gendered responses to passion? How does sexual abstinence serve feminism? Does freedom from conception award autonomy or sexual slavery?' – *Women's History Review*

'Bland wants to know how feminists were able to speak. She inves-tigates the languages and ideas they drew on and the implications of drawing on concepts and representations that were not their own, and asks whether the contradictions were too great or whether they managed to subvert those discourses to their advantage. Bland is particularly skilled at showing the contradictions they experienced when reworking profoundly masculinist discourses to accommodate women's concerns...This book is informative and elegantly writ-ten and takes on a vital issue.' – *Journal of the History of Sexuality*

'Bland is deft at showing the ways in which the various feminist campaigns cut across and often undermined one another...In a moving conclusion, she argues that this cat's-cradle of contradict-ions still tangles up feminists today – most obviously in the vexed questions of pornography and censorship.' – *New Statesman*

BANISHING THE BEAST

Feminism, Sex and Morality

LUCY BLAND

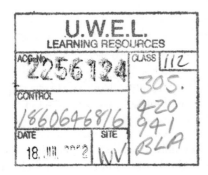
TAURIS PARKE PAPERBACKS
LONDON ● NEW YORK

Published in 2001 by Tauris Parke Paperbacks
an imprint of I.B.Tauris & Co Ltd
6 Salem Road, London W2 4BU
175 Fifth Avenue, New York NY 10010
www.ibtauris.com

In the United States of America and in Canada distributed by
St Martin's Press, 175 Fifth Avenue, New York NY 10010

First published in 1995 as *Banishing the Beast: English Feminism and Sexual Morality 1885–1914* by Penguin Books

ISBN 1 86064 681 6

A full CIP record for this book is available from the British Library
A full CIP record for this book is available from the Library of Congress

Library of Congress catalog card: available

Typeset in 10½/12pt Bembo by Q3 Book Work, Loughborough
Printed and bound in Great Britain by MPG Books Ltd, Bodmin

To my mother Deirdre with much love

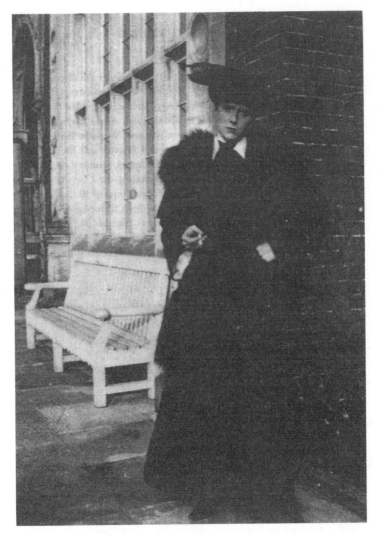

The author's grandmother, Sybil Cooper: a new woman

CONTENTS

ILLUSTRATIONS

ACKNOWLEDGEMENTS TO THE 1ST EDITION

This book has taken an embarrassingly long time to complete. Initially, I set out to write a doctoral thesis on 'Femininity in the 1950s'. I then proceeded to move ever backwards, finally coming to rest at the turn of the century. I received a book contract and the idea of a PhD temporarily faded into the background. So for a time did the book as well, as the demands of academic teaching took precedence. Later I returned to the book, and indeed the thesis too, for now it appeared to me that I could write the PhD as a dry-run for the book itself. My supervisor Richard Johnson thus deserves the first acknowledgement and heartfelt thanks. He saw me through the long, arduous process of thesis production with unfailing encouragement, patience and incisive critique. My thesis examiners, Hiranthi Jayaweera and Anna Davin, also gave useful and perceptive advice. Anna Davin, far beyond the call of duty, offered many detailed comments and suggestions, including the correction of my appalling spelling!

Numerous others have helped in different ways, through their encouragement, support, knowledge and intellectual stimulation. David Doughan of the Fawcett Library is in every feminist historian's acknowledgments! I too wish to thank him for his contagious enthusiasm and wealth of knowledge. Thanks too to the staff of the British Library, the Library of Political and Economic Science, the British Newspaper Library, Sheffield Central Library, the Library of the Wellcome Institute for the History of Medicine, and the Manuscripts Room of University College Library. Norma Clarke read the entire thesis; Catherine Hall, Mariana Valverde, Angela McRobbie, Frank Mort, Deirdre Inman, Dave Phillips, Charlotte Brunsdon, Paula Krebs, Helen Crowley, John Tosh, Lorraine Gamman, Joy Dixon, Micky Burn and Susie Balfour have all read one or more chapters in draft and I am grateful for their helpful comments, encouragement and sound advice. Judy Greenway has been very generous in the time given to reading more draft chapters than I would care to remember. She has always been enormously supportive and her knowledge of the period has been invaluable. Martin Durham has likewise read nearly every chapter, been consistently enthusiastic, encouraging and helpful, and offered to undertake the generous and Herculean task of proof-reading the entire thesis manuscript.

Thanks to Liz Stanley for sharing her ideas and information on Olive Schreiner, and to Hilary Frances for doing likewise with Edith Watson. Thanks too to Wendy Bradshaw for her supportive friendship, to Charlotte Brunsdon for invaluable discussions about the processes and agonies of writing, and to Arthur Hill for much needed rock-climbing diversions. At Penguin's, my commissioning editor Margaret Bluman not only displayed the greatest patience and tolerance at the non-completion of the book, but remained helpful and enthusiastic throughout. I thank her for her confidence in my ability. Thanks too to Jennifer Munka for her meticulous copy-editing and to Linda Rozmovits for the excellent index.

Finally, my deepest thanks to Dave Phillips for all his encouragement and support. When we first met, the book was supposedly about to be finished; only three and a half years later did the long, creaky process come to a close. His belief that I could and finally would manage to complete made it all seem possible, just as doubts were beginning to set in.

For the use of the picture of Edith Lanchester, many thanks are given for the permission granted by The Motion Picture and Television Fund of Woodland Hills, California.

Banishing the Beast was first published in 1995 (with a slightly different sub-title) by Penguin Books. In the intervening six years there
has been a proliferation of excellent studies of turn of the century
feminism, including feminist engagement with issues of imperialism.[1]
There have also been a number of important historical texts on sexuality, sexology, social purity, sexual abuse and prostitution.[2] Despite
this valuable new scholarship, I would suggest that there has been
nothing to date which has substantially challenged the main arguments of *Banishing the Beast* or rendered them obsolete. However this
is not to argue that further research is not needed. The relationship
between turn of the century British feminism's concern with sexuality, and issues of nation, race and imperialism, requires detailed study.
The beginnings of such an investigation are seen in Antoinette
Burton's pivotal text *Burdens of History*[3], while Philippa Levine's
forthcoming book on gender, race, empire and prostitution will make
a further significant contribution. But analyses of the ways in which
Empire impinged upon, and were reflected in, British feminists' views
of sexuality, are still underdeveloped. It is to be hoped that future research will be undertaken along these lines.

Finally, I wish to thank Lesley Hall for suggesting the republica-
tion of this book to I.B. Tauris, and Philippa Brewster for her
enthusiatic response.

1 For example, Kumari Jayawardena *The White Women's Other Burden,* Routledge
   1995; Clare Midgley (ed.) *Gender and Imperialism*, Manchester University Press
   1998; Julia Bush, *Edwardian Ladies and Imperial Power*, Leicester University Press
   2000; Antoinette Burton (ed.) *Gender, Sexuality and Colonial Modernities*,
   Routledge 2000.
2 For example, Shani D'Cruze *Crimes of Outrage*, UCL Press 1998; Lucy Bland and
   Laura Doan (eds.) *Sexology in Culture,* Polity Press 1998; Angus McLaren *Twentieth
   Century Sexuality,* Blackwell 1999; Sue Morgan *A Passion for Purity: Ellice Hopkins
   and the Politics of Gender in the Late Victorian Church*, University of Bristol 1999;
   Paula Bartley *Prostitution: Prevention and Reform in England, 1860–1914*, Routledge
   2000; Louise Jackson *Child Sexual Abuse in Victorian England*, Routledge 2000; Lesley
   A. Hall, *Sex, Gender and Social Change in Britain since 1880*, Macmillan 2000; and
   a 2nd edition of Frank Mort *Dangerous Sexualities*, Routledge 2000, with a new
   introduction and useful extensive additional bibliography.
3 *Burdens of History: Feminists, Indian Women, and Imperial Culture, 1865–1915*,
   University of North Carolina Press 1994.

In 1911 feminist Lucy Re-Bartlett prefaced her book *The Coming Order* with the following allegorical narrative:

> Once upon a time there was a terrible dragon which held the whole countryside in terror, for it devoured the men, and the women, and even the little children. And though many knights went against it, none could slay it. Instead it vanquished all of them, killing some outright, and sending others back to their villages wounded and with a terrible fear in their hearts. And this fear spread among the others of their village, until all at length believed the dragon to be unconquerable. Then a child came forward – a girl child. 'I will go against the dragon,' she said . . . She armed herself with no shield or sword, for in her heart was a conviction . . . that the power of the dragon was largely illusion, and that it was <u>fear</u> which had destroyed all the knights . . . Presently she reached a cave where the monster often dwelt, and he was there, and heard her coming, and rushed out, belching fire upon her as he advanced. But the little girl stood firm and felt not even a sensation of fear, so great was that conviction in her heart. And sure enough, though the flames encircled her as the monster drew near, they did not scorch or hurt her in the least . . . And the Beast, amazed at seeing her thus standing unaffected by his approach, stopped short. Then it was the little girl who moved forward – forward until she was near enough to touch the monster and gaze into its face . . . while it stood petrified. 'Who are you that terrify human beings so?' she said. 'They call you the greatest force in nature – they say you are invincible – and yet you stand thus before me.' And indeed the Beast seemed to have lost all force . . . More – it seemed to be shrinking visibly with every moment that her gaze continued . . . 'It is as I thought,' she said. 'Your power lies only in men's fears – when any human being stands upright before you, as I stand, you have no power at all.'
>
> And the Beast shivered, and bowed down before her, for indeed he felt his power broken . . . the child bound the Beast with a little sash which she wore, and led it back to the village thus . . . And then a great force sprang up among the men and women of that village – they had learnt a life-giving truth – that no brute force, no brute

force whatsoever, could stand against the human spirit when it rose.[1]

The 'beast' tamed by the girl-child (womanhood) was the 'lower self'; the metaphor was familiar currency. To rise to the 'higher self' necessitated the taming/curbing, or according to some commentators, banishing, of the 'beast within'. In the period from the 1880s to the First World War, a key attribute of this 'beast' was its selfish, egotistic, sexual lustfulness. The 'beast' supposedly lay within us all, but to many, including most feminists, it was closer to the surface in men, more contained and submerged in women. Linked to the idea of 'natural' male lustfulness was the double moral standard so hated by feminists: that lack of chastity was understandable and excusable in men, but unforgivable in a woman. Inherent to the double standard was the assumption that women were the sexual property of men.

From the 1880s onwards, the feminist demand for a single standard became central to the women's movement; as one woman expressed it: 'There is nothing in the feminist programme about which the feminist feels so keenly as the double standard of morality.' Feminists sought transformed sexual relations between men and women in which women were equal and independent and men took responsibility for changing the oppressive aspects of their sexual behaviour – their 'beast within'. Feminists wished for the eradication of women's experience of sexual objectification, sexual violence, and lack of bodily autonomy, to be replaced instead by a new sexual morality in which men lived by the same ethical precepts as women.

The taboo on speaking about sex had begun to be broken with the feminist-inspired campaign against the Contagious Diseases Acts. The Acts had been introduced in the 1860s in certain ports and garrisons in an attempt to address the problem of venereal disease among the military. They had permitted the compulsory examination, detention and treatment of suspected prostitutes. Feminists, led by Josephine Butler, opposed the state sanctioning of 'vice', restrictions on women's civil liberties and the injustice of examining the prostitute and not her male client.

After a protracted and arduous campaign through the 1870s, in which middle- and upper-class 'lady' members of the repeal campaign were regularly attacked, verbally and physically, for daring to speak on a subject so highly 'unsuitable', the Acts had been eventually suspended in 1883 and repealed three years later.[3] The courageous actions of these feminist repealers became an important heritage for subsequent suffrage agitation.

By the early 1880s the repealers had also become concerned with juvenile prostitution and what was termed 'white slavery' – the traffic in women, abducted through deception or force, for the purposes of prostitution. That the legal age of consent was thirteen meant that juvenile prostitution was not against the law: any man with impunity could engage in sex with a consenting girl of thirteen or over. In response, feminists and others had attempted to get the age of consent raised. Several versions of a Criminal Law Amendment Bill on this issue had been before Parliament since 1883, but all had failed, filibustered out. There were a number of MPs and Lords who were determined to retain their age-old prerogatives; as one member of the Lords was reported to remark: 'Very few of their Lordships . . . had not, when young men, been guilty of immorality. He hoped they would pause before passing a clause within the range of which their sons might come.'[4] In their search for something which would 'rouse the nation' into supporting the Bill, Josephine Butler, along with Bramwell Booth of the Salvation Army, visited the offices of W.T. Stead, editor of the *Pall Mall Gazette*.

W.T. Stead was the instigator of 'New Journalism', a style of narrative and sensationalist reporting which he had adopted from the popular Sunday papers and had extended to a more élite readership, exposing poverty and inequality on the one hand, generating sexual scandal on the other.[5] A supporter of feminist and radical causes, he saw himself as the people's preacher, with 'the editorial chair . . . the most powerful pulpit in which to preach'.[6] In response to Butler and Booth he undertook a six-week investigation of London's underworld, interviewing prostitutes, brothelkeepers, procuresses and other 'expert witnesses'. Drawing on the genres of melodrama, Gothic tale and pornography, he presented his findings in a series of four prurient and titillating articles entitled 'The Maiden Tribute of Modern Babylon'. The 'Maiden Tribute' referred to the ancient Greek myth in which seven boys and seven girls were sent from Athens every nine years as a tribute to the Minotaur, a monstrous creature, half-man, half-bull. In Stead's analogy, the sacrificial victims of his day were the young girls (the boys no longer featured) forced into the brothels of London and abroad. Drawing centrally on the notion of the sex-crazed 'Beast', Stead's Minotaur represented 'the foul product of unnatural lust'.[7]

Prior to the appearance of the articles, Stead whetted his readers' appetites with the following 'WARNING':

> All you who are squeamish and all who are prudish, and . . . prefer to live in a fool's paradise of imaginary innocence and purity . . . will do *well not to read the Pall Mall Gazette of Monday and the following three days.*

The articles were subdivided under various salacious headings such as: 'The Violation of Virgins', 'How Girls are Bought and Ruined', 'Why the Cries of the Victims are not Heard', 'Strapping Girls Down', 'A Child of Thirteen bought for £5'. Stead began by announcing: 'The maw of the London Minotaur is insatiable, and none who go into the secret recesses of his lair return again'. He then documented something of this 'insatiable' maw: revelations of girls

> snared, trapped and outraged, either when under the influence of drugs, or after a prolonged struggle in a locked room . . . Others are regularly procured, bought at so much per head . . . or enticed under various promises.

He had been told of the 'violation' of 'unwilling virgins, purveyed and procured to rich men', which 'although it ought to raise hell, does not even raise the neighbours'. In underground rooms, or rooms with thick walls, nightly floggings were undertaken; 'to some men . . . the shriek of torture is the essence of their delight'. It was the familiar story of debauched aristocrats ruining the 'daughters of the poor', but this time presented in more (porno)graphic detail. He heard from an ex-brothelkeeper of trips to the country disguised as a parson in order to lure girls to London. He was informed by two procuresses of the endless demand for virgins, a demand often met through the buying of girls from drunken parents in the East End.[8] To verify the ease with which young girls could be 'bought', he wrote of his actual purchase of thirteen-year-old 'Lily' (Eliza Armstrong) from her mother.[9]

The articles caused uproar – 'an Earthquake has shaken the foundations of England', according to the Bishop of Truro.[10] These 'revelations', as they were known, generated an intense, emotional response of fear (in women at least), fury and horror. The anger was at once channelled by feminists and others into the campaign for the current bill to raise the age of consent and to tighten up on procurement and 'white slavery'. A gigantic petition of nearly 400,000 signatures – two and a half miles long when unrolled – was carried from Clapton to Parliament in a carriage drawn by four white horses, draped in banners inscribed 'This Inquity Shall Cease' and 'Beware', and flanked by soldiers of the Salvation Army.[11] In August a demonstration in Hyde Park attracted nearly a quarter of a million, with feminists, socialists, trade unionists and Anglican priests walking side by side.[12] This new movement of diverse constituencies managed almost immediately to force through the Criminal Law Amendment Bill which, in addition to raising the age of consent to sixteen and tightening up the law on brothels, contained a last-minute amendment to criminalize male homosexuality.[13]

One of the more positive effects of the 'Maiden Tribute' articles and the subsequent campaign for the age of consent bill was that women felt to some degree empowered to speak on issues of sex. As one feminist expressed it:

> Things are changed now, everything lies more open, especially I think since the Pall Mall revelations, which however questionable, did I believe break down a great barrier for women – after them no one was supposed of necessity to be in ignorance.[14]

The 'Maiden Tribute' articles, along with the success of the repeal campaign against the Contagious Diseases Acts, encouraged feminists to place a number of sexual issues squarely on the agenda: firstly, changing the law in relation to sexuality – increasing the legal protection of women and girls, and amending the divorce law; secondly, consideration of how to change men's sexual behaviour and to arm women against undesired sexual encounters, thereby giving greater control to women over their own person; thirdly, discussion of what constituted sex and sexual morality, and of how relationships between men and women might be transformed. From 1885 up until 1914, such issues remained central to the feminist agenda. With the First World War came a host of changes, not least a refocusing of feminist activity; it was the end of an era for feminist sexual politics.

This book is concerned with the various and contradictory ways in which English feminists discussed and campaigned around issues of sexual morality. Part 1 examines the dominant definitions of femininity, sex and morality in order to understand the context within which feminists developed their language of political activism in relation to sexuality. Chapter One presents a narrative account of a club composed of feminist women and socialist and radical men set up in the 1880s to discuss relations between the sexes. The possibility of speaking in a mixed group about such a 'sensitive' subject was not unrelated to the effects of the 'Maiden Tribute' articles. Club debate on issues such as female chastity, the differences between male and female sexual instincts, male (ir)responsibility in sexual relations, the definition of morality, and the role of motherhood, prefigured subsequent controversies in the 1890s and 1900s arising both between the sexes and between feminists; the club can thus be seen as a microcosm of wider debates. Chapter Two contextualizes the club debate through detailed consideration of dominant definitions of femininity, sexuality and morality. This chapter also considers the feminist appropriations of these definitions – the subject positions which informed feminists in their campaigns around the double moral standard.

Parts 2 and 3 examine the key areas of feminist sexual politics: marriage, prostitution, fertility control and sex. Part 2 focuses on the beliefs and practices of feminists campaigning around issues of sexual morality in both public and private – the

feminist attempts at the 'purification' of marriage and prostitution. Feminists recognized the inter-relationship of the so-called
'separate spheres'. They were aware that women within these
two spheres – the 'public woman' (the prostitute) and the
'private woman' (the wife) – were interconnected both by the
ideology which reduced all women to mere physicality, and by
the men who passed between them, sexually serviced in one
quarter, 'morally' serviced in the other. Part 3 examines the
politics of fertility control and sex, considering feminist ambivalence towards the campaign for contraception, the contribution
of eugenics to feminist thoughts on reproduction, the consequent
contradictions around class and race, and the various feminist
debates and disputes about what constitutes sex, how sexual
relations should be transformed, and what sex should mean to
women.

The relationship of feminism to sexual morality in the late
nineteenth and early twentieth centuries has been to some extent
the subject of previous historiography. Sheila Jeffreys's *The
Spinster and Her Enemies: Feminism and Sexuality, 1880–1930* makes
an important contribution to 'reclaiming' feminist social purity
as a crucial aspect of feminist politics. The book also demonstrates
the inappropriateness of labelling these feminists as 'prudes'.
However, it 'whitewashes' the more contradictory aspects of
social purity, in particular the racist assumptions and the contribution made by social purity to the policing of the working classes.
Frank Mort's *Dangerous Sexualities: Medico-Moral Politics in England since 1830* has a different object of analysis than my own,
namely an historical investigation of the intersection of health,
morality and sexuality, but it gives some space to an examination
of feminist resistances, particularly those of social purity. While
largely in agreement with Frank Mort's excellent analysis, my
project is different in that I take these resistances as my *central*
focus. *Sexual Anarchy: Gender and Culture at the Fin de Siècle* by
Elaine Showalter makes exciting and suggestive parallels between some of our own contemporary predicaments, and those
of a hundred years ago. But the book is concerned less with
feminist politics as such, and more with the implications of
culture, particularly literary culture, for a politics of sexuality.

Judith Walkowitz's latest book, *City of Dreadful Delight*, a brilliant piece of cultural history, has as its focus 'narratives of sexual danger in late Victorian London'. While touching on some of the same concerns as *Banishing the Beast*, it sets itself a more specific remit, and a briefer historical period, namely the 1880s.

The two texts which come closest to my project are Susan Kingsley Kent's *Sex and Suffrage, 1860–1914* and Margaret Jackson's *The Real Facts of Life: Feminism and the Politics of Sexuality, c. 1850–1940*. *Sex and Suffrage* takes feminist sexual morality as its key concern. Kent's focus is on the crucial place of morality politics within the female suffrage campaign, with the feminist assault on the double moral standard as the unifying component of the women's movement. While agreeing with her general thesis, I disagree with what I would term her 'homogenization' of feminist positions. Rather than recognizing the important differences *between* feminist moral arguments, as well as the contradictions at play *within* feminist sexual moralities, she presents the feminist understanding of what constitutes an 'equal moral standard' as a unitary phenomenon.

Margaret Jackson's *The Real Facts of Life*, published as this book goes to print, argues that feminists in this period challenged the sexual basis of male power through their politicizing of sexuality. While agreeing in general with this characterization, I am in less agreement with her specific representation of these politics. Like Sheila Jeffreys's *The Spinster and Her Enemies*, and indeed Kent's *Sex and Suffrage*, Margaret Jackson completely ignores the class and race agenda of these feminists. She also sets up what I see as a false dichotomy between social purity feminists and feminists supporting sex reform. As I hope to demonstrate, many feminists moved between positions; on some occasions, where they deemed it useful, they used the language of sex reform, on other occasions they deployed a language and politics of social purity. While disagreeing with Kent's homogenization of feminists, I am in no more agreement with Jackson's (and Jeffreys's) polarization. Feminist politics were complex, contradictory, and not easily compartmentalized into two opposing camps. There was greater fluidity in positions held by feminists than seems to be appreciated by Jeffreys, Kent or Jackson.

In examining and analysing the feminist politics of sexual morality at the turn of the century, I draw frequently on biographical material. The feminists who people this book, while in no sense free agents operating upon the world at will, nevertheless made history, although not under conditions of their own making, to paraphrase Marx. My approach to these individuals is thus neither one of hagiography, nor of a crude determinism which reduces individuals simply to 'bearers' of structures. I am concerned to understand the context within which feminists thought and acted, with all the restrictions and possibilities therein.

February 1994.

PART ONE

DEBATING AND DEFINING
THE TERMS

CHAPTER I

The Men and Women's Club

I PEARSON SETS THE TONE

In November 1885, a spinster mathematics teacher wrote to a bachelor professor of applied mathematics and mechanics of her impressions on the divide between the sexes:

> Men seem to say: by long descent, by unparalleled power, by race necessity, physical instincts *must* be obeyed . . . Women . . . say: we *must* have the precious things of life; love and sympathy are a thousand times more valuable than the gratification of physical instinct . . . How must we work towards harmony?[1]

She was referring to the dominant rationale for male sexuality, namely that it was compelled by a powerful physical instinct to perpetuate the species. In contrast, she offered a feminist vision of an ideal future in which men lived by the same standards they demanded of women. In this vision, unchastity would no longer be excusable in a man, yet unforgivable in a woman; both sexes would subordinate 'the gratification of physical instinct' to 'love and sympathy'.

How was it the case that these two mathematicians – Isabella Clemes and Karl Pearson – were corresponding on such an issue? The key to the answer lies in their joint membership of a London club composed of radicals, socialists and feminists of both sexes. Formed a few months earlier that year, the club aimed to discuss 'all matters . . . connected with the mutual position and relation of men and women'. In late Victorian England, where sexuality was seen by many as 'base' and 'animal' and ignorance of women's bodies and all things concerning sex was widespread, discussion of such issues was indeed radical. There were, of course, other mixed groups of socialists and feminists in existence. The Fabian Society had been set up the year before, and the Hampstead Marx Circle had its first meeting

3

at the beginning of 1885 (starting with a reading of Marx's *Das Kapital*, vol. 1, in the French edition; it was not yet translated into English).[2] But neither of these organizations, nor indeed any other organization, was taking relations between the sexes as its object of study. Yet although radical, the club's radicalism was decidedly élitist. Only the select few were allowed within its ranks, and its objectives lay not with the practical or political application of knowledge, but with disinterested 'objective' debate.

Over its four-year life-span the club discussed a host of topics: from the position of women among early Indian Buddhists, women of old Russia, and sex relations among the Romans, through to more contentious and contemporary considerations of the sex instinct, morality, marriage, prostitution, family limitation and women's emancipation. The heart of its concern, however, lay with morality and sexuality, or rather heterosexuality, for it was this that was implicitly assumed in club discussion of sexual instinct, sexual behaviour and sexual feelings. Not only did the issues raised in the club highlight many of the difficulties feminists were having with thinking about sexual morality, especially in debate with men, but it could be argued that the club prefiguratively rehearsed some of the major struggles between feminists, as well as between men and women, which were to surface in the 1890s and early twentieth century. This was partly because several of the club members were themselves to become influential in debates about sex and morality. Thus Karl Pearson, for example, was to become a leading eugenist (an advocate of selective breeding) and writer on questions of sex difference. Olive Schreiner, another member, was already having an impact as a novelist with *The Story of an African Farm*,[3] and her later books (especially *Dreams* and *Woman and Labour*) were to be held in high esteem by many feminists. Other club members and associates were on the brink of fame and influence, as 'new woman' novelists for example. In the rehearsal of ideas and conflicts, the club can be seen as a microcosm of wider struggles already on the agenda. Careful analysis of the club offers us a useful opening to the exploration of some of the period's key issues concerning sexual morality.

The 'Men and Women's Club', as it was soon to be named, was Karl Pearson's brainchild. Pearson was a highly educated, ambitious young man of twenty-eight. He had trained as a barrister, but his additional scientific qualifications had led to his recent appointment as Professor of Applied Mathematics and Mechanics at University College, London. With the help of an older female friend, Mrs Elizabeth Cobb (the wife of a solicitor and future Liberal MP), he gathered together fourteen middle-class men and women for the club's first meeting in July 1885. As indicated, club members had been chosen with extreme care. Dr Elizabeth Blackwell was rejected for being a 'Christian physiologist'; her faith 'prostitutes the name of science', declared Pearson. She came once as a guest, however. Another woman doctor, Kate Mitchell,[4] was thought 'too unrefined', while Kate Mills, who nearly became a member, was rejected in the end due to her deafness. The chosen members were mainly freethinkers, prepared to abide by the club's constitution in discussing all subjects 'from the historical and scientific, as distinguished from the theological standpoint'.[5]

Initially, the club was composed of six men and eight women. The male members were colleagues of Pearson's, radical liberal or socialist in their politics, and employed as lawyers, doctors or university lecturers. They shared similar public-school and Oxbridge backgrounds and were further linked through membership of the same West End men's clubs: the Savile, the National Liberal Club, the Athenaeum. Two of the men were married, another married man soon joined, and a further three married during the club's four-year lifetime. In contrast, of the women members, both initial and subsequent, all but two were single, and one of these, Constance Parker, the wife of the club's president, was to cease attending almost immediately. The club's constitution announced that it would meet monthly, consist of no more than twenty members, and be composed of equal numbers of men and women. They met in each other's homes, although generally at the house of a male member, with half of the club's thirty-six meetings taking place at the house of the club's President, Robert Parker. He was a barrister living in Brunswick Gardens, Kensington, the heart of respectable London.

Many of the women felt themselves to be intellectually inferior to the men. Although a number of them were economically independent as teachers, writers or journalists, only one had been to university. They were mostly middle-aged and untrained, conscious of being outside 'the younger rising student generation'. All were feminists of one kind or another, active in philanthropy, reform and women's suffrage, with members variously involved in the Charity Organisation Society, the London School Board, the National Vigilance Association, the Fabian Society, the Ladies National Association for the Repeal of the Contagious Diseases Acts, the Personal Rights Association and the National Society for Women's Suffrage. Olive Schreiner was the only woman member with any reputation at the time (although she was to leave the club after its first one-and-a-half years), but the club's guests included Annie Besant, Jane Clapperton, Dr Elizabeth Blackwell and Eleanor Marx, all established figures within radical and feminist circles. Another two club associates – Mona Caird and Emma Brooke – were on their way to becoming well-known 'new woman' novelists.

Members' objectives

Why did these men and women wish to join such a club? The women appear to have had rather different objectives from the men. This may not have initially seemed the case. In his opening paper, Pearson quoted club member Annie Eastty (but without acknowledgement): 'There is little hope of real reforms unless men and women know one another's aims and views in detail and accept to some degree the same standard – the same ideal for the community.' As we shall see, Pearson managed to get the ideal of his choice declared the club's, but it becomes obvious that many of the women were not in full agreement. Club members clearly also wished to break down the barriers to men and women, especially *unmarried* men and women, forming friendships and freely exchanging ideas; this was generally inhibited by the middle-class etiquette of the period. Some of the members may have also seen the club as a site for meeting and courting the opposite sex outside the traditional middle-class confines of Church, chapel and family circles.[6]

Maria Sharpe, one of Elizabeth Cobb's younger unmarried sisters, had a further expectation: the club was to be 'a means of serving the women's cause'.[7] Other women seem to have thought likewise. On examining club discussion and correspondence it becomes clear that what inspired the women more than the men was the desire for transformed relations between the sexes, including a transformed sexual morality. To many of the women, Annie Eastty's hope for a common ideal that would aid reform seems to have referred to a vision of an emancipated femininity and a moralized masculinity – a 'new woman' and a 'new man'. The women hoped that the club would prove to be a site for the building of this common ideal. They were to be disappointed.

Despite the men's initial lip-service to feminism, once the women became more forthright in their views some of the men began to condemn the women's movement as individualistic and the women activists as too partisan for club participation. This was to become a point of irreconcilable tension between the sexes. So too was the men's desire to take *women* as their object of study. Maria Sharpe soon realized that while

the women ... wanted knowledge of acts generally ... the men wanted primarily to add to their knowledge a special branch, i.e. knowledge of the way in which women looked at things.[8]

Pearson indeed later confessed to Maria that his view of the club 'has always been selfish, namely a desire to understand women's standpoint and modes of thought.'[9] Unsurprisingly, this focus on women as objects of scrutiny, both in general and as participants in club discussion, dismayed many of the female members.

There was also divergence between the sexes in the club in relation to the 'Maiden Tribute' articles, which were published the week preceding the club's opening. The club could not have come at a better moment for the women whose membership was sought by Elizabeth Cobb and Pearson. Maria Sharpe wrote inquiringly to Pearson: 'I wonder if you realize how grateful many of us are for the channel which work for the club supplies us for the feelings let loose by the consideration of the late painful revelations.'[10] These 'feelings let loose' were of intense anger at the existence of such atrocities mixed with fear of the sexual dangers facing *all* women. They were behind Elizabeth Cobb's boast to Pearson that 'I can now find women for the club you could not match in men'.[11] Olive Schreiner composed a letter of thanks and admiration to Stead for women to sign. In the end the letter was replaced by a more 'business-like' one from Millicent Fawcett, since several women, including Fawcett, found the letter too emotional. The core of Olive's letter dealt with women's complicity:

> To some of us your words have come as a revelation. They have shown us what lay behind our smooth lives: they have filled us with remorse. Have we not too been guilty? Have we not made it easy for man to smite down with the right hand, while he honours us with the left? Have we cried out 'All women are one! In the saddest girl-child that is wronged I too suffer'? *Have we been content to be ignorant?*[12]

Elizabeth Cobb told Pearson how much she liked Olive's 'All women are one!', but she added: 'I dare say *you* too will think the letter too passionate.'[13]

Elizabeth Cobb was right; Pearson neither liked Olive's letter nor shared the enthusiasm for the articles and the 'agitation' they were engendering, particularly objecting to the religious element involved: the role of the Salvation Army and the Anglican Church. He was also concerned that the new movement would tend to blame men in general. He wrote to Maria Sharpe: 'Glad as I am that the *Pall Mall* should reveal the extent of the evil . . . I fear [that] all women . . . will not recognize that the majority of men are as guiltless as the women of these atrocities.'[14] Robert Parker had similar fears, worried lest the movement's desire to expose men involved in prostitution would create 'an outcast class of men'. To Parker this was unjust, since it was 'an undoubted fact . . . that doctors do extensively recommend sexual indulgence to a certain class of male patients.'[15] In other words, men were not wholly responsible for their actions, since they were merely acting on medical advice. Of the male club members, only Ralph Thicknesse shared the women's optimism about the effects of the *Pall Mall* 'revelations'. Ralph Thicknesse was a barrister and Secretary of the Minors' Protection Committee, an organization concerned to implement the 1885 Criminal Law Amendment Act in relation to child sexual abuse. He believed that the articles and their aftermath would 'lead to freer discussion between men and women of what was before considered an undiscussable subject, and freer thought must follow freer discussion'.[16] He presumably had hopes that the club would become one site for this 'freer discussion'.

Whatever their sensationalism and prurience, the *Pall Mall* articles, in pointing to the existence of prostitution, some of it enforced, among young girls barely in their teens, raised crucial issues of sexual coercion and exploitation. The 'revelations' highlighted power imbalances between the sexes which were exacerbated by inequalities of class and age. Stead, a radical rather than a socialist, presented an anti-aristocratic bias – the sordid picture of upper-class rakes corrupting innocent young working–class girls – instead of examining the economic reasons for women in a capitalist society turning to prostitution, or acknowledging the fact that many of the prostitute's clients were of the same class as the prostitute. Nevertheless, *in theory* the articles provided a way-in for discussion of male sexual desire, prostitution and the question of what constituted informed consent. In practice, apart from a painful and fraught discussion of prostitution and the Contagious Diseases Acts, these other two issues barely surfaced in the four years of club debate.

The hostility of Pearson and Parker to the movement engendered by the *Pall Mall* articles pointed to deep divides that were to surface and resurface during the life of the club: the men's avoidance of male responsibility for sexual behaviour versus the women's (unsuccessful) attempt to encourage accountability; the men's disparaging attitude towards religion versus some of the women's realization of its power of expression; the men's dismissal of feeling and emotion as valid responses versus the women's desire for the validation of feeling.

Pearson and 'The Woman's Question'

The club's minutes, papers and correspondence are available to us in archives scrupulously kept and left for posterity in the Pearson collection in University College, London. It makes for fascinating, if sometimes frustrating, reading. While the minutes of the club's meetings are minimal, giving a tantalizing but limited glimpse into club interaction, our vision is widened by a reading of the preserved correspondence. The club members and associates appear to have been tireless letter-writers. They were writing in the pre-telephone age, but at a time when the speedy postal service allowed letters to be posted and delivered on the same day. These letters clearly demonstrate that club debate extended beyond the boundaries of official meetings; they also give some sense of the passions, conflicts and grievances of club members. Letters seem to have been one location for the working through and articulation of discontents, especially for the women. Unfortunately, while much of the correspondence to Karl Pearson is preserved, as well as correspondence to the club secretary, Maria Sharpe (Pearson's future wife), we have few of the letters sent *by* Pearson – save to Maria. Nevertheless, we are still able to sense how Pearson's presence pervaded and dominated the club at every turn.

Karl Pearson was the son of middle-class Quakers. He had attended King's College, Cambridge, on a mathematics scholarship and then studied law, mathematics and philosophy as a postgraduate in Germany. Following in his father's footsteps, in 1881 he was called to the Bar (his father was by this time a QC). In 1884, however, aged only twenty-seven, he became Professor of Mathematics and Mechanics at University College, London. Women found him physically attractive, but he lacked warmth and tolerance, and was 'apt to attribute intellectual differences of opinion to stupidity or even moral obliquity'.[17] Although denying the intention, Karl Pearson's paper 'The Woman's Question', given at the club's first meeting in July 1885, outlined not only many of what were to be the club's key questions and concerns, but also the *mode* in which they were to be debated. As Maria Sharpe later commented, it 'set the tone of the club'.[18]

He started by defining what he took as the fundamental distinction between the sexes: women's child-bearing capacity. He then posed the question:

If we admit the inferiority of women at the present time ... is child-bearing a check on intellectual development, and so the subjection of child-bearing women a part of an inevitable natural law?[19]

Given that 'race evolution has implanted in woman a desire for children', Pearson argued that it was possible that non-fulfilment might also check the intellectual development of the '30–40% of womankind' who were childless. 'Thus either child-bearing or its absence may possibly act as a hindrance to woman's development.'[20] In other words, women might well be in a no-win situation simply by virtue of being women!

Pearson's nascent eugenics added another depressing ingredient to this already dismal scenario. Reproducing in large numbers meant power: 'Those nations which have been most reproductive have ... been the ruling nations in the world's history'. Women must therefore reproduce, so 'if child-bearing women be intellectually handicapped then the penalty to be paid for race predominance is the subjection of women'. But reproduction had to be confined to the eugenically 'fit'. He asked rhetorically:

Shall those who are diseased, shall those who are nighest to the brute, have the right to reproduce their like? Shall the reckless, the idle ... those who follow mere instinct without reason, be the parents of future generations?

Turning his attention to prostitution, he asserted:

Every attempt hitherto to grapple with prostitution has been a failure. There is only one thing which has not been tried – namely to bring its existence forcibly before the mass of women. What women will do when they thoroughly grasp the problem, I cannot in the least foreshadow.[21]

(Interestingly, this was written shortly before the *Pall Mall* articles and its mass educating of men and women on the horrors of London's underworld. What many women did with this knowledge, particularly their demand for male continence, was not to Pearson's liking.) He contrasted the 'woman of the night' with the frivolous middle-class woman found in London's day-time streets – the 'shopping doll', 'gazing intently into shop windows at various pieces of ribbon'. He scorned the latter, pitied the former. Having initially implied that women's subjec-tion might be inevitable, Pearson contradictorily surmised a more hopeful future:

> When woman is truly educated, is developed equally with man . . . the highest ideal of marriage [may] be perfectly free and yet, generally, lifelong union. May it not be that such a union is the only one in which a woman can preserve her individuality?

He argued, however, that:

> Most . . . is . . . to be hoped for from a higher moral tone of general society, a tone which can only be produced by a truer education of both men and women, especially in their mutual relations and duties.[22]

One gets the distinct impression that these 'duties' for women included the duty to breed. Furthermore, concern with a woman's *individuality* stood uneasily beside his concern with duties. The contradiction between a woman's *social obligations* and, a woman's *individual rights* was to become another key point of tension between the club men and women, as too was the definition of this 'higher moral tone'. And Pearson's contradic-tory approach to women and their emancipation was to feature frequently in subsequent discussion. He had set the terms of debate: women were to be the primary object of study (however much the women protested) and women's subordination to the interests of the 'race' had to override their demands for emancipation.

At the next meeting of the club, in October, after the summer gap, Henrietta Muller presented a paper entitled 'The Other Side of the Question'. Henrietta Muller was in her early thirties and the only female club member to have gone to university, one of the first batch to have attended Girton College, Cambridge, where she read classics. According to Elizabeth Cobb, she was a 'manhater', 'onesided' and 'warped in her moral nature' and Elizabeth did not want her joining the club at its beginning in case it was she who 'set the tone'.[23] At the huge demonstration in August, in support of the Criminal Law Amendment Bill, Henrietta had headed the Women's Trade Unions' contingent. She was highly committed to the Women's Movement, being active in a host of feminist organizations including membership of the executive of the National Society for Women's Suffrage. She had also served on the London School Board. Elizabeth Cobb might have labelled her a 'manhater' but she knew how to deploy femininity for political ends, amusing Maria Sharpe by telling her 'how she was compelled to descend to the level of the men's taste on the School Board and wear smart bonnets, because a good speech in a smart bonnet made more effect than without one.'[24]

To Pearson, the key divide between the sexes and between women was motherhood. To Henrietta, the fundamental distinction between the sexes could be summarized as 'man's license and woman's self-control'. Henrietta thereby moved sexual difference away from biology and located it within the realm of morals. Pearson had mentioned the necessity for 'a higher moral tone' without being clear what this entailed. To Henrietta Muller it was obvious – it was self-control: 'Self-control is the basis of all moral life and ... the characteristic which distinguishes Humanity from the rest of the animal world.' Rather than following Pearson in assuming 'the inferiority of women at the present time', she shifted the focus on to *men's* inferiority. If men and women's sexual instincts were equal (which she doubted), then men were inferior to women in self-control and there was no excuse for prostitution and the Contagious Diseases Acts 'by which a hideous and unspeakable outrage is perpetrated on women in the supposed interests of the health of men'. If sexual instincts were not equal, men were inferior 'by reason of a natural slavery to sexual instinct'. Men had to get to know these truths about themselves: 'Women must learn the difficult and disagreeable task of saying fearlessly what they think even if it is not very welcome; men must learn the equally disagreeable task of hearing it.' She looked to women as the moral saviours of humanity: 'The sons of earth have done their task and nature now calls upon her daughters to fulfil theirs – as the one has conquered the physical world, the other shall conquer the moral . . .'[25]

The club minutes (written at this stage by Robert Parker) noted that her paper was followed by 'a somewhat desultory discussion'. This lukewarm response upset Henrietta, but at least she had impressed Olive Schreiner, who announced to Pearson: 'She is a plucky, fearless, brave, true little woman'.[26] The following month's meeting saw various 'notes' of response to the talks of Pearson and Henrietta. There was criticism of Henrietta; Maria Sharpe, for example, had suggested that her paper had not been written 'in the spirit of scientific inquiry so much as in the spirit of a rebel'. Henrietta acknowledged that this was indeed true, but 'justified by the slavery of women and by the fact that our danger lies in too ready submission to the claims of men'.[27] The 'note' of response from Mrs Walters, a close friend of Olive Schreiner's, was more complimentary. Back in the summer Mrs Walters had been courted by Elizabeth Cobb as a potential member, but she had eventually declined, possibly because of geographic distance (she lived outside London) and her other commitments which included active suffragism. In her paper Mrs Walters agreed with Henrietta's view of 'woman the slave to man, man to his own passion'. She saw two possible solutions: one was the economic independence of women which would lead to women refusing marriage, sex and child-bearing; the other was a change in men – their becoming 'altruistic, in which case sexual instinct would be no longer ugly, but directed towards getting beautiful children, its only natural *raison d'être*'.[28] Although this was a particularly narrow view of sex to which few of the women members subscribed,[29] it was one of the few demands made *of men*. Reaction to Mrs Walters's demand was unfortunately not recorded.

Talking of Sex

In the light of Henrietta Muller's suggestion that men's sexual instinct was greater than women's, the club decided to assess the comparative strength of this instinct between the sexes. Although on the surface this might have appeared to have been an objective search for 'truth' – indeed, this was the way in which the male members presented it – the hidden agenda was surely a concern with Henrietta Muller's claim that men were 'slaves to sex instinct', and thus morally inferior.

As it happened, no subsequent paper discussed the comparative strength question directly, but it was one of the issues, along with the question of the relationship of chastity to health, which was to come up repeatedly in club debate. Pearson and Parker were keen for these questions to be 'scientifically' answered and the 'facts' thereby established, as too was Olive Schreiner. She had told Elizabeth Cobb in March that although she was against the double moral standard, its undesirability could 'only be proved or disproved by showing how like or unlike the nature of men and women are, especially on the sexual side'. She thought the likeness to be great, 'but I should like to know as well as to feel.'[30] For the other women, ability 'to feel' seemed to be sufficient; they were less interested in establishing 'scientific' answers to these two issues. It was true that in wanting men to change their sexual behaviour they would have liked it established that chastity was not unhealthy. 'I want someone to say men can be healthful . . . without constant indulgence or without any at all if necessary, as women can,' Maria Sharpe had told Kate Mills earlier in the year.[31] But most of the women were convinced that men *could* change and no 'proof' was needed. Mrs Walters believed so; an associate of the Club, Fabian and novelist Miss Emma Brooke, warned Pearson that once women had economic independence, men would be forced to learn self-restraint and 'to stop being a beast of prey.'[32] As for the relative strength of sexual instinct, the women were divided: some thought that men's instinct was stronger, others that the instincts were equal. Either way, they were in agreement that male sexual *behaviour* needed to change; the relative strength was not the burning issue.

At the December meeting, club member Dr Reginald Ryle's brief was the broad one of 'some physiological facts which bear upon the relations of the sexes'. He included 'the relation of activity or inactivity of sex relations to general health of individual'. To Ryle there was no proof of a relationship between the two. Not everyone agreed. Two other doctors had been asked as guests to the meeting, due to their supposed expertise on the relation of sex to health. Bryan Donkin was doctor and friend of Karl Marx's family and of Olive Schreiner, with whom he was currently – and unrequitedly – in love. He joined the Men and Women's Club soon after the December meeting. Dr Louisa Atkins, one of Britain's first women doctors, was a widow of about forty. Elizabeth Cobb liked and respected her, and approved of her reaction to Stead's 'Maiden Tribute'. While sympathizing with Stead, Dr Atkins 'much disapproved of his manner of working and writing', although she was certain that there was no exaggeration in his claims. In her keenness to recruit any suitable married or widowed woman, especially a doctor, Elizabeth Cobb encouraged Dr Atkins to join the club. Dr Atkins described herself as 'a heterodox in religion and everything', but she declined the invitation, finding the club insufficiently practical.[33]

After Ryle's paper, the two guests were asked their opinion on the health and chastity issue. As was frequently the case, the question was predominantly considered in relation to women. Dr Atkins was 'very decided that men and women are not different in strength of sexual feeling'.[34] 'That sexual inactivity injures the general health of most women ... experience has convinced me', she informed the club. Olive and Dr Donkin agreed, although Olive expressed her beliefs in relation to *both* sexes: 'A person might stifle their sexual desire by diverting their energy into other channels and yet suffer in health.'[35] Doctors Atkins and Donkin both seemed convinced that it was chastity and not absence of child-bearing, as Pearson had suggested, which injured women's health. Apart from Olive, the female club members were not so sure. Maria Sharpe later recorded that 'I would not bear to assent to this' – perhaps unsurprisingly, given that she was a single woman in her mid-thirties expecting to remain a spinster for the rest of her life.[36] In club discussion she suggested that inactivities other than sexual might contribute to women's ill-health. Elizabeth Cobb agreed, telling of a girl whose health had been vastly improved by an active college life.

Members Isabella Clemes and David Rhys Davids both bravely spoke out on a personal note in declaring themselves celibate yet happy.[37] (They did not mention whether they were healthy, however.)

The relative strength of men and women's sexual instinct and the relation of chastity to health came up again in May 1887, although the two delivered papers, by Henrietta Muller and Kate Mills, were on neither subject but on family limitation. The discussion plunged at once into the chastity and health issue. Ryle held to his conviction that there was no reliable evidence of chastity being harmful. Parker disagreed, referring to Doctors Atkins and Donkin as authorities. Pearson held both family limitation papers to have assumed an unproven fact: that sexual desire was stronger in men. He asserted that women's desire was equal, presenting some fairly odd 'evidence' to substantiate this assertion. For a start, he claimed to have supporting statistics, although there was no mention of their source. Further, he announced that 'widows and women who have once experienced sexual intercourse find it extremely hard to restrain their desire', and that women in general were easy to seduce, thus showing 'great physical appetite on their part'. He also made claims to personal knowledge: 'considering healthy peasant women, as I have known them in the Tyrol, I should say the evidence was in favour of the sexual impulse in woman being on a par with that of a man.'[38] In what way Pearson had 'known' such women was unclear.

Among the club minutes there is a loose sheet of paper on which Henrietta Muller had written, alongside Pearson's above assertions, a list of her own points of 'evidence that men have stronger sexual desire than women'. Her points were as follows:

1 Prostitution
2 CD Acts
3 Polygamy (polyandry scarcely exists)
4 Incest – always fathers and daughters – never mothers and sons
5 Violation of little girls – see Stats [sic]

6   Seduction and rape of girls and women – see police reports and stats [sic]

7   Consensus of opinion – State, law, religion, society, medicine

8   Personal experience, e.g. evidence of acquaintances[39]

There is no indication that these comments of Henrietta's were discussed by the club.

Several of the other women members wrote responses to the family limitation papers. None of them agreed that men and women's sexual desires were of a similar strength. Maria's sister Loetitia Sharpe felt that 'in a state of nature' women's sexuality would probably be stronger than men's, but that as products of years of suppression by 'civilization', women's instinct was checked while men's sexuality had been encouraged. Maria Sharpe and active suffragist Florence Balgarnie made similar points. Maria added that it was women's greater sense of *responsibility* in relation to the sexual act which had inhibited their sex instinct, while Florence hypothesized that women had developed more control over 'animal passions' because 'they suffer the consequences in child-bearing'. Florence understood sex as evolving from the physical through to higher mental and moral stages, with our becoming more human the higher the stage we attained. This was a fairly widely held view at the time. Implicit in their discussion of sexual desire was the assumption of hetero-sexuality. For all its claims to radicalism, the club did not mention homosexuality, except when Parker read 'An Ode to a Youth' during his paper on 'Sexual Relations among the Greeks of the Periclean Era'. Lesbianism as a term was not yet in current use, and intimacy between women was not generally thought of as *sexual* as such. In the club there were two women whose rela-tionship in another era might have been labelled lesbian: Maria Sharpe and her close friend Lina Eckenstein had what was termed a 'romantic friendship'. Lina wrote Maria letters of love, devotion and admiration, even after Maria was married; Maria's letters are not available so it is unclear whether she replied in kind. There was certainly no idea of impropriety in their intimacy.[40]

The women's feelings and fears about sex had been forced

into articulation back in January when the discussion of the pros and cons of 'preventive checks' – one of the current terms for contraceptives – had been initiated by birth controller Annie Besant in her talk on 'The State and Sexual Relations'. All the men, save possibly one, were in favour of 'checks'; the women were split on the issue. Yet even those in favour saw them as a necessary evil. They appeared to agree that women were likely to 'prefer self-control and long periods of abstinence'.[41] The trouble was, it could never be assumed that men would take any notice of women's preferences. Hence for some women, although 'checks' were 'very odious', they were preferable to continuous child-bearing. To Henrietta for example, 'checks' were 'a mere *pis aller* [a last resort or stopgap] till men have self-control and women have freedom'. It made a lot of difference if the birth control was in the *woman's* hands: 'She should be able to apply it at her own will, without the knowledge of the man.'[42]

Weighing up involuntary child-bearing against non-consensual sex, other women members felt that contraceptives worsened the situation for women. They believed that 'checks' were brutalizing in their effects for they 'vulgarized the emotions' and encouraged promiscuity, and it was feared that once women no longer had the excuse of possible pregnancy, they would be subjected to their husbands' every sexual whim. Indeed, many women of this period looked on artificial birth control (especially the sheath, the standard male form of contraceptive) as a means of reducing a wife to a virtual prostitute. While Pearson viewed 'checks' as a means of placing the woman in the *same* position as the man with regard to the sexual act, namely as a means to physical pleasure without fear of pregnancy, Loetitia Sharpe, although believing 'checks' to be an unfortunate necessity for the present, felt that they made women more than ever a *vehicle* of men's pleasure. To Henrietta, 'family limitation' should be about the right of a woman over her own person and the right of a child to be well-born; pleasure of the *man* should not be the priority.[43]

Given that all the women, save Elizabeth Cobb, were unmarried, etiquette dictated that they could not speak of sex from personal experience – even in a club as supposedly radical as this.

It is anyway unlikely that they had had personal experience of sexual intercourse (Olive may have been the exception). Instead, they drew on their knowledge of other women. The majority of female members had a clear sense that for most women marital sex was not primarily about pleasure: it was frequently non-consensual and entailed involuntary child-bearing. 'To many women sexual intercourse is an unpleasant and fatiguing obligation', asserted Henrietta.[44] Or, as a married female friend of Maria's expressed it in a letter, quoted to the club, 'men are . . . brought up in the tacit understanding that marriage secures sexual intercourse whenever *they* are the least inclined for it, and I am perfectly sure most women give way to them for the sake of peace.'[45]

One woman member felt rather differently: Olive Schreiner clearly believed that many women experienced sexual pleasure. During the summer of 1886 Olive engaged in an unselfconscious correspondence with Pearson on questions of sex. She was the only member of the club who could be described as 'bohemian'. Having grown up in South Africa, she was untrammelled by English middle-class etiquette. As her close friend the sexual radical Edward Carpenter described her, she was 'a pretty woman of apparently lady-like origin who did not wear a veil and seldom wore gloves and who talked and laughed in the streets quite naturally.'[46] In 1881 she had arrived in London in her mid-twenties and found a publisher for *The Story of an African Farm*. The novel concerns the rebellious search of a woman for self-expression and religious certainty; its powerful language and imagery were widely admired. Olive was warm and generous, but her outspokenness sometimes shocked a number of the female club members. As Elizabeth Cobb related to Pearson: 'My sisters have always felt Olive Schreiner thought too much that purely animal feeling *must* sway, and could not be mastered.'[47]

Having questioned married women on their sexual experiences, Olive felt compelled to put Pearson right on a number of matters: 'After the great mass of evidence I have collected from married women . . . I cannot doubt that you are wrong in saying that women feel *any* dislike to intercourse with their husbands during pregnancy.'[48] Two days later she was correcting another of his misconceptions:

> One of my friends told me that her husband liked her to suckle her children long, because then, owing to the absence of the period ... they could more frequently have intercourse. It is strange how wrong you are in these small physiological matters.[49]

As for sexual pleasure, she made 'a *wild* supposition', that in the future, human reproduction would be possible without sex, similar to the propagation of a rose tree by cuttings: 'Then the sexual systems might be used exclusively aesthetically for purposes of pleasure; for sympathy and union between human beings'. She thought that the 'aesthetic' function was already supplementing the reproductive.[50]

In contrast, Pearson's views of sexual pleasure did not seem particularly about 'sympathy and union'. He proposed that sex, even among animals, was never solely for procreation, but was also a 'physical pleasure like climbing a mountain'.[51] All the woman members were horrified (note that Olive was no longer attending the club at this point); to Maria this equated 'a taste of a strawberry and a kiss of a friend'.[52] While devaluing the sanctity of sex on the one hand, it denied the sufferings on the other. Most of the women club members' view of sex stood in stark contrast to that of Pearson: it was about suffering and the reduction of women simply to being 'mere bodies', with preventive checks as a means of protection not pleasure.

Although their woeful reflections were implicitly critical of the male view of women, little *direct* challenge was made of men to put their house in order. But one woman who did openly criticize masculinity was the novelist and Fabian Miss Emma Brooke. In one letter to Pearson she vehemently turned on him: 'The truth is, you men have murdered Love ... you have killed the inspiration in the woman's heart by abuses of all kinds.'[53] Unfortunately, although she submitted two papers to the club and was in regular correspondence with Pearson, she was never asked to become a member. Elizabeth Cobb was disparaging: 'I have never thought of her as a character commanding much respect. We thought of her for our club at the beginning, but I believe considered her not sober enough.'[54] Emma Brooke's letters to Pearson were certainly filled with passionate anger; some might have called it intemperance, to others it was feminist realism. In the club generally it was not men's sexuality that was under scrutiny but women's. In their adoption of an evolutionary understanding of sex (the 'years of suppression by civilization'), the women inadvertently contributed further to the deflection of attention away from men and *their* responsibility for sexual behaviour. Any critique of male sexuality was additionally under-mined by the early establishment of the club's definition of morality.

Morality

The club's constitution declared that discussion would be from a 'scientific, historical and non-theological standpoint'. Not only was religious argument out of court, but implicitly so too was any argument springing from personal, subjective *feelings* or emotions. Such an argument was deemed 'non-scientific' and seen, by the male members at least, as mystical and sentimental, akin to a religious response, and typically 'feminine'. In arriving at a definition of morality, these club parameters of 'legitimate' discourse came fully into operation. At the November meeting in 1885 Parker minuted a voiced desire 'for discussion of the meaning of morality'. He noted that there had been two conflict-ing criteria at play within the various papers: on the one hand, self-control, on the other, welfare of the community.[55] He could have added that this represented the view of some of the women and the view of Pearson respectively.

In January 1886, teachers Annie Eastty and Isabella Clemes gave papers on the meaning of morality. Unfortunately, neither Henrietta Muller nor Mrs Walters were present – the two women whose papers had earlier held morality to involve self-control. Annie Eastty, an unmarried, free-thinking schoolmistress from Bermondsey, argued that for Darwin 'the "moral sense" was due to the survival in the struggle for life of social instinct. This justifies inclusion of *feeling* as well as *reason* in our use of the word.'[56] Isabella Clemes saw morality as concerning both 'social duties' '(to others)' and 'individual duties' '(to the laws of nature as they concern himself alone)'.[57] A few months earlier, Robert Parker had dismissively commented on Isabella Clemes's ideas to Pearson: 'There is a danger of her viewing morality as mysterious intuition, or revelation, a divine (she believes in Providence and God . . . the capitals included) and not purely human law.'[58]

It is clear that Pearson would not have agreed with either Annie Eastty or Isabella Clemes. Speaking as a freethinker in a recently delivered public lecture, he asserted:

> Morality is a matter not of feeling but of knowledge and study. *The ignorant cannot be moral* . . . Morality to the Christian is a matter of feeling, of obedience to a code supernaturally revealed . . . The only practical method of making society as a whole approach the free-thinker's ideal of morality is . . . to teach it to use its reason.[59]

At the end of the January 1886 meeting the club drew up its definition of 'moral'. Neither 'self-control' nor 'feeling' were mentioned. Yet if 'feeling' was decreed irrelevant and illegitimate in questions of morality, 'self-control' could not be dismissed so easily. After all, it was widely held in this period that self-control was obtainable *via* the application of reason. As we have seen, in the club's discussion of the relative strength of sexual instinct, medical opinion had been presented as to the desirability of a sexual 'outlet' for both sexes. This obviously undermined a demand for sexual self-control. Furthermore, such a demand was clearly felt by some of the men to entail an unsettling demand *of them*. Parker, for example, warned Maria:

> 'You women' are purer than we . . . Must you not take care lest in trying to make us as you are, you fall into the habit of dividing men into two classes only, pure and impure (as we have divided women) . . .?[60]

He had expressed the same sentiment about the response to the 'Maiden Tribute' articles, where he had feared the creation of an 'outcast class of men'.

In the minutes for the January 1886 meeting we find the underlined statement:

> It was agreed ... that an action could not be considered moral which left out of view the welfare of future society ... NB It was further agreed that morality neglected the good of the individual in so far as such good was ... incompatible with the good of society.[61]

'It was agreed', the statement ran, but Annie Eastty and Isabella Clemes could not have wholly agreed, for the definition omitted both 'feeling' and the moral responsibility of the individual to him/herself. Did these women or others present not raise objections?

A week later, Robert Parker reflected on the meeting to Maria:

> It was almost inevitable that we men should agree in defining morality with reference to the welfare of the Society ... I had hoped for someone who would boldly maintain the position which women often take up, when they place the essence of morality in the emotions.[62]

Maria replied somewhat testily:

> I am sorry I could not supply the need you felt of a strong advocate of emotional morality. I don't think anyone there felt the least inclination to take that character, and I must confess that it a little grieves me that you should expect it of me.[63]

The women may not have held morality to be simply about emotions, but there is some indication of at least a muted resistance to the club's definition. A few months after the definition had been coined, Parker commented in the club minutes that there was 'a distinct tendency ... observable to use such words as morality and duty in senses other than those determined by the Club'.[64]

At the end of the year, the equation of *moral* with *social*, and the evolutionary basis of such, was spelt out by Pearson:

> There is a principle lying at the basis of all growth ... the 'survival of the fitter'. [He preferred this to survival of the *fittest* since 'the fittest is never reached'.] The moral or good action is that which tends in the direction of growth of a particular society ... In this sense I should use the word *social* for moral, and *anti-social* for *immoral*.

The 'moral', the 'social', the 'welfare of society' and the 'direction of growth of society' were thus all equated; they were in turn conflated by Pearson with 'socialism':

> Socialism . . . is essentially a new morality, it denotes the subjection of all individual action to the welfare of society; this welfare can be ascertained only by studying the direction of social growth. To judge whether or not beliefs or actions were moral or social or socialist, one judged it against the 'ideal'. By 'ideal' I do not denote some glorious poet-inspired Utopia . . . but . . . the outcome of our reading of the past . . . of the tendency and forces at present developing humanity in a definite direction.[65]

It all seemed to come down to one's ability (or power?) to read the past and ascertain the direction of society's growth. It is probably obvious by now who it was that felt confident and authoritative enough to claim this ability.

The Inequality of Club Discourse

Matters were made worse for the women by the constraints of the club's dominant discourse. Reflecting back on the club's four years, Maria noted that the women of the club 'even in general discussion . . . had to learn a partially new language before they could make themselves intelligible'.[66] One could add that they also needed it to make the men intelligible to *them*. Maria was referring to the particular reading of Darwin adopted by the men; this was the 'scientific standpoint' to which the club was committed. As will be discussed later, Darwinism was open to many interpretations. In the club the women were as active as the men in drawing on evolutionary theory to develop an argument; they were not ignorant of Darwin *per se*, but of the men's particular positivist usage, and they found difficulty with the impersonal mode of presentation. It was surely not irrelevant that the majority of the male members were lawyers and thus highly familiar with the dry objectivity of legal discourse. On one occasion, for example, Olive Schreiner complained to Maria of Parker's 'legal technicality'.[67]

The women tried hard to conform to the men's dictates.

Maria spoke for the women members as a whole: 'We are all equally anxious to use the scientific method in our inquiries . . . none of us being able to apply it readily to some of the more complex facts of thought and feeling.'[68] Most of them were adamant that it was not desirable to speak from a subjective stance. Annie Eastty confided to Maria: 'I do always in discussion – not only at the club – try to repress my merely personal feelings.'[69] Maria likewise noted: 'In discussion I hate what I do generally because it is so subjective.'[70] But their attempts at the 'scientific method' were frequently misunderstood. Again Maria was not alone in being

> unacquainted with the phraseology and methods of arguing in which they [the men] were all so much at home . . . and if I used an expression in a letter that was not perfectly clear I found that both Mr Parker and Mr Pearson gave it some turn towards supernatural-ism with which I was totally unsympathetic.[71]

The attempt to speak 'objectively' was not simply about conforming to the men's mode of discourse; the women recognized that speaking personally rendered them more vulnerable. As Maria noted, to 'discuss questions from the personal stand-point' led to 'the raising of distinctive sex feeling in women'. I am unsure what she meant by this exactly, but she was certain that it 'must lead to pain if not bitterness'.[72] Personal feelings also impeded research. In her (unpublished) 'Autobiographical History' written in 1889 at the closing of the club, Maria recalled how when researching the laws on prostitution AD 800–1500:

> I used to sit at the [British] Museum and collect myself before I could summon up courage to go to the counter to return my books on prostitution or to ask some question about them. However I got used to it. I determined all through to treat the subject as objectively as possible and to let the personal feeling not into my work at all.[73]

Constrained on all sides by the club's object of study, its dominant definitions, its mode of speech and its manner of inquiry, we might suppose that the women were never able to set the agenda or to raise issues of pressing concern to *them*. Yet in various ways the women managed not only to level criticism

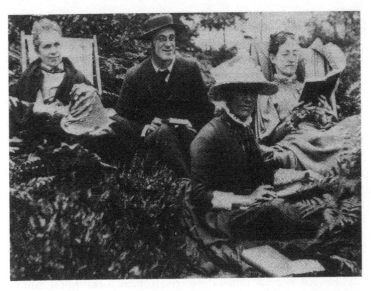

A Men and Women's Club picnic: Maria Sharpe in the foreground, Elizabeth Cobb reading a book, Ralph Thicknesse, and Mrs Wickstead, friend of the Club

of the men, and of Pearson in particular, but also to call into question the very legitimacy of the club's obsession with establishing objective, rational and politically neutral knowledge.

2 THE WOMEN OF THE CLUB ANSWER BACK

Despite the correspondence in time between the 'Maiden Tribute' articles and the club's opening, sexual morality as such was never directly on the club agenda. Within the club's definition, sexual behaviour, unless viewed as having a bearing on the welfare of society as a whole, was not deemed of relevance to issues of morality. Consequently the morality/immorality of specific sexual behaviour barely got a mention, despite the attempts by some of the women members, such as Henrietta Muller, to raise the subject in club debate. Pearson had, in effect, defined sexual morality as the morality of breeding. But his idea of 'moral motherhood' was not to go unchallenged. The women also challenged the club's veto on emotion and feeling, both in terms of the desirability of speaking with and from one's feelings, and in terms of the value of emotions within human evolution. And when some of the men rounded on the women via an attack on feminism, the women rallied to its defence. They also tried to raise the issue of masculinity, but to little avail. All these small attempts to shift the focus, redefine the definition of 'moral' and change the terms, mode and object of debate were little more than pinpricks in the sides of Pearson and Parker's inflated egos. But they rocked the boat, and in the end, I would suggest, contributed to rendering the club's continuation impossible.

Motherhood

The female club members barely mentioned motherhood, possibly because as predominantly single women it was not a dominant issue in their lives, although they were certainly aware that excessive child-bearing was a problem for many women. The few women who did write of motherhood drew on women's experience. In relation to sexual desire, Pearson had taken 'experience' as valid proof – he had drawn on his own and the experience of doctors and other unnamed sources. But in relation to motherhood, Pearson used evolutionary argument to 'explain' women's 'maternal instinct' and to 'justify'/rationalize women's past and (possibly) future subordination – that society's 'need' for child-bearing might necessitate continued handicapping of women.

In her 39-page handwritten response to Pearson's 'The Woman Question', Emma Brooke took issue with his ideas on motherhood. Her evidence was

> founded on stored-up observations . . . and incessant watchfulness
> . . . To learn, you must listen to their [women's] words, observe
> their faces in the unconscious moments when nature and feeling
> speak for themselves.

She thus took women's experience as her starting point; her access to that experience lay in unobtrusive observation.

Henrietta Muller's paper of response to Pearson had suggested, in contradiction to Pearson, that many women were entirely without a maternal instinct.[74] Emma Brooke elaborated further. She maintained that children were often *dreaded* – one had only to look at the infanticide rate. Further, women's ill-health frequently resulted not from lack of children but the bearing of too many. To Pearson's claim that race predominance relied on reproduction, she angrily retorted: 'Show me any logical reason why I should go on bearing children at your order only to perpetuate wretchedness.'[75]

Pearson proposed state financial support for motherhood; the women club members were against it. To Maria Sharpe, for example, it would act to undermine a father's sense of responsibility. Emma Brooke was all for the state supporting mothers, but not for the same reason as Pearson. He was in favour of *selective* support, the state eugenically regulating 'the quantity and quality' of the population. Emma wanted a *woman's* choice, not the state's. In our present society, she argued, 'a woman's body is ... not her own', but once a woman can possess herself and *choose* motherhood:

> the difference to the child in being the centre of thoughtful and leisured care instead of being the victim of the mother's exhaustion and worry and secret discontent will be untold.[76]

Emma Brooke not only indirectly challenged Pearson's definition of morality by suggesting the *immorality* of his proposed scheme of reproducing to order, but she also indirectly questioned the legitimacy of his calling himself a socialist. She commented bitterly on his portrayal of women in his 'The Woman's Question' paper:

> I think your attitude towards women in general 'unsocialistic'. Towards those you describe ... as 'dolls' ... you manifest a degree of scorn and hardness which somehow gives me pain ... And then in your attitude towards the better women there is ... a distinctly dominant tone, an inclination to lay down their duty for them ... You underrate women, you do indeed. You are hard because you have so little knowledge of that very woman nature you cannot keep from despising.[77]

Speaking Politically, Speaking Personally

Emma Brooke never attended the club and thus did not face some of the constraints it imposed. We have seen how difficult, undesirable, even dangerous it was to speak from a personal stance at the club, how it engendered in the women a sense of inferiority, ignorance and vulnerability. The club also thought it inappropriate to speak from a sectarian stance. Inability to be politically detached from the subject matter, in this case the Contagious Diseases Acts, drove Florence Balgarnie to hand in her resignation (although she was later to withdraw it). She wrote to Pearson:

> I am too much a *partisan* myself to continue. I have been a worker in, as well as a student of, these problems and I feel that, by the part I took in the CD [Contagious Diseases] debate, I was guilty of want of loyalty to some of my best friends and co-workers. To me that question cannot have two sides. I would just as soon believe there were two sides to the question whether there is a right to murder![78]

(One could legitimately say that Pearson held definite partisan views himself, but they, of course, masqueraded as 'objective science'.)

Henrietta Muller's resignation earlier in the year had not surprised Parker:

> She is a person of strong convictions and those convictions do not perfectly harmonise with the sceptical or enquiring spirit which rightly dominates our discussions. She cannot live without her faith ... I have never thought the club quite suitable to persons already committed to a definite creed.[79]

Henrietta and Florence's 'creed' was not religious but political: a strong commitment to the 'cause' of women. The other women club members were also feminists, but Henrietta and Florence were dedicated activists, each involved in a variety of organizations. Both were prominent in the National Society for Women's Suffrage (Florence as Secretary, Henrietta as Executive member) and the Personal Rights Association (an anti-statist organization rooted in the Butlerite campaign against the Contagious Diseases Acts). Henrietta was also a member of the National Vigilance Association (which sprang up in the wake of the 1885 Criminal Law Amendment Act), was the first secretary of the Society for Return of Women as Poor Law Guardians, and had been a tax resister in 1884. Both women had served on School Boards, Florence in Scarborough for two years, Henrietta in London for six years from 1879, having topped the poll with 19,000 votes, the first woman elected. Florence was one of the founders of the Women's Trade Union Association, and an active member of the British Women's Temperance Association (BWTA). She was later secretary of the Anti-Lynching Committee which was set up in London in 1894, inspired by the recent British tour of the African–American Ida B. Wells.[80]. It was not surprising that the club's 'neutrality' was frustrating to such politically active women.

The problem was, if the response was not to be personal or partisan, if their familiarity with 'objective' discourse and the men's particular brand of positivist Darwinism was insufficient, if the discourse itself was inadequate to allow them to say what they truly thought, the women were sometimes reduced to silence. Henrietta believed this occurred because 'woman's long subjection has taught her silence'.[81]. But she felt that the *men's* behaviour did not help. Writing to Pearson to explain why she had resigned from the club, she accusingly declared:

> at the last meeting . . . it was the same old story of the man laying down the law to the woman and not seeming to recognise that she has a voice and the woman resenting in silence, and submitting in silence.[82]

Maria resented Henrietta's accusation of silence. As we have seen, the women did speak, but it was often with difficulty. If the club had ruled out 'feeling' as a legitimate basis from which to act or speak, this did not prevent the women's occasional amazement at its *absence* among the men. Parker's talk on 'Sexual Relations among the Greeks of the Periclean Era' in February 1886 prompted this response from Maria:

Never shall I forget the frozen impression which it left in me ... it was the coolness with which Mr Parker seemed to treat the whole subject, showing no warmth.[83]

The club women appear to have again experienced precisely this 'frozen impression' on hearing three papers on the Contagious Diseases Acts. Parker presented the first two papers, claiming the effects of the Acts to have been largely beneficial. Noting disparagingly that the opposition to the Acts had been primarily religious, he suggested that the club might discover if there was a *rational* reason for opposition. Thereupon he listed all the supposedly rational arguments against the Acts and answered each with what he took as clear-cut refutation. For example, in answer to the claim that the Acts unwarrantably interfered with liberty, he replied that women generally *chose* prostitution freely, and as for police abuse of power, there was no satisfactory evidence. Rather than seeing the Acts as unfair to women, he argued that they should be viewed not as penal but preventive.[84]

Ralph Thicknesse, possibly the only male club member opposed to the Acts, gave a paper on their 'social aspects' the following month. He was supposedly one of the male members most supportive of feminism. Maria found his lengthy paper 'very painful' – not least because, despite his opposition to the Acts, he saw prostitution as 'beneficial' to society. Prostitution haunted relations between men and women during this period. As Maria expressed it, it was 'the great unknown subject to girls which fills them with an enquiring fearfulness ... the region where women are possibly bodies only to men, casting a dark shadow across all their own relations to the other sex'.[85] To Olive Schreiner – and Maria agreed – 'no-one can grasp the position of woman and its meaning unless they look at the fact of prostitution that is the terrible core lying at the heart of the matter'.[86] Women's fear of prostitution spoke in part of their fear of the dangers of sex with men.

The women were asked to write personal responses to the three papers so that the men might understand their opposition. A little over a year earlier Maria had admitted to Pearson:

It is impossible for women not to feel [discussion of the Contagious Diseases Acts] an intensely personal matter. It is perhaps well that men should not realise how personal if there is to be any attempt at dispassionate consideration.[87]

By 1888 they were still dubious about giving their personal views, Annie Eastty agreeing with Maria that 'in writing the sort of note suggested we do come down to a lower level of argument',[88] while Maria suspected it was 'a request to take up the "performing task" . . . that whatever we did as women was something worth listening to' and that this was their only value to the men. Further, the women felt burdened with the men's expectation that they would respond emotionally and express views which they held 'no more than the man in the moon'.[89]

Nevertheless, despite these reservations, they now recognized the impossibility of disinterested 'objective' speculation on a subject which moved and angered them so deeply. They thus agreed to present short personalized replies. This was one issue over which there was a clear gender divide in the club; as Judith Walkowitz points out, the club debate of the C.D. Acts re-enacted the recent public battle between regulationists and their feminist opponents.[90] Loetitia Sharpe opened the various responses by pointing to the Acts' *anti-social* nature – that they facilitated promiscuity, prostitution and disease. She validated her opposition in terms of the club's declared concern with the welfare of the 'race' and its equation of immorality with the 'anti-social'. 'Women would of course be willing that their sex should be sacrificed for the good of the race', she declared (sarcastically?), but concluded that they had not yet been convinced that the 'good of the race' would be promoted by the Acts. Annie Eastty claimed that prostitution, encouraged by the Acts, was 'a step backward into the mental life of brutes', for 'it acknowledges and provides for sexual appetite disassociated from any distinctively *human* feeling'.[91] Although voicing her opposition in terms of a Darwinian standpoint, her reference to 'feeling' was of course at variance with the dominant view of evolution in the club.

Maria's contribution pursued a rather different tack, one relating directly to her feelings, emotions and sense of vulnerability.

She took issue with the condescending way in which Josephine Butler's use of prayer had been condemned by Parker and Thicknesse as 'by-gone superstition . . . strengthening the ignorant and unreasoning party against the Acts.' (Parker had also mocked Mrs Butler's 'propriety': 'one shudders to think of the agony she would endure if present at one of our club meetings.')[92] Maria, on the other hand, defended prayers as 'the unconscious expression of our strivings after our highest ideals'. She claimed that 'any woman – even an agnostic – opposed to the Acts, will find herself in sympathy with many of Mrs Butler's utterances'. She also strongly objected to the state sanction of prostitution, which encouraged men to 'pass from intercourse . . . with . . . prostitutes to intercourse with other women [carrying] with them habits mental and other . . .' In other words, the state encouraged the treatment of all women as virtual prostitutes, as destined 'merely to satisfy the bodily needs of men'.[93] Loetitia had spoken of women's identification with the prostitute, that the degradation of one was the degradation of them all. Maria in effect revealed the foundations of this collective degradation.

Pearson claimed not to understand what they could possibly mean by the Acts *degrading women*. As far as he was concerned, 'the stamina of the race in the future is far more to me than the sentiment that to deal with an anti-social class of women must degrade all womankind'.[94] Like Parker, in asking for *rational* grounds for opposing the Acts he meant grounds that demonstrated their 'anti-social' nature. But to Pearson the Acts appeared far from anti-social, and if they entailed a limitation on certain women's rights, so be it; like the handicaps of motherhood it was the price to be paid.

If bemused by the women finding the Acts degrading, Pearson was more worried about Maria's reflections on Mrs Butler and prayer. He wrote to her the day after the meeting to advise her, rather pompously, that in calling concern with human welfare 'prayer', 'we place ourselves in union with a past stage of development'.[95] To freethinking Darwinians like Pearson, religion had evolved from the lower stages of human development to the present higher stage of science and rationalist ethics. Seeing religion as a 'lower' form which could not co-exist with

34

science, Pearson had accused Dr Elizabeth Blackwell of 'prostituting' science with her Christianity. In contrast, Annie Eastty (also a freethinker incidentally) wrote to Maria declaring:

> I feel more and more my indebtedness to the club for the opportunity it has given me of discovering that I am not so completely out of sympathy with a 'religious' element in feeling as I thought.[96]

Rationality versus Emotions

The women had broken the taboo on speaking with feeling, but they had not thereby directly confronted the men's *dismissal* of feeling and emotion as important human attributes. Annie Eastty had included 'feeling' in her definition of morality and human sex, but it had been rejected. Olive Schreiner was one of the few women at the club who stood as Pearson's intellectual equal. She felt no compunction in gently mocking his distrust of the emotions. After giving a long description of the novel she was currently writing (later entitled *From Man to Man* and published posthumously),[97] she requested it be dedicated to him. She then, in brackets, concocted a caricatured response:

> KP: Dear me! Dear me! . . . Emotions, unmixed, unmitigated emotions! I must write to my respected friend OS at once. I, Karl Pearson, sworn enemy of the emotions, Professor of Applied Mathematics, to have my name appended to so emotional an effusion . . .![98]

Another woman prepared to challenge Pearson's disparaging attitude towards emotions was the Fabian and anarchist Mrs Charlotte Wilson. Not strictly a club associate in that she neither attended club meetings nor contributed a written paper, she was nevertheless in touch with club affairs via friendship and correspondence with Pearson and Olive. She read much of Pearson's published and unpublished writings and was frequently in agreement. But his attitude towards emotions riled her. She wrote in disbelief:

Surely you did not express your actual conviction when you said that the higher – the desirable – development of man implies the destruction of emotions. Surely you admit that the basis of society is the social feeling of its individual members – among the less developed a semi-conscious gregariousness, among the more developed a passion of sympathetic understanding. The capacity to feel destroyed, society is destroyed it seems.[99]

She thought that Pearson's ideal of 'intellectual asceticism', as she called it, was a harmful restraint. In contrast, she had a 'vision of the fully developed human animal, leading a full and intense emotional life and in the strength of it, doing the widest and deepest intellectual work, tasting to the full the keen joys of thought . . .'[100] She was arguing for a balance between emotions and intellect, between feeling and rationality; Pearson's subsequent work does not indicate that he took much notice of her advice.

Individualism and the Emancipation of Women

In the club discussion of the Contagious Diseases Acts, Pearson and Parker were clearly disturbed by the women members' talk of religion, feeling and 'bodily needs of men'. The two men were quick to condemn the women's responses as 'thoroughgoing individualism', labelling the women 'individualistic', the men 'socialistic'. (The accusation that feminism was 'individualistic' was a common one among socialist men of this period.) Pearson was also locating women lower on the evolutionary scale, for in a recent public lecture he had presented a three-tier model of human evolution: the progressively higher stages of individualism, socialism, and humanism. He believed that women were individualist partly because of the constant struggle between 'freedom of the individual' and 'subjection of the individual to social stability'. Women's subjection had not been 'a result of mere caprice of men' but 'a sacrifice of individual freedom to a more imperative social end. It [had] inaugurated a new era in family life and checked a promiscuity which was not a stable social form.'[101] Once again women's subjection was explained and rationalized in terms of evolutionary needs and men were without blame. In reaction to Maria having claimed that the C.D. Acts hindered women's emancipation – hindered 'the full use of their powers' – Pearson proposed that:

> *The emancipation of women is not an end in itself*, but only a means to greater social efficiency and stability ... [the latter] will depend entirely on the increased use of women by the society and not on the extent to which they gain the 'full use of their natural powers'. These powers must instead be ... limited ... by the need for the individual subserving the whole.[102]

Was this a response to the women becoming too uppity for Pearson; were their 'natural powers' in need of rational limitation?

The committee meeting later that month decided that the recent references to 'emancipation of women' 'showed vagueness and ... the club should arrive at a more precise definition'.[103] Accordingly, Florence Balgarnie opened the discussion on this theme in October. She argued that the first stage must be women's economic independence, along with the control of passion by reason. (She did not say *men's* passion but from her statements elsewhere this was clearly what she meant.) Maria, her sister Loetitia, and club member Lina Eckenstein all strongly disagreed with the idea that economic independence was the most important part of women's emancipation. Clearly gaining in confidence, they shifted attention on to the men. To Maria, women's first requirement was 'a mental revolution in men'. Loetitia likewise felt the main problem was men's attitude towards women: 'men spoke [to women] always with condescension.'[104]

In November it was Parker who presented his ideas on women's emancipation. The women's movement was reactionary, he argued, since it encouraged women on to the labour market. Because of their children, married women should not work, but neither should unmarried women, for 'if only unmarried women can work, this might encourage the ablest women to stay single, and the race to be perpetuated by inferior women'.[105] The following month he patronizingly added:

It is to be hoped that through study and knowledge they [women] will arrive at a rational view and will see that it is important for the race that they shall not enter into competition.[106]

Parker's concern with healthy breeding was echoed in Thicknesse's paper, also given at the November meeting and entitled 'Claims of Children'. 'The vast majority of women not only ought to but will have children and ... they ought to devote their entire time to them', he asserted.[107] Maria noted in the club minutes that 'many members objected to the way he emphasized the child-bearing function of woman as the whole of her life aims and education.' It is perhaps significant that if we look at attendance at this meeting we find women in the majority, with eight women to six men. (Although the initial membership in 1885 had also had a majority of women, this was not always the case, given new members, resignations, non-attendance and the presence of guests.) Unsurprisingly, women members were much less likely than the men to agree with this idea of a 'social' demand on women to be child-bearers. Some of the men were also opposed, however. To Rhys Davids, Parker and Pearson appeared to be against women's emancipation. He appealed to the meeting:

Surely what we as a club agree on is that women do not in the present ... have the same chance as men and we want them to have it. Then we are told that the having of children makes this impossible.[108]

Pearson may not have openly said that he was against women's emancipation, but in the past three years he had begun to see such emancipation as highly contingent. When he came to rewrite his 1885 paper 'The Woman's Question' for his book *The Ethic of Freethought* (published in 1888), he added several new paragraphs on the rights of women. He was now arguing that these rights had to be totally subservient to, even absorbed into, society's reproductive 'needs':

We have first to settle ... what would be the effect of her emancipation on her function of race reproduction before we can talk about her 'rights', which are, after all, only a vague description of what may be the fittest position for her, the sphere of her maximum usefulness in the developed society of the future.[109]

The women members certainly did not think of their 'rights' in this way, and they rallied in defence of feminism. In December, in sharp contrast to Pearson, Parker and Thicknesse, Maria Sharpe presented the women's movement as 'part of that struggle for life which has raised the human race in the scale of being'. Evolutionists were always speaking of 'stages'; Maria did likewise. She suggested that there were three stages to women's emancipation: the first, a demand for better training and education; the second, for social and political rights and increased work opportunities; the third, a need for change in 'the relation of the sexes to each other and in marriage and the house'. This last stage was reached 'when the education women receive in the outside world of men ... must act backwards on her inner home life with men'.[110] Unlike the men's view of emancipation, she was pointing to the crucial need for a shift in personal and sexual relations, especially the 'mental revolution in men' that she had mentioned in October. Similarly, Loetitia's 'note' on women's emancipation that month expanded on 'men's attitudes towards women', which she had problematized in October:

> The worst disability that women suffer from is the average public opinion in matters of sex. Women are still judged and valued by their bodies rather than their minds . . .[111]

In the subsequent discussion, Pearson returned to the issue of women as child-bearers. In familiar vein he argued that if women's 'subjection [as mothers] is for the general good they had better remain in subjection'. What if, in seeking their emancipation, women 'injure the race'?[112] Again the gulf between the sexes was blatantly revealed: the women trying to break from their reduction to 'mere bodies'; the most vocal and dominant men returning women to the physical status of child-bearers.

39

Invisible Masculinity

Maria and Loetitia had raised the 'problem of men' a couple of times but, on the whole, masculinity was given little considera-tion in the club. Henrietta had tried unsuccessfully to get it on the agenda; Olive had challenged Pearson's first paper 'The Woman's Question' for assuming that the object of study – the problem – was woman and not man as well. The women had resisted the club name of 'Wollstonecraft' (after the late eighteenth-century feminist Mary Wollstonecraft) partly for the same reason. Even in the club's early days, Elizabeth Cobb had been doubtful that the men would co-operate: 'We want to study men as well, I am so afraid our men members will not help us to do that.'[113] It was the *Men* and Women's Club after all, but it felt to Elizabeth 'as if *man* were the only human being and woman only another species of monkey'.[114] And monkeys could not study men.

Olive, however, attempted her own study of male sexuality, asking Pearson how many men he knew 'who have reached . . . thirty and been absolutely celibate', what was the proportion of celibate men in the English middle classes generally, and was their ideal a union with one person or more than one?[115] We do not have Pearson's reply, but Olive's next letter disbelievingly wondered whether he had understood what was meant by celibate, given the high numbers he had given. Writing to Maria the following year, Pearson returned to this question of Olive's:

> Looking round a considerable number of male friends . . . I be-lieve that more than 50% of them are chaste; some 10% more would probably have been so, only at eighteen or nineteen they have been practically seduced by prostitutes, servants or other women.[116]

The woman was blamed again. As for woman's subordination, it was not anyone's fault, but due to evolutionary 'needs'. Either way, the club avoided scrutiny of masculinity, and the men avoided the taking of responsibility.

Towards the end of the club's life, Maria, who had greatly

gained in self-confidence during the past four years, wrote to Pearson accusing men of helping to perpetuate weakness and passivity in women. 'How many men really *desire* women strong in all directions? Is it not really passive women that they want ... so that they might have their own way with them.' She added sardonically: 'Where you have life and vigour you have variety, and it is not at all pleasant to have a wife doing the unexpected.'[117] She had touched a raw nerve. Many 'radical' men, Pearson included, waxed lyrically of Mary Wollstonecraft, George Eliot and other women who had lived outside society's dictates. But when it came to women in their own lives, they did not want them to be so unconventional that they might make demands of *them*, the men.[118]

The Club's Ending

The club had its final meeting in June 1889. Earlier that year Pearson explained to Maria why he thought the club's end was nigh:

> The problems with which it [the club] has dealt are problems which can't be solved by 'opinion' but only by real scientific research, and this is just what the individual members cannot find the time to give.[119]

In truth, the club had thrown up problems that could be solved neither by opinion nor by 'scientific research', whatever Pearson might have meant by the latter. For club debate had revealed an unbridgeable chasm between the desires and aspirations of women and men. It was with definitions and visions of morality, sexuality and the future that the true differences lay. The dominant men of the club looked to a specific kind of state-socialist future, in which rationality and reason reigned and women performed their duty as eugenic breeders for the nation. The definers of morality were to be those with the power and ability to 'read' the evolutionary direction of society – by definition an educated elite. As for sex, the men's ideal was of the separation of reproduction from sex, with sex involving pleasure 'in moderation'.

Today this may sound reasonable, even radical, but it disavowed the nonconsensual side of women's sexual experience – their reproductive sufferings and sexual abuse.

The women were more concerned with a future in which women were emancipated and economically independent, and in which men and women related to each other as equals, giving and receiving respect and consideration. Above all, they longed for men to transform their sexual practices and thus help to eradicate the double moral standard. To many of the women, in relation to sex, the ideal was one of *love* not lust, of spirituality not physicality. Since love concerned emotion and feeling, its discussion in the club was taboo. Loetitia, when listing the difficulties of club debate about 'artifical checks' (birth control) included 'the obvious necessity of omitting all considerations of love'.[120]

The women had many thoughts about ideal love. Henrietta, for example, had a vision of a new kind of spiritual yet passionate love, far surpassing the limitations of the physical body. She explained to Pearson:

> If our past race experience [in relation to sex] has failed then nothing is left to us but to try another way and to see whether the spiritual basis doesn't answer better; a spiritual love between a man and a woman would certainly ... develop a passionate feeling, but one which differs so widely from the average feeling as to be almost of another kind. It is only then that passion can be 'as intense as fire, as clear as the stars, as wide as the universe'. It stands to reason because the physical in us is definite, limited, mechanical; the mental and spiritual alone is infinite in power and unlimited in its range.[121]

Kate Mills' vision, also of a higher plane of being, was possibly even more startling and radical. She explained to Maria:

> I am not an ascetic or a prude but ... I say it is the cursed thing that pulls men and women down and holds them down ... this mad craving to find a heaven in the absorption in to another life which takes the form of sexual intercourse ... It is fatal because it does it while it throws over us a beautiful, incomprehensible, mysterious feeling of devotion and self-surrender ... But since we are Darwinians ... may we not reasonably suppose that the animal kingdom in its highest genus may evolve a more perfect specimen of the perfect

man (which would surely be hermaphroditic – only man and woman together forming the perfect creature . . .)

After all, she observed, 'the body of every man and woman bears the trace of the bisexual physical structure from which possibly man has descended and to which possibly he will re-ascend'.[122]

At the club's last meeting Parker presented a list of the club's achievements. The club had 'broken the barriers which in conventional society prevent all free discussion to be both possible and profitable'.[123] It had set out 'the proper use of word "moral"' and had found 'the men to have socialistic, the women individualistic tendencies.'[124] Did the men get to understand women better, given that the club's object of study had in effect been women? Pearson doubted it:

> Sometimes I have thought I did see them [women] more clearly, but then Miss Muller's old statement to me, that I should never hear the truth from any of its members, has recurred.[125]

To Emma Brooke, it was not so much women's concealment of the truth as man's inability to *see* that was the barrier: man's projected expectations of women: 'He looks at them through his own mental image.'[126] As we have seen, it was these male assumptions of what women did and thought that so perplexed and angered Maria.

Had the women gained anything from the club? Henrietta had resigned, informing Olive that 'the club is a piteous failure'.[127] Isabella Clemes and Agnes Jones both left the club early on. Isabella Clemes, mathematics teacher to one of Elizabeth Cobb's stepdaughters, had told Maria that at the club 'I feel something like despair at marking the gulf between our [men and women's] ideas'.[128] As we saw at the beginning of the chapter, she had conveyed her sense of this gulf to Pearson. Agnes Jones's departure was probably related to her being an Hintonian: a follower of the late James Hinton, a writer on sexuality and morality. Initially impressed by Hinton's ideas, Pearson had turned violently against him in the early days of the club, accusing him of immorality because of his apparent advocacy (and practice) of polygamous relationships.[129] Florence Balgarnie had threatened resignation but was persuaded to stay when asked to speak on her special interest – women's emancipation. However, after giving her paper in October 1888, she was absent from half the subsequent meetings. She was uneasy in the club, telling Maria that she felt 'a mere cumberer [an awkward burden] . . .'[130] And to Henrietta Muller in an interview for the *Woman's Penny Paper* she admitted: 'I do not prefer speaking at drawing-room meetings. I am more at home when addressing working people, especially working men.'[131] Club meetings were clearly of the 'drawing-room' kind.

Olive Schreiner had left the club early, and indeed left England. Her departure in December 1886 has been interpreted by historians as due to unrequited love for Pearson, and Pearson's horror at her sexual advances.[132] By her own account she certainly loved Pearson, but she strongly denied that she felt 'sex love', and 'Karl would never misunderstand me on this point', she later told her close friend Havelock Ellis.[133] At the time, however, she did feel misunderstood; she also seemed unsure as to whether she could *recognize* her own sexual feelings, for she inquired of Pearson:

> If ever you thought you saw an element of sex creeping into my thought or feeling for you why didn't you crush it? See, I love you better than anything else in the world, and I have tried to keep far from you that nothing material might creep in between my brain and yours, and you have not understood me.[134]

She told Ellis that her departure was partly due to a terrible row with Elizabeth Cobb, who had been spreading rumours about Ellis being an Hintonian. Pearson, who had only heard one side of the quarrel, informed Olive that Mrs Cobb was 'true in word and thought and deed, and that if I would quarrel with her, he could have nothing more to do with me'.[135] Whatever her overt explanation for the rift between Karl Pearson and herself, a short story written two years later ('The Buddhist Priest's Wife', which she thought to be her best piece of writing) seems likely to have drawn upon the incident. The heroine expounds her views to a man (bearing certain affinities with Pearson) for whom she has unrequited love:

If a man loves a woman, he has a right to try to make her love him because he can do so openly, directly . . . There need be no subtlety, no indirectness. With a woman, it is not so; . . . the woman who had told a man she loved him would have put between them a barrier once and for ever that could not be crossed; and if she subtly drew him towards her, using the woman's means – silence, finesse, the dropped handkerchief, the surprise visit – then she would be damned; she would hold the love, but she would have desecrated it by subtlety . . . Therefore she must always go with her arms folded sexually; only the love which lays itself down at her feet . . . is love she can ever rightly take up. This is the true difference between a man and a woman. You may seek for love because you can do it openly; we cannot because we must do it subtly.[136]

Whether or not Olive was writing about herself and Pearson, her account of the cultural restrictions on a woman openly declaring her sexual attraction to a man is as relevant today as a hundred years ago.

The women who left the club clearly felt deeply ambivalent about the whole experience for one reason or another. Those who stayed on however appear to have benefited – or so Maria told Pearson:

As far as I know the opinion of the women, the dissolution of the whole thing would be an immense loss in their lives. To me the one gain that has no loss, has been the intellectual stimulus which contact with minds immeasurably cleverer than mine has given me. Stupid as I still feel, I no longer feel the absolute despair I used to experience after club meetings at first.

Although in her late thirties, Maria still lived in her mother's house. But here the club had also helped her: 'In my home life too I have established a right to "a room to study in" . . .'[137] It appears that those who lasted the course may well have gained in assertiveness and self-confidence. What some of them undoubtedly also gained was the realization that a joint ideal between men and women was virtually impossible and that the only way for many women was to struggle for their emancipation separately from men. In her fury at Pearson's laying down the law for women, Emma Brooke had retorted:

In this women's question it cannot be solved unless women be allowed distinctly to work out for themselves their own idea of what their duty or ideal is.[138]

On her resignation from the club Henrietta wrote to Olive:

Men are like gardeners who have ... clipt [sic] women into shapes like this: [she had drawn below a picture of a tree with a lot of thin, identical branches] ... therefore the *only* chance for a woman to find out what her own shape is, is for her to grow *alone*, according to her own sweet will, under the open sky of Heaven.[139]

She wrote to Pearson at about the same time, announcing that she would start a rival club for women only: 'You will say "this is prejudice"; I will not deny it. I will merely say that in my club every woman shall find a voice and shall learn how to use it.'[140] As this book will reveal, women did indeed find a voice, or rather many voices. With each came a different use and a different set of contradictions and obstacles.

Conclusion

As we have seen, women's difficulty in forcing masculinity on to the agenda was due, in part, to their powerlessness, especially their unfamiliarity with the men's positivist use of Darwinism and their sense of being uneducated. Although drawn to the club by the feelings aroused by the *Pall Mall* revelations, no expression or channelling of these feelings was really possible given the way in which Pearson and, to a lesser extent, Parker dictated the Club's legitimate and illegitimate modes of debate and agenda. Women's difficulties were exacerbated by the club's definition of *morality*. Opposition to the widespread resort of men to prostitutes, including young girls, had no place within a discussion of immorality in which the *moral* was defined in terms of healthy breeding for the future of the 'race'. Pearson's eugenism pervaded the club and cast the gaze ever back on women as reproducers. And women's claims to individual rights, as opposed to social obligations, were undermined further by the disparaging way in which the male members professed to have demonstrated that the women could not be proper socialists because they were too preoccupied with individualism.

The Men and Women's Club represented in microcosm the tensions and difficulties which were to confront feminists in the years up until the First World War. Feminists themselves argued over the validity of chastity and the definition of sexual morality. Not only did eugenics challenge aspects of feminism, but a number of feminists themselves began to adopt a eugenical perspective, including a language of race and nation. They debated the thorny issue of a woman's right over her own body (the language of liberalism) versus her social 'duty' to bear healthy offspring (the language of eugenics and state socialism). The defining of male and female sexuality also became a crucial site of struggle at the turn of the century, with attacks on feminists, spinsters and lesbians in terms of their 'deviant' sexuality. Feminists retaliated by challenging male sexual practices, although for some of those feminists eager to claim a sexual identity, ridiculing 'frigidity' appeared more emancipatory than confronting male 'sexual excess'. Before examining these various feminist debates and campaigns, however, it is necessary to contextualize them (and indeed the Men and Women's Club) in terms of the dominant definitions of femininity, sexuality and morality.

CHAPTER 2

Women Defined

The current and dominant definitions of femininity, sexuality, and morality provided not simply 'raw material' for the new feminist ideas, but they of course also represented many of the assumptions about women which feminists were reacting *against*. The dominant constructions of femininity were used to justify women's exclusion from political power and public space on the one hand, and the 'naturalness' of their location in the private sphere of the family on the other. Nineteenth-century religion made a central contribution to the ideological construction of moral womanhood. By the late nineteenth century, however, the Church was beginning to be rivalled by medicine and natural science as the key self-declared definers of sexuality, femininity, masculinity and, to a lesser extent, morality.

In drawing upon the languages of their culture, feminists frequently combined concepts from evolutionary theory and science with concepts from religion. A synthesis of ideas from religion and science was not in itself unique; the novelty lay with placing the Christian moralizing role designated to women within an evolutionary narrative which posited women as the agents of change. To touch both the heads and the hearts of women, a combination of ideas was thought to be needed which allowed the realm of feeling as much validity as the realm of thought. This was attempted by feminists in their uniting of religious and scientific ideas; they were also constructing a feminist ethics which, in explaining the basis of existing immoral practices, pointed the way to greater morality in the future. Such ideas were a kind of 'sociology' of women. It was not for nothing that feminist doctor Elizabeth Blackwell entitled her main collection of articles *Essays in Medical Sociology*.[1] In Britain in the late nineteenth century, the term 'sociology' was frequently used to refer to the attempt to discover the laws of social development with the aid of Darwinist concepts. By 1902, sociology was defined in the *Encyclopaedia Britannica* as 'the science of social evolution'.[2] A number of women were constructing a feminist version of such a 'science'. What were these religious and scientific constructs which provided feminists with their repertoire of ideas?

Religious Constructions of Femininity

The early nineteenth century saw a revival of Anglican evangelicalism, with its emphasis on female obedience and submission as laid down by Genesis and St Paul. A favourite passage in collections of nineteenth-century family prayers was St Paul's Epistle to the Colossians, with its hierarchy of subordination:

> Wives submit yourselves unto your husbands ... Husbands, love your wives and be not bitter against them. Children obey your parents in all things ... Servants, obey in all things your masters...[3]

Evangelicalism also had implications for the construction of female sexuality. Prior to the late eighteenth century and the rise of evangelicalism in Britain, women were thought to be as licentious as men, if not more so, for their rational control was deemed weaker. The Evangelicals opposed aristocratic profligacy, sanctified family life, and advocated chastity and prudence in both sexes, but especially in the woman. Women were designated what Nancy Cott terms 'passionless'[4] – lacking carnal motivation – although the idea of women's inherent licentiousness never fully disappeared. Within Christianity generally the Fall 'explained' women's subordination to men: Eve's transgression had led to women's suffering, including the pain of childbirth. Yet childbirth, or rather women's role as mother, also provided the avenue to women's salvation.[5] Indeed, her familial responsibilities, emphasized heavily by the Evangelicals, aided the suppression of the dangerous sexual aspect of herself – her Mary Magdalene side subordinated to the Madonna. As 'pure' and 'passionless' wife and mother, a woman could be redeemed.

Evangelicals shared with other Christian denominations a

belief in separate spheres for men and women – the home and women's role within it as the foundation of moral order, standing as a bulwark against the immorality of the market. As Davidoff and Hall convincingly establish, by the 1840s this ideology of separate spheres which had originally been linked to evangelicalism had become increasingly secularized – become in fact 'the common-sense of the English middle class'.[6] As we shall see, feminists drew on aspects of this 'common-sense' for their own ends.

Feminist Appropriation of Religion

One important way in which feminists challenged the claim of female inferiority and incapacity was to argue that women had been disadvantaged not by nature but by a culture created predominantly by men. Feminist journalist and trade unionist Edith Simcox, for example, suggested that 'purity and religion', supposedly the 'natural heritage of women in all but the lowest grade of culture', was simply a product of circumstance:

> The intellect of women, as a class, has been concentrated and expended upon the incidents of private life and the domestic relations, and within these limits, as a natural consequence, their sense of moral obligation has been developed.

She also pointed to the relatively recent arrival of the idea of women's greater morality, and the continuation of the older 'typical view of the typical woman', namely 'as a daughter of Eve, on intimate terms with the old serpent and given to the beguiling of men'.[7] But although feminists may have blamed male culture for women's subordination, they nevertheless drew upon the languages of that culture for their analysis.

At face value, being among the most patriarchal of discourses, the theological doctrine and orthodox institutions of Christianity appear to offer little to women. Yet, despite the emphasis of Anglican evangelicalism on female obedience and submission, the religion provided women with certain advantages. The church or chapel was one of the few public arenas from which middle-class women were not excluded. Association between women, for religious and philanthropic purposes, gave them important practical skills such as public speaking, committee chairing, and the writing of reports, which they could subsequently use within feminist organizations. The nonconformist religions tended to have more direct implications for feminism, not least because nonconformists' sense of being different and at odds with the world was likely to have fostered an awareness of injustice. Given that a number of prominent feminists, including part of the leadership of the repealers of the Contagious Diseases Acts, were raised as Unitarians or Quakers, these two small but influential denominations (the Unitarian Society and the Society of Friends) seem to have been particularly significant for feminism.[8] Among Quakers, with neither formal creed nor professional ministry, the spiritual equality of all human beings was assumed. Institutionally, women were, in fact, treated differently from men, but meetings were open for both sexes to speak and there was a history of famous female preachers. Quakers, particularly women, had been active in anti-slavery work. This was also the case with the Unitarians, who had strong allegiance to the egalitarian ideas of the Enlightenment – the power to reason and a belief in natural rights, toleration and freedom. While Anglicanism explained women's subordination in terms of the Fall, Unitarians rejected the doctrines of original sin and essential human depravity, for which women were usually blamed.[9] The daughters of Unitarians also received a relatively superior education, for Unitarians saw intellectual and moral education as interdependent and necessary for the development of human goodness.[10] Mention must also be made of the Salvation Army. Founded in 1875, it was the first British organization, religious or political, in which women were placed not as subordinates but as principals. The conspicuous presence of 'Hallelujah lasses' on the streets made an important contribution to women's emancipation.[11]

Whatever the emphasis that nonconformism might have given to equality, it shared with Anglican evangelicalism the desire for a moralizing role for women within the home. Yet this view of women's 'proper' destiny gave women a language with which to demand of those within that home, including husbands, a sexual practice of the same 'purity' as that demanded of women, namely sexual chastity outside marriage and self control within. Women's supposed lack of carnality was the cornerstone of the argument for women's moral superiority.[12] By emphasizing women's moral, as opposed to sexual and carnal, characteristics, feminists were thereby raising women's status and self-esteem. The idea of women as 'moral protectors of the home', while ideologically contributing further to women's domestic confinement, simultaneously gave women a sense of mission, spiritual worth, and strong incentive to engage in philanthropic works – to morally protect others' (the working classes') homes. This moralizing role for women was a crucial component both in the inspiration of many women *into* feminism, and also in the very nature of their subsequent feminist mission. It was perhaps no surprise that many of the daughters of Unitarians, with their relatively superior education as well as their view of women's moralizing role, became both philanthropic workers and social purity feminists. Maria Sharpe and her sisters were among them. ('Social purity' was the contemporary euphemistic term for 'sexual purity' – the 'purity' or 'sexual continence' of both sexes. The social purity movement was intent on changing society's sexual behaviour and attitudes.) From religion, feminists took the ideas of women's moral superiority and of passionlessness and used them in their demand for transformed relations between the sexes. What did medicine, the 'new' challenge to religion as the designator of femininity, have in its turn to say to women?

Medicine's Gaze on Women

From the late eighteenth century, Western science has placed the act of 'looking' at the heart of scientific inquiry; this 'look' has implicitly, if not explicitly, been male.[13] In the early to mid-nineteenth century, when medicine was struggling to establish itself as a profession, part of this professionalization entailed defining medicine as part of science: as the domain of rationality, reason and *men* rather than the older association of medicine with healing, superstition and women.[14] By the late nineteenth century, medicine as science was not simply claiming the human body, especially that of woman, as the main object of its medical look or gaze, but also asserting that the defining and understanding of womanhood should lie within its domain. While science was presenting itself as *the* arbiter of knowledge in general, medicine, now claiming to be a branch of science, was beginning to challenge religion as the arbiter of knowledges: in particular, those of femininity, sexuality and, on occasion, morality.

The scientific/medical claim to understand Woman and render her intelligible was part of science's wider project: the understanding and controlling of Nature. From the time of the Enlightenment women have been designated *part of* Nature – both as the repositories of natural laws to be revealed and understood, and as unknown, potentially disruptive and wild creatures, 'outside' Culture. This identification of man with Science and Culture, woman with Nature, and the assumption that the gaze of science and medicine is male, is cogently illustrated by a late nineteenth-century statue standing in the Paris medical faculty, drawn to our attention in a perceptive article by Ludmilla Jordanova.[15] Entitled 'Nature Unveiling before Science' the statue is of a bare-breasted woman removing a veil from her head and body. The medical male onlooker stands for Science; his gaze anticipating the 'seeing' of Nature – the gaining of full knowledge of Nature – through the unveiling of Woman.

The professional status of medicine rested on its claim to specialized scientific training. Until 1876, women were excluded from such training through the refusal of British universities and medical schools to grant them medical degrees. Elizabeth Blackwell and Elizabeth Garrett managed to bypass this restriction. Blackwell, who had trained as a doctor in America, was able to practise in England under the Medical Act 1858 which permitted the registration of physicians with foreign degrees. In 1860 the requirement of a British medical degree was introduced. Elizabeth Garrett managed to obtain a licence to practise in 1865 by qualifying for the diploma of the Apothecaries Society, and then obtaining a degree in Paris. The regulations were again quickly altered to prevent the entry of further women. After a long struggle by women to gain access to the profession, the Medical Act 1876 enabled all British licensing bodies to confer diplomas on women. But social and ideological barriers to their entry into medicine still persisted. To all extent and purposes, medicine remained a male profession.[16]

Female Sexuality and the Medical Profession

Before the Enlightenment women were seen as lesser men, with the retention, inside, of structures that in the male were visible without. So, for example, the vagina was viewed as an internal penis. By the beginning of the nineteenth century, however, the sexes were generally believed to be incommensurable and opposite. Before the 1800s, women were assumed to be as sexual as men, indeed more sexual; after the 1800s, this began to change to a view of women as lacking carnal desire, as already mentioned in reference to evangelicalism. Yet the idea of a basic similarity in male and female sexuality (what Thomas Laqueur refers to as the 'one-sex' model) never fully disappeared, but co-existed with this new 'two-sex' model.[17] As far as the medical profession was concerned, the result was internal disagreement over the definition of female sexuality. The profession did agree however on the unquestionability of heterosexuality. Lesbianism was rarely mentioned by nineteenth-century doctors (or anyone for that matter) until the rise of sexology at the end of the century, a development which will be considered in a later chapter.[18]

Despite doctors' divergence of opinion on the question of female sexuality, the views of William Acton have been taken by some historians as representative of the period.[19] He was one of a number of doctors who transformed the moral state of passionlessness into a *somatic* condition of womanhood. Acton asserted that 'women (happily for them) are not very much troubled with sexual feeling of any kind. What men are habitually, women are only exceptionally'. He added this statement to the third edition of his book in 1861 which, until that time, had contained nothing at all on women since its main subject was the functions and disorders (especially the disorders) of the male sexual organ.[20] Like most doctors of the period, Acton's views on *male* sexuality demonstrated a distinctive tension between viewing the male sexual urge as a powerful and inevitable physiological process of evacuation on the one hand, and as in need of definite self-control on the other, for seminal loss debilitated the body.[21] Although many doctors paid lip-service to the idea of male continence, many simultaneously believed that a regular sexual 'outlet' for men was necessary for their health: 'A man must not expect to be in health, if he neglected to exercise a natural function.'[22] Sexuality was assumed to be naturally heterosexual; the 'outlets' of homosexuality or of masturbation (the latter known as 'solitary vice' or 'self-abuse') were deemed most *un*natural.

In 1871, in the fifth edition of his book, Acton inexplicably changed the parenthesis of his statement 'women (happily for them) are not very much troubled with sexual feeling . . .' to 'happily for society'.[23] Given the increasing encroachment of the women's movement on the male domain, perhaps the possibility that women might also become *sexually* active was alarming; he was certainly alarmed by a contrasting demand which he explicitly attributed to feminism. This he also mentioned in his fifth edition:

> During the last few years, and since the rights of women have been so much insisted upon . . . numerous husbands have complained to me of the hardships under which they suffer by being married to women who regard themselves as martyrs when called upon to fulfill the duties of wives. This spirit of insubordination has become intolerable.[24]

The nature of this 'insubordination' was spelt out in his sixth edition four years later: 'I was lately in conversation with a lady who maintains women's rights to such an extent that she denied her husband any voice in the matter whether or not co-habitation should take place . . .'[25] In stark contrast stood his ideal woman, who though 'seldom desires any sexual gratification for herself . . . submits to her husband's embraces . . . only to please him . . .' For she is 'so unselfishly attached to the man she loves as to be willing to give up her own wishes and feelings for his sake'.[26] Thus to Acton, although a woman did not normally desire sex, expression of this lack of desire in refusal of her husband was unacceptable: a wife should selflessly submit to her husband's sexual 'needs'.

If Acton's views on men typified the medical profession of the period, this was less true of his views on women. An examination of British doctors' views on female sexuality from the 1850s to the 1900s reveals a wide range of opinion.[27] Those that agreed with Acton included the famous gynaecologist Lawson Tait, who asserted that 'as a matter of fact, women are not sexual at all',[28] and the psychiatrist Charles Mercier, who noted that 'the impulse towards sexual intercourse is in the great majority of women but slight'.[29] Those that disagreed included J. Matthews Duncan who, in complete contrast to his fellow gynaecologist Tait, proclaimed that 'it is an almost universal opinion that in women desire and pleasure are in every case present.'[30] Dr Willoughby Wade informed the *Lancet* in 1886 that 'it is far from exceptional to find that there is an extreme enhancement of concupiscence [lust] in the immediately pre-catemenial [menstrual] period',[31] and Dr T.L. Nichols, writing in the previous decade, declared that a healthy menstruating woman 'is full of ardour, has a great capacity for enjoyment, and is seldom satisfied with a single sexual act'.[32] (As an example of the wide variance of opinion, we find Tait announcing that any sign of 'sexual eccentricity' in a girl at the time of her period must be treated as insanity – 'the best and safest explanation . . . of what looks like mere lust.')[33] T.L. Nichols, however, although believing all *healthy* women capable of strong desire, held that 'a great many women . . . never have pleasure in the sexual embrace . . .' This defect was either hereditary or caused by learning bad habits, in particular the 'early excitement of the amative faculty',[34] i.e. masturbation, which Nichols thought killed desire through blunting sensibility, unlike most doctors who believed the opposite.[35]

Most doctors in this period blamed heredity and bad habits not for lost desire but lost *modesty* and the possibility of subsequent *uncontrolled* desire. While men had will-power to restrain their sexual desire, women had the essentially 'feminine' quality of modesty – the 'womanly propriety of behaviour'.[36] Modesty as a protection was highly precarious: numerous factors could lead to its loss. Modesty was threatened by anything which 'in some way roused [a young girl] to unholy passion'. The 'bad habits' which led to the loss of modesty included masturbation, the reading of 'licentious novels', or mixing with 'lewd' companions. Modesty was an *unconscious* quality, unrelated to will-power; it was thought of as an inhibitory force which ensured women's 'purity' through protecting them from their 'lower' sexual selves. Once lost or destroyed, modesty, and its foundation of sexual innocence, could never be regained.[37] 'The innocent girl once outraged', the matron of a Lock Hospital (a hospital for venereal diseases patients) told W.T. Stead, suffered 'a lasting blight of the moral sense.'[38]

The prostitute was seen as the ultimate immodest woman and the embodiment of sexuality. In the late nineteenth century, a number of scientists were declaring prostitutes' sexuality and lack of modesty as signs of 'atavism' – reversion to a more 'primitive' stage of evolution. To most evolutionists, contemporary black people (termed 'savages' or 'primitives') were thought to be 'living fossils' – relics of an earlier evolutionary stage. In examining the sexual and moral behaviour of contemporary 'savages', anthropologists claimed to have access to the behaviour of the 'savage' ancestors of whites. There was much talk of 'primitive promiscuity'.[39] Although the term was used by anthropologists to refer to an early stage of human development, it was also used as a description of contemporary 'primitives'. In this latter respect, Karl Pearson's view was representative: 'the lives [of "primitive races"] are often ... little less than a carnival of sexuality'.[40] Atavism, along with lost modesty, 'explained' the prostitute's supposed lasciviousness.[41]

According to psychiatrist Dr Charles Mercier, prostitution was both a moral failure of character (of the prostitute, not her client of course!) and a mark of insanity, which in itself was a sign of atavism. For many psychiatrists of this period, all insanity involved retrogression, frequently referred to as 'degeneracy'.[42] As Mercier expressed it, this involved 'a peeling off of those superimposed layers . . . deposited by the process of evolution'. In the mentally sane, judgement, reason and will inhibited the 'lower' centres of 'primitive', childlike desires and instincts. Prostitutes, already lacking will-power by virtue of being women, also lacked modesty, women's sole inhibitory force protecting them from falling into vice and insanity. Prostitutes lacked 'the power of foregoing immediate indulgence which is the foundation of morality'. To Mercier they were 'moral imbeciles'.[43] The prostitute's 'moral imbecility' had implications for all women. If a woman's modesty once lost could never be regained, presumably *all* women risked moral imbecility. Behind the veneer of the dominant nineteenth-century ideal woman – the domestic 'angel in the house' – lurked the earlier representation of sexualized femininity: the Magdalene behind the Madonna.

The 'Maiden Tribute' and the Medical Press

Concern lest women lose their modesty was central to the medical profession's response to the 'Maiden Tribute' articles of 1885. On the face of it, the two main journals of the medical profession appeared to occupy polar opposite positions. The *Lancet* and the *British Medical Journal* (*BMJ*) fundamentally disagreed about the advisability of an exposé of London's underworld. To the *Lancet*:

> The publicity which has recently been given to the subject of sexual sin . . . is in itself an enormous evil . . . There are things 'done in secret' which 'should not be so much as named' in family circles or in newspapers which have an entrance into private houses . . .[44]

The *BMJ*, however, edited by the 'radical' Ernest Hart, welcomed the *Pall Mall*'s articles, believing that 'a great end will be served by this exposure . . . of practices which have too long secretly prevailed in our midst . . .'[45]

The two journals also had differing 'solutions' to the horrors revealed. To the *Lancet*:

the remedy will come only from the cultivation of purity in habit, in books, in newspapers, in schools, in the home ... It is to the religious subjection of the body that we must look for the spread of personal purity and sexual innocence.[46]

In contrast, the *BMJ* called for immediate legislation, particularly to raise the age of consent (which is, of course, what occurred). Although it also strongly advised the introduction of school sex education, it clearly felt ambivalent about such education for *girls*: 'Innocent ignorance is always attractive', it claimed, but suggested that 'if it be the means of luring the innocent victim to her doom, it is surely most dangerous.' This faced the *BMJ* with a dilemma, posed in the form of 'a difficult question to our readers': 'How ... is the girl approaching ... sexual maturity to be made acquainted with the solemn facts of the creative act, and guarded against associating them with the base impulses of passion?'[47]

I want to look in more detail at this 'difficult question'. What was meant by '*associating* [the solemn facts of creative act] with the base impulses of passion?' Was the girl to be told of – warned about – these 'base impulses'? Assuming for the moment that she was to be told, was it feared that she would *confuse* them with the 'creative act' and thus possibly be put off, even repelled by, the prospect of conjugal sex? Or was there anxiety that knowledge of these 'base impulses' would 'defile' her purity, even unleash 'passions' in the girl herself? Did the journal fear that a girl or young woman could lose her modesty through receiving *any* sexual information, that even if she was not told of the 'baser' side of sex, it would reveal itself to her by virtue of the removal of her protective innocence, her modesty's foundation? Even a modicum of sexual knowledge might make her more responsive to sexual advances, or more open to picking up 'vicious habits' such as masturbation. Such speculations as to the article's meaning draw upon some of the questions engaging the medical profession at the time, in their various attempts to define and thereby 'understand' women and their sexuality.

The *Lancet* and the *BMJ* might have differed in their views on the value of the 'Maiden Tribute' revelations, but in relation to questions of 'purity', modesty and female sexuality, the two main journals of the medical profession had more in common than was at first apparent. They were unanimous that great care was needed to retain the modesty of women and girls. For once lost, a woman became transformed: she crossed the boundary on which the entire female sex already hovered and entered a state of pathology and/or vice. Prostitution, 'nymphomania' and insanity all converged as the possible outcomes of the lost 'inhibitory power' of modesty.[48] The medical representation of femininity was thus inherently contradictory: if a woman retained her modesty she was defined by her morality; if she lost her modesty she was defined and ruled by her sexuality.[49]

Spinsterhood, Chastity and Dangers to Health

Many doctors and feminists appeared to share the belief that chastity for the unmarried of both sexes was necessary (although not sufficient) for their purity and sexual morality. Chastity was not quite sufficient since *true* morality necessitated a pure mind as well as a pure body.[50] But although many doctors theoretically advocated this doctrine, in practice some of them held to a double standard: that unchastity for men was understandable and even necessary for health, but for women it was unforgivable. Several doctors advised young men to keep a mistress or go to a prostitute until they married.[51] By the 1880s, feminists were challenging the hypocritical co-existence of a lip-service paid to chastity for both unmarried sexes, with a reality in which male promiscuity was tacitly accepted while anything less than total female sexual abstinence was thoroughly condemned.

There were, of course, doctors who strongly advocated chastity. To T.L. Nichols, for example, 'the law of a pure and unperverted nature is the law of chastity ... consistent with the highest health, and the best bodily, mental and moral conduct of men and women'.[52] Men could restrain themselves if they really wanted to; even their dreams could be controlled through the application of will: 'It is not that men have not the power of self-restraint ... it is that they lack the motive ... Vice is considered manly.'[53] Although Nichols wrote vehemently against the double moral standard, he nevertheless thought chastity far easier for women – not only, he suggested, for the majority with their unhealthiness and thus their minimal sexual desire, but also for those 'of passionate natures', since '[a] woman is continent without the least difficulty so long as she does not love'.[54] The implication was that since female chastity was easy, female unchastity was all the more reprehensible. William Acton also professed to advocate the healthiness of chastity outside marriage and of continence within, but faced with the married feminist who maintained that the *woman* should decide on the timing of sexual intercourse (the 'lady who maintains women's rights to such an extent that she denied her husband any voice in the matter whether or not co-habitation should take place'), he warned her that this might be 'highly detrimental to the health of the husband'.[55]

Whatever their hypocrisy, neither Acton nor Nichols suggested that chastity or continence might be detrimental to *women's* health. But by the late nineteenth century, as we saw in the Men and Women's Club, a growing section of the medical profession was suggesting that the chastity of unmarried women was as harmful to their health, if not more so, as the chastity of unmarried men.[56] Unlike their advice to the bachelor, however, doctors did not advocate the spinster's search for a sexual outlet, but dolefully charted the inevitable dangers of her 'unnatural' state. Was this a backlash against the feminist confrontation of the double moral standard – an attack especially on the feminist spinster? A woman in this new medical 'understanding' did not even need to lose her modesty to become sexually 'overcome'. By 1891, Dr Harry Campbell was pointing out that most of the medical profession blamed any 'disordered nervous function in the unmarried woman' on 'unappeased sexual craving'.[57] And it was the psychiatrists who were at the forefront of such pronouncements. Henry Maudsley, for one, claimed that 'between the instinctive sexual impulses ... and the conventional rules of society which prescribe the strictly modest suppression of them ... a hard struggle is ... maintained'.[58] One possible outcome was 'sexual hallucinations'; these were 'the characteristic features of a form of insanity which attacks unmarried women'.[59]

Maudsley believed that women could escape such a fate through religion, 'the only channel' which allowed women to express their sexual instincts 'freely without impropriety'. He was not advocating religion, for he thoroughly opposed the power of the Church, but he viewed women's 'religiosity' as nothing but an expression of their sexual desires.[60] Dr T.S. Clouston, however, saw religion not as providing an outlet, but as encouraging unmarried women's sexual obsessions. He wrote of 'ovarian or old maid's insanity' – a madness occurring

> in unprepossessing old maids, often of a religious life, who have been severely virtuous in thought, word and deed, and on whom nature, just before the climacteric, takes revenge for too severe a repression of all the manifestations of sex, by arousing a grotesque and baseless passion for some casual acquaintance of the other sex whom the victim believes to be deeply in love with her, or who has actually ravished her after having given her chloroform. Usually the clergyman is the subject of this false belief.[61]

An incident involving one woman accusing another of this type of 'insanity' is mentioned in Vron Ware's *Beyond the Pale*.[62] Forty-five-year-old spinster Catherine Impey, founder of the Anti-Lynching Committee (of which Florence Balgarnie was secretary), wrote in 1895 to a younger man, a dental student from Ceylon, declaring love and proposing marriage. He was so shocked by her letter that he forwarded it to his benefactor Isabella Mayo, one of Catherine's co-workers in anti-racism. Isabella in turn tried to get African-American journalist Ida B. Wells to denounce Catherine, which she declined to do. Isabella refused to work with either Ida or Catherine ever again, declaring Catherine mentally unstable, 'the victim of hallucination'.[63] Vron Ware speculates as to why Isabella reacted so violently. Was the issue simply one of Catherine's transgression of respectable femininity, or was the objection primarily to do with racial transgression? Ware suspects that it was both.[64] Isabella asserted that Catherine's behaviour would have led to a lynching in the southern states of America, where it was the black man, not the white woman, who got punished for any cross-race relationship. But while Ida B. Wells demanded the acceptability of voluntary relationships between black men and white women, Isabella, despite her involvement in anti-racism, seems to have assumed that cross-race relationships were always unacceptable. As we shall see, assumptions about racial difference regularly inflected debates about sexuality and gender.

The Afflictions of Reproduction

Unlike women, men could supposedly rule their bodies (and much else besides) with their minds. As Ornella Moscucci points out, since instinctual functions in men, including sexual ones, were believed to be controlled by the brain, head injuries were assumed to cause impotence and 'wasting of the testicles'.[65] Women, however, were ruled *by* their bodies; their reproductive physiology guiding their every move. Until the late nineteenth century, the uterus was held as a woman's central controlling organ, closely connected to the nervous system. With the beginnings of endocrinology at this time, it was no longer the uterus but a woman's ovaries which were said to dominate her body and mind. According to leading obstetricians R. and F. Barnes (father and son):

> The active or dominant organ of the sexual system is the ovary ...
> The ovary reigns supreme until conception ... then the uterus ...
> rules until the child leaves it ... The breast rules ... until ...
> supplanted by the ovary, which is ever struggling for supremacy
> and cannot long be kept in subjection.[66]

To most doctors, the ovaries were thought to have their greatest impact on the days up to and during menstruation. Menstruation was erroneously assumed to be the period of potential fertility, although not all doctors believed ovulation and menstruation to correspond exactly in time.[67] Whatever the medical confusion and disagreement over the matter, doctors were unanimous that women were driven this way and that by the dictates of their cyclical system, with crises at puberty and menopause and regular monthly disruptions in between. While male sexual desire and behaviour were subject to will, the desires and behaviour of women, sexual or otherwise, were largely beyond their control. Menstruation was held to exacerbate women's tendencies to capriciousness and instability, even to bring on madness. The supposed physical and mental disturbances of menstruation, indeed womanhood itself, as has already been pointed out, were deemed to lie on the borders of pathology.[68]

As if it were not enough to suffer the regular 'disorders' of menstruation, woman's reproductive system also rendered her susceptible to numerous other afflictions, especially that of hysteria. With hysteria's outbreak, woman's volition, meagre at the best of times, left her completely. Thought to be almost exclusively female,[69] it was defined as 'a disease of will',[70] 'the loss of inhibitory influence exercised on the reproductive and sexual instincts of women by the higher mental and moral functions'.[71] Hysteria was uniquely tied to femininity, its symptoms echoing the various physical and emotional characteristics deemed the hallmark of womanhood. Thus the hysterical patient exhibited a wide repertoire of unstable behaviour, rapidly moving, for example, from sobbing to laughter, wild tantrums to muteness and paralysis. In other words, hysteria was an exaggeration of the emotionality and capriciousness of woman. But it was also woman's supposed childishness that rendered her susceptible. Imitative, lacking willpower, acting on impulse and confusing fantasy and reality, woman's 'child-mind' was 'the most apt soil for hysteria ... the hysterical state ... a *mêlée* of childish peculiarities'.[72] It is perhaps not surprising that with the appearance of militant suffragism at the beginning of the twentieth century, suffragettes were quickly labelled hysterics.[73] Freud's theory of hysteria was not accepted in England until the First World War, only adopted with the advent of male hysteria in the form of 'shell shock'.[74]

In 1892 Dr Bryan Donkin (Men and Women's Club member and unrequited suitor of Olive Schreiner) wrote the section on 'Hysteria' for *A Dictionary of Psychological Medicine*. The 'typical subject of hysteria' was the young woman. In viewing her susceptibility to hysteria as linked to the stress of puberty, his argument was conventional. Less conventional was his recognition of the contribution of social factors: 'The educational repression and ignorance as regards sexual matters ... [and] all kinds of other barriers to the free play of her powers ... set up by ordinary social and ethical customs'.[75] While Donkin viewed *barriers* to 'the free play of [a young woman's] powers' to be an instigator of pathology, many other doctors declared the instigator to be the *removal* of such barriers. The latter argument was centrally used in the medical profession's attack on women's higher education, with claims that women's deployment of intellect would fatally injure their procreative capacity.[76]

Gynaecology and Ovariotomy

By the late nineteenth century, gynaecology was presenting itself as the legitimate specialism devoted to the study as well as the treatment of women's reproductive and sexual physiology. It characterized its scientific 'penetration' of women as parallel to the colonizer's penetration and conquest of an alien land.[77] But its claims went even further: it was to be the final arbiter in all kinds of issues relating to the role of women. Thus to Lawson Tait: 'Some of the questions raised by the advanced advocates of woman's rights are to be settled, not on the platform of the political economist, but in the consulting room of the gynaecologist.'[78]

Whatever the pretensions of gynaecology, its methods were highly contested within medicine, especially its controversial surgical interventions of ovariotomy, clitoridectomy and hysterectomy. Indeed, gynaecologists' very right to operate was challenged by surgeons, for as obstetric *physicians*, gynaecologists were formally not allowed to perform surgery, reflecting the traditional division of labour between surgeons and physicians. Their eagerness to operate was also objected to by many others inside and outside the medical profession. Ovariotomy, introduced into Britain in the 1840s, was by the 1880s seen by gynaecologists as their greatest achievement. The case was different with clitoridectomy. In the 1860s, obstetrician Isaac Baker Brown's zeal for the operation had led to heated controversy. Although he had been removing the clitorises of numerous women for a range of afflictions including epilepsy, hysteria,

insanity and masturbation, the medical profession were concerned less with the extent of his operating than the public
rumour that he operated without the women's consent. In 1867,
when Baker Brown was expelled from the Obstetrics Society,
clitoridectomy was largely abandoned in Britain, although it
continued to be occasionally performed.[79]

As for ovariotomy, its opponents accused its enthusiasts of
zealous 'over-treatment' and the 'unsexing' of women. In 1886 a
well-publicized legal case, brought by a woman against a Dr
Imlach, for improperly removing her ovaries, raised wider ethical
questions. To the *Lancet*, opposed to ovariotomy, the trial's
interest lay 'in the broad question [of] whether the frequent and
almost indiscriminate spaying of women suffering from diseases
which are not fatal, and which are often only trivial, is justifiable.'[80] The epithet 'spaying' was popular with opponents of
ovariotomy; they sometimes also labelled the operation 'vivisection', with women and animals both victims of the monstrous
vivisector.[81] The *Lancet*'s accusation of 'spaying' led to a lengthy
and vitriolic debate in its letters column, with Lawson Tait
angrily differentiating the operation performed on animals
('spayed before puberty to prevent . . . development of a sexual
appetite and the powers of procreation') from the human operation, which he termed 'the removal of the human uterine
appendages'.[82] According to Tait, the latter was performed after
puberty, and it neither destroyed sexual desire nor procreative
power, given that the woman was already usually sterile from
the disease for which the operation was performed. He informed
the British Gynaecological Society that his ovariotomy patients
never lost their sexual appetites, gleaning his evidence from the
husband of each patient, 'a better witness than the patient
herself'.[83] The Society warmly received Tait's encouraging evidence, apparently unaware of the fact that in other contexts Tait
was most insistent that women *lacked* sexual desire, whether or
not they had been operated upon.

To label ovariotomy 'spaying' was also an accusation that
healthy as well as diseased ovaries were being removed. Indeed,
given the belief in the destabilizing effect of a woman's reproductive system, some gynaecologists recommended ovariotomy as

the cure for epilepsy, excessive sexual desire, hysteria and certain kinds of insanity, as well as for painful periods and uterine tumours. While a number of doctors implied that these very afflictions *indicated* ovarian disease, others were aware that the ovaries were organically healthy but believed that such was the domination of a woman by her ovaries, their mere presence could mentally and physically disable the woman concerned.[84]

The Feminist Challenge to the Medical Designation of Women: the Case of Dr Elizabeth Blackwell

Although feminists may have drawn upon religion as an important component for their construction of a theory and politics of sexual morality, they were less inclined to turn to medicine for similar provision.[85] Feminists were adamant that women should not be continually reduced to their physicality. Loetitia Sharpe's complaint that 'women are still judged and valued by their bodies' can be read as an objection to the idea that women were basically nothing *but* their bodies. Elizabeth Blackwell was a key example of a feminist who challenged the medical profession's legitimacy to define and control women. Being herself a doctor, she was in a stronger position than most women to do so. As Susan Kingsley Kent points out,[86] feminists set great store by the admission of women into the medical profession in the hope that women doctors, with their knowledge of biology and psychology, would establish the 'true' nature of femininity, masculinity and sexuality. To Blackwell, women should become physicians because of the distinctly moral contribution they could make to the profession – countering the male, materialist science of bacteriology.[87]

Born in England in 1821 to nonconformist and abolitionist parents, Elizabeth Blackwell emigrated with her family to America in 1832 where she eventually managed to train as a doctor. She was later able to practise in England under the Medical Act 1858, which permitted the registration of physicians with foreign degrees. (The Act was quickly amended, as explained earlier.) Elizabeth Blackwell was Britain's first woman doctor. She was a member of numerous philanthropic and social purity organizations, such as the Social Purity Alliance, the Moral Reform Union and the National Vigilance Association. She also belonged to several feminist groups, including the Ladies National Association (for the repeal of the Contagious Diseases Acts) and the National Society for Women's Suffrage, of which she was a vice-president. She wrote extensively on questions of morality, sex education and the medical profession. Her writings were suffused with an explicit commitment to the eradication of the double moral standard through the beneficial teachings and practice of ethical medicine, and through women's role as moral guardians and teachers of children and men.[88] Religion was central to her writings. She saw 'true' science, including 'true' medicine, as that which was informed by, and confirmed, Christian morality. Her views on Christianity, however, were far from orthodox. Raised as a Congregationalist, she became a Christian Socialist in 1882, then joined the Christo–Theosophical Society in 1891.[89]

Elizabeth Blackwell took issue with the dominant medical view of women as physiologically inferior and ruled by the demands of their reproductive system. She argued that men and women's physiology was in most respects equivalent, claiming, for example, that testes were analogous to ovaries, and men's involuntary emissions were directly parallel to menstruation. In this she followed the pre-Enlightenment way of thinking, in which men and women were essentially the same. But in two respects she held simultaneously to the post-Enlightenment view of crucial *difference* between the sexes: the significance of having or not having a uterus, and the nature of sexual desire.[90] According to Blackwell, in lacking one key organ, namely a womb, men were rendered inferior to women. Women's superiority did not rest on literal motherhood; their potential motherhood, and their concomitant maternal instinct, could take the form of what Blackwell termed 'spiritual motherhood': an altruistic approach towards humanity in which a whole nation represented a woman's progeny, to be 'protected' and 'saved'. In viewing women's 'maternal instinct' as potentially 'spiritual', she inverted the dominant medical view of this instinct, namely that it rendered women closer to 'lower' animals by virtue of their shared 'animal' experience.

Although viewing maternity as the key attribute of femininity, Blackwell was appalled by the widespread medical opinion that women were ruled by their reproductive system, and that therefore a host of afflictions could be treated via treatment of this system. Opposed to the general increase in surgical intervention – the '*prurigo secandi*' (the itch to cut) – she saw bilateral ovariotomy (the removal of both ovaries), which she termed 'female castration', as especially heinous because it rendered women incapable of childbearing.[91] Like other feminist anti-vivisectionists, she drew parallels between the medical treatment of women, especially ovariotomy, and the medical treatment of animals. She believed that vivisection inevitably dehumanized the doctors and students involved, and thereby contributed to gynaecologists' willingness not simply to perform unnecessary operations on women, but also to submit women to 'degrading' vaginal examinations.[92]

While opposing the medical practice of ovariotomy, Elizabeth Blackwell also challenged the Acton view of women as sexless beings. Differing from many other social purity feminists, she believed women to be as sexual as men, if not more so, although sexually distinct. Here was the other crucial way in which she saw men and women differing: women's sexual desire was principally mental, with greater capacity for self-control, while men's desire was physical, their will-power subordinated to their passions. This association of woman with the mind and man with the body represented another reversal of dominant ideology. Although aware of women's potential for sexual pleasure, her work as a doctor had taught her that many women had bad experiences: 'Injury from childbirth or brutal or awkward conjugal approaches may cause unavoidable shrinking from sexual congress, often wrongly attributed to absence of sexual passion.' If only there was wider realization that 'the special act necessary for parentage' was not the whole of sex: 'It is the profound attraction of one nature to the other which marks passion; and delights in kiss and caress – the love touch – [is] its physical expression, as much as the special act of the male'. Be that as it may, she still saw the latter as 'the ultimate physical expression of love.'[93]

In their potential for motherhood and their greater capacity for sexual self-control, women were seen by Elizabeth Blackwell as men's moral, if not mental, superiors. Women's moral superiority rested on their maternity (literal and spiritual); it gave them the key role in the 'future regeneration of the race' – as teachers (of children), doctors and transmitters of hereditary 'purity'. Like many feminists of the period she utilized the 'common-sense' concept of 'race',[94] with the implicit slippage between human race, white race, and Anglo-Saxon race, and the assumption of white superiority and supremacy. In her concern with women's pivotal role in the future of the 'race', she foreshadowed the language of eugenics. The idea of 'Woman as Mother' was mobilized by many feminists. It both empowered women, giving them a vantage point of superiority from which to speak, while simultaneously locating that vantage point within a discourse of racial superiority. For women were superior not as mothers in general, but as mothers of 'the nation' and of 'the race'. Such constructions were inevitably placed within an Imperialist framework of which the vast majority of feminists were blithely uncritical.[95] The idea of women as 'mothers of the race' drew centrally on the language of evolution.

Evolutionary Theory, Darwin and Sex Differences

The evolutionary challenge to religion had started earlier than Darwin, but it was his writings – in particular *The Origin of Species* (1859) and *The Descent of Man* (1871) – which in the late nineteenth century entered popular consciousness and speech. Darwinism, with its concept of random selection, its denial of individual free will, in addition to its obvious refutation of a literal reading of the Bible, pushed many a contemporary thinker into religious doubt and the search for a new ethical understanding of the world. Yet on the whole, most evolutionists were not wanting to oppose theology. As Robert Young has pointed out, they wished to reconcile nature, God and humankind.[96] Young suggests that in this period there were three possible ways of characterizing the relationship between science and theology. Firstly, each new scientific discovery could be seen as additional proof of the Deity's power; Dr Elizabeth Blackwell, for example, held to this view. Another position, that of Henrietta Muller among others, saw the apparent conflict between scientific findings and a scriptural passage as necessitating a re-interpretation of the passage's meaning, taking it as symbolic rather than literal truth. A third position, held to, for example, by Karl Pearson, saw science as refuting theology. But if Pearson was dismissive of religion, there were many who viewed an ardent belief in science as itself religious. To the Fabian Beatrice Webb, science *was* a religion, and mid to late nineteenth-century intellectuals displayed an 'almost fanatical faith . . . that by the methods of physical science, and by these means alone, could be solved all the problems arising out of the relation of man to man and of man towards the universe'.[97] Others, including Herbert Spencer, suggested that a true grasp of evolution's magnitude *induced* religious feeling.[98] Whatever the challenge of evolutionary theory to the biblical Creation narrative, religion, or at least a religious sensibility, still had a significant hold on the British psyche.

Unsurprisingly, evolutionists made pronouncements on the nature of femininity and masculinity. Thus, by the late nineteenth century, belief in innate, 'natural' differences between the sexes was being compounded by belief in *evolved* sex differences – differences which had arisen over time and were part and parcel of evolution. These differences were claimed to have been pivotal both to the evolutionary processes leading to the rise of humankind and to its particular subsequent development. It was further widely claimed that evolution to higher stages had entailed *increased* differentiation between the sexes. To many Anglo-Saxon evolutionists, the 'highest' stage had been reached with white Victorian bourgeois society.

Charles Darwin's ideas on sex differences were rooted in his concept of 'sexual selection', developed in *The Descent of Man and Selection in Relation to Sex*. To explain what appeared to be otherwise inexplicable characteristics specific to one sex, such as deer's antlers or peacocks' tail-feathers, he hypothesized that competition was not just for food and space (the process of natural selection) but also for mates. According to Darwin, 'sexual selection depends on . . . success . . . over others of the same sex in relation to the propagation of the species'. Success entailed winning two kinds of struggle: one, generally between males, involved driving away or killing rivals, the females remaining passive, while the other, again generally between males, was a competition to excite or charm those of the opposite sex. The females, now no longer passive, were the selectors of the more agreeable partners.[99] Differences 'not directly connected with the act of reproduction' he termed 'secondary sex characters', and proposed that the majority had arisen through this process of sexual selection. Although not directly connected with the *act* of reproduction, they were nevertheless fundamentally about the process leading up to reproduction. Darwin's stress on sexual selection suggested that reproductive success (and the sex differences associated with it) was the key to evolutionary survival and sex differences were central to this.

Although sexual selection as a biological theory did not win wide acceptance,[100] Darwin's views in *The Descent of Man* on differences between the sexes became highly influential, and a starting point for a new psychology of sex difference. What were these views of Darwin's? He began by suggesting that males fighting over females required more than bodily strength and size: 'courage, perseverance and determined energy'[101] were also needed. He acknowledged that men today no longer usually fought for their wives; however,

> during manhood they generally undergo a severe struggle in order to maintain themselves and their families [a particularly middle-class view of the world], and this will tend to keep up or even increase their mental powers and as a consequence the present inequalities between the sexes.[102]

This combination of natural and sexual selection had resulted in 'the man attaining to a higher eminence, in whatever he takes up, than can woman – whether requiring deep thought, reason or imagination, or merely the use of the senses and hands'.[103]

Did women have *any* superior abilities? Darwin conceded that women had 'greater tenderness and less selfishness', and that 'it is generally admitted that with woman the powers of intuition, of rapid perception, and perhaps of imitation, are more strongly marked than in man ...' However, lest one was to think this suggested female superiority on any score (although 'imitation' does not sound too wonderful), he added the proviso: 'Some at least of these faculties are characteristic of the lower races, and therefore of a past and lower state of civilization.'[104]

Women, the 'Lower Races', and Children

Although referring to 'lower races', and accepting the claim of greater intelligence of whites, Darwin was passionately opposed to slavery and to overt racism. However, aspects of his theory were pressed into the service of political views with which he had little or no sympathy. In particular, his ideas on race were taken as supportive of the newly developing race science – 'scientific racism' – in which races were seen as biologically differentiated on a fixed and graded scale of intelligence, moral worth and closeness to animality. Scientific claims of an evolutionary hierarchy and 'proof' of the physical and mental inferiority of 'primitive' peoples added an important rationale to, and reconception of, existing racist beliefs and practices. And Darwin's notion of 'the struggle to survive', along with the concept of 'the survival of the fittest' (not, in fact, a term of Darwin's but of Herbert Spencer) were deployed in justification of colonial expansion and exploitation.[105]

The comparison and equation of women and 'lower races' was widespread. A plethora of nineteenth-century scientific writings, especially those of the new sciences of anthropometry and craniology, 'discovered' that women shared with negroes a narrow, child-like skull and head in comparison to the rounded-head, small-jawed males of the 'higher' races.[106] (The term 'lower races' was frequently used interchangeably with 'primitives', 'savages', negroes and black people, although 'lower races' did include other racial groups. To Britain, however, the colonized negro represented the epitome of the 'lower' race.) The equation of white women and 'lower races' was reinforced by the supposed similarity of both groups to children. Posture was taken as one indication of this proximity. As sex psychologist Havelock Ellis expressed it:

> Verticality . . . is in direct ratio with evolution . . . the human infant is as imperfect a biped as the ape; savage races do not stand so erect as civilised races . . . women are more curved forwards than the men.[107]

Women, 'lower races' and children shared not simply physical characteristics, but also mental ones: lack of willpower, emotionality, dependence, imitativeness, and little capacity for abstract thought.[108] If 'lower races' represented the female type of the human species,[109] females represented the 'lower race' of gender. 'Lower races' were thought of as the children of the human race, while the white child represented an ancestral (primitive) stage of human evolution (the theory of recapitulation).[110]

The dependence of both women and black people was thought to necessitate their 'protection' – by white, Western man. But although childlike, both women and blacks were simultaneously the unknown 'Other' – '*terra incognita*', the 'dark continent' – to be 'discovered', dominated and controlled.[111] If civilization – white, masculine and adult – was to be maintained, its antithesis – primitive, female and childlike – needed containment.[112] The enthusiasm with codifying and thus defining women and black people was in part a concern to control an 'alien' grouping, in the same way that there was widespread codification of other 'outside' groups, such as criminals, the insane and the urban poor.[113] Indeed, these latter groups were also constructed in analogy with 'lower races', as biologically 'races apart', whose differences from the white male and likeness to each other 'explained' their lower position in the social hierarchy.[114] The desire to 'know' and control both women and black people was also related to the fact that both groups were currently challenging their subordination. The British women's movement had began in the 1860s, while the Indian mutiny of 1857, the Jamaican revolt of 1861 (the General Eyre case) and other black uprisings raised the spectre of the 'threatening native'.[115] In speaking of women in a 'racialized' language, scientists were able to claim that just as races were distinctive 'species', incapable of successfully crossing the social and cultural boundaries proper to their race, so too were women a distinct species whose individual members risked degeneracy should they try to cross the boundaries proper to their sex.[116]

Women and black people were not always equated in their evolutionary development however. Progressive differentiation of the sexes was held as the hallmark of evolutionary progress, and it was thus assumed that there was greater similarity between black men and women than white men and women. Black men and women were thought to have similar brain sizes, for example, unlike white men and women.[117] Thus, although white women were frequently equated with black people generally, this idea of progressive differentiation implied a definite distinction between white and black women. The prime distinctions were presented as sexual and reproductive. Black women were said to lack modesty and display sexual desires similar to black men. They were also thought to have smaller pelvises than white women. According to Havelock Ellis:

> while in some of the dark races it [the pelvis] is ape-like in its narrowness and small capacity, in the highest European races it becomes a sexual distinction which immediately strikes the eyes ... It is at once the proof of high evolution and the promise of capable maternity.[118]

Wider pelvises were necessary, it was argued, to accommodate the supposedly bigger heads (with the bigger and cleverer brains) of white babies. Along the way, however, evolution was also thought to have inexplicably disadvantaged women. While the 'uncivilized' woman lacked reproductive disabilities, with her menstruation apparently scanty, even non-existent, and her child-bearing without complications, the reproductive experience of the 'civilized' woman was of such 'profound suffering' that Lawson Tait felt 'a devout thankfulness' that he belonged to the opposite sex.[119]

White and black women generally may have differed sexually and reproductively, but there was a section of white women declared to be like black women in one crucial respect: the lower-class woman, above all the prostitute, resembled the lower-race woman along the lines of a shared 'primitive' sexuality. And the prostitute, atavistic and degenerate, with her supposed arrested development, morbid heredity and physical and mental stigmata, such as skull deformities, protruding jaws and oddly shaped ears,[120] stood as a 'race apart' in the heart of British society, the most 'Other' of the urban poor. While 'Otherness' entails distancing of the peripheral from the central norm (here the norm of white, middle-class masculinity), the very separateness of the 'Other' promotes curiosity and desire.[121] Middle-class male resort to the working-class prostitute was partly related to this attraction to – and repulsion from – the 'Other'. Similarly, the role of anthropological accounts and photographs of 'primitive' peoples provided a surrogate pornography for European middle-class males – a fascination and prurient interest in the 'exotic' and 'repulsive' sexual customs of aliens.[122]

Sex Differences in the Mind

In 1887 the comparative psychologist, naturalist and Darwinist George Romanes wrote an influential article on 'The Mental Differences between Men and Women'.[123] He brought together a number of widely held beliefs about femininity and presented them as a scientific compilation of the mind's 'secondary sexual characters' – the beginning of the new psychology of sex differences mentioned above. He divided the mind into three components: intellect, will and emotion. In relation to intellect, women lacked originality and their judgement was inferior, being superficial, partial and emotional. Women's intellectual inferiority was to be expected, argued Romanes, given that their brains weighed approximately 5 oz less than men's. Here Romanes was drawing on craniology – a branch of physical anthropology concerned with measuring the human skull, with particular reference to differences between races and sexes. By the late nineteenth century many of craniology's earlier claims were being challenged, including the belief that mental ability could be gauged

76

from brain size, and that the size of men's brains relative to body weight was greater than women's. This reference to brain weight was the one aspect of Romanes's article rejected by the *British Medical Journal*; otherwise they were 'thoroughly with him in his condemnation of the fatuous notion of some feather-brained reformers that there is no such thing as sex [difference] in mind'.[124]

As for will or volition, Romanes informed his readers that 'we rarely find in women the firm tenacity of purpose and determination to overcome obstacles which is characteristic of what we call a manly mind . . . their minds are more prone to wandering', as well as displaying 'proverbial fickleness'. Afflicted with insufficient will, women were overpowered by their emotions. Negatively, 'this tendency displays itself in the overmastering form of hysteria or in the more ordinary form of childishness, ready annoyance, or a generally unreasonable temper . . .' Coyness, caprice and vanity were added to the list. More positively, women showed 'affection, sympathy, devotion, self-denial, modesty . . . reverence, veneration, religious feeling and general morality'. However, whenever evolutionists and doctors presented positive attributes of femininity, there tended to be a negative, obverse side. Thus women's greater 'sensibility' and 'delicacy' spelt physical and mental weakness and a proneness to imbalance, their greater 'morality' and 'religiosity' labelled them superstitious and possibly prudish, their 'intuitiveness', one of the more positive-sounding attributes, meant immediate mental apprehension *without reasoning*, for women's intuition had to compensate their inability to reason. As for female 'receptivity', this had the negative connotation of 'suggestibility'. Taken as a whole, the mental characteristics of women were 'those which were born of weakness', while those of men were 'born of strength'.[125]

Sex Differences and the Sex Cells

Two years after the publication of Romanes's essay, Patrick Geddes and Arthur Thomson's *The Evolution of Sex*[126] presented an all-encompassing theory of sex difference. In contrast to

Darwin, who saw most sex differences as functional and dynamic
– existing for a specific purpose (to aid sexual selection) and
changing with the changing interaction between organism and
environment – biologists Geddes and Thomson presented a view
of sex differences which was static, essentialist and ahistoric.
They claimed that all sex differences were simply reflections of
the basic divide between the primary sex cells, the egg and the
sperm, and had nothing to do with 'sexual selection'. The sex
cells, they argued, displayed contrasting metabolisms: the sperm
was small, active and dissipated energy and was thus 'katabolic',
while the egg was large, passive and energy-conserving and thus
'anabolic'. Thus, they argued, males everywhere, among all
animals including humans, were 'more active, energetic, eager,
passionate and variable; the females more passive, conservative,
sluggish and stable'.[127] Geddes and Thomson's book was hugely
popular among scientists and social critics of the day. Havelock
Ellis, for example, endowing Geddes and Thomson's claims with
an additional 'race' element, argued that if women were the
'conservative' force to men's 'progressive', women were the
preservers of the more 'primitive' traits found in lower races,
while the men of the higher races led the way in new biological
and cultural directions.[128] Although Geddes and Thomson professed support for women's rights, the logic of their argument
was deeply conservative, for sex differences were so ingrained in
our evolutionary history that 'to obliterate them it would be
necessary to have all the evolution over again on a new basis.
What was decided among the prehistoric Protozoa cannot be
annulled by Act of Parliament'.[129]

Feminists, Heredity and Evolution

Feminists approached evolutionary theory as a guide to the
future and an explanation of the present and the past. As
expressed by one associate of the Men and Women's Club, the
writer Jane Clapperton: 'The doctrine of evolution . . . must be
regarded as: *explanatory* of things as they are, and *prophetic* of
things as they will be and should be.'[130] Feminists were not, of

course, alone in such a view; for example, the radical liberal David Ritchie reflected in 1889 that 'evolution has become not merely a theory but a creed ... a guide to direct us how to order our lives'.[131] If Karl Pearson wished to use evolutionary theory to aid the development of a kind of national state-social-ism, his future wife Maria Sharpe held other priorities: Darwin had put

> instruments in our hands by which we may help ourselves. It is ... my earnest conviction that it is through the right understanding of these laws that women alone will be able to solve the problem of 'herself, her mission and her end'.[132]

To solve the 'woman problem', many feminists believed that it was not enough simply to understand these evolutionary laws; women as active agents of change had a role to play in determining evolution's *direction*. A number of feminists, frequently with the aid of anthropological writings, constructed the evolutionary past in the form of a narrative. They drew upon various anthropological hypotheses concerning the existence of a period of Matriarchy. Feminists suggested that under Matriarchy women had been men's equals, maybe even their rulers, and had undoubtedly played the central role in the creation of human culture. At some point, however, the women had been subordinated to men. Such a hypothesis acted to counter the view that women were *naturally* passive and eternally under patriarchal rule.[133]

Narratives of Transgression

Why had women become subordinated? One popular theory held to by a number of feminists, including Annie Besant, Henrietta Muller, Kate Mills, Elizabeth Blackwell, and especially Ellis Ethelmer,[134] proposed that women's subordination was due to men's past and present transgression of 'physiological truths' or 'natural laws'. These God-given 'natural laws' were those by which humans should live if they were to remain in good health, and, in the long term, realize their true humanity. Such ideas were rooted in the earlier sanitarian or moral environmental tradition in which health and disease were viewed holistically, seen as bound up with environmental, bodily and moral 'cleanliness'. Health was the natural state; ill health was the result of the violation of these 'physiological truths'. The nineteenth-century idea of the 'physiological' conflated mind and body. Indeed, other technical medical terms, such as 'habit' and 'constitution', referred to aspects of human physiology which were both mental and physical, and seen as the products of the interaction of biology, psychology and the environment.[135]

Belief in such 'physiological truths' was widespread in the nineteenth century, but viewing women's oppression as due to men's trangression of these 'truths' was a new development. In contrast to, and a subversion of, the Christian precept of Woman's original transgression (Eve in the Garden of Eden), it was Man who had committed the original sin – that of sexual excess: the demand by men of an inordinate amount of sex from women, largely against women's will. Feminists holding to this hypothesis followed the theory associated with late eighteenth-century biologist Jean Baptiste Lamarck, namely, that organisms evolved by acquiring characteristics and then passing them on to their offspring in the form of altered hereditary (later called genetic) information.[136] Feminists used Lamarck's theory to argue that male transgressions, originally acquired as wicked habits, had become implanted into men's very beings through heredity. In having transgressed the natural law of sexual continence at some point in early human history, man ever since had inherited 'an exaggerated and abnormal amount of sensual desire ...'[137] Man was therefore less truly human than his female counterpart, in that only women held to the 'natural law' of humanity.

Within dominant culture, Woman was designated part of 'Nature', and 'Other', in contrast to Man and Culture. Late nineteenth- and early twentieth-century feminists played upon and subverted the idea of women's relation to nature. In confronting men's transgression of the natural laws of continence, and in attempting to get men to learn to live by such laws, feminists saw women as the transformers of the social order. Women were the civilizers, leading men to their 'true' *human* nature. And within this construction, it was *Man* who was 'Other' – as less truly human than his female counterpart. Man as 'Other' took one of two forms. Men were either on par with non-human animals – at the same stage of bestial carnality – or, in their sexuality at least, they were *lower* than other animals on the evolutionary scale, for the latter, unlike humans, were believed to live by an ethical 'natural law' of sexual continence in which the female dictated the timing of all sexual intercourse. In either construction, men were 'unnatural' in the sense that they were other than fully human, where to be human included the 'natural' ability to control carnality.[138] Such a view subverted the dominant equation of Woman with Nature, Man with Culture and Humanity. Within this alternative model, Woman was equated with human, civilized nature – essential for the development of *moral* culture – Man with non-human, uncivilized nature. Nature in the sense of *human* nature was thus not in opposition to culture, but the crucial contributor to it.

There was another dimension to these sets of oppositions between human and non-human, namely the dimension of race. Those who viewed non-human animals as sexually licentious often simultaneously held this view of 'primitive' peoples, thereby effectively equating non-human animals and contemporary black people. Those who viewed non-human animals as sexually moral tended likewise to claim that primitive peoples had a higher sexual morality than the so-called 'civilized' – a romanticized eighteenth-century Rousseau-like image of the 'noble savage'. For example, in a paper to the Men and Women's Club in the 1880s, Kate Mills had asserted that like the 'lower' animals, the 'easy parturition' and lack of menstruation of 'savage' women was due to their living by the 'natural law' of sexual abstinence during pregnancy.[139] The 'civilized' man, in breaking this law, had brought painful childbirth and menstruation upon their women. Although ostensibly praising the 'primitive' lifestyle, this equation between 'primitive sexual morality' and 'animal sexual morality' was inherently racist for, as with the negative portrayal of animal and 'primitive' sexuality, it asserted the virtual *equivalence* of animals and black people.[140] The biological and social hierarchy of humanity and race remained unchallenged, whether the 'savage'/beast be noble or otherwise.

The Lamarckian view of male sexual excess held by feminists had as its complement the idea that women had acquired an aversion to sexual relations. It was argued that in the far distant past, women's experience of the dangers and pain of childbirth had acted as an inhibitory factor on their sexual 'urges'. In some explanations it was claimed that such pain had come into being as a result of male transgression. The pain, combined with the social responsibilities of motherhood and the cultural denial of female sexuality, led to a reduction in women's sexual desire: 'The incumbent sequences and sufferings – the burdens and pains of motherhood – developing on her [woman] a natural deterrent.'[141] This lessened desire was then inherited by subsequent generations. We saw how such arguments were put by the women of the Men and Women's Club.

How did the feminists who held to this theory envisage the ending of these male transgressions, and thereby the eradication of the roots of women's subordination? If the tendency to male sexual excess was the product of inherited habit, the learning of *new* habits of sexual continence could put heredity on a new and 'purer' road, thereby transforming the tendencies of future generations of men. Men would henceforth have a different attitude towards women, and although this alone would not eliminate women's oppression, it was a crucial step towards that end. Science, meanwhile, should ideally be committed to delineating these 'natural laws' and informing the public accordingly. And the 'aversion' of women to sexual intercourse would presumably go once men were practising self-control (thereby reducing involuntary pregnancy) and once sex was transformed from being a solely physical phenomenon into something more spiritual.

In their narratives of evolutionary descent, the fact that the sexuality of 'lower' animals and primitive people was perceived as *different* from the sexuality of white people – whether better

82

or worse – but also as *comparable* because connected through evolution, enabled feminists to deny the inevitability of current masculine sexual behaviour, and the eternal victimized sexuality of women. It was more appealing to 'explain' male sexual excess in terms of evolution than biology. To accept male biological 'needs' as the explanation for this 'excess' (the dominant position within medicine) was to accept its inevitability. Women faced such biological reductionist arguments in relation to themselves; their reproductive systems supposedly confined them to the domestic sphere if not the sickbed, while sexually, women were constructed as 'mere bodies', passively available for male consumption. Thus, it is no surprise that feminists were keen to challenge the claims of biological determinism, both to take issue with the idea of male sexual 'necessity' and to counter the dominant view that women were the inevitable victims of their biology. Evolutionary narratives provided an explanation *and* a solution; they 'explained' the origin of male sexual excess (in itself the explanation for female subordination) and offered the means to its eradication. Lamarckian theory permitted feminists to argue that biology, including supposedly 'innate' sexual difference, was *transformable*. As we shall see, evolutionary theory, through the idea of sexual selection, also provided a means of speaking about female agency in the past and the future.

Women as Sexual Selectors

Most feminists were in favour of the learning of new habits – new ways of living and behaving – even those who did not think that women's subordination was due to past male transgressions. Learning these new habits would entail an extensive programme of education – of children, men and women. Children were to be given a basic programme of sex education while men were to be taught the value of living by an equal moral standard.[142] Women needed to be educated about human physiology and sexuality, both for their own protection, and also to equip them, as mothers, for the task of teaching their children.

Armed with such knowledge, women would be more discerning in their choice of future partners, and, as wives, they would insist on the highest morality from their husbands. Sexual selection would again come to the fore. When women were economically independent, feminists believed, sexual selection would at last be truly possible, with the female playing the leading role as her ancestors had done, and as non-human females were still doing. The final plank in this women-centred vision of the future lay with heredity: through the law of inheritance, women would pass on to their offspring the moral tendencies of their husbands and themselves.

Such was the optimistic view of a number of feminists in the 1880s and 1890s, an optimism increased by their view of evolution's future. For along with a number of other theorists of the time, Alfred Wallace and Herbert Spencer among them,[143] these feminists believed that the human evolutionary process was moving from natural selection to conscious, moral selection, from physical struggle to survive towards a time of co-operative and moral order. For feminists, the women's movement was part of this 'inevitable movement forward', and it was women who were the central agents of change[144] – they were the moral guardians of the future. As Henrietta Muller had informed the Men and Women's Club:

> The sons of earth have done their task and nature now calls upon her daughters to fulfill theirs – as the one has conquered the physical world, the other shall conquer the moral.[145]

The Multivalency of Darwinism

How was this view of evolution reconcilable with Darwinism which, in allowing chance to be the only sure determinant, had supposedly put paid to the idea of human agency, or indeed any agency, moving history forward under its own volition? The answer lies in the very nature of Darwin's writings: full of ambiguities and contradictions, they were open to a variety of different readings and evaluative positions.[146] For example, Darwin's metaphorical notion of 'natural selection' was ambiguous and imprecise. His frequent resort to anthropomorphism, as in the depiction of 'Nature' as the 'Great Mother', implied an agency with active intent. Further, whereas in *The Origin of Species* he concentrated on the mechanism of 'natural' (that is, non-human and unwilled) 'selection', in *The Descent of Man* the main mechanism was sexual selection, the *choosing* of mates (and it was the females who did the choosing). The idea of active, determining agency was also encouraged by the narrative form in which his texts were written, and what Gillian Beer calls 'a form of imaginative history'.[147] After all, evolutionary theory could not, and still cannot, be 'proved' at any particular moment in time. And the state of genetic knowledge in the late nineteenth century left many of the processes of inheritance inexplicable. This meant that although the idea of natural selection contradicted the Lamarckian idea that will and habit could generate change, Darwin fell back on Lamarck's theory to explain certain aspects of inheritance. And given that the language of intention was still present in Darwin, Lamarck's theory that conscious endeavour and inherited habit were the agents of evolutionary change continued to be adhered to by many. This remained the case even after the discovery by Weismann in the 1880s that the soma (body) cells were unable to influence the germ cells (and thus that physical and mental changes in one's lifetime could not be passed on via inheritance).[148]

Darwin's theory was so multivalent that it allowed feminists to make readings in stark contrast to the dominant readings of the day. Those happy with the status quo chose to assume that Darwin's theory implied that the present age, of white, male, capitalist supremacy, was evolution's pinnacle. Feminists questioned this assumption; they saw the future as a potentially far superior alternative, in which patriarchy had been abolished, and, for some feminists, capitalism as well. And it was to be women who would lead humanity forward to this new and glorious age. Yet although the call was for 'women', most English feminists implicitly qualified the collective noun: the future female leaders of humanity would be white and, ideally, Anglo-Saxon.

Feminists, Morality and Darwin

A further example of the multivalency of Darwin's writing lay in the use of his work to construct a new morality. By the 1880s, the growing numbers of atheists, agnostics and freethinkers no longer saw morality and religion as inevitably related. The official line of the Men and Women's Club, for example was 'the possibility of morality without reference to religious creeds'.[149] While Darwin's theory contributed to many Victorian intellectuals' spiritual crises,[150] for others, including many feminists, religion and evolutionary theory co-existed as different, but possibly equally valid and complementary, ethical guides. There were at least three ways in which the hypotheses and reflections on morality in Darwin's *The Descent of Man* were drawn upon. One approach perceived support for the notion of 'self-control', another focussed on his ideas of 'altruism', love and sympathy as the basis of morality, while a third emphasized Darwin's functional view of morality as maintaining social unity and solidarity. The first and second were definitions held to by many feminists who thereby found vindication in Darwin's writings of their beliefs and politics. Within Victorian culture generally, while the 'lower self' was conceived as purely appetitive and impulsive, and hence selfish and egoistic, the 'higher self' (the *moral* self) was held to display restraint/self-control and altruism.[151]

In the first reading, Darwin was held to have presented the currently dominant definition of morality (and of sexual morality in particular), namely 'self-control'. The idea of self-control had long been central to many religious codes. The higher part of human nature – the spirit, soul or 'reason' – was believed to be in constant battle with the lower part – the demands of the flesh and bodily passion. Conquering this passion through self-control was the true mark of human morality. In the Men and Women's Club, Henrietta Muller and Mrs Walters were examples of adherents to this view; likewise the *Lancet*'s concern with 'the religious subjection of the body'. Darwin could be interpreted as a fellow adherent in his statement:

A moral being is one who is capable of reflecting on his past actions and their motives ... [A]fter some temporary desire or passion has mastered his social instincts, he reflects and compares ... and ... resolves to act differently for the future – and this is conscience.[152]

Darwinian psychiatrist Charles Mercier, in equating morality with self-control, defined both as 'the capacity to forego the immediate gratification of a desire for the sake of obtaining a greater but more distant benefit'.[153]

If women were having difficulty in claiming greater morality on the grounds of their chastity, given the assertions of chastity's dangers to health, it was no easier for them to claim greater morality on the grounds of possessing more self-control. Where feminists claimed that women were both more chaste than men and innately less sexual, their claim to greater self-control was undermined by the observation that according to their own beliefs, women lacked any sexual desire *to* control. (Indeed, in the discussion of Henrietta Muller's talk 'The Other Side of the Question', Parker had commented that if one accepted her hypothesis of greater male passion, then men could be seen as *more* moral than women, given they had more to control.)[154] Where feminists held women to be both more chaste than men and potentially *as* sexual as men, their claim of greater self-control was up against the question of will-power. Self-control was thought to necessitate will-power, but this was a quality believed by many scientists and medical men to be relatively lacking in women. If one accepted this view, it became nonsensical to speak of women possessing greater self-control than men – women simply did not have the *capacity* for self-control.

There was some disagreement, however, as to what constituted will-power, and how it could be developed and strengthened. For example, leading naturalist and physiologist William Carpenter (an authority cited by Kate Mills in her argument for continence) held that to develop will-power one needed both to train the 'intellectual faculties', and to build 'moral character'.[155] Religion was central, he believed, in the formation of the latter. It was here that women could claim an advantage: they might lack training of the intellect (although this could be remedied in the long run), but many women had the edge over men in relation to training in religion. Elizabeth Blackwell declared that:

> We see that under the effect of training to a moral life and the action of public opinion, a great body of women in our own country constantly lead a virtuous life, frequently in spite of physical instincts as strong as those of men, and always in spite of mental instincts still more powerful.

Women might have as great a sexual instinct as men, she believed, but because they were trained to apply 'constant watchfulness' they had greater self-control.[156]

A second reading of Darwin pointed to his ideas on altruism:

> The moral sense of conscience ... is the most noble of all the attributes of men, leading him without a moment's hesitation to risk his life for that of his fellow-creature.

He also claimed that the foundation of 'the moral qualities ... lies in the social instincts, including ... family ties ... [T]he most important elements are love, and the distinct emotion of sympathy'.[157] It would have been this quote that led Annie Eastty in the Men and Women's Club to claim that Darwin had intended the 'moral sense' to include feeling as well as reason.[158] Despite four years of subjection to Pearson's domination in the Club, and her avowed allegiance to his definition of morality, in 1889 Maria Sharpe was still adhering to this particular reading of Darwin (and to her nonconformist religious upbringing?), in her claim that 'love to our fellowmen is the motive of our moral conduct'.[159]

Many feminists, particularly religious feminists, singled out this emphasis of Darwin's, as well as his allusions to self-control, to justify their own definition of morality. Women's potential maternity and its associated attributes of love and care appeared to make this notion of morality of particular relevance to women. For women to take morality as altruism was in fact highly congruent with the dominant 'separate spheres' ideology. Within this ideology, men were allocated to the public and political, women to the private and domestic, where they acted as moral guardians of the home. This notion of separate spheres had developed in the early nineteenth century as part of the 'making' of the middle classes, with the ideology as pivotal to the development of a distinctive middle class identity.[160] In the late nineteenth century the philosopher Herbert Spencer elaborated upon the idea of separate spheres in proposing that they corresponded to two entirely opposed arenas of morality: an ethics of the family and an ethics of the state. In the family, the guiding moral principle was that of the greatest benefits given where merit was least; in the state, benefits were given proportionate to merits. To Spencer, women's nature was 'to give most where capacity is least'; their entry into the public world would therefore be disastrous, since it would lead to 'the fostering of the worse at the expense of the better'.[161] Many opponents of women's suffrage and of women's access to the public world thought likewise. In contrast, feminists argued for the *extension* of this altruistic morality, or indeed a morality of self-control, into the public world, thereby transforming that sphere for the better – the public sphere would be 'purified' and women's entry into wider political life, via the suffrage, was an important starting point for this 'purification'. As we shall see in the next chapter, some feminists believed in beginning this 'purification' process even before receiving the suffrage.

The Men and Women's Club Revisited

A third reading of Darwin selected out his reference to the functional role of morality in cementing a society together. This was not a reading made by many feminists, but it was the reading favoured by Karl Pearson, and it informed the definition of morality laid down by the Men and Women's Club. Darwin argued that with the evolutionary development of reason, moral behaviour became less instinctive and more open to conscious choice. This idea was not original to Darwin; Herbert Spencer and Walter Bagehot had said something similar.[162] Nevertheless, the idea became central to what was later termed 'Social Darwinism' in which Karl Pearson was a key figure.[163]

As a young man, Pearson's main mentor had been the brilliant mathematician William K. Clifford, who died an untimely death in 1879 at the age of thirty-three. A colleague of Clifford, reflecting back on their time together in Cambridge in the 1860s, remembered how 'natural selection was to be the master-key of the universe . . . Among other things, it was to give us a new system of ethics'.[164] In building this new system of ethics, Clifford drew on Darwin to construct a 'scientific basis of morals'. He developed a notion of the 'tribal self': a tribe or group having a sense of itself *as* a unified entity. Observable in 'the simpler races of mankind', this tribal self lay buried within us all, hereditarily transmitted. 'With the settlement of countries and the aggregation of tribes into nations, it takes a wider and more abstract form'.[165]

We can see how these ideas informed those of Karl Pearson and Robert Parker, in particular the link between morality and nationalism. Parker explicitly linked the club definition of morality to a racial 'struggle to survive': 'We [in the Club] have fully accepted the Darwinian theory of development . . . that morality has been evolved in men and women by the struggle of race with race.'[166] Within this definition of morality, women were again described in terms of a language of race, but this time it was not an equation of women with other 'lesser' racial groups, but a designation of their destiny as racial breeders – literal carriers of the future. As we shall see, many feminists in addition to Elizabeth Blackwell subscribed to this racialized role for women, not least because it appeared to offer a subject position of significant importance. But by confining women to the realm of motherhood, such a position inevitably set limits to women's potential. It also had implications for those women who did not 'fit' the image of ideal 'racial mother', whether due to disinclination, designated unsuitability or racial classification.

I have shown how the Club's ideas on morality were informed by Darwin's various pronouncements on 'the moral sense'. The Club's other concerns and its mode of debate also become more explicable in the light of the wider context given by this chapter. Its focus on women as the object of study clearly reflected the obsession of the period; likewise its concern with the questions of the relative strength of male and female sexual instinct and the relation of chastity to health. It is also easier to understand the female club members' ambivalence in speaking from a position of subjectivity. In the late nineteenth century, many women were attempting to enter the world of public discourse. If they spoke in the manner appropriate to femininity, they were labelled irrational, emotional, sentimental and subjective; if they dared to attempt to speak in a discourse of 'science', they were warned that they were taxing their fragile bodies and minds, and were thereby courting the dangers of ill health and insanity.

While feminists challenged medicine's biological reductionist view of women as little more than walking wombs, they appropriated a construction of femininity from religion, namely woman as morally pure. They thus used the assumption of sexual difference (a difference in moral aptitude) for their own ends. They also shifted the allocation of blame for 'original sin' from woman as Eve to man as transgressor of natural laws. They confronted the equation of woman with Nature and 'primitives' by claiming that it was man, in his sexual excessiveness, who was closer to the 'beast' of Nature, while woman was humanity's civilizer. Here they turned to evolutionary narrative as 'explanation' for women's subordination. They took from Darwinism not the construction of woman as such, but the potential within evolutionary narrative for female agency: females as sexual selectors. The multivalence of Darwin's writings also permitted feminists to claim Darwinian backing to their definitions of morality, be it self-control, or altruism. Feminists developed a compelling explanation of the 'origin' of women's subordination and an optimistic prognosis of women's future, dependent on women's active participation in running the country as well as the introduction of changes in male habits and male heredity. That there were limitations to this explanation and to the feminist appropriations from religion and evolutionism will become apparent in the next few chapters.

PART TWO

PURIFYING THE PUBLIC AND PRIVATE: WOMEN AS MORAL AGENTS OF CHANGE

'Purifying' the Public World: Feminist Vigilantes, Prostitution and 'Protective Surveillance'[1]

In 1894, two American male guests of social purity feminist Mrs Laura Ormiston Chant complained to her that on their recent visit to the Empire Theatre of Varieties, a large and famous music-hall in Leicester Square, they 'were continuously accosted and solicited by women and . . . very much shocked by the want of clothing in the ballet'. In autumn of that year, along with Mrs Amelia Hicks, national organizer for the British Women's Temperance Association, Mrs Chant set off for the Empire music-hall to establish the veracity of their claims. Bonneted and in smart but 'discreet' evening dress, she was determined not to stand out as an outsider, a 'prying prude'; in an earlier visit, her 'day' dress betrayed her as other than a regular patron of the music-hall – 'I was a marked woman'. Her disguise did not stretch to the wearing of *décolletage* however:

> No one has carried on a more consistent campaign against the normal style of evening dress than I have. Ever since I was 21 I have abjured bare neck and arms.[2]

She was appalled by what she witnessed. Not only were some of the performers revealing too much flesh, but worst of all, prostitutes were present in the audience – or rather, in the auditorium, since they were not strictly a *part* of the audience. According to Mrs Chant, they were not there to watch the performances; they came to watch for potential clients. The *Vigilance Record* related her account of the visit:

> The women complained of were very much painted and more or less gorgeously dressed; they did not go into the stalls; they either sat on the lounges or sofas, or took up positions on the top of the stairs and watched particularly the men who came up to the promenade.

> In no case were these women accompanied by gentlemen, or by any others, except of their own type. She noticed a middle-aged woman who introduced the others to a number of gentlemen ... The attendants appeared to be on very friendly terms with many of the women.[3]

By this it was implied that the Empire knew well enough the intentions of these women – they were regulars and part of the music-hall's attraction.

On 10 October 1894 the London County Council (LCC) Licensing Committee met to consider applications for the renewal of music-hall licences. Licensing of London's approximately 400 music halls, a function formerly held by magistrates, had passed to the Council on its inauguration as administrator of London under the Local Government Act 1888. Mrs Chant attended the meeting in order to challenge the renewal of the Empire's licence, on grounds of indecency on the stage and disorderliness in the auditorium. Although bent on eliminating 'demoralizing' entertainment, Mrs Chant was at pains to stress that she was not against amusement *per se*, insisting: 'I am no Puritan.' 'We don't want to lessen the amusements ... but we will have them decent. They will not be as highways of ruin to the young, licensed opportunities for the vicious.'[4] A number of feminists were called upon by Mrs Chant as witnesses, including Lady Isabel Somerset (President of the British Women's Temperance Association) and Mrs Sarah Amos (a fellow temperance worker and a campaigner for the rights of working women).

Not all feminists applauded Mrs Chant's actions however, Josephine Butler, for example, informed a close friend:

> I tried hard to keep out of the 'Empire' conflict ... I continue to protest that I do not believe that any real reform will ever be reached by outward repression ... [L]et individuals alone, not ... pursue them with any outward punishment, nor drive them out of any place, so long as they behave decently.[5]

A 'repressive' response to moral matters was of particular concern to Josephine Butler; it had been troubling her for several years. Her concern was all the greater because a number of *feminists*, once apparently *laissez-faire* and anti-statist in matters of sexuality and morality, were now, in the 1880s and 1890s, adopting a more repressive stance and were taking to closing brothels, clearing the streets of prostitutes and attempting to 'clean up' indecent leisure pursuits, from literature to music-halls. Why were these women acting in this way?

The Criminal Law Amendment Act and the National Vigilance Association (NVA)

Many feminists in this period held as one of their key objectives the 'purification' and 'civilization' of both public and private worlds. As predominantly middle and upper class, feminists' wish for greater 'civilization' and morality can be seen as partly related to their classes' current fear of a working-class uprising. The 1880s was a period of low profit, high unemployment, severe cyclical depression and a chronic housing shortage. This economic instability, combined with political developments – the rise of socialism, trade unionism and the immigration to the East End of foreign anarchists and socialists – prompted the propertied classes to attempt a remaking of working-class culture, especially the encouragement of the working class into a 'middle-class' respectability. This was to be achieved through legislation and philanthropy.[6] Immoral behaviour was viewed with as much suspicion as overtly political beliefs and activities. Indeed, Victorian moral and social reform converged,[7] with the desire for moral reform present even in the pursuit of what might appear to us today as essentially *material* reform. For example, the concern to improve working-class housing partly related to the belief that overcrowding encouraged incest and juvenile prostitution.[8]

While the respectable working classes were wooed, the casual poor – the 'dangerous classes' – were policed more coercively, and their behaviour subjected to greater intervention. The social purity movement of the 1880s was part of this new intervention-ist approach. As Walkowitz points out,[9] although still holding to an older rhetoric of liberal reform and voluntary effort, the movement was now much more willing to turn to the state for the enforcement of its moral objectives. And it was not surprising that prostitution should be a key site of intervention, since prostitution was viewed as emblematic of the danger and disorder of the city.[10] All this may give us a small part of the explanation for the interventionist activities of certain middle-class social-purity feminists. However, these women were not simply acting as members of the middle class, but also, and crucially, as religious feminists with a history of philanthropy.[11] Thus, for a greater understanding of their actions, it is important to look at what informed their vision of purified public and private worlds, and what *means* appeared appropriate to further the desired end. The vision of social-purity feminists was partly shaped by certain religious beliefs, and frequently by adherence to 'temperance', in which women were seen as the victims of male alcoholic abuse. That some of these feminists' actions took a repressive and statist form needs to be related in part to their heritage of philanthropy, their views concerning female sexuality, and their attitude towards local government and the state. But first, what exactly was this 'repressive' activity in which a number of feminists were now engaged?

The story of this apparent volte-face needs to start earlier, in the 1870s. Through the 1870s, Josephine Butler's energy was directed towards the abolition of the Contagious Diseases (C.D.) Acts. The legislation had been introduced in the 1860s to regulate prostitution in the hope of countering venereal disease among the army and the navy. By the 1870s, opposition to the Acts had sprung up in the form of a coalition of middle-class evangelicals, working-class radicals and an active group of feminists headed by Butler. Despite the difficulties entailed in such diverse groups attempting to work together, sufficient MPs had been converted to the repeal cause to win the C.D. Acts' suspension in 1883.[12]

In 1885, after fifteen years of fighting for the abolition of the C.D. Acts, there was much optimism that their repeal was close at hand. In her address to a meeting in the spring of that year, Josephine Butler spoke of a new concern – 'repressionists' in their midst: those bent on abolishing prostitution and introducing moral behaviour through repression. At this point, however, she was adamant:

> These people are not our enemies . . . mistaken as we think they are
> in their methods, [they] are still honestly desirous of getting rid of
> prostitution; . . . the advocates of the Contagious Diseases Acts desire
> the very opposite. They believe prostitution to be a necessity . . . It
> is the fervent desire of my heart to win and gain over entirely to our
> side all that crowd of repressionists who are now . . . going in a
> distinctly wrong direction, but who may be won.[13]

The C.D. Acts were repealed in 1886. A year later, Butler's
concern with repressive actions remained. It was now voiced
specifically in relation to Britain's central social-purity organization, the NVA, which at this time numbered many repealers
among its members,[14] Josephine Butler included, although her
membership was always only nominal. The NVA's work had
many dimensions. It provided support to victims in numerous
cases of indecent sexual assault, rape and 'seduction', including
the offer of a solicitor's services. It argued for the introduction of
women magistrates and women police, and campaigned to
change various aspects of the law concerning sexual offences.
Like most social-purity organizations, it saw the law as 'schoolmaster to the nation'.[15] Josephine Butler praised the NVA's
activities in all these respects; her unease lay primarily with
another aspect of its work: the enforcement of those clauses of
the Criminal Law Amendment Act concerning brothels. While
viewing legislation as potentially educative, she opposed repressive application.

Butler was not alone in her concern. Veteran feminist and
repealer Elizabeth Wolstenholme Elmy was similarly worried
about 'those with whom for 17 years I have worked for the
Repeal of the Contagious Diseases Acts', who, 'by a strange
perversion, now sanction and command the means and the
methods of a cruel repression'.[16] Mrs Chant was one such example – a member of both the feminist repeal organization the
Ladies National Association, and the NVA. Ten years later,
having lost hope long ago of winning such people, Butler
warned her colleagues:

> Beware of 'Purity Societies' . . . ready to accept and endorse any
> amount of inequality in the laws, any amount of coercive and

degrading treatment of their fellow creatures in the fatuous belief that you can oblige human beings to be moral by *force*, and in so doing . . . promote social purity.[17]

It was still the NVA to whom she was principally referring.

The NVA had been set up by social purists in order to ensure the enforcement of the Criminal Law Amendment Act of 1885. As we have seen in Chapter One, the Act had hurriedly passed through Parliament in the wake of W.T. Stead's sensationalist 'revelations' in the *Pall Mall Gazette* in July of that year as to the extent of London's juvenile and coerced prostitution. There had been unsuccessful attempts to secure a Criminal Law Amendment Bill for a couple of years, each bill aiming to raise the age of consent and reform the law on sexual assault. Most feminists supported these measures, but the bills also contained various repressive clauses relating to soliciting and brothels. The Vigilance Association for the Defence of Personal Rights (known since its beginnings simply as the 'Vigilance Association'), of which Josephine Butler and many other repealers had been founder members in 1871, had always been wary of each new version of the bill. Despite its chief aim being opposition to 'over-legislation' in the name of personal freedom, it gave guarded support to the version of the bill which finally got through. (Incidentally, it made no reference to the clause which criminalized 'acts of gross indecency' between men.) Nevertheless, it warned that

> a law however just, must be justly and wisely administered . . . In the present case there is far more than the usual amount of probability that mischief may be done, on account of the formation . . . of voluntary associations to put the law in motion, and the difficulty of ensuring . . . that they shall always act with prudence and justice.

Most of such voluntary associations affiliated themselves to the NVA. The Vigilance Association for the Defence of Personal Rights was also far from happy with the NVA's choice of title. Since the NVA had 'filched from us our good name',[18] the following year the Vigilance Association changed its own to the 'Personal Rights Association'.

The Vigilance Association for the Defence of Personal Rights may have initially been supportive of the new Act, but it soon had misgivings. By January 1886, it was as worried as Josephine Butler about the enforcement of certain of the Act's clauses, in particular the clause dealing with 'places of vicious resort', namely brothels.

Suppression of Brothels

The Criminal Law Amendment Act 1885 outlawed brothel keeping and the procurement of women for prostitution. Under summary proceedings, brothel keepers and their agents could be sentenced with a fine up to £20 or three months' imprisonment with hard labour for the first offence, and £40 or four months for the second and subsequent convictions. Prosecutions of brothels rose dramatically: in the ten years prior to the Act, an average of 86 brothels were prosecuted in England and Wales each year; from the year of the Act up to the First World War the average number rose to more than 1,200.[19] Landlords could be held responsible under the Act if they knowingly let houses for the purpose of prostitution. Rising pressure on such landlords from vigilance groups led to a wariness about letting property to 'suspect' women (such a label would apply to most women living without men). This thus created a housing problem not only for women working as prostitutes and living in lodging-house brothels, but also for any women living with other women, and even women living on their own, although the latter did not constitute a 'brothel'. (Self-contained flats did not come under the legal definition of a 'brothel' either, but over-cautious landlords apparently did not make – or know about – the distinction.)[20] The situation resulted inevitably – and ironically, given the aims of the instigators of the Act – in many prostitutes being forced to resort to setting up house with pimps, or, as they were called, 'bullies', to provide a cover for their work. Pimps were only too eager to provide the 'protection'.

The Personal Rights Association (the PRA) deplored the closures of brothels and pointed out how the result 'accentuated the double standard ... for it persecutes the women and leaves the men unmolested' (although to be fair to the NVA, many members did wish for prostitution legislation to be applied to both sexes equally). And the PRA objected too to the class bias of the closures, for upper-class brothels – 'fashionable houses' – remained virtually untouched. It also condemned those organizations who were aiding the legislation's enforcement.[21] Henrietta Muller was a member of both the NVA (the chief instigator of brothel closures) and the PRA, but on the issue of the harassment of prostitutes, she knew where her loyalty lay:

> It seems to me that a woman has rights *as a woman*, even though she be a prostitute ... I am not in the least ashamed to say that when I do go to those places where these women are, and which men haunt (and I have been to such places in Paris and London), I have not the least hesitation in saying that I feel towards the women who pass me with their faces bearing traces of such sorrows and sadness, that these women are my sisters, and they may be in some cases morally superior to myself.[22]

As brothels closed, women were being thrown out into the streets with nowhere to go. Some of these women were being subsequently sent to prison on charges of vagrancy. Elizabeth Wolstenholme Elmy, another member of the PRA, pointed out that brothels 'after all, are the only "homes" known to many hapless women', and 'the very first step will be that she is "taken up" by some policeman as "an idle and disorderly person"'. She also predicted the virtual re-introduction of the Contagious Diseases Acts, presenting this forewarning to 'those old fellow-workers' who 'now sanction ... a cruel repression'. Although it was 'painful to differ so profoundly', she felt compelled to ask them:

> Have you protested against the arbitrary *arrest and examination* of women as 'unconstitutional and unjust' [when campaigning against the CD Acts] solely because they were inspected in the name of public health? Do such things become constitutional and just because they are done in the name of public morals? ... I say advisably '*arrest and examination*' because ... under the Prisons Act, such examinations are perfectly possible ... In the name of public morality and social purity our mistaken friends will have brought us back

to that cruel oppression of women which they denounced and resisted when enforced in the alleged interests of the public health.[23]

In contrast, over the following two years the NVA's *Vigilance Record*, edited by Mrs Chant, was full of the 'good work' being done by vigilance groups in closing brothels. Yet the NVA faced a recurrent problem: prostitutes' lack of inclination 'to leave their sinful life'. At a conference of 'London Societies of Vigilance Committees', the NVA Secretary William Coote warned that

> there was a grave danger lest Vigilance Committees should concentrate solely on the closing of bad houses. To do this alone would only drive the evil deeper down . . . and it was essential that every effort should be made to draw the women who lived in . . . disorderly houses into a better life.[24]

Yet despite Coote's directive, attempts at 'rescue' work seem to have been decidedly unsuccessful so far as the inhabitants of closed-down brothels were concerned. Mrs Chant described one 'closing of an evil house' in 1887, location unspecified: 'The girls had to be rescued somehow and the house to be cleaned up . . . But as they showed no inclination to leave their sinful life . . . it was resolved to attack the house.' A group of them barged in,

> and one of the girls was handed over to the rescuers of her own sex, to be entreated, reasoned, coaxed . . . into giving up the life that meant her ruin. She . . . obstinately reiterated her wish to live the life she'd chosen 'of my own free will'.[25]

The outcome of the NVA's closing of a 'colony' of brothels in Aldershot the following year was another disappointment to the NVA. The 'colony' was composed of more than thirty 'immoral' houses in three adjoining streets, with a public house in the centre. Asked what would happen to the 400 girls and children rendered homeless by their action, Coote replied in an open court that 'he was prepared to take charge of the whole of the girls and children . . . provided they were anxious to make an effort to lead an honourable and honest life.' This offer was repeated several times elsewhere, but according to Coote, no more than five or six girls took up the offer.[26]

A later and highly critical account given by the *Personal Rights Journal* suggested that the number was possibly even lower. The journal quoted an NVA report on its response to the homeless girls:

> The Association bravely [!] determined to take care of them, but although 34 were taken into the local hospital, only one other was found desirous of accepting the Society's PROTECTION and leading once more a pure and honest life. [The *Personal Rights Journal*'s exclamation and capitals]

The *Personal Rights Journal* sarcastically commented:

> It is difficult to say whether the *bravery* of a powerful society, cramming homeless and helpless girls into a hospital where surgical outrage . . . awaits them, or the eccentricity of those who were not willing to accept such *protection*, is the more remarkable. We should like to know what became of the remainder of the 400, and also whether the one lamb 'willing' to be led to the slaughter was led by the gentle hands of the Aldershot police.[27]

The journal christened the NVA 'vigilant stampers upon the feeble', and observed that these 'stampers' unfortunately included women, notably Mrs Millicent Fawcett[28] and Mrs Chant.

In contrast to the *Personal Rights Journal*, the *Hants and Surrey Times* declared sanctimoniously:

> It is not only the reputation of the town, but also the moral well-being of our young people that is imperilled by the toleration of this flagrant vice . . . Demoralization must attend the sights and sounds of vice to which we are constantly exposed in our principal streets.[29]

Yet the contradiction of which the *Hants and Surrey Times* (and the NVA?) seemed unaware, was that the closing of brothels was likely to increase the amount of soliciting taking place in the streets. The immediate outcome of this particular case was a definite *rise* in 'the sights and sounds of vice'. For of those prostitutes unwilling to be 'led to the slaughter', ninety marched through Aldershot in protest, four abreast, with a drum-major at the head and singing as they went. The *Aldershot Gazette* was shocked: 'A very bad sight was witnessed.'[30]

Music Halls and Mrs Laura Chant

Born in 1848, Laura Chant was a prominent speaker for women's suffrage, temperance, purity and Liberal politics, on the executive committee of the Women's Liberal Federation. She also wrote poems and songs. In 1888 the *Woman's Penny Paper*, edited by Henrietta Muller, referred to her as 'the most popular of our lady speakers'.[31] The *Adult*, journal of the anarchist group The Legitimation League, was less polite:

> Mrs Ormiston Chant . . . is a middle-aged lady, of strong sympathies with oppressed women, considerable powers of eloquent speech, limited range of intellect, and a plentiful lack of imagination, humour and perspective.[32]

She belonged to the feminist repeal organization the Ladies National Association, and was an advocate of women's participation in local government. She was also a committed member of the NVA and editor of its journal, the *Vigilance Record*.

Given her commitment to the NVA, her support for the closing of brothels was no surprise. Her support for such action was part of a wider vision involving the regulation and censoring of all public 'temptations to vice'. Brothels stood on the border of the worlds of the public and the private – to the uninitiated, they could 'pass' as private residences; as part of the culture of an area and a community, their presence was public knowledge. Brothels needed abolishing not regulating, as far as Laura Chant was concerned, but other public places needed active supervision. Here the law was required to stand hand in hand with active 'protection' and 'guidance' from those in the 'know': 'What is wanted . . . is the appointment of inspectors of both sexes, especially of capable women, to supervise the moral conduct of the streets and public places.'[33] She no doubt saw her own music-hall inspections as a contribution to this moral supervision, not least because music-halls were no marginal form of entertainment: by the early 1890s there were over 500 in London alone, with the 35 largest halls catering to an average nightly audience of 45,000.[34]

When Mrs Chant visited the Empire in 1894, it was not the first time that she had 'inspected' a music-hall. From June 1888 until April 1889 the *Vigilance Record* ran a series entitled 'Amused London', chronicling the sallying forth of Mrs Chant and a woman companion to various music-halls in both the West and East Ends. What she found there may have amused London, but it certainly did not amuse Mrs Chant. The worst case was a West End Theatre of Varieties (unnamed by Mrs Chant, but probably either the Empire or the Alhambra), where the lack of clothing in the ballet and the indecent suggestiveness of other performances were 'surpassed in indecency by the conduct of the audience. The whole was nothing but an open market for vice ... the wretched painted women openly plying their horrible trade ... the guilty, foul-eyed men, seeking whom they might devour'. The scene struck her as unearthly in its nastiness:

> It was as though we had seen with Dante the vision of ... the unhallowed victims of their own lusts, swept round and round in never-ending circles by the storming gusts of their unchained passions.[35]

In contrast, a well-known working-class music-hall in Paddington 'was immeasurably superior, in moral tone and decency' to the 'fashionable' West End equivalent:

> Of course there was vulgarity, but vulgarity of a downright honest, homely kind, unseasoned by vicious jests or indecent allusions. Indeed the audience seemed of a fresher and more wholesome type, more childlike in nature, easily amused.[36]

Unlike the 'educated gentlemen' of the West End, they did not require 'either vice or indecency to whet their jaded appetites'. Nevertheless, Mrs Chant held to the general principle that it was still necessary to step in 'to provide amusements for the people'.[37]

In this account she was reflecting the philanthropist's view of the working classes as 'child-like' and in need of direction. Here it was the performances that were the main problem: the demoral-

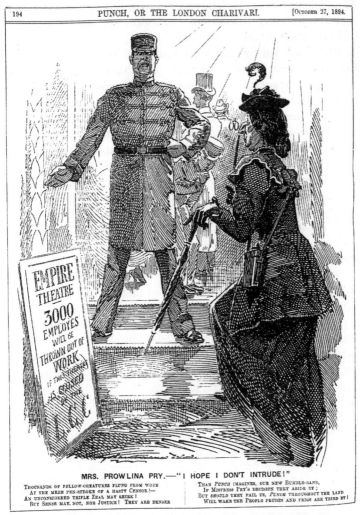

MRS. PROWLINA PRY.—"I HOPE I DON'T INTRUDE!"

THOUSANDS OF FELLOW-CREATURES FLUNG FROM WORK AT THE MERE PEN-STROKE OF A HASTY CENSOR!— AN UNCONSIDERED TRIFLE ZEAL MAY SHIRK ! BUT SENSE MAY, NOT, NOR JUSTICE ! THEY ARE DENSER	THAN *PUNCH* IMAGINES, OUR NEW BUMBLE-BAND, IF MISTRESS PRY'S DECISION THEY ABIDE BY ; BUT *SHOULD* THEY FAIL US, *PUNCH* THROUGHOUT THE LAND WILL WAKE THE PEOPLE PRUDES AND PRIGS ARE TRIED BY !

Mrs Laura Chant portrayed by Punch, *27 October 1894*

izing effects on audience and performers alike of near-nakedness, and the insidious sexual innuendo imparted to certain songs. Music-halls were predominantly working class, but the West

End 'Palaces of Varieties', of which the Empire was one, attracted many upper- and middle-class men, including aristocrats, army officers, students and clerks. Like other social-purity feminists, Laura Chant was equally concerned with the leisure pursuits of her own class, viewing the male aristocracy as lascivious and debauched. In contrast to her concern with working-class music-halls' stage performances, in upper- and middle-class halls her attention was drawn more to the behaviour of the audience, above all the behaviour of those who came to service the men's debauchery: 'Women openly plying their horrible trade.' Unfortunately, 'the streets of London' were no better: 'The presence of large numbers of women who are there but for one purpose, the sale of themselves' was 'a perpetual menace to the home life of the people'.[38]

Prostitution on the Streets

It was with precisely such a sentiment that the NVA wished to remove prostitution not simply from brothels and music-halls, but also from the streets. In a pamphlet written in the 1880s, feminist NVA member Dr Elizabeth Blackwell differentiated between three methods of dealing with prostitution. Firstly, she referred to the 'let alone' system (*laissez-faire*). In operation in London, it encouraged the streets to be 'a public exchange of debauchery for vicious men and women, [with] brothels allowed to flourish and multiply'. This system 'permits great and dangerous evil to run into licence'. Secondly, she presented the female regulation system – the system favoured on the Continent and in operation in this country under the Contagious Diseases Acts. She was adamantly opposed to this method too – it fostered 'corruption and . . . moral degradation'. The third system – 'the only righteous method of dealing with vice by means of law' – was the repressive system. However, she wanted the system to operate only where it had public backing, and the police were subject to citizens' control – where they were 'servants of the people'. She was greatly opposed to greater discretion being given to the police.[39]

By the early twentieth century, the NVA clearly thought that the time was ripe for the 'repressive system'. (Dr Blackwell's opinion on this is unknown; she was in her eighties, and had retired to Hastings.) In 1901 the NVA and the Watch Committee of the newly founded London Public Morality Council, backed unanimously by Westminster City Council, recommended to the Home Secretary that 'vigorous action should be at once taken to clear the streets of prostitutes'.[40] The Home Secretary complied. The Watch Committee included feminists Lady Isabel Somerset (President of the British Women's Temperance Association), Millicent Fawcett (President of the National Union of Women's Suffrage Societies) and Salvationist Mrs Florence Booth. The years 1901–6 saw the most intense repression of prostitutes in London, with women being convicted *without* proof of annoyance. According to the current law (the Metropolitan Police Act 1839 and Town Police Causes Act 1847), solicitation was outlawed if there was 'annoyance' to an inhabitant or passer-by, and the annoyed party was meant to appear in court. But women were being convicted on police word alone. (This had always been objected to by Elizabeth Blackwell, incidentally.)[41] Indeed, the NVA and the Public Morality Council were recommending that this practice be enshrined in law through the abolition of the 'annoyance' clause.[42] The campaign also deployed the language of race, both organizations claiming that a large majority of prostitutes and brothelkeepers were foreign – French, Belgian and increasingly Jewish. They welcomed the Aliens Act 1905 (which gave power to control 'undesirable and destitute aliens' entering the country). The Act was fuelled by anti-Semitism.[43]

By the early twentieth century the NVA and the Public Morality Council had developed excellent relations with the police. NVA branches throughout Britain co-operated with local police over the prosecution of brothels, street prostitution, obscene books, pictures and displays, as well as exchanging information in relation to cases of sexual offences. In its annual report in February 1903 the Public Morality Council observed that 'during the last 2 years the moral condition of our main streets has improved. This must be attributed to the excellent work . . . done by the Metropolitan Police'.[44] 'The moral condition of our main streets' referred primarily to the removal of prostitutes. As Judith Walkowitz points out, it was an historical irony that the Criminal Law Amendment Act 1885, welcomed at the time by feminist repealers, had given the police greatly increased summary powers over poor working women – a trend that Butlerites had always opposed. Under pressure from vigilance associations, the police acted against women rather than the white slavers and seducers of children whose journalistic portrayal had instigated the Act in the first place.[45] In 1885 the *Journal of the Vigilance Association* had warned that 'a law however just, must be justly and wisely administered'.[46] The *unjust* administration of the 1885 Act was clearly aided by the work of the NVA and later the Public Morality Council, especially in relation to the harassment of women prostitutes, whether in brothels, music-halls or on the streets. Although by the early twentieth century few feminists were still involved, their more repressive actions in the 1880s and 1890s had made their contribution.

Religion, Temperance and Feminism

As I have already suggested, Christian feminist philanthropists applied the idea of women as moral guardians of the home to their moralizing work within the public sphere. It was nonconformist feminists above all who instigated such work, often in tandem with others of their religious persuasion. To Laura Chant it was 'the calm steady voice of righteous public opinion. The Non-Conformist conscience, as some call it . . .'[47] These feminists frequently united their religious beliefs with a belief in 'temperance'. By 'temperance' was meant 'moderation in the consumption of alcohol', although by the late nineteenth century for many temperance workers it meant 'total abstinence'. The United States saw the direct linking of feminism with evangelical religion and temperance teachings – 'Gospel Temperance' – in the form of the Women's Christian Temperance Union. The British Women's Temperance Association (BWTA) made similar connections, although the religious rhetoric was less pronounced. Set up in 1876, by 1892 the BWTA claimed 570 branches and 50,000 members.[48] Feminists cited male alcoholism as a major instigator of men's violence towards women. As Philippa Levine points out, it was again a challenge to a double standard 'that privileged male preference and pleasure over female health, safety and liberty'.[49] The emphasis of the temperance movement earlier in the century had been on women using their influence at home to turn their husbands, brothers and sons away from drink. Now feminists called for women to move their temperance campaign into the *public* sphere, both in defence of the home (a 'maternal struggle'), but also in the quest for greater safety for women on the streets. In addition, they demanded greater moral 'purity' of male politicians, including a commitment to the aims of temperance.

Feminist temperance workers were not necessarily 'repressive' in their quest for abstinence. For example, feminist activists Henrietta Muller and Florence Balgarnie, and Henrietta's sister Eva McLaren, were all temperance workers, but none of them supported the more repressive actions towards drinking and other 'vice'. Henrietta was initially an active member of the NVA, on its executive and its legal sub-committee, but in 1888 she resigned. One of her disagreements with the NVA, as I have already mentioned, was its zest for brothel closures. She also objected to its attempted prosecution of birth-control pamphlets (defined by the NVA as 'vicious literature'), to be discussed in a later chapter.

Women's Work within Philanthropy and Local Government

Whatever their differences, one area uniting these feminists was the belief that women should use their local government vote to urge candidates into support for temperance. Yet their interest in local government went beyond this common concern. Earlier I suggested that women's role within philanthropy and local government played a part in the move of certain feminists towards a 'repressive' moral politics. Nineteenth-century feminists, including feminist repealers, frequently engaged in philanthropic activities.[50] Whatever the benefits to its recipients, philanthropy clearly entailed their subjection to specific forms of surveillance, including the imposition of middle-class norms of domesticity.[51] It is in this sense that philanthropy has been analysed as involving a 'familialist strategy' – intervention at the level of the family in order to control women's and children's sexual and social behaviour and to remake working-class culture.[52] To transform the character of a class, it was thought necessary to influence the disciplining of children, and to persuade mothers to play a key role in such disciplining. Positively, as Judith Walkowitz points out, the encouragement of 'women's home influence' provided the rationale for a mother's right to control sexual access to her daughters, thereby subverting the man's authority in the home.[53] Negatively, it promoted a custodial, if caring, relationship between mothers and daughters, relating to the middle-class Victorian idea of the sanctity of childhood (which working-class parents were frequently thought to be violating), and a view of adolescence as a period of social dependency – in contrast to the reality of most working-class (employed) adolescents' lives. To the middle classes, *all* girls needed 'protection', or rather 'protective surveillance' – from themselves, from men, and from 'unsuitable' company. These attitudes tended to pervade the actions of those feminists involved in social-purity campaigning, and their desire to administer 'protective surveillance' was likely to be repressive in its implications.

Philanthropy was, above all, about the surveillance of, and possible co-operation with, the working-class woman at the heart of the working-class family. Philanthropy was not solely concerned with policing the family of course, but the other areas of what constituted the 'social' – that 'blurred ground between the private and the public', namely housing, hygiene, demography, etc. – all had woman as the key object of the philanthropic gaze. Given that philanthropic workers ('social workers') were predominantly female, with the ascent of the 'social', women became both agents and objects of reform.[54]

By the end of the century, many female philanthropists began to move into local government. It was a logical move, for they saw local government as they saw philanthropy, namely as involving the extension of women's home influence – their domesticating and 'civilizing' role – into the wider world. It was an engagement with municipal housekeeping. Feminists and anti-feminists tended to agree that the womanly domestic approach was appropriate for local government, but they parted company over its appropriateness at the *national* level. Although women were excluded from central government until 1918, they were able to play an important part in local government several decades earlier. From 1869, unmarried and widowed female ratepayers were able to vote in local elections, although it was not until 1907 that women were finally allowed to stand for election in borough and county councils. However, from 1870 *any* woman could stand for the new school boards, but they had to be a ratepayer to vote for them. (Thus, in this case it was easier for a woman to stand as a candidate than be a voter!) Female ratepayers could vote for Poor Law boards, but for some time it was unclear whether women were eligible to serve on them. However, in 1875 one woman stood successfully for a London Poor Law union, and by 1895 there were over 800 elected women, encouraged by the Society for Promoting the Return of Poor Law Guardians, or Women Guardians Society as it was known.[55]

As Hollis points out,[56] by the mid-1880s women on school boards and Poor Law boards were helping to shape education and poor relief, but the built environment – its streets, houses, public health and policing[57] – was still outside their remit, and in the hands of (male) town councillors. Women's concern to influence the management of public spaces stemmed partly from the desire to facilitate women's entry into a world hostile to their presence. In the meantime, if women could not be councillors themselves,[58] a number were at least determined to pressurize male councillors as much as possible in the pursuit of certain objectives. What objectives were these?

An examination of the membership of the Women Guardians Society and the Women's Local Government Society reveals that members were involved in a network of Liberal, philanthropic, temperance and social-purity organizations, including allegiance to the NVA. Mrs Chant, for example, belonged to the Women's Liberal Federation, the Ladies National Association, and the British Women's Temperance Association, and she was a founder member of both the Women Guardians Society and the NVA. (Indeed, the NVA actively supported the election of female Poor Law Guardians.) There were many women with similar cross-cutting membership. Thus, the objectives of women active in local government tended to relate to issues of morality, or 'social purity', to use the term of the period. The LCC was perceived as a possible vehicle for the furtherance of social-purity concerns, not least in its role as the licenser of London's music-halls. To ensure 'decency', Mrs Chant and other members of the NVA encouraged the newly created LCC's 'Theatre and Music Halls Committee' to 'vigilantly watch our entertainments, and vigorously repress whatever is clearly contrary to good morals'.[59]

The LCC did not need much encouragement, for until 1907 it was controlled by the 'Progressive' Party, an alliance between Liberal, Fabian and Labour representatives. Known as 'Municipal Puritans', the Progressive councillors were mainly nonconformist and in favour of 'temperance', seeing alcoholism and moral corruption as the chief causes of working-class social unrest.[60] They were as keen as any member of the NVA, indeed several of the councillors *were* members of the NVA, to rid music-halls of impropriety, vice and alcohol and turn them into sites for 'wholesome' family entertainment. They were supported by, among others, Keir Hardie and John Burns.[61] The Progressives institutionalized vigilance in 1890 with the introduction of an LCC inspectorate: twenty-three inspectors 'to devote their attention chiefly to the nature of the performance and to the character and conduct of the audience, especially the female portion thereof'.[62] The LCC was also in favour of responsible and morally concerned citizens engaging in voluntary inspection – precisely the civic activity being undertaken by Laura Chant.

Given its moral politics, it was no surprise that the LCC upheld Mrs Chant's complaint at its Licensing Committee in October 1894. After all, the Empire was the most notorious of upper-class Englishmen's pleasure grounds,[63] anathema to the Municipal Socialist ethic. The Empire was informed that its licence would only be renewed if alcoholic drink was banned from the auditorium, and the Promenade – the site of Empire assignations between prostitutes and clients – was abolished. Mrs Chant and her allies would have preferred the premises to have been closed to prostitutes, but the next best thing was the separation of the audience (and show) from the prostitutes, thereby preventing men from moving freely between the two sites of erotic entertainment.

The public's response to the proposed ban was one of outrage – if the 170 letters sent to the *Daily Telegraph* are anything to go by. A number of these letters labelled Mrs Chant a dangerous example of the New Woman.[64] The Empire's response was the erection of a canvas screen between the auditorium and the bar, thus fencing off the audience from the drink and the prostitutes. The prostitutes' response appears to have been indifference, for as one nonchalantly remarked, they could simply switch to other music-halls: 'We can give all a turn.' As for their male clients, a week after the ban the music-hall was invaded by a band of upper-class men, headed by the youthful Winston Churchill, who proceeded to tear down the fiimsy screen.[65] The partition was rebuilt, but the following year the Empire was able to secure an unconditional licence once again. This time, protest from various social purity feminists was to no avail.[66]

Female Modesty and Sexuality

Josephine Butler and Elizabeth Wolstenholme Elmy may have been horrified by their former colleagues' repressive actions, but most Butlerites and repressive moralists shared an attitude towards female sexuality that had 'protective surveillance' within its logic. Judith Walkowitz describes feminists' response to girls that they came across during their philanthropic work:

> Butlerites . . . registered the same feelings of repugnance and ambivalence toward incorrigible girls as they had earlier toward unrepentant prostitutes. For them as well as for more repressive moralists, the desire to protect young girls thinly masked coercive impulses to control their voluntary sexual impulses.[67]

The 'repugnance and ambivalence' stemmed from their view of women as 'pure', inherently modest, and barely sexual – unless they had the misfortune to 'fall'. As was discussed in the last chapter, to say a woman had 'fallen' implied that she had lost her modesty, and become thereby transformed. However, many social purists were aware of the vulnerability of working-class women to the vagaries of the labour market. For example, when the NVA asked for rescue workers' views on the causes of prostitution, the replies cited 'extreme poverty' as well as 'vanity, idleness and frivolity' in relation to women; for male clients, it was 'sensuality'.[68] And most feminists did recognize that it was men's sexual demands which created prostitution in the first place.

Despite recognizing the likely contribution of financial hardship in women's resort to prostitution, many feminists tended to follow orthodoxy in viewing a woman's 'fall' as heralding her total transformation. The position of the feminist social purity organization, the Moral Reform Union, was not atypical:

> Modesty and a chaste deportment are a young girl's birth right and her choicest adornment ... But when the beast and the harlot have taken the woman's place, there is no depth of shameful sensuality into which she is not prepared to sink.[69]

Before 'the beast and harlot' had 'taken the woman's place' however, the prostitute who was a *victim* of circumstances could still be saved – whether the circumstances be economic hardship or male 'seduction'. She could never of course be *fully* saved, for 'purity and innocence once lost we know but too well can never be regained'.[70] According to Dr Elizabeth Blackwell, prostitutes, if *not* caught in time, became 'demons'– 'human tigers who delight in destruction and torture.' Blackwell had clear ideas on the need to distinguish between the woman who was determined to remain a prostitute and the woman who was prepared to change. She offered this advice:

> The tenderest compassion may be shown to the poor creature who *ceases* to be a prostitute; ... but do nothing to raise the condition of prostitutes as such, any more than you would try to improve the condition of murderers and thieves.[71]

The distinction between the reclaimable and the unreclaimable prostitute was part and parcel of philanthropy's distinction between the deserving and the undeserving poor.[72]

Such ideas informed Laura Chant's view of the performers and prostitutes at the Empire. In relation to the performers, she was sure that 'the unhappy girls in the ballet and choruses ... had lost something if they did not feel the loss of clothing'. She was implying, of course, that they had lost their modesty and sense of shame. And if 'the unhappy girls' were 'rescued' in time, they might still be saved. Her attitude towards these women reflected the general attitude towards actresses and female performers, namely the presumed proximity of their trade to prostitution. Actresses had enormous difficulty in claiming and retaining respectability.[73] Mrs Chant's greatest condemnation of fallen womanhood she reserved for the Empire prostitutes. She was insistent that there was a clear distinction to be made between women such as these, who were engaged in 'gilded vice', and poor women who worked the streets. 'High-class' prostitutes, supposedly making good money from their trade, transgressed the ideals of femininity: to Laura Chant they had calculatingly chosen their profession. Streetwalkers, however, she saw as hapless *victims* of economic circumstance and/or unscrupulous men.

When accused of forcing the Empire prostitutes back out on to the streets and thus *adding* to street prostitution, Mrs Chant defended herself by claiming that these women were not off the streets in the first place, since the Empire explicitly stated that streetwalkers were refused entry. (Indeed, prostitutes entering the Empire had to be able to pay the high five-shilling entrance fee, as well as to purchase smart evening attire.) She referred to the Empire prostitutes as those 'who minister entirely to the demands of lust, and who love darkness and secrecy because their lives are evil.'[74] They were Dr Blackwell's 'demons'. As for the streetwalker, Laura Chant was at pains to emphasize that her house had 'always been open as a refuge to the poor creatures'. Although innocence could never of course be regained, some streetwalkers were reclaimable; the Empire women were beyond the pale. This justified her belief that 'the stern aid of the magistrate must be invoked against the persistent transgressor, the hand of Christian charity must be the remedy to help not yet hardened and repentant ones'.[75] Dr Blackwell and Mrs Chant may seem extreme examples, but the vast majority of feminists in this period constructed an image of the prostitute as either passive victim of seduction, betrayal or economic hardship, eager to be reformed (the preferred construction of Josephine Butler and most of the LNA), and/or evil unrepentant woman bent on vicious immorality. The woman who had temporarily and voluntarily drifted into prostitution was inconceivable within this ideological framework.[76]

Women and Public Spaces

Laura Chant's concern was partly about the danger of demoralization, but it was surely also about the desire to transform the streets and sites of public entertainment into places where women could move freely without fear of attack or the accusation of non-respectability. As Judith Walkowitz demonstrates so convincingly in her book *City of Dreadful Delight*, if London was becoming a place of possibility for women, it was also a place of danger. As a daily irritant, respectable women complained of male 'pests'.[77] More disturbingly, women's presence on the streets could spell their death – the 'moral' message of the 1888 Jack the Ripper murders.[78] There was also the charge of impurity. As Elaine Showalter notes: 'Victorian ladies were not permitted to cross urban, class and sexual boundaries.'[79] The term 'public woman' was used interchangeably with the terms prostitute, streetwalker and actress; they all implied that the public world excluded respectable women. The 'public' was reserved for men and those women who 'immorally' serviced them; only the male *flâneur* had the right to gaze upon the city and the 'public' women therein.[80] Indeed, the term 'public' was shocking in its juxtaposition with 'woman', the very antithesis of 'public'.[81] Women were literally excluded from many male public preserves, such as men's clubs and public houses. Yet 'respectable' women in this period were increasingly entering the public domain of both West and East Ends; they were there in various guises on their way to and from work – as philanthropists, missionaries and Poor Law guardians, or as clerical workers, civil servants and teachers. They were also there as shoppers, attending the new department stores, or as visitors to museums, libraries, theatre and music-halls – all public spaces opening up to women. Ironically, women charity workers in the East End experienced greater social freedom than ladies in the West End bothered by male 'pests'.[82]

Feminists then, as now, wanted the streets and other public places to be safe and accessible for women, both literally and symbolically. For a woman to be unable to venture into such places without fearing attack, being labelled 'immoral', or suspected of being a prostitute, necessarily acted as a constraint upon her freedom of movement. The prostitute and 'respectable' woman, supposedly recognizably differing in dress, could well be confused.[83] Olive Schreiner, for example, related how in December 1885 she was suspected by a policeman of being a prostitute when walking home one evening in London with a male friend (Dr Donkin). Her lack of gloves and hat were additional signs of her 'unrespectability' to the policeman concerned.[84] Two years later, feminists, including Josephine Butler and Laura Chant, rose to the defence of Miss Elizabeth Cass, a respectable Northern milliner, falsely arrested for soliciting in Regent Street. On the evidence of Miss Cass's employer as to her virtue, the charges were dismissed, but not before the incident had become a *cause célèbre*. Judith Walkowitz points to the ironic support for Miss Cass of W.T. Stead, who took her case as vindication of the rights of respectable women to walk the streets alone at night, but whose 'crusade', instigated by the 'Maiden Tribute' articles, had intensified the police harassment of prostitutes in the first place.[85]

Breaking down the barriers of constraint was obviously part of the feminist agenda. As one feminist journal expressed it:

> It is our business to see that in this nineteenth century there is not a street in London where a woman may not walk safely, and even not be afraid to ask her way.[86]

Some feminists believed that the removal of both prostitutes and alcohol from public places would contribute to this safety. Many of these feminists were Liberal in their politics; their demand for state attention to women's safety fell within the logic of the classic Liberal view of the state. For although a *laissez-faire* approach implied minimal state intervention, it held that the state should guarantee the conditions under which individuals freely pursued their own interests. Women were demanding that it was *their* interests and *their* freedom which needed guaranteeing on the streets; it was a basic civil liberty.

Victims of Vice and their Liberty

What about the liberty and civil rights of the prostitute? According to Josephine Butler, the repressive activity of the NVA entailed

> a constant tendency towards *external* pressure, and inside that a tendency to let the pressure fall almost exclusively on women, because it is difficult, they say, to get at men. It is dangerous work, in reference to personal liberty, but few people care for liberty or personal rights now.[87]

In contrast, the NVA, and the feminists active within it, such as Laura Chant, Millicent Fawcett and Elizabeth Blackwell, never thought of their vigilance work as the curtailment of prostitutes' liberty. On the contrary, they assumed that the removal of 'vice' and the alternatives which they presented, *helped* the victims: their actions offered the hand of reclamation to reclaimable prostitutes, and gave freedom from immorality to that other group of 'victims of vice', namely 'ordinary citizens', including respectable women like themselves, who wished to be able to enter public spaces without fear of immoral sights and dangers. To Laura Chant:

> A great deal of well-meant nonsense is talked about the 'liberty of the subject', whenever there is . . . effort to clear the streets. Some good people seem to be so zealous in defending the vicious from injustice that it seems as if they were in danger of forgetting that

vice is in itself a colossal injustice, an infringement of the liberty of the subject.[88]

Millicent Fawcett made a similar point in viewing as polar opposites the liberty of 'vice' and the liberty of the subject, especially where the subject was a woman.[89]

While the liberty of the 'ordinary citizen', the citizen as ordinary *woman*, was at risk in the face of the unregenerate prostitute and other agents of vice, the regenerate prostitute needed *her* 'liberty' *rescued from* a life of vice. 'Saving' the prostitute was seen as the restoration of her liberty. The Personal Rights Association however did not think that the NVA's repressive actions were likely to 'save' prostitutes or restore their liberty. On the contrary, it accused the NVA of 'crushing its [immorality's] victims'; the NVA called this 'morality', but to the PRA it represented 'nothing better than outward decency'.[90] Perhaps surprisingly, some NVA feminists were well aware that 'outward decency' was not enough. Mrs Mary Bunting, for example, told the National Union of Women Workers (an umbrella organization for women's philanthropic groups):

> If we insist on merely clearing the streets of the women so that our eyes may be less pained than they are at present, and our youth less exposed to temptation, we lull ourselves into a false security, and the disease, for which the state of our streets is an outward manifestation, will get more thorough hold of the system from being driven inwards.[91]

False security or no, the NVA continued with its repressive activities, and even where prostitutes were clearly not being 'saved', but rendered homeless, it did not view the project as a failure. The prostitutes concerned were labelled hardened and unreclaimable, as in the case of those whose marching protest in Aldershot presented such a 'very bad sight'. In the case of the prostitutes at the Empire, repressive purity feminists did not think of them as victims either, but as women who had calculatingly chosen a life of 'vice', and whose livelihoods deserved to be destroyed. Deborah Gorham suggests that there were two distinct and opposing attitudes among social purity reformers:

on the one hand, those who held that legislation was to force people to be moral, by compulsion if necessary, and on the other, those who believed that defending individual rights was as important as combating vice.[92] In relation to feminists involved in 'rescue' work the distinction is too sharp; feminists like Millicent Fawcett and Laura Chant argued that the defence or achievement of certain rights and freedoms (such as the freedom for women to walk unmolested on the street) *necessitated* the combating of certain types of vice. Also at issue was the question of whether 'vice' could be defined as 'crime'; while coercive 'immoral' acts *against* women were clearly in the category of crime, some feminists were inclined to feel much the same about 'immoral' acts committed *by* women, if seen as anti-women in their effects.

The repressive purity feminists shared with their less repressive sisters the desire to bring about a transformation in public and private morality, especially in the sexual relations between men and women. They appeared to believe that one of the best means to this end lay with the 'domestication' and 'civilizing' of the public world through philanthropic and statist interventions. Their wish to transform the public world for the benefit of all, though especially, of course, for women, was rooted in a wider feminist vision in which women had freedom of movement in all spheres of society, and the issue of men's behaviour towards women was squarely on the political agenda. One part of their work entailed campaigning for women's entry into government – at both local and national levels. Another part of their work involved addressing issues of sexual violence – providing support to victims of male assault and campaigning for changes in unjust laws. In their attempt to eliminate prostitution, they focussed predominantly on the *prostitute* rather than her male client. Their attitude towards the prostitute tended to be one of 'protective surveillance'; this related to their views on female sexuality, and their concomitant distinction between repentant and unrepentant prostitutes, or victims and calculating 'demons'. Coupled with their optimistic belief that their own presence within state bodies would radically change the nature of these bodies, repressive purity feminists acted in and through the state in an effort to transform the sexual morality of the time. In their campaign for the implementation of the law and its reform, and in their philanthropic and local government work, these feminists saw both the law and women as educators and protectors of other women. They combined a liberal stress on their right to freedom of the streets, with a religious emphasis on the moral superiority of the 'pure' woman (but the fallen state of the 'impure'). In their attempts to challenge the practice of prostitution, and to protect the innocent *victim* (the reclaimable prostitute and the respectable woman on the street), they ended up both denying other's women's agency – their ability to act on the world – as well as controlling those women they defined as 'unreclaimable'.

CHAPTER 4

Marriage: Its Iniquities and Its Alternatives

In August 1888 the *Daily Telegraph*, London's best-selling news-paper, requested its readers' response to the question: 'Is Marriage a Failure?' Over the next month, and much to its amazement, the paper received 27,000 replies.[1] Although enthusiastic support for the institution of marriage was declared by a few, the vast majority revealed discontent and sometimes profound unhappi-ness. The correspondents, almost exclusively middle-class, usually blamed their individual spouses, but their complaint of difficulties in extricating themselves from bad marriages or in meeting potential partners demonstrated their more general dissatisfaction with marriage as an institution and a market.

Daily Telegraph readers were not alone in their ambivalence towards marriage. Feminists had been criticizing marriage for some years, not so much in a general sense, but in terms of its injustices: a woman's economic dependency, loss of legal and political rights, an unequal divorce law, and, above all, the assumption of a husband's *ownership* of his wife. Their campaigns had led to the Infant Custody Acts 1873 and 1886, which gave mothers certain rights to appeal for custody of their children, the Married Women's Property Acts 1870 and 1882, and the Matri-monial Causes Act 1878. The Property Acts allowed a married woman to retain her own wages, possessions and capital, rather than renounce them to her husband, thus giving her the same rights over property as an unmarried woman. The Matrimonial Causes Act gave magistrates' courts the power to grant a separa-tion order, with maintenance and custody of children under ten, to a wife who had been beaten by her husband, extended in 1886 to wives who had been deserted.[2] Yet despite these legal victories, feminists felt that gains for the married woman were lagging somewhat behind those of her single sister. Coverture remained firmly in place: the condition of a married woman as legally under the 'protection' of her husband, with her legal existence subsumed within his. It was, above all, a married woman's right over her own person that needed to be won, and it was this which became the main focus for feminists in their discussion of marriage and its discontents.

With all their campaigns around marriage in this period, feminists drew on the liberal principles of freedom, liberty and bodily autonomy. As Mary Lyndon Shanley points out, feminists argued that the idea of liberty was meaningless if it excluded the fundamental right to control over one's own body. Liberal theory's distinction between the public world of politics and the private world of family was thereby undermined, for feminists were demanding that the same standards of freedom and equality operate in both spheres.[3] I would suggest further that, while feminists drew upon liberal theory, they *simultaneously* drew upon the idea of a woman's purifying role, and applied it to their political demands for the transformation of both public and private spheres. In relation to their demand for a purified marriage and home, feminists constructed a new marital ethics which combined liberal and religious principles.

By the late nineteenth century, feminist strategy to purify marriage and reconstruct it as a site of true liberty for women was composed of three interrelated components: a campaign to change the law on coverture, divorce and a woman's bodily rights (a legislative tactic); an attempt to change beliefs and practices both through providing children and adults with a basic grounding in sex education and through warning young women of the seamier side of marriage (a protective and educative tactic); the construction of an ideal relationship of emotional and spiritual unity (a utopian, imaginative tactic). The distinctions were not mutually exclusive, for the legislative tactic was itself informed by a concern to extend the legal *protection* of women. Through all three elements ran the central theme of a married woman's right over her own person – her personal autonomy – and a transformed, purified and *moral* relationship between the sexes. This three-pronged feminist strategy did not, of course, develop out of thin air; its basic tenets were argued at length in articles, pamphlets, and public talks, as well as explored in feminist novels – a wide-ranging discussion which became known as 'the Marriage Debate'. Prior to this, nineteenth-century novels had already prepared the ground in their exploration of the contradictions and conflicts in women's lives.[4]

Mona Caird and the Marriage Debate

The debate on marriage in the *Daily Telegraph* had been instigated by a recent article in the *Westminster Review* by the feminist Mrs Mona Caird.[5] According to the *Daily Telegraph*'s theatre critic Harry Quilter, the *Telegraph* had posed the question 'Is Marriage a Failure?' in order to discover readers' reactions to Mona Caird.[6] He did admit that Mona Caird had never actually asked the question – her article assumed that marriage as presently practised *was* a failure. She was more concerned with why and in what way this was the case, and how the problem might be remedied. She developed her ideas on marriage in a number of essays, starting with the *Westminster Review* article mentioned above.[7]

Mona Caird was a journalist and writer, on the brink of becoming a well-known 'new woman' novelist. She was a freethinker, an anti-vivisectionist and a member of the Personal Rights Association, with its roots in the campaign against the Contagious Diseases Acts and its programme of radical individualism. She acknowledged the influence of J.S. Mill, Shelley, Herbert Spencer, T.H. Huxley and Charles Darwin, as witnessed in her own particular ideological marriage of concepts drawn from liberalism and evolutionary theory. In the Men and Women's Club's first year she was seriously considered for membership, but she was never finally asked, partly because Olive Schreiner was very much against her at the time (although she later changed her mind), describing her as 'a narrow, one-sided woman, violently prejudiced against men'.[8] She did add, however, that she thought her 'clever and likely to add life and interest to our discussions'.[9] Mona Caird attended the club's May

1887 meeting; it considered birth control of which she, unlike most of the female club members, approved. Her association with the club did not stop here. To Maria Sharpe, as well as to other club members:

> The correspondence in *The Daily Telegraph* ... on 'Is Marriage a Failure?' and Mrs Caird's article in *The Westminster Review* ... seemed in a way connected with our Club because Mrs Caird's first article was so evidently founded on Mr Pearson's first woman articles in *The Ethic of Freethought*.[10]

(This collection of Pearson's, published early in 1888, contained his paper 'The Woman's Question'.) Indeed, Mona Caird drew heavily on the anthropological and historical arguments used by Pearson.

Mona Caird claimed that the current institution of marriage had its roots in the earlier evolutionary stage of 'barbarism', a period in which male hunters had raided neighbouring settlements and captured the women. This, she argued, represented 'the origin of our modern idea of *possession* in marriage. The woman became the property of the man, his own by right of conquest. Now the wife is his by right of law'.[11] Linked to the idea of woman as man's possession was the double moral standard – the idea that 'a man's trangressions are regrettable necessities, and a woman's detestable aberrations, to be fiercely punished and rooted out'.[12] The 'half-savage' in humankind had been sustained and encouraged by the teachings of Luther. His strict marriage system, supposedly to curb 'sensuality', was responsible for setting up the rigid divide between two classes of woman: the married woman and the prostitute. To Mona Caird, however, the mercenary quality of the marriage market rendered it *equivalent* to prostitution. Indeed she believed that marriage and prostitution

> are the two sides of the same shield and not the deepest gulf ... can prevent the burning vapours of the woman's inferno ... from penetrating into the upper regions of respectability and poisoning the very atmosphere ... The same idea – the purchase of womanhood ... rules from the base to the summit of the social body.[13]

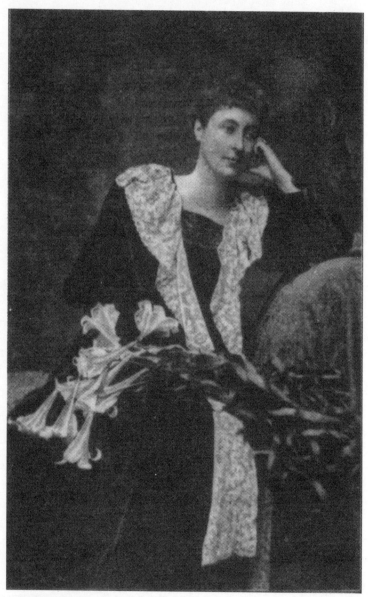

Mona Caird in the Lady's Realm, *vol. 5, November 1892 – April 1899*

Luther was guilty on another score: having 'preached the devastating doctrine which makes it a duty to have an unlimited number of children', he was thereby also responsible for women's consequent nervous exhaustion and ill-health.[14]

How was marriage to be transformed? To Mona Caird, it was first necessary to conceive the desired alternative, to construct a new ideal. The ideal needed to be based upon the principles of freedom, equality, love and sympathy. It would entail a 'free contract' outside the domain of Church and state, to be framed by the couple themselves. Here she drew on the liberal principle of freedom of contract, but applied to marriage it had far-reaching implications. This new kind of marriage was to be not simply predicated on full independence and equality, but on a woman's right to self-possession – the 'full understanding and acknowledgement of the obvious right of the woman to *possess herself* body and soul, to give or withhold herself . . . exactly as she wills'. This was to represent the 'fundamental principle' of the new ideal. Allegiance to such an ideal, let alone its realization, could only develop slowly. To facilitate contact and open friendship between the sexes, she advocated co-education, and the breaking-down of sex segregation at the work-place. She envisaged a slowly growing resentment towards state interference, paralleled by the winning of economic independence for women ('the first condition of free marriage'),[15] and legal change, including the granting of women's franchise and the equalization of parental rights and divorce. All these reforms were necessary for women to gain true equality. But it was essential that men change too: 'The enemy has to be met and fought within men's own soul, not merely by laws from without.'[16] Additionally, women's labour within the home had to be recognized as real *work*[17] (although like other feminists of the period, Caird did not question the gendered nature of this division of labour).

The feminist optimism in evolution discussed in Chapter Two was echoed in Mona Caird's belief that the 'primitive impulse' (pre-human and non-rational) which she equated with the 'savage' and sensual side of humankind, was being undermined by the evolution of 'sympathetic and rational impulses', and thus the move towards the ideal marriage was already underway.[18] But it was a vision implicitly restricted to the 'civilized' West, for the 'primitive impulse' remained pronounced among 'non-civilized' peoples. What today we would call the 'racism' of her vision was accepted in the late nineteenth century unproblematically; it was part of the imperialist rhetoric of racist 'common-sense'.

The Opening Up of Debate

The marriage debate continued on into the 1890s, with numerous contributions from feminists and non-feminists alike. As James Hammerton observes, just as middle-class marriage had become established as the site of privacy and domesticity, a bulwark against the market-place, it was opened up for public scrutiny – not simply by feminists, but by a wide spectrum of commentators. Working-class marriage was under attack too, including in the form of music-hall songs, although more in a spirit of 'comic disaster' and resignation than critique – male songs such as 'At Trinity church I met my doom', and 'She was one of the early birds and I was one of the worms', and female songs such as 'Girls, we would never stand for it'.[19] Mona Caird's depiction of wives as the 'property' of their husbands struck chords with many. Mary Lyndon Shanley rightly suggests that Victorian feminists would have been amazed by the claim of many modern historians that 'companionate marriage', characterized by 'romantic love' and 'a conscious ideological egalitarianism' was the norm in England by the mid-nineteenth century.[20] The spectre of male violence in marriage had already been raised by the feminist Frances Power Cobbe who, in 1878, had written a stringent attack on the complacency shown towards the widespread existence of wife battering. Commentary on the disparity between the light punishments meted out to wife-beaters compared to other criminals became a regular feature of the *Woman's Suffrage Journal* and later, in the early twentieth century, of *The Vote* and *Votes for Women*. Frances Power Cobbe's class bias, typical of most middle-class commentators of the period, led her

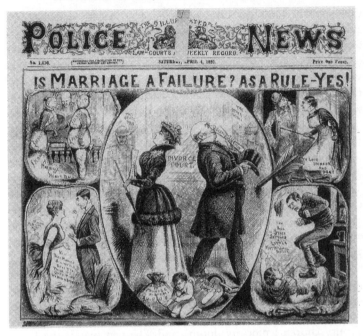

The Police News, *4 April 1891, portrays the 'Marriage Debate'*

to assume that it was predominantly the working classes who were violent – brutalized by their surroundings and their alcoholic consumption. Yet Cobbe saw one of the roots of such violence lying in 'the notion that a man's wife is his PROPERTY', a notion common to all classes.[21] (Her article, 'Wife Torture in England', reprinted as a pamphlet, was partly responsible for the introduction of the Matrimonial Causes Act 1878.) In many ways conservative in her views, Cobbe nevertheless argued *against* marriage for women, because of married women's frequent unhappiness, abuse and illness.[22] She herself lived for many years in a happy relationship with another woman.

Some feminists suggested that if marriage rendered women the property of men, the system was a form of slavery. (The equation was not new – it had been made years earlier in 1825 by William Thompson and Anna Wheeler in their *Appeal of One Half of the Human Race, Women, against the Pretensions of the Other Half, Men*.)[23] Given that marital rape went unrecognized in law, the slavery of marriage was sexual as well as economic. One feminist posed the rhetorical question: 'Does the English girl know, when a man asks her in marriage, that he asks her to become for life, not merely an unpaid household servant, but his sexual slave?'[24] The analogy between marriage and slavery was being drawn in feminist fiction as well. For example, in her novel *A Superfluous Woman*, Emma Brooke informs her readers that 'lovely girls are bought and sold in the London marriage market very much as Circassian slaves are sold to a Turkish harem'. (Note that feminists were as likely as anyone to subscribe to the dominant view of the Orient as sexually depraved.) The book's heroine has been taught to think of herself as 'a dainty piece of flesh which some great man would buy'.[25]

Feminists likened marriage not only to slavery, but also to prostitution. Indeed, feminists saw the two institutions of marriage and prostitution as inextricably interlinked, the supposed 'purity' and sexual passivity of the middle-class woman existing at the expense of the working-class prostitute who served the sexual 'needs' of the middle-class man. Feminists were thereby also recognizing the inseparability of the public and private spheres. The relationship between marriage and prostitution went further: the mercenary nature of many middle-class marital transactions, the frequent absence of love in marriage and the husband's 'right' to his wife's sexual services all contributed to a view of marriage as itself a form of 'legalized' prostitution.[26] As one feminist doctor asked rhetorically: 'If a wife has not got the control of her own person, in what respect is she better than those most unhappy members of our sisterhood, who are pathetically defined as "unfortunate"?'[27] In some ways the married woman's position was viewed as worse, for she exchanged all she had – her legal rights, her independence, her labour power and her body – simply for a home, a ring and the 'respectability' of the marital status. Like the parallel to slavery, the equation between marriage and prostitution was often best expressed in feminist fiction. George Egerton (pseudonym of Mary Chavelita

Dunne) has one of her heroines bitterly remark:

> As long as a man demands from a wife what he must sue from a
> mistress as a favour . . . marriage becomes for many women a legal
> prostitution, a nightly degradation, a hateful yoke under which they
> age, mere bearers of children conceived in a sense of duty, not of
> love.[28]

If marriage in its current form forced women into being 'mere
bearers of children conceived in a sense of duty', feminists held
women's *choice* of motherhood (and, indeed, of when to have
sexual intercourse) as central to the *ideal* marriage. Feminists
wanted men to restrain their sexual desires and let women set the
terms. As one commentator expressed it: Women 'want to *own*
themselves, to dispose of their bodies as seems to them best, not to
have maternity forced upon them.'[29]

Despite seeing present marriage as immoral, most feminists
did not reject marriage *per se*. On the contrary, they wished for
it to be radically reformed. Part of such reform relied on women
actively challenging the double moral standard by disassoci-
ating from any man of 'doubtful record'. 'The time has come',
wrote one commentator, 'when women should *demand* that the
men they marry, the men their daughters marry, the men whom
they receive into the sanctuary of their homes, shall be free of
taint.'[30]

Yet feminists recognized that individual women's demands
were not enough; to destroy the mercenary quality of marriage,
they agreed with Mona Caird on the need for full economic
independence. As Clementina Black (President of the Women's
Industrial Council and the Secretary of the Women's T.U.C.)
expressed it: 'Economic dependence means personal subservience;
and economic independence means personal freedom.'[31] There
was little exploration, however, of what wives' economic independence might entail, or recognition that class difference was
crucial in any analysis of the economics of marriage.[32]

Many feminists also agreed with Mona Caird in wanting a
change in the current divorce law – a law viewed as itself
contributing to the immorality of marriage. Since 1857, at great
expense, divorce had been available in England and Wales to a

husband on the grounds of his wife's adultery alone, to a wife on the grounds of her husband's adultery plus additionally either his cruelty, desertion, or bestiality. Thus a husband, in contrast to his wife, was free to engage in extramarital sex with impunity. Such explicit inequality was a clear example of the double moral standard. Not all feminists were in favour of easier divorce; indeed, quite a few opposed divorce in *any* form, assuming it to be of more benefit to straying husbands than their economically dependent wives. And divorce was still considered scandalous. Elizabeth Chapman, for example, viewed it as 'an unmixed evil . . . It tends to undermine monogamy . . . encourages hasty choice, puts a premium on temporary liaisons.'[33] Yet given that divorce was a current reality, she supported its equalization between the sexes as an important blow to the condoning of husbands' adultery. While a few feminists favoured divorce by mutual consent, others wished to retain the idea of marital fault. Mrs Millicent Fawcett sweepingly asserted:

> People who . . . think marriages should be dissolvable at will . . . are in effect anarchists . . . none of the leaders of the Woman's Movement in England have ever countenanced for a moment anarchic methods or anarchic aims.[34]

Nevertheless she too wished for the equalization of the divorce law. It was generally agreed by feminists that rather than increasing marital breakdown, such a change would raise moral standards through the indirect raising of women's status. Feminists arguing for or against specific divorce law proposals always did so in terms of the *morality* of their position.

Alongside the feminist critique of marriage there developed practical tactics for marriage's transformation, in particular, campaign work to change marital law on the one hand, and feminist literature for women's empowerment on the other. In addition, feminists strove to construct a new and inspiring vision of the ideal marriage in which the sexes were equal, an equality that included female bodily autonomy and a sexual relationship of the highest morality.

Changing the Law: the Clitheroe Case, Marital Rape and Divorce

> What is the best action for those who desire to see a healthier and
> purer sexual morality . . .? The first step is to agitate for a reform of
> the marriage laws.[35]

Marriage in Britain has traditionally involved the sanctioning by
the Church, and more recently by the State, of what has been
declared the only form of legitimate sex: sexual intercourse
between a man and a woman. Not only have sexual relationships
between the sexes outside marriage been deemed illegitimate,
but sexual intercourse *within* marriage has been seen as part of a
husband's 'conjugal rights'. In 1869 J.S. Mill had condemned the
fact that a husband could 'enforce the lowest degradation of a
human being – that of being made the instrument of an animal
function contrary to her inclinations'.[36] In 1878 and 1880, Annie
Besant and Elizabeth Wolstenholme Elmy respectively had both
spoken out against the non-recognition of marital rape.[37] At the
end of the century, with marital rape still unrecognized (indeed,
to remain unrecognized in this country right up until recently),
veteran feminist Elizabeth Wolstenholme Elmy reflected angrily:
'The wife . . . is in a different position from any other woman,
for *she has no right or power to refuse consent* [here she was quoting
the ruling of a judge]; anything more infamously degrading it is
impossible to conceive.'[38] There had, however, been one important legal victory in the intervening period; the verdict of the
Clitheroe or Jackson case in 1891.

Immediately after his marriage to Emily in November 1887,
Edmund Jackson had left for New Zealand to establish a business,
while she remained living with her sisters and brother-in-law.
Although it had been arranged that she would join him shortly,
she wrote asking him to return. He did so in July 1888 but she
refused to see him. He began proceedings for restitution of
conjugal rights, he wrote her letters, but still she would have
nothing to do with him. Then one Sunday in March 1891,
Edmund Jackson, with two accomplices, grabbed Emily as she
was leaving church in Clitheroe, dragged her backwards into a
carriage, took her to his uncle's house in Blackburn and locked

her in. Her sisters immediately applied for a writ of habeas corpus on her behalf. The husband claimed that common law entitled him to his wife's custody, and although the lower court agreed, it was unanimously held by the Court of Appeal that 'where a wife refuses to live with her husband he is not entitled to keep her in confinement in order to enforce restitution of conjugal rights.'[39]

Reaction to the verdict was mixed. Mrs Jackson was booed and jostled on her return to Clitheroe for defying her husband, and her sisters' house was stoned. *The Times* dramatically exclaimed that 'one fine morning last month marriage in England was abolished'. The *Law Times*, however, referred to the verdict as 'the charter of the personal liberty of married women',[40] while to feminists it was seen as a great victory. Elizabeth Wolstenholme Elmy wrote gleefully to her close friend Harriett McIlquaham:

> Let us rejoice together . . . 'coverture' is dead and buried . . . It is the grandest victory the women's cause has ever gained, greater even than the passing of the Married Women's Property Act . . . [B]y the law of England a husband has no more right over the person of his wife than over the person of any other woman.[41]

She immediately sent a series of five letters to the *Manchester Guardian* on the case, its future implications and the legal position of women generally. These she reprinted as pamphlets, distributing 100,000. Not all feminists were so optimistic. One, for example, although hoping that the Clitheroe case had 'purged from the law of England . . . the husband['s] right of property in the person of his wife', nevertheless feared that the popular view remained, namely 'that both chastisement and imprisonment are the natural prerogative of the husband'.[42]

By the time of the Clitheroe case, Elizabeth Wolstenholme Elmy had had a long career in feminist politics. She appears to have been the most extraordinary woman, with boundless energy and an unfailing commitment to the emancipation of women. She was born in 1833, the daughter of a Methodist minister from Eccles. She was active in the women's movement from 1861 in a host of concerns including women's entry into higher

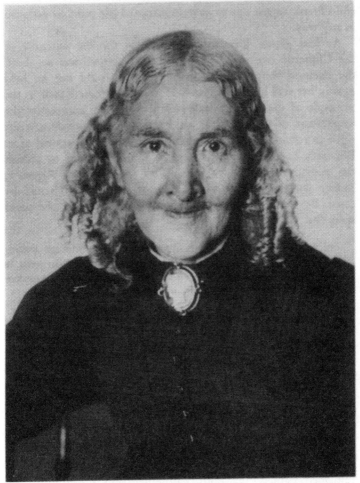

Elizabeth Wolstenholme Elmy

education, the campaign for the Married Women's Property Acts, maternal custody and guardianship rights, the campaign against the Contagious Diseases Acts, the struggle for women's suffrage, as well as being central to the feminist campaign in the 1890s to transform marriage legally, practically and ideologically. Her marriage to Ben Elmy and the birth of her (only) child Frank appear not to have interrupted her political activism in any way.

At first glance Elizabeth's enthusiasm for the outcome of the Clitheroe case seems misplaced.[43] Coverture was *not* dead: the decision simply ruled that a woman could not be held against her will by her husband. However, Elizabeth took as the principle of the ruling a wife's right to bodily autonomy; the implication of this principle was that it would include a wife's right to refuse her husband sexual intercourse. For several years Elizabeth had been trying to get a Bill introduced to abolish the marital exemption of rape. With the ruling of *Regina* v. *Jackson* she hoped that the passage of such a Bill would be eased. By 1897, reflecting back on her futile attempts, she noted sadly that

> one woman, [herself], deeply indignant at the iniquity of the existing marriage law of England ... has, during the past fourteen years, in vain asked some 40–50 different Members of Parliament to introduce a Bill ... for the abolition of this infamy.[44]

If non-recognition of marital rape implied a husband's ownership of his wife's body, so too did the divorce law's sexual double standard. Concerned to abolish the marital rape exemption, Elizabeth was also determined to reform the law on divorce. In 1889 Elizabeth at last succeeded in inducing a Dr Hunter to bring in a bill which equalized divorce between the sexes and proposed desertion as an alternative to adultery as grounds for divorce. But Dr Hunter seemed uncommitted to the project. She bitterly reflected: 'For four years he merely played with it, never bringing it in ... during which time *I* had circulated some 200,000 leaflets and worked hard to develop opinion.' In 1892 the bill was before Parliament but Dr Hunter only told her at the last minute and it fell. The main argument put against it was that it was wrong for a Scotsman to be in charge of a bill addressing English law (divorce law in Scotland was different – and better: adultery or desertion by either spouse constituted grounds for divorce). She found someone else (Sir Frank Lockwood) who promised to introduce the bill but he too made no effort. Three years later she cynically remarked: 'It has often been said of Sir Frank "that he never broke a promise". I suppose this refers to promises made to men . . .'[45]

Feminist Sex Education

Although feminists proved unable to win the legal recognition of marital rape, they were determined to lessen its occurrence. To many feminists, the central means to such an end lay with the provision of sexual information to both sexes. It was nothing new to want sex education for *boys*, but until the 1880s, girls' sexual innocence-cum-ignorance had been widely believed to provide their 'protection'. (I noted the medical profession's deep ambivalence towards sex education for girls in Chapter Two.) The equation between sexual innocence and purity was also being challenged:

> Purity! There can be no purity where there is no knowledge . . . Those women who face the world bravely every day, seeing its dark as well as its bright side . . . and passing through all unscathed – these are the pure women . . . the others are mere ignoramuses.[46]

Feminists were aware of the high likelihood of a woman entering marriage ignorant of the 'marital intimacies, which, unless of reciprocal impulse, may prove repugnant and intolerable to her'.[47] One commentator noted cynically: 'It is not indelicate to train up daughters to catch eligible husbands . . . But give them a sound practical knowledge of their own physiology? . . . Shocking! Most improper!'[48] Sex education was to be the crucial strategy in transforming potential sexual abuse into actual sexual harmony. It was also seen by feminists as a central means by which women could be protected from unwanted sex and at last be able to demand that sexual encounters take place on their *own* terms. Boys, meanwhile, would learn from this new sex education of the need for sexual continence and respect for the body of both sexes.

The first sex education book written by a feminist in this country was that of Dr Elizabeth Blackwell, although one may be forgiven for wondering how her feminism informed her text.

The subject matter was certainly controversial, however: before its acceptance by Bell and Sons, the work had been rejected by thirteen publishers. Hatchards had initially accepted it, until a senior member of the firm (the wife of a bishop) burnt the proofs.[49] Despite being entitled *Counsel to Parents on the Moral Education of Their Children in Relation to Sex*,[50] it was the mother who was addressed throughout. The text encouraged maternal education and maternal surveillance, all part of 'the great work of maternity'. On the one hand she was advised to impart 'physiological truths' to the child, centrally the indispensability of chastity, as well as a celebration of the body – 'a wonderful and sacred thing, intended for important and noble ends.'[51] As Mariana Valverde points out,[52] social purity educators such as Blackwell did not argue for the denial of sexuality but its recognition as normal and necessary, in need of correct channelling. In this Blackwell was indeed radical. The mind had to be trained in 'early purity', she insisted: the mother must 'prepare the young mind to shrink from the debasing literature with which society is flooded'.[53] This was even more necessary for girls than boys, for 'it is only by securing mental purity that young women will unconsciously address themselves to the higher, rather than the lower, instincts of their male companions.'[54] (It was an indirect reference to the age-old theme that women were partly, if not wholly, responsible for male sexual behaviour.)

On the other hand, keen watchfulness was advised: 'The mother's eye . . . must always watch over her children . . . The mother should caution the child not to touch or meddle with himself more than is necessary.' The child needed protection from corrupting influences, in particular working-class women, who as nurses and servants (and here her class prejudice is palpable) 'bring back to the respectable home the evil associations of their own lives'.[55] Mothers needed to transmit 'pure', 'right' knowledge before the 'impure', 'wrong' knowledge of others was revealed to the child. (Elizabeth Blackwell clearly thought the 'wrong' knowledge was being transmitted at the Men and Women's Club when she attended as a guest in November 1886 and listened to Ralph Thicknesse's paper on 'State Interference with Marriage and the Domestic Relations'. She wrote to Pearson afterwards, accusing him of 'leading young girls astray with pernicious doctrines.')[56] To Elizabeth Blackwell's credit, she did recognize the existence of female sexuality and women's potential for sexual pleasure, although of course to be solely within marriage. And she also stressed the need to give basic physiological information ('true' physiology always being 'pure'), although she was very vague as to how mothers were to undertake such a task which was presumably daunting to most Victorians.

Blackwell's text was published in 1878. Three years later the Moral Reform Union was established, a feminist organization committed to the distribution and publication of 'Literature of Moral Education', which on the whole meant sex education. Until the publication of Ellis Ethelmer in the early 1890s, however, there was little explicitly feminist material available. Ellis Ethelmer was the pseudonym of Elizabeth Wolstenholme Elmy's husband, Ben Elmy, although it is very possible that the writings were a collaborative venture between husband and wife.[57] As well as two sexual education manuals for adolescents and children (*Baby Buds* and *The Human Flower*), the writings consisted of two poetic pieces (*Woman Free* and *Phases of Love*) and a prose tract (*Life to Woman*).[58] Together these works presented a coherent analysis of why and in what manner women were subordinated, and how this subordination might be overcome. The texts also offered a utopian picture of a future in which women were men's equals and humanity had moved from the level of the 'brute' and was on its way to a higher 'psychic place and purpose' with a transformed relationship between the sexes.

As one of the feminist evolutionists mentioned in Chapter Two, Ethelmer argued that the roots of women's present oppression lay in male sexual abuse of women in the past. This tendency to abuse had become hereditary in man in the form of 'an exaggerated and abnormal amount of sexual desire'. One of the consequences of sexual abuse was the development of menstruation in women, an 'abnormality' parallel to man's abnormality of 'acquired excess of passion'. As we have seen in the discussion of medicine, Ethelmer was not alone in viewing menstruation as, in effect, pathological. To Ethelmer, menstruation – 'a kind of modified abortion' – was initially the result of 'the forced intercourse of young brides', but had become hereditary. (Elizabeth Blackwell agreed that male sexual abuse had become hereditary, but she differed from Ethelmer in thinking menstruation was beneficial to women.) Men's sexual excesses had also forced women into the slavery of endless childbearing, argued Ethelmer; woman 'by mother's burden forced to slavish fate'. Women's physical subjection in the form of menstruation and involuntary motherhood was reinforced by ideological subjection.[59]

How was women's subjection to end? Ethelmer (like Elizabeth Blackwell and many other feminists) saw a crucial part of the solution lying with sex education, given by mothers to their children. Armed with sexual knowledge, including of the 'duties' expected of wives, young women would demand their right to 'physical inviolability'. Women also needed to educate men into 'psychic love'. By this Ethelmer appears to have meant a union of hearts and minds in which the physicality of sexual intercourse was merely a lesser part. Ethelmer believed women to have less sexual desire than men. In an argument similar to that presented by several of the women in the Men and Women's Club, it was claimed that 'uncompelled profligacy is rare in women; the incumbent sequences and sufferings – the burdens and pains of motherhood – devolving on her a natural deterrent influence'.[60] For woman to become her own person, she also needed to gain the social, economic and political rights so long denied her. Indeed, no woman could become sexually equal without equality being sought and won in all aspects of her life.

Ethelmer's two sex education manuals, *Baby Buds* and *Human Flower*, were revolutionary in presenting (rather elliptical) information on sex and the body for the child and adolescent of *both* sexes to read for themselves. However, like Blackwell, Ethelmer was first and foremost encouraging sex instruction to be undertaken by the mother, with the manuals to aid her. Unlike Blackwell, the surveillance aspect was absent. What were to be the consequences of sex instruction? For the boy:

The voice of lower passion will be overcome by the higher pleadings of justice, while the youth will be no more deluded by false counsel and evil example into the ways of heartless and thoughtless wrong-doing.

As for the girl or young woman, sex education was largely seen in terms of providing full information of the dangers – 'the surest safeguard' against undesired approaches from men, *including* husbands. To Ethelmer, it was essential that women had complete control over their bodies: 'The function of wifehood and motherhood must remain solely and entirely within the wife's own option'.[61] The consequences of this 'fuller knowledge' for both sexes would be 'the worthier man, the happier woman.' Dr Alice Ker similarly advised:

> The girl must be taught that her body is her own ... and that she has no right to make the undue ownership of it over to her husband ... In the marriage relation, the choice of time and frequency is the right of the woman, by reason of the periodicity which characterises her being.[62]

The feminist journal *Shafts* recommended Ethelmer's work, and noted that women were now realizing 'the urgent need for moral and physiological training for their children'. A Mrs Kapteyn of Hampstead was 'organising classes for the instruction of the young'.[63] Sex education was not centrally, if at all, about a woman's right to sexual pleasure. To feminists, the main purpose of sex education was to empower the married woman sexually by providing knowledge of her body, the man's body, and what he was likely to 'expect' of her, and by encouraging the conviction that her right to refuse any undesired sexual advance was inviolable. Yet Ethelmer's ideal of 'psychic love' suggested the inclusion of pleasure, although possibly nothing as mundane as simply physical delight!

'New Woman' Writings and Marriage Exposed

Although the 1890s witnessed a smattering of sex education pamphlets addressing girls as well as boys, the consequences of young women's sexual ignorance was explored more fully in fictional form, especially on the pages of the 'new woman' novel. The term 'new woman' had just entered the English language, apparently invented by the feminist novelist Sarah Grand. In one sense the 'new woman' was a journalistic and literary construction, but she also had a basis in reality: the increased opportunities for middle-class women to enter higher education and employment and the various gains made by feminism more generally. The term 'new woman' was not equivalent to the term 'feminist', although a self-defined 'new woman' was likely to hold certain feminist convictions. She was generally thought of as a middle- or upper-class young woman, concerned to reject many of the conventions of femininity and to live and work on free and equal terms with the opposite sex. She was given to reading 'advanced' literature, smoking cigarettes, and travelling unchaperoned, often on a bicycle. Her hallmark was *personal* freedom.[64]

The 'new woman' novels had as their subject matter the doubts and dilemmas surrounding the 'new woman': her experience of work and higher education and her challenge to conventional marriage and sex. But the novels were also largely written by women who themselves epitomized the 'new woman' stereotype. Many of these novels by women are today unknown, but at the time they sold in their millions. These female 'new woman' writers thought of their fiction as didactic in intent and as a political contribution to the women's 'cause'. They aimed high: 'In women's hands – women writers' hands – lies the regeneration of the world.'[65] The novels were an important site for the imaginative exploration of relationships between the sexes. Feminist journals (and not simply those that were literary) extensively discussed 'new woman' fiction and 'new woman' authors. (The feminist *Shafts*, for example, presented lengthy reviews of certain 'new woman' novels, and the *Woman's Penny Paper* regularly interviewed certain 'new woman' writers.) Feminists drew on incidents or quotations from this fiction in their more overtly political writing.[66]

The female 'new woman' fiction writers were markedly distinct from their male equivalents. While the male 'new woman' writers, such as George Gissing, Grant Allen and George Moore, tended to focus on the sexual 'freedom' of a 'new woman' heroine (Thomas Hardy was an exception in this respect), the woman writers concentrated more on the sexuality of men.[67] It was male sexual behaviour which was singled out as the key problem: demanding, selfish, frequently injurious to its female 'recipient', it was seen as the central cause of many married women's unhappiness. '"What brutes men are!" is the never-ceasing burden of new woman's song', remarked one hostile reviewer sarcastically.[68] The 'brutishness' of male sexual behaviour was exacerbated by women's sexual ignorance. In *The Beth Book* of 1897 the author Sarah Grand informs the reader:

> There are marriages which for the ignorant girl preached into dutiful submission, whose 'innocence' has been carefully preserved for the purpose, mean prostitution as absolute, as repugnant, as cruel, and as contrary to nature as that of the streets.[69]

In the short story 'Virgin Soil', George Egerton's 'Florence' believes sexual ignorance is the key to her disastrous marriage. She turns accusingly on her mother:

> 'I say it is your fault because you reared me a fool, an idiot, ignorant of everything I ought to have known . . . my physical needs, my coming passion, the very meaning of my sex, my wifehood and motherhood to follow. You gave me not one weapon in my hand to defend myself against the possible attacks of man at his worst. You sent me to fight the biggest battle of a woman's life . . . with a white gauze' – she laughed derisively – 'of maiden purity as a shield.'[70]

And the heroine of Emma Brooke's *A Superfluous Woman* reflects: 'As to her nature, of that she had heard nothing; passion, she had been taught, was an offensive word.'[71]

If the feminist participants in the 'marriage debate' had begun the process of opening up marriage for public exposure, scrutiny continued and extended through this 'new woman' novel. Despite 'its flippancy, its garish crudity, its edification of selfishness' the social-purity feminist Blanche Leppington praised the 'new woman' novel in 'helping to carry the pressure of the moral question into the sacred enclosure of marriage itself, from which all questioning had been too long excluded'.[72] In its depiction of the double moral standard at work within marriage, the non-consensual sex, the incessant child-bearing, the 'new woman' novel was spotlighting a host of horrors lurking behind the veneer of marital respectability. But the novels went further than the contributors to the 'marriage debate' – they pointed to one further parallel between marriage and prostitution: the risk of venereal disease shared by wives and prostitutes alike. Unlike the prostitute, however, the wife, with her sexual 'innocence', was largely unaware of the danger. I say 'largely unaware', for the extensive reporting of divorce cases since the 1860s, including those alleging 'the communication of a loathsome sore',[73] must have given at least some women a sense that husbands could be health risks to their wives. In their exposure of the hypocrisy of double moral standards, feminists also revealed an irony: a man's resort to prostitutes for the 'purity' of his wife in reality rendered her ill and sterile.

Serious fictional depiction of venereal disease had already greatly shocked the London 'Establishment' in 1891, with the first showing of Ibsen's *Ghosts*, a play depicting a family haunted not simply by the disastrous effects of congenital syphilis upon a middle-class family, but also, as Elaine Showalter points out,[74] the degenerate prohibitions of bourgeois morality. The play was noisily condemned by the press. To the *Daily Telegraph*, for example, it was nothing but 'an open drain, a loathsome sore unbandaged, a dirty act done publicly', to the *Daily News* it was 'naked loathsomeness'.[75] Such a verdict did not deter the feminist 'new woman' writer Sarah Grand from taking venereal disease as a central theme for her novel *The Heavenly Twins*.

Sarah Grand was born Frances Bellenden Clarke in 1854, the daughter of a naval lieutenant. She married David McFall, a 39-year-old army surgeon, when she was aged 16. They finally settled in Norwich where McFall had some involvement with the local Lock hospital (a hospital for the treatment of women with venereal disease) – or so Gillian Kersley (Grand's biographer) surmises.[76] Frances McFall left her husband in 1890, after the anonymous publication of her first novel *Ideala*. She changed her name to Sarah Grand and published her best-known novel, *The Heavenly Twins*, in 1893, and her autobiographical novel

The Beth Book four years later. She began lecturing for various feminist causes, including the Women Writers Suffrage League. She was also an enthusiastic cyclist, and a member of the Rational Dress Society. 'Rational dress' referred to the abandonment of tight lacing and all restrictive feminine garments; another assumed characteristic of the 'new woman' was indeed her adoption of loose-fitting, comfortable clothes. In 1922 Grand moved to Bath, later to become its mayor.

In her foreword to the 1923 edition of *The Heavenly Twins*, Sarah Grand reflected back on how her attempts at its publication had led one publisher to comment: 'All delicately-minded women must feel themselves aggrieved, if not insulted, by the prominence which is given to the physical side of marriage . . .' Once a publisher was found, the book's Press reception was no better. The book was denounced as 'a product of hysteria and wilful eccentricity, with something more than a savour of indelicacy'. Whether this acted as an inducement to sales is unclear, but within a year 20,000 copies of the book had been sold, and it was to be reprinted six times, bringing Sarah Grand letters of praise from women (and doctors) worldwide.[77]

The Heavenly Twins is an immensely long and fascinating book composed of a number of interlocking narratives. Despite the title, the central figure is Evadne; indeed, the novel opens and closes with her story. Evadne represents the 'new woman': she is inquisitive and self-taught, her reading ranging from medical and sociological texts through to J.S. Mill and Mrs Gaskell, and she holds 'views'. Her mother is deeply shocked by the latter: 'Well I don't know where she got them from . . . for *I* haven't any.' Only hours after marriage to Major Colquhoun, Evadne learns of his profligate past; at thirty-nine he is already 'a vice-worn man', 'a moral leper'. For appearances' sake, she agrees to live with him, but on the condition that it is a marriage in name alone. She reprimands her aunt for suggesting that she forgive her husband:

> So long as women like you will forgive anything, men will do anything. You have it in your power to set up a high standard of excellence for men to reach in order to have the privilege of associating with you.

It was of course a theme being raised in the marriage debate: women to veto all men of suspect morals. In contrast to Evadne, Edith, the daughter of a bishop, was all innocence and ignorance, 'fitted by education to move in the society of saints and angels alone'. Her marriage to Sir Mosely Mentieth, a debauched syphilitic, results in a diseased child and her own decline into madness, culminating in agonizing death. As one Nurse Griffiths remarks: 'It's the dirty men makes the misery.'[78]

Outside the realm of fiction doctors and scientists minutely analysed the physiognomy and physiology of the prostitute and 'explained' her choice of profession in terms of her 'primitiveness' and degeneracy;[79] the 'new women' novel writers applied the art of physiognomy to a study of their fictitious men. They read the facial signs of male debauchery. Thus in Sarah Grand's *The Heavenly Twins*:

> Evadne noticed something repellent about the expression of Sir Mosely's mouth. She acknowledged that his nose was good, but his eyes were small, peery and too close together and his head shelved backward like an ape's.[80]

(Fortunately, when a contemporary physiognomist turned her eye on to Sarah Grand herself, the account was highly flattering, including mentioning that her 'clear-cut upper lip indicates purity and a total absence of coarseness and sensualism'.)[81] In Emma Brooke's *A Superfluous Woman*, it was the voice which betrayed Lord Heriot: 'A thread ran through it like the twang of a broken wire – a thin trickle of disease dropped out with every syllable'.[82] Venereal disease was harming not simply the innocent wives of the new woman novel, but their children also – the inheritors of the 'sins of the fathers' in the form of congenital syphilis. While feminists saw their role as saviours of the future, the very possibility of a future was threatened by the diseased constitutions of profligate men. As is noted by Evadne of *The Heavenly Twins*: 'There is no past in the matter of vice. The consequences become hereditary, and continue from generation to generation.'[83]

While not the only new woman writer to mention venereal disease, Sarah Grand was the first. At the time of her death in

1943 one admirer reflected: 'She was the real pioneer of public enlightenment on venereal disease. Participants in the Ministry of Health's campaign today can only guess how much courage this took fifty years ago.'[84] She was certainly courageous, but she felt herself misunderstood. She was at pains to emphasize that not only was she *not* against marriage or men as such, but she was actively in favour of 'true' marriage and virulently against divorce. Dissolute men, however, should be given short shrift: 'I hope that we shall soon see the marriage of certain men made a criminal offence.'[85]

Constructing an Ideal Relationship

There was much to be won before women could meet men on an equal footing, but this did not deter feminists from constructing a future ideal of emotional and spiritual unity between husband and wife. In her 1878 tract on marriage, Annie Besant argued that a 'true marriage' necessitated 'satisfaction for mind, heart and tastes as well as for body'.[86] Few could have disagreed. Few could have disagreed either with Eleanor Marx and Edward Aveling's definition of 'the highest ideal', namely 'the complete, harmonious, lasting blend of two human lives'.[87] (Sadly, their own free union, far from harmonious, ended with Eleanor's suicide.)[88] Again and again, feminists described the ideal relationship between the sexes as one based on love, sympathy, companionship, mutual attraction, monogamy, fidelity, permanence, mutual responsibility, equality, and, above all, women's autonomy. The vision had its limitations, of course. An ideal of emotional blending or unity offered no *practical* help for the handling of emotional (or other) dependency within marriage. There was, it seems, little recognition of the complexity of psychic structures. It was also assumed to be a heterosexual ideal. Further, it portrayed a very middle-class view of marriage, for as Ellen Ross points out, many working-class women did not view marriage as (potentially or actually) involving romantic love or emotional 'intimacy'; 'intimacy' was confined to children, female kin and female neighbours. But although the ideal husband for

the working-class woman was the man who 'provided' economically, gave his wife a generous share of his pay-packet, and made
few sexual demands, affection and compatibility of temperament
were also highly prized, reflecting an ideal not dissimilar from
that of her middle-class counterpart. Similarly, gender specific
obligations and responsibilities were seen as part of a 'good'
marriage by most women, although the nature of such obligations varied between classes.[89]

If feminists agreed on certain abstract, high-sounding principles
pertaining to an ideal relationship, disagreement arose as to its
proposed legal status. The central issue was whether the relationship should be sanctioned publicly by law and the state or based
solely on a *private* contract, as advocated by Mona Caird. Further,
for those feminists for whom a private contract was the ideal,
there was disagreement as to whether this should be simply a
future ideal – to come into effect once women were truly
emancipated – or an ideal to be embarked on now, in the
present. The proposed private contract was generally termed a
'free union', 'free alliance', 'free marriage' or 'free love'. Those
feminists adhering to such an ideal insisted that their notion of
'free love' was one of monogamy, and, if love persisted, of
permanence. The term had negative connotations for many
however, and was frequently equated with promiscuity, even
polygamy, so that sometimes an advocate of 'free unions' might
defensively argue that this did not mean she supported 'free
love'.[90]

Marriage was the socially sanctioned destiny of all women. Of
those women who did not marry, many might well have wished
it otherwise, but there were others for whom the alternatives to
marriage, namely spinsterhood or free union, were welcomed,
even actively sought. For many the choice related to their
feminist critique of marriage. What part did consideration of
such choices play in the feminist politics of sexual morality?

2 THE ALTERNATIVES TO MARRIAGE: FREE UNIONS AND SPINSTERHOOD

Free Unions

Despite their criticism of marriage, most feminists were generally opposed to any current formation of free unions, even though some of them considered it a *future* ideal. For example, in the early days of the Men and Women's Club, a number of the women had refused the name initially proposed for the group – the 'Wollstonecraft Club' – partly on the grounds of the possibly damaging association with Mary Wollstonecraft's 'immoral' lifestyle (meaning her 'free love' relationships). The women members were resolute that *for the present*, given women's vulnerability and disadvantage, *reformed* legal marriage was infinitely preferable to a non-marital relationship between the sexes. While Henrietta Muller informed Maria Sharpe in private that she was against marriage, at a club meeting Maria was surprised to hear Henrietta argue for legal reform alone. Henrietta held that only in the future, *after* women were free, would alternatives to marriage be possible. But Annie Besant, who came to speak to the Club in January 1887 on 'The State and Sexual Relations', disagreed; she was a feminist openly in favour of free unions.

Annie Besant was born in 1847. Her father, a doctor, died five years later, leaving his wife and three young children almost destitute. Initially very religious, Annie made a disastrous marriage to clergyman Frank Besant in 1866. She later implied that she was raped on the first night of her honeymoon. She described her existence with him as 'degraded by an intolerable sense of bondage', for he had 'very high ideas of a husband's authority and a wife's submission'.[91] In the 1870s she lost her faith, left her husband and joined the Secular Society. She became an active birth controller, atheist and radical liberal, and in 1877 she and Charles Bradlaugh were tried in court for the distribution of a birth-control pamphlet. Her former husband, who already had custody of her son, now won custody of her daughter, Mabel. In the 1880s Annie Besant converted to socialism and joined the Fabian Society, and later the Social Democratic Federation,

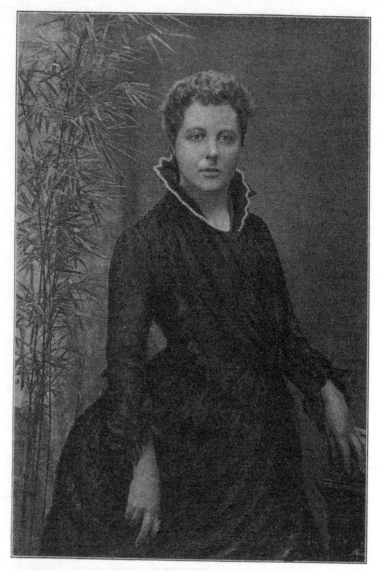

Annie Besant, 1885

Britain's first Marxist party.[92] To Beatrice Webb, generally disinclined to compliment, Annie Besant was 'the only woman I have ever known who is a real orator, who had the gift of public persuasion'.[93] From 1887 to 1888 Besant worked closely with W.T. Stead, with whom she fell unrequitedly in love. On his part, he delighted in unconsummated 'harmless flirtations'.[94] In 1888 she was elected to the London School Board for Tower Hamlets as a Progressive (the Progressives were a loose alliance of radicals, liberals and the left) and in the same year she organized the famous Bryant and May matchgirls' strike. In 1890 she converted to Theosophy, and a few years later became the head of the Theosophical Society in Europe and India. She moved to India and continued her political involvement in the espousal of Indian Nationalism.[95]

Club members were familiar with Annie Besant's 1878 pamphlet on marriage in which she had argued that

> side by side with [an] effort to reform marriage abuses, should go the determination not to contract a legal marriage while the laws remain as immoral as they are ... Women have a fairer chance of happiness and comfort in an unlegalised than in a legal marriage.[96]

She informed the Club that she was against state regulation of personal relationships save where children were involved. Anticipating the usual arguments in opposition, she had various replies to hand. For example, in answer to the suggestion that permanent marriages would not take place but for state support, she suggested firstly that if that was the case, they stood condemned, and secondly that with free unions there would be *more* permanent relationships, because it was unhappy indissoluble marriages which led to immorality. And to the suggestion that once a man in a free union tired of the woman he would throw her off, she replied that it would be worse for the woman if she *were* legally tied to him. To Annie Besant, free unions were the moral and rational alternative to current mercenary marriage.[97]

Annie Besant may have seen free unions as the desired alternative to marriage, but most feminists disagreed. Why? The main reason, it seems, was that they feared such unions would allow men unrestrained sexual licence and would thereby render women more vulnerable. Until men's sexual impulses had been curbed through the inheritance of lesser lustful inclinations, marriage law at least gave women some protection; given the reality of the double moral standard, it was better to increase rather than decrease the taboo against non-marital sex. The feminist Moral Reform Union took an uncompromising stand: 'Against the practice of the self-styled "free love" – which really means the substitution of lust for love – we shall wage an unremitting war.'[98] A female contributor to the *Daily Telegraph*'s 1888 correspondence on marriage declared:

> it would be a bad day for my countrywomen if in the case of 'Marriage v. Free Love', a verdict should be given for the latter. What would become of wives over 40, if they could be thrown on one side like broken toys?[99]

But not all women agreed. For example, a female reader responded:

> The moral ties of love, reverence, sympathy and ... oneness should be sufficient, and where people are so far apart morally that they require *fetters* to keep them together they would be far better parted altogether.[100]

A woman's vulnerability in a free union also related to the risk of her being left to fend not only for herself but for her children too:

> it [a free union] absolves the man from all legal parental responsibility... [A] woman who accepts a free union has now the choice of remaining childless or accepting the final responsibility for the children she bears.[101]

There was also the question of children's need for permanence, less assured, according to some, if the parents' relationship was without legal ties.[102] But there was disagreement here too. One woman informed *Daily Telegraph* readers:

> 'Free love' sounds like an excuse for licence, but I honestly believe that the children of a marriage in which the only ties were love and respect would be better cared for, better trained and ... become

better citizens than the offspring of a legal union where love and respect had become impossible.[103]

If feminists were primarily opposed to free unions on the grounds of women's vulnerability, the question of respectability came a close second. Fear of free love in part related to its equation with the highly disreputable cause of anarchism.[104] Further, as predominantly middle-class, many feminists shared a class disgust with anything which challenged bourgeois respectability. The bourgeoisie had historically consolidated itself and constructed a class identity through the disavowal of the non-respectable, the 'low'.[105] But the class identity was also gendered, and lack of respectability in a *woman* had sexual connotations with no equivalence in a man. An 'unrespectable' woman implied a woman with a 'reputation', a 'loose' woman. Feminist Lady Cook (sister of American anarchist feminist Victoria Woodhull) contrasted the sex bias in the epithet 'free' as applied to women, with its application to men:

> A 'free' man is a noble being; a 'free woman' is a contemptible being . . . Freedom for a woman is . . . escape from those necessary restraining conditions which prevent the sinking of her soul into degradation and vice, which it is, all unconsciously, assumed is her natural tendency.[106]

In other words, the woman freed of the 'restraints' on her sexuality (legal marriage) crossed the threshold into vice; it was similar to the argument about the restraints of modesty. It is thus perhaps explicable why many feminists looked especially aghast at a woman from their own ranks entering a free union, fearing that scandal of impropriety would harm the 'woman's cause'.[107] Elizabeth Wolstenholme's free union was a case in point.

Elizabeth Wolstenholme had set up house with anarchist poet and crêpe silk manufacturer Ben Elmy in the early 1870s, inspired, according to Sylvia Pankhurst, by Mary Wollstonecraft, and aware of the disabilities suffered by married women. However, on her becoming visibly pregnant, 'there was much fluttering in the suffrage dovecotes'[108] and she had finally been induced to marry. But the pressure had not stopped here. In December 1875 Mrs Millicent Fawcett had written to Mrs Wolstenholme

Elmy (now formally married; rather than renounce her name, she had joined it to that of her husband)[109] asking her to resign as secretary of the Married Women's Property Committee on the grounds that 'the prospects of the women's movement will be materially affected by what you do at the present time . . . What happened before you married has been and is a great injury to the cause of women'.[110] Other feminists did not take such a harsh line, but nevertheless seem to have wished her not to hold office until the scandal had blown over.[111] (She resigned temporarily but soon returned, becoming the main force behind the Married Women's Property Act 1882.) Feminist ambivalence towards free unions was to continue into the late nineteenth century, as we shall see in relation to an infamous free-love case in the 1890s.

The Legitimation League And The Questioning Of Free Love

The Legitimation League was one organization which explicitly supported free love. Originally set up in 1893 'to create a machinery for acknowledging offspring born out of wedlock and to secure for them equal rights with legitimate children',[112] in 1897 it formally adopted as its primary aim the education of public opinion 'in the direction of freedom in sexual relationships'. (The issue of illegitimacy was relegated to second place.) Free love was made to sound highly honourable: 'Free love is simply two of the noblest principles of human relations – freedom and love – merged together.'[113] A number of members, including the President (Wordsworth Donisthorpe), promptly resigned. W.T. Stead informed the League that he was sorry to hear that it had undertaken the championing of free love, for

in ordinary interpretation it means an attempt to break down the securities . . . which the human race has . . . evolved . . . for the protection of the weaker sex against the unrestrained licence of the stronger.[114]

Undeterred, and with its new aim blazoned, the League launched its journal the *Adult* in the same year. It was anxious to dispel any fears that support for free love would be at a woman's expense: 'One of the fundamentals of our position is the equal sex freedom of man and woman. "Free love" for one sex at the expense of the other means neither freedom nor love.'[115] Although it is clear from various articles in the *Adult* that not all members (who were of both sexes) were especially supportive of feminism, the League's formal commitment was explicit. The *Adult*'s editor George Bedborough assured the readers of the feminist journal *Shafts*: 'The League holds to the precious principle that a woman belongs to herself, that neither priest nor lawyer has any right to dictate to her.'[116] And in the *Adult*'s first issue it was stated that 'we protest . . . against the theory underlying laws, marriage settlements and popular practice that a woman's person can be the "property" of her husband'.[117] It appears that about half of its members were women, as were the holders of official posts (or at least so the *Adult*'s editor claimed). The League's treasurers were both women, and its president from 1897 was the American anarchist feminist Lillian Harman, who had been imprisoned in Chicago for living with the father of her illegitimate child. According to Detective Inspector John Sweeney of Scotland Yard, who had infiltrated the organization for several years, the League had 'a very large and influential membership', containing a lot of anarchists, although many members did not allow their names to appear in public. When Lillian Harman visited London in 1898, membership increased and branches of the League were formed in various provincial cities.[118]

The *Adult*'s editor might have been convinced that feminism and free love were reconcilable, but not all its members were so sure. In addition to a woman's economic vulnerability within a free union and her sole responsibility for the children, several of the female League members elaborated upon the effects of lost respectability, namely entering the ranks of the social outcast. Mary Reed told readers of the *Adult*: 'To my mind "free love" offers no honourable or happy solution to the woman. It certainly leaves her freedom, but at the cost of what makes life endurable – the respect of the men and women of character whom she admires'.[119] At a League dinner another feminist League member, Edith Vance, focused on how this loss of respect was particularly difficult for women. Speaking of Gladys Heywood, common-law wife of the League's founder Oswald Dawson, she addressed the men:

> I did not know until I had a talk with Mrs Dawson . . . what a very great deal she has to endure. It is very easy – perhaps it is fun for you gentlemen – to be twitted about your connection with the League . . . If the conversation gets too bad, you can knock the man down or threaten to do so, but Mrs Dawson is not in a position to thus deal with her slanderers.[120]

A woman labelled a 'free lover' was likely to have been slandered not simply as a 'sinner' for living with a man outside wedlock, but also as a 'promiscuous woman', sexually available to all men. That free love gave all men potential property rights in a woman's sexuality was an idea held to even by certain League members. J.C. Spence, a vice president of the League, who later resigned once the League adopted free love as its main aim, objected to free love because 'the idea that we are to share the woman we love with other men is repulsive'.[121] And Lillian Harman recounted a talk given by Mr W.M. Thompson, editor of *Reynolds*, to a recent gathering of the League in which he had asserted that 'freedom in love is impracticable because no man can love and respect a woman who is the "common property of the herd"'. To Lillian Harman, Mr Thompson seemed to possess 'a very hazy conception of what Free Love really means. It is impossible for him to realize that a woman may be the property of herself.'[122] Indeed, a woman's desire to be her own person, free to enter a relationship in which no man held property rights in her sexuality, was at the heart of why certain women supported free unions. More negatively, for other women their support related more to their rejection of current marital law than their espousal of sexual freedom. But women feared that the support of at least some men for free love was in terms of the potential sexual access to more than one woman, and the facilitated avoidance of financial responsibilities for children and partner. If Mr Spence and Mr Thompson are anything to go by, men's *objection* to free love was in terms of their disinclination to give up sole ownership rights in a woman's body.

Edith Lanchester

The extreme hostility of many to free unions, be they feminist, socialist or simply 'ordinary' members of the middle class, is illustrated by the negative reactions to Edith Lanchester's unmarried alliance. Edith was a self-declared 'new woman', and she certainly epitomized the image. Born in 1871, the daughter of a prosperous architect, she had an honours degree in science from London University and was an ex-teacher (dismissed for 'advanced opinions'), now working as a clerk. She was a feminist, a socialist prominent in the Social Democratic Federation, a close friend of Eleanor Marx and firmly against marriage. In 1894 she had stood as a socialist candidate for the London School Board. In 1895 Edith decided to live openly with a railway clerk and fellow SDF member, James Sullivan. When her family heard of her plans they were so horrified that they arranged for a specialist in mental diseases, Dr George Blandford, to come to her lodgings in Battersea and certify her 'insane'. 'Over-education', according to her father, was the cause of her insanity. To the doctor, her 'insanity' was manifested in her obvious seeking of 'social' suicide: her choice of entering a free union. (To medical science generally, conformity to socially acceptable behaviour was taken as the criterion of mental health.) Class, of course, also came into it. Dr Blandford recounted in the *British Medical Journal* how Edith had intended to 'live in illicit intercourse with a man in a station of life much below her own'.[123] When asked by the doctor whether she would marry Mr Sullivan, she replied that she would never marry, since marriage was immoral. Her father and brothers then pinioned her arms to her sides with a rope, forcibly dragged her into a waiting carriage, and took her off to a private lunatic asylum in Roehampton. With the help of colleagues, Sullivan applied for a writ of habeas corpus. Support and wide publicity were organized through press reports and

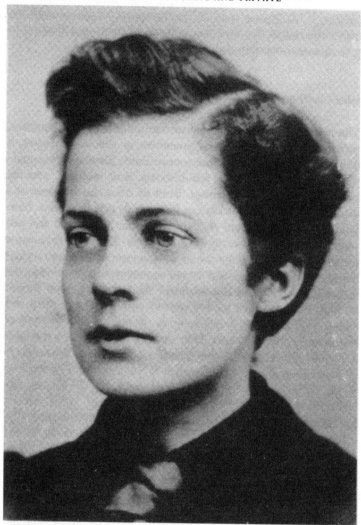

Edith Lanchester

'Lanchester meetings' (in which the Legitimation League played an important supportive part), and three days later she was visited by two Commissioners of Lunacy who proclaimed her perfectly sane if somewhat foolish. The next day she was released. From then until his death she lived in a free union with Sullivan. She never saw her father again.[124]

The Social Democratic Federation did not back Edith Lanchester (although several individual members gave her their support).[125] The Federation's leader Hyndman deplored her action on the grounds that its identification of socialism with free love would alienate the working classes. Most feminists were similarly unenthusiastic, although for different reasons. Given that by the 1890s there was relatively greater openness on issues of sexuality, we might have expected feminists' attitudes to have changed since the 1870s condemnation of Elizabeth Wolstenholme and Ben Elmy's unorthodox relationship. However, feminist lack of interest in the Lanchester case clearly indicated the continuity of ambivalence, even hostility towards those engaging in free unions. The feminist paper, *Woman's Signal*, while granting that Edith Lanchester was clearly an intelligent and sane young woman, did not support her actions. 'She appears to have been misled by the example of Mr Grant Allen's theoretical "Woman Who Did"' (Allen's notorious novel *The Woman Who Did* concerned a woman who chose to bear an illegitimate child). The *Woman's Signal* continued:

> It is natural enough that this decision should cause great distress to her parents, who . . . are old enough to know the terrible and life-long martyrdom which their daughter would bring upon herself by such conduct.

However, while they could 'sympathise with the position of her father', they did not approve of his use of the lunacy laws, which they held to be in need of immediate reform. Indeed, their interest in the case rapidly became one of interest in this latter issue, rather than the question of a woman's right to self-determination.[126]

The vast majority of feminists were critical of the current legal status and practice of marriage, but few were prepared to countenance the alternative of a free union. For many however, the alternative of spinsterhood held more appeal.

The Choice of Spinsterhood

For a woman who rejected the inequality of marriage and the instability of free unions, the mantle of spinsterhood was the only alternative. It has been suggested by a number of historians that feminists in this period were predominantly unmarried. Philippa Levine's survey of 194 Victorian feminist activists, however, reveals that nearly half of them married at some stage in their lives.[127] While some women consciously opted for spinsterhood, for the majority of single women it was not a choice. Given the so-called 'surplus' of women – in 1881 there were 1,055 women to every 1,000 men, by 1911 the figure had risen to 1,068 – for many, marriage was simply not possible in the first place. In 1892 Clara Collet estimated that one in six of all women in England and Wales were likely to remain unmarried, while in London the figure rose to one in five.[128] This demographic imbalance was largely due to the higher death rate of males, and the higher rate of male emigration, three males emigrating for every one female.

While the majority of girls were still being brought up to expect marriage, the new and reformed girls' secondary schools were encouraging girls to view the future prospect of earning their own living as a viable alternative.[129] For many years factories and domestic service had provided paid employment for working-class single women, but there had been little for their middle-class equivalents. Now, largely owing to feminist pressure, various doors were slowly opening for women into higher education and several professions, while changing economic conditions provided job opportunities in new areas such as clerical work, teaching and nursing. There was a rapid expansion of the respectable 'white blouse' job market;[130] although such work tended to be poorly paid, it was at least becoming more possible for the single woman, whatever her class, to exist outside the boundaries of the nuclear family in conditions better than abject poverty. Martha Vicinus has shown how single women, forced to redefine themselves in terms outside both the nuclear family and the institution of prostitution, developed a new role for themselves in which they could operate in the public world as paid workers while retaining their domesticity, respectability and femininity. They transformed the passive labels of purity and goodness into 'active spirituality and passionate social service'.[131] This was precisely how Henrietta Muller saw her role and that of other single women. In an article in the *Westminster Review* in 1884 she called on single women to work in the public sphere to protect 'the social, legal, political interests of women, children and young girls' – the work of 'the "femme libre" of the future'.[132]

'New woman' novelist Sarah Grand may have been enthusiastic about 'true' marriage to a 'right-minded man', but she did admit that marriage was no longer the only respectable career for middle-class young women: 'Thinking . . . for herself, the modern girl . . . knows that a woman's life is no longer considered a failure simply because she does not marry.'[133] This changing attitude went still further: by the end of the nineteenth century a number of women were consciously rejecting marriage, not merely making the best of a bad deal. Although Annie Besant argued for free unions over the inequality of current marriages, she was convinced of another alternative: 'Women are beginning to desire to emerge from a life crystallised around the idea of sex, and to find open to them careers other than dependence on a man as a wife or mistress.'[134] Men might have regarded the spinster as 'some man's wife that should have been',[135] or, along with Grant Allen, have viewed her as 'a deplorable accident of the passing moment',[136] but single women were starting to develop a pride in their status; they were discarding the image of the 'old maid'. For example, to one woman: 'An Old Maid is a woman *minus* something; the Glorified Spinster is a woman *plus* something.'[137] A self-defined 'glorified spinster' elaborated on what this 'something' might be: 'The glorified spinster . . . earns her own living . . . lives honestly, dresses plainly . . . [T]here does not exist on this earth a more respectable character than a woman who can stand alone and make her own way.'[138]

Feminists, Chastity and Theosophy

Those spinsters who embraced chastity with enthusiasm as opposed to regret claimed that a chaste life, and the greater ability to exercise sexual self-control, rendered women the moral superiors of men. In Chapter Two we have seen how such claims were undermined both by the assertion that women's moral capacity was less than men's, and by the medical proposition that chastity was injurious to health. In the advocacy and defence of chastity and singleness for women, there were two main bodies of argument, in parallel to the two primary modes of attack: that chastity represented a spiritual state of moral worth, and that its observance rendered women not only healthy, but generally healthier than their married counterparts.

On the question of spinster's health, M.A.B. informed the *Englishwoman's Review* that many women

> are happier and better off as spinsters than as wives ... [the spinster] busy and active ... in her chosen vocation of letters, art or science, or ... social and philanthropic labours. She is most likely ... far healthier and stronger, and suffers far less physically than the broken-down and worn-out mother of a large family.[139]

To Henrietta Muller, 'To do any consecutive work, to avoid the terrible waste of energy, wear and tear upon the health consequent on interrupted mental labour, single life is almost necessary for a woman.' As for the moral worth of chastity, we have seen how for Henrietta Muller, self-control represented 'the basis of all moral life and ... the characteristic which distinguishes humanity from the rest of the animal world.'[140] She believed that men's attitude towards chastity was quite different from women's. Discussing Pearson's 'The Woman Question' with Olive Schreiner, she reflected: '"The Woman Question" is not bad ... but page 3 is a male view of chastity, "something very hard to maintain", not an unconscious stage of mental and bodily ease.'[141]

Henrietta Muller was born in Chile in the early 1850s, daughter of a German *émigré* businessman. She was fluent in six languages. In 1873 she was one of the first batch of students to attend Girton College, Cambridge, where she read Classics. As I have already mentioned, she became extremely active in a host of feminist organizations. She was a tax resister in 1884 and sat for six years for Lambeth on the London School Board, where, in 1879, she topped the poll with 19,000 votes, the first woman elected.[142] Fortunately she was affluent, for she estimated that her elections cost her £12,000. (Elizabeth Cobb thought Henrietta disposed of her wealth frivolously: 'A woman who can spend £50 and half a day over one dress, cannot have taken the sorrows of our race to heart.')[143] Henrietta founded the Society for the Return of Women as Poor Law Guardians and she wrote frequently for the journal the *Westminster Review*. When she resigned from the Men and Women's Club in March 1888, she told Karl Pearson that she would start a rival club for women only in which all women would find a voice. I do not know whether she managed to start such a club, but she did start a paper. The weekly *Woman's Penny Paper* was launched in October 1888 with Henrietta as editor (under the pseudonym of Helena B. Temple), and the proud boast that it was 'the only paper in the world conducted, written, printed and published by women.' The paper defined its policy as 'progressive' and it covered 'general English and foreign news', including news of feminist activity, prostitution, 'rational dress' and the position of women in India.[144]

I have already mentioned Henrietta Muller's view of women as the moral saviours of the future. She believed that women were only now starting to become fully human as they broke from the roots of their subordination: endless male sexual demands and the shackles ('the *curse* might one not say?')[145] of continual motherhood, where they fulfilled 'one function only, that of race preservation'.[146] When she referred to women breaking from their subordination she was thinking not of those married women who avoided such a fate through birth control or insistence on their husbands' continence, but the single woman, herself included: 'A new sturdy and vigorous type, we find her neither the exalted ascetic nor the nerveless, inactive creature of former days.'[147] At last such women were filling 'worthily a wide sphere of social and public usefulness'. Women must hold onto their unique qualities, such as 'quickness of insight, grace, gentleness and a self-control wonderful to think of'. This was 'far better . . . than to offer to humanity a mere repetition of manhood.'[148] A single woman might not bear a child, but she was able

> to secure better conditions of life to a nation of children . . . Thus, in rejecting the personal or grosser forms of love, a woman only leaves herself more free to give a larger, holier and deeper love to those who need it most.[149]

Kate Mills was another advocate of chastity for both sexes, outside marriage at least. A social worker, she was a close associate of the Men and Women's Club, writing papers for the club and in regular correspondence with Maria Sharpe. She seems to have been highly respected by the Club members who knew her. Before the opening of the club, Maria informed Pearson that Kate Mills 'has apparently studied the question of the relation of the sexes on many sides for some years'.[150] Kate Mills demonstrated a clear recognition of the influence of social attitudes on sexual behaviour:

> The very fact that a body of people look upon lust as a necessary attribute of humanity . . . has a very decided tendency to bring about the evil it recognises . . . In short: as you think, so you are . . . let lustfulness be considered *natural* and it will soon become prevalent.

The logic of this argument was that if men could be persuaded to see lust as unnatural and harmful, they would be able and prepared to be as chaste as any woman and lust's prevalence would thereby cease. She did not deny that women might experience sexual pleasure, but she believed that 'the incomprehensible power of magnetic currents . . . that draw men and women together' was a snare: 'This fatal attraction which overcomes reason [and] instincts of self-preservation in the woman'[151] and encouraged a 'feeling of devotion and self-surrender'.[152] It also generated an illusion in that 'this mad craving to find a heaven in the absorption in to another life' could not be realized. 'I believe celibacy to be infinitely higher than any existing form of marriage', she announced, although she did admit that 'there must be even now . . . at least some men and more women quite fitted for a more perfect marriage, where mutual help, work and friendship . . . form the basis'.[153]

By 1891, if not before, both Kate Mills and Henrietta Muller had become members of the Theosophical Society.[154] Their membership was not atypical among feminists; indeed, many feminists either joined the Theosophical Society or demonstrated a definite interest in its teachings, for example, Charlotte Despard, Edith Lees and Annie Besant, to name but three. The Theosophical Society had been founded in New York in 1875 by Russian *émigré* Helena Blavatsky and American Henry Steel Olcott; by the 1880s it had an active branch in London. Theosophy claimed to have distilled in its Secret Doctrine the basic truths underlying science and all world religions. Diana Burfield suggests a two-fold appeal of theosophy to women.[155] Firstly, there was the Theosophical Society's first objective which read: 'To form a nucleus of the universal brotherhood of humanity, without distinction of race, creed, *sex*, caste or colour.' [Italics are my emphasis.] Secondly, theosophical teaching weighted the two sexes equally. The body, a temporary vehicle for an eternal spirit, evolved through all material forms up to the spiritual, reincarnating numerous times as male and female. This evolutionary process required the interaction of two opposite principles, male and female, which were two halves of one whole, the Absolute. An additional attraction of theosophy to women was the provision of a basis from which to criticize the male domination of the Anglican church. And theosophists' attempted synthesis of religion and science had affinities with the project of those feminists who were also attempting the harmonization of the spiritual and the material. In addition, as Joy Dixon points out,[156] for those in the Theosophical Society's 'Inner Section', commitment to a more spiritual life included physical celibacy for both sexes, surely an appeal to those women committed to chastity. All these different aspects of theosophy partly explain its popularity with feminists.

Henrietta Muller moved to India and worked alongside Annie Besant. In 1895 she adopted a young Bengali man as her son and protégé. She planned for him to become a lawyer and politician, and to devote himself to social and political reform. Rumours circulated concerning her 'public exhibitions of affection for her adult son', but the *Theosophist* was convinced of 'the purity and unselfishness of her motives, however eccentric her actions might at times appear'. As for Kate Mills, by early 1891 she was married – to a fellow theosophist, a Mr Arthur Cobbold. They were both members of the Theosophical Society's 'Inner Section'.[157] I am unsure how long she had been a theosophist, but she must have become one in the previous two years, for in April 1889 she had informed Maria that 'I do not know theosophical views on this subject [sexual intercourse] at all beyond that they advocate chastity'. Her ignorance on this matter surely implies that she had not yet joined the Society. In her husband she had 'gained a friend and ally to the cause of women of purity'.[158] As well as finding a philosophy and religion in harmony with her views on sexual morality, she seems to have found a way of combining marriage and chastity.

Romantic Friendships

If many women wished to marry and dreaded the loneliness of spinsterhood, there were many others for whom spinsterhood spelt not loneliness but emotional commitment. The ground-breaking research of Lillian Faderman, Caroll Smith-Rosenberg, Martha Vicinus and others[159] has revealed the importance for many nineteenth-century women of close, long-lasting emotional ties with other women. Such ties included both loving support between sisters, and passionate declarations between unrelated women. The latter, termed 'romantic friendships', involved explicit pronouncements of love in letter and diary (indispensable sources for the historian of today). Such romantic friendships might also have involved kissing, fondling and sharing a bed. Until the late nineteenth century, such relationships were generally viewed benignly. Many of these women, as documented by Martha Vicinus, lived in women-only communities: residential housing, religious sisterhoods, women's colleges, boarding schools and settlement houses. A number set up house together as a loving partnership, although familial obligations and economic dependency made this an option open to few until the end of the century.

There were clearly many women who loved other women passionately and may well have had erotic relations with each other, which we would now term 'sexual', but who did not identify themselves as lesbian at the time. Whether or not women saw their relationships with other women as 'lesbian' depended on many factors, not least a familiarity with such a notion in the first place. Unlike Berlin or Paris, London, as far as historians can discover, had no visible lesbian subculture in the years before the First World War. Whether or not women saw their relationships with other women as 'sexual' depended, in part, on what the term meant to them. As I have already suggested, sexual feeling was often assumed to be heterosexual *by definition*, most obviously in the case of the widely held view of sex's function as reproductive. Educationalist Constance Maynard, born in 1849, passionately loved a number of women in her lifetime, but to her the idea of sexual feeling was self-evidently heterosexual. In her 1887 unpublished autobiography she reflected: 'It is all very well to call [my] loneliness "sex feeling", but I can honestly say my thoughts never strayed to a man.'[160]

Maria Sharpe's old childhood friend Lina Eckenstein was devoted to Maria, writing to her in terms we would today interpret as those of a lover. On one occasion she sent what she called an analysis of her admiration:

> My Sweet Ria . . . when I say certain things to you, you take them as the outcome of momentary infatuation, where you see them written you must grant them more than the transitory existence of words wafted to oblivion . . . When I say you are beautiful do you think I do so just because your hair is especially luxurious against a dark wallpaper, or the colour of your cheeks heightened by the reflection of the fire . . .[161]

When Maria married (of which, more below) Lina wrote to

Pearson of 'my darling who is now yours'.[162] Even after Maria had been married several years, Lina felt no hesitation in writing 'Dearly beloved Ria', ending 'Goodbye, beloved Ria ... Love me always dearest'.[163]

Even where there was clearly a physical relationship between two women, they did not necessarily see it as sexual, let alone lesbian. In the early twentieth century, working-class feminists Eva Slawson, Ruth Slate and Minna Simmons formed a close friendship, beautifully chronicled in Tierl Thompson's *Dear Girl*. For three years, until her sudden death from undetected diabetes in 1916, Eva had a passionate relationship with Minna. They declared their undying love, they slept together, they embraced and caressed and they 'decided that we were both passionate and sensuous. How I love the body', Eva wrote in her diary, 'too much spiritual and physical love is reserved for sexual union. We ought to be able to mingle soul and body, woman with woman, man with man ... embracing with the whole body'.[164] Yet despite her closeness to Minna, she 'longed for a child and lover' (not seeing Minna as lover) of her 'very own'. She told Minna that 'if she were a man, I should feel absolutely completed'.[165] Maybe the incompleteness was the fact that Minna and she could not have a child together. Despite Eva having read writings of the homosexual radical Edward Carpenter, it does not appear that she identified as a 'Uranian' (the word used by Carpenter for homosexual).[166]

Sexological writings aside (to be considered in a later chapter), sexual expression outside a heterosexual relationship, such as in the case of masturbation or homosexuality, was generally believed to be a *male* aberration – possibly a mark of degeneracy, a sign of bestial lust. In late Victorian Britain, although women were thought to harbour many aberrations, to most people homosexuality was not yet thought to be among them. It is important to stress the *normality* of same-sex loving relationships in many women's lives. Those women who saw themselves as a committed couple may have been termed 'spinsters' in that they were unmarried, but they were 'single' only in the sense that they were without a man.

By the early twentieth century, and certainly by the interwar years, same-sex relations between women had become suspect. This did not mean, however, that women or girls 'knew' about the phenomenon of lesbianism. In the 1920s the sixteen-year-old Valentine Ackland (later the lover of Sylvia Townsend Warner) fell in love with Lana, aged nineteen. They became inseparable. In bed together

> We were both totally ignorant (innocent is a better word) and all we knew of love-making was to lie close together and kiss; but no two have ever loved more and been more completely passionately fulfilled.

Her father eventually found out and furiously questioned her.

> I told him that we were in love. I remember vividly the expression of disgust on his face . . . he asked if I realised that what Lana and I had done was the worst, filthiest . . . the most unforgivable thing that anyone could do?

She replied that they had done nothing wrong: 'We had only loved each other.'[167]

Assault on Spinsterhood and Chastity

Negative images of spinsterhood abounded in late Victorian England. Since the nineteenth-century woman's 'destiny' was assumed to lie with marriage and motherhood, the unmarried woman had long been seen as a social and emotional failure, if not yet a sexual misfit. But alongside positive portrayals of spinsterhood negative ones grew in their ferocity. Why? It was partly due to the rising strength and 'threat' of feminism and the increasing number of single women entering the public arena. Given Britain's sense of imperialist challenge from Germany, Japan and the United States, there was also a new emphasis on breeding healthy children for the empire; spinsters' 'barrenness' was unacceptable. And although there was still no unanimity among the medical profession as to the harmfulness of chastity, there was a gradual pathologizing of the spinster, physically, psychologically and sexually. Along with the sexologists' 'discovery' of lesbianism,[168] the single woman was being constructed as an unwanted and unnatural deviant.

Feminists themselves were also involved in these debates. In relation to chastity's harmfulness for women, for example, the majority of feminists probably discounted the claim, but a growing number, especially among the new generation, were not so sure. If women were to have an active sexuality, the definition of chastity as the lack of a sex life necessary for both sexes did at least appear to involve recognition that women had active sexual needs *to* harm. But the medical voices pronouncing on the dangers of female chastity did not, as a concomitant, acknowledge a woman's *right* to sex. For those feminists wishing to claim this right on their own terms, it was difficult to avoid considering the 'health and chastity' issue. Given that the anarchist Legitimation League advocated 'free love', some of its members, perhaps unsurprisingly, accepted the view that female chastity was injurious. Its journal *The Adult*, appearing in the late 1890s, was certainly fascinated by the topic, advertising on the back of one of its pamphlets a competition, with prizes of 100 and 50 guineas, for 'the 2 best works on the psychological, physiological and pathological effects of CELIBACY on women.' Dora Kerr informed a League meeting that 'women suffer as much from enforced celibacy as men ... We cannot suppress sex. If suppressed, it always takes some morbid form.'[169] Similarly, socialist Eleanor Marx, in a joint article with her lover Edward Aveling in 1886, claimed that 'ungratified sex instincts' in a young woman lead to 'morbid virginity', 'lunacy', even suicide.[170] And the writer Jane Clapperton, supporter of the League and one-time Men and Women's Club associate, while merely declaring in 1885 that women's chastity 'not freely chosen ... is a *cruel lot*',[171] elaborated further in 1904: a woman's lack of sex led to 'hysteria, chlorosis, love melancholy and other unhappy ailments'.[172] Another anarchist female columnist, in stark contrast to those feminists who saw marriage itself as a health risk, claimed that on entering a railway carriage: 'The face of the mated woman bears a look of quiet rest, in contrast to the ... unmated woman who glances inquiringly at each male figure ... with a dull sense of despair.'[173]

The Choice for Maria Sharpe: Spinsterhood, Free Union or Marriage?

On her own admission, it was not until 1887 that Maria Sharpe began to think seriously about marriage – not so much as an option for herself (although this may have crossed her mind), but in terms of its political and ethical meaning, in particular its immorality. She was not yet convinced that a free union was the desired alternative. While concerned with 'the false immorality they [marriage laws] draw between two classes of women and children', she feared that 'anything like a direct attack on them seemed like an attack on the ideal of monogamy, an encouragement of want of responsibility in the future'.[174] At the club's outset in 1885 Maria had been explicitly opposed to free unions. She had been one of the women who had objected to the name initially proposed for the group, the 'Wollstonecraft Club', and had also opposed the proposed membership of Karl Marx's daughter, Eleanor, who was then living in free union with Edward Aveling. Maria felt that people living in relationships outside marriage were in a constant 'state of antagonism which makes open-minded reason impossible'.[175] Olive Schreiner, a close friend of Eleanor's, had been upset, but had not wanted Eleanor joining the club if anyone objected.[176] In contrast, Karl Pearson appeared to support free unions. In his 1885 paper 'The Woman's Question' he suggested that 'the highest ideal of marriage [may] be perfectly free and yet, generally lifelong union.' At the time he wrote to Maria Sharpe: 'To me the noblest union must be a free contract.' He added, however: 'Such a bond is impossible in our modern life',[177] although he gave no indication as to why.

By March 1889 Maria had changed her mind about free unions. She wrote to Pearson:

> I have come to the stage now of feeling ... legal marriage is a hindrance rather than a help to the development of a healthy and reasonable morality in the relations of the sexes.[178]

She was unaware that Pearson was at the time contemplating asking for her hand in marriage. Pearson's reply to her letter indicated his anxiety. He asserted that her beliefs held great risks:

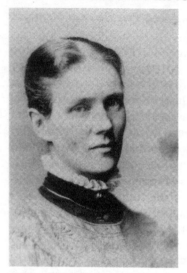 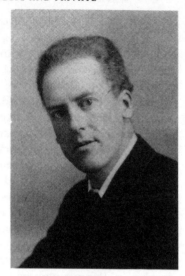

Maria Sharpe   *Karl Pearson*

Should she [a woman holding such views] put her views in practice, or to venture to teach them, she will be a social outcast . . . Believe me, no woman ought *at the present day* to disbelieve in marriage, unless they had £10,000 a year, or a saleable beauty, or the power to write *Adam Bede*.[179]

(Its author, George Eliot, had herself lived in a free union.) Pearson advised Maria to keep her thoughts to herself. Maria replied testily that 'speaking out seems to me the very thing we want nowadays . . . I will take no one's advice to keep my opinions secret . . . Concealment . . . is a poison to life'.[180] Unlike most of the female club members, Maria never deferred to Pearson's arrogant assertions.

In her late thirties, Maria, like many unmarried women of her age, probably expected to stay single for the rest of her life. Indeed, women were considered to be 'on the shelf' if still unmarried at thirty. Daughter of a solicitor, brought up as a Unitarian, she had left school at seventeen and subsequently lived 'in a philanthropic and domestic atmosphere' with her widowed mother and sisters in Highbury Fields. To Olive

Schreiner, Maria 'seems to have (a rare quality in a woman owing to her narrow life!) an impartial mind'.[181] Yet in the opinion of Annie Besant, writing to Karl Pearson in January 1887, it would be better if Maria 'knew a little more of the condition of the masses of decent workers by coming into contact with them'.[182] Maria had begun to carve out a meaningful future for herself of what she saw as 'useful' work. At this point in her life, as well as shifting her views on marriage, Maria was both converting to socialism, and undergoing a crisis of religious faith. But although no longer happy with the doctrine of Unitarianism, Freethinking (espoused by Pearson) appealed even less: it lacked 'definitive moral purpose'.[183]

Maria appears to have had a number of close friends, had won 'a room of her own' in her mother's house in which to study, and, to her own amazement, the club had given her sufficient confidence to undertake research and writing. As Judith Walkowitz suggests, she was perhaps the most transformed female club member.[184] She was delighted when her club paper 'Henrik Ibsen: his Men and Women' was accepted by the *Westminster Review* and published in June 1889. Her expectations remained low however: 'I have schooled myself so well to expect nothing.'[185] Her article's publication coincided with London's first unbowdlerized production of Ibsen's *The Doll's House*, privately staged at the Novelty Theatre on 7 June. Pearson booked a dozen tickets in the dress circle, and many Men and Women's Club members and associates attended, including Maria, Olive Schreiner, Emma Brooke and Eleanor Marx. The play generated heated controversy, not least because at the end the heroine Nora leaves her husband, children and confining 'doll's house'. Her destiny is left unclear – as Norma Clarke wittily remarks: 'We aren't told she's off to join the Norwegian Women's Movement'[186] – but she is definitely set on gaining freedom and self-knowledge. Edith Lees recalled how after the play: 'A few of us collected outside the theatre breathless with excitement . . . What did it mean? . . . Was it life or death for women? . . . Was it joy or sorrow for men?'[187] Five years earlier, Olive had enthused about the play to Havelock Ellis: 'It is a most wonderful little work . . . It shows some sides of women's nature that are not often spoken of, and that some do not believe exist – but they do.'[188] By 1889, Ibsen's heroines were becoming an inspiration to many feminists, Maria Sharpe included; she was determined to study his plays in greater depth.

In late July of 1889, and a month after the club's ending, Pearson declared his love and asked Maria to marry him. He had pursued her to Norway where she had gone on holiday with her sister Loetitia, and her close friend Lina Eckenstein; she also wished to learn Norwegian so as to translate Ibsen's play *Brand*. Five years younger than Maria, Pearson was the son of middle-class Quakers. In his childhood he had experienced his father, a barrister, as authoritarian and his mother, with whom he had sided, as loving, but weak and ineffectual. As already mentioned, he was something of a polymath, having studied mathematics at Cambridge and law, mathematics and philosophy as a postgraduate in Germany. His love of all things German led to his changing the spelling of his name from 'Carl' to 'Karl'. In 1881 he was called to the bar, but in 1884 he shifted career and, aged only twenty-seven, became Professor of Mathematics and Mechanics at University College, London.[189]

Maria gave no definite answer to Pearson's proposal, and he left her in Bergen to think it over. His first few subsequent letters, however, indicated his confidence in an eventual affirmative, not least the transformation in his address from 'Dear Miss Sharpe' to 'Dearest One', signed 'Ever thine, Karl'. He wrote at great length as to why he had asked her to *marry*, rather than enter a free union. It was an elaboration of their earlier correspondence in March, when, according to Pearson, she had 'unconsciously nearly upset it all'. He wrote now:

> I do think that if we are to seek . . . the ideal life for an independent man and woman, it would be absolutely free union . . . But I am not sure that . . . it is best merely to live in revolt . . . it is more hard to make others believe your gospel is not the outcome of the step you have yourself taken in life, not the converse . . . [C]an we so well write on sex relations if we have placed ourselves outside the world's sanctions[?][190]

In other words, Pearson was worried that forming a free union would endanger his and Maria's credibility – that their beliefs would be taken as nothing but justification of their own unorthodoxy. In her pamphlet 'A Noviciate for Marriage', written in 1892, Edith Lees Ellis suggested that so far as alternatives to marriage were concerned, 'we shall inevitably have to try experiments which will bring social ostracism on those who have the honesty to put their principles into practice'.[191] Pearson, perhaps understandably, could not face the ostracism.

Unfortunately Maria's letters for the next two months were later destroyed at her request, although one gathers from his replies that they expressed increasing doubts. Indeed, by late September when they met briefly again, she was adamant that she could not marry him. To her sister Elizabeth Cobb, who was in constant correspondence with Pearson at the time, Maria had become 'utterly unlike herself',[192] and to another sister, Loetitia, 'she has lost balance and cannot judge ...'[193] Lina Eckenstein told Pearson that he was 'entirely wrong' in thinking she was opposed to his feelings for Maria, but she wondered: 'Can it be that you have not cared for what is really herself but for a creature of your dream ...?'[194] Elizabeth's question to Pearson was less accusing:

> Is it somehow that you have not won her over, somehow not given the touch, which makes the self-surrender there must be for even the *most* independent marriage possible? A self-surrender I believe as much on the man's as on the woman's side.[195]

Whatever the implications of the latter statement, lack of 'self-surrender' on Pearson's side was not seen as the issue: Maria was the problem. Elizabeth Cobb wrote a month later: 'I am *sure* she puts you above all other men, but yet does not feel irresistibly impelled to surrender herself, and she is terribly unhappy that she cannot.'[196]

An earlier letter to Pearson in May, before his marriage proposal, may indicate why Maria did not feel so 'irresistibly impelled'. She had written that 'the purely physical side of [women's] sexual desires ... is so closely connected with the desire for self-surrender',[197] yet self-surrender was an enemy of women's emancipation. This was why women striving 'to realize their own individuality' frequently renounced their sexuality. Did she fear that the sexual side of marriage would entail *her* self-surrender and thus loss of individuality?

Even today there are still vestiges of the idea that a virginal woman, in sexual intercourse with a man, 'gives' him not only her virginity but her very being. In the nineteenth century, such a belief co-existed with, on the one hand, the assumption that a woman's sexuality lay passively awaiting the touch of a man, and on the other, the Christian emphasis upon female self-sacrifice or martyrdom.[198] It is hardly surprising that feminist spinsters such as Maria Sharpe were wary of the sexual side of marriage. If they were to sacrifice themselves at all, for many it was better to do so for the good of the 'Woman's Cause' than in the line of marital duty. Whether or not Maria feared sexual self-surrender, she must have dreaded loss of independence. Her involvement in the Men and Women's Club had prompted her to explore her politics, religion and intellectual potential.[199] Now she faced the choice of continuing with her state of spinsterhood and her new-found freedom, including the various recent openings into writings and research, or marrying, aquiring respectability, but also economic dependency, the loss of legal and political rights, and the possibility of having to relinquish her intellectual pursuits for the duties of housewife and mother. To Maria, Ibsen had acute awareness of the dilemma she now faced: he possessed 'a vivid realization of the difficulties ... of that half of the human race, for whom the problem of self-realization or self-sacrifice must always be the most difficult to work out.'[200]

Maria's predicament was paralleled to some degree in the dilemma facing Beatrice Potter (later to become Beatrice Webb) as to whether or not to marry Joseph Chamberlain. Beatrice met Chamberlain in June 1883 and fell in love. She was in her late twenties, he in his late forties. A widower, a prosperous Birmingham manufacturer turned radical politican, Chamberlain was the darling of the Liberal party. While tempted to marry him because of 'great personal attraction and the immediate gratification of a woman's longing for love and support and for settled and defined occupation',[201] Beatrice recognized the danger:

His personality absorbs all my thought and he occupies a too prominent position for me . . . I shall be absorbed into the life of a man whose aims are not my aims; who will refuse me all freedom of thought in my intercourse with him.[202]

He talked of requiring women's 'intelligent sympathy'; 'Servility, Mr Chamberlain, think I, not sympathy', was Beatrice's silent response.[203] She was well aware that marriage to this man would render impossible the independent career and personal freedom she so ardently desired. She opted for personal freedom.

In some respects, Pearson was less obviously patriarchal than Joseph Chamberlain. Indeed, he was insistent that he did not *want* Maria to be the kind of wife who surrendered herself, as his mother had done (although I do not think he was thinking of *sexual* surrender at this point). After all, they had 'formed the ideal to take marriage with perfect freedom for both – no surrender of the individuality of the one out of affection for the other'. Further, 'keeping the ideal of free expansion of your own individuality ever before me', was the one way, he said, in which Maria could curb his hereditary tendency to selfishness and thereby help him 'to a much fuller and healthier life'.[204] But Maria may not have believed that the 'free expansion' of her individuality was what Pearson really desired. In her letter in May, she had inquired of him, rhetorically: 'Is it not really passive women that [men] want . . . so that they might have their own way with them[?]'[205] There was also the fact that Pearson made the prospect of marriage to him sound a grim and demanding ordeal, including a *sexual* ordeal. 'If you feel strong enough to be my wife', Maria was informed, she had to come to terms with his 'inherited tendencies':

My father comes of a sturdy peasantry, strong and passionate to almost ruthless selfishness. I have inherited some of his strong physical nature, much of his selfish and passionate tendencies, and a life of study and too much loneliness has only enabled me to repress them by an almost equally vicious tendency to periods of depression and moroseness. Add to this a hypersensitiveness derived from my mother and you will have a picture which may look black.[206]

Indeed. It may well have contributed to Maria's admission that 'I am more paralysed than I can say, but seem to see clearly that I cannot now give you love.'[207] 'We must not go on writing to one another . . . I cannot be your wife'.[208] '. . . [my love] is too poor now to make me the strong woman you need.'[209] She told him she had a dread that she would 'wreck his life';[210] perhaps she also dreaded that he might wreck hers.

Elizabeth Cobb was certain that Maria did love Pearson, but she was suffering from 'hysteria': 'It is *most* common when a woman is in love . . .',[211] '. . . sexual feeling has in a strange way overpowered her. It is very very strong in us poor weak human beings'.[212] Pearson must be patient. This statement of Elizabeth's on 'sexual feeling' appears to have contradicted her earlier position at the club where she had argued that women had lesser sexual needs than men, and that chastity was unlikely to be the cause of a woman's ill-health, hysteria included. I would suggest, however, that to Elizabeth, sexual feeling was overpowering Maria not so much as a driving desire, but as a *fear*: of sex itself and of self-surrender and loss of individuality. Maria later admitted that during this period: 'A well-known nervousness which has marred all my life had become exaggerated into a terror.'[213] She had also told him back in November 1885 that unlike men, women entered marriage with 'repulsion toward the exercise of the sex function'.[214]

After a seven-month period in which she refused to see him, Pearson and Maria Sharpe met again several times in April 1890. At some point in this month she agreed to marry him. Gaps in the available correspondence leave one unclear as to why she changed her mind. We do know, however, that a few days before she accepted him she wrote: 'Self doubts alone trouble me now, and only being with you and feeling it is right for you, can quiet me.'[215]

Back in September 1889, Elizabeth had inquired of Pearson whether or not he had 'won her'. Thirty-seven years later, when Maria was dying, the question was answered in the form of a long, tragic letter to Elizabeth which he asked her to destroy immediately, but which he never finally sent. He sadly and movingly reflected on his marriage:

As I look back on it now I think life has been largely a failure. I have sacrificed everything – Maria would say wife and children included – to the idea of establishing a new tool in science [eugenics and statistics] which would give certainty where all was obscurity . . . I have made many enemies and few friends . . . It is not so much the waste of mine but of others' lives, in particular Mia's. She has been a splendid wife, if you mean by that, that she has ever worked for her husband's purposes. But she has done it from her inbred sense of duty . . . I have never actually won her . . . Marrying as we did, after what had happened previously, I ought to have realised that I had still to win her, but I spent my life over my work and she sacrificed her life in looking after home and children . . . I cannot let you of all people believe that our marriage has been an ideal one. It wanted delicacy of handling to make it so, and I have given too little of my time and thought to it. I have never won Mia, and that is the tragedy of it, when it is too late to remedy.[216]

I have dwelt at some length on the case of Maria Sharpe and Karl Pearson because it seems to highlight some of the difficulties and ambivalences facing women in this period who were contemplating marriage, and within it, sex, especially feminists keen to retain a strong sense of their own independence and identity. The difficulty and possible reluctance in breaking from the roles assigned by convention (and by middle-class male psychic development?) cannot be overestimated. John Tosh suggests that middle-class men born in the second half of the nineteenth century were likely to have been handicapped by a childhood experience of an undemonstrative father.[217] The confining of tenderness to femininity (in the form of affectionate mother and/or nanny), reinforced by public school ethos, resulted in boys' distrust of such 'unmanly' feelings in themselves, and the emotional reticence which appears to have been a marked attribute of Pearson's. This reticence may have been exacerbated by Maria's original rejection. At the time, his close friend Robert Parker feared that the experience would result in Pearson being 'still more impressed with his old idea that a man who allows his affections to be roused, incapacitates himself for serious work'.[218] In addition, as Judith Walkowitz points out, the fact of Pearson's mother being dominated by his father may have bred contempt as well as sympathy for women.[219] Whatever his intentions, by his own account Karl Pearson sounds like a typical late-Victorian paterfamilias. The inherited selfish passion of which he had warned Maria seems to have been obsessively directed into his

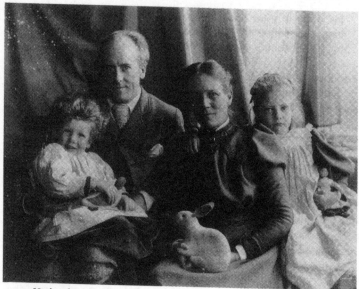

Karl and Maria Pearson, their son Egon and daughter Ilse, about 1896

research, with what one commentator referred to as 'demonic energy'.[220] Before their marriage, Maria had alerted Pearson to the contradiction between women's emancipaton and women's self-sacrifice; in his turn, he had voiced a commitment to women's independence, his future wife's included. At work it was true that he employed unmarried professional women as his assistants.[221] But as for Maria, Pearson's subsequent absorption into his own research to the exclusion of her intellectual and emotional needs meant that her time and energy were indeed 'sacrificed' to the care of her husband, and 'looking with slender means after home and [three] children'. She gained the pleasures of motherhood, but what of her losses?

Feminist Strategy on Marriage in the Early Twentieth Century

In the early twentieth century, the feminist debates and campaigns around marriage developed and shifted in certain ways. The two feminist tactics in relation to marriage reform, namely, attempts to change the law (the legislative tactic) on the one hand, and the development of sex education and marital warnings (the protective and educative tactic) on the other, were elaborated and extended. In relation to the feminist protective strategy there was an increased focus on the sexual dangers of marriage, especially venereal disease. Several feminists now began to speak on the issue more factually as opposed to confining the subject to the realms of fiction. Stressing the need for protection from such dangers was part of a wider campaign against women's and children's sexual vulnerability. The vote was seen as a central means of transforming sexual morality; once women had the vote, the argument went, not only would they be stronger, more independent and self-respecting, they would also be able to introduce legislation to deal with male immorality.

A new element in the feminists' protective strategy took the form of concern with the economic independence of married women. As Mary Shanley points out, nineteenth-century feminists, while addressing married women's lack of economic and legal rights, rarely considered the problems arising from wives' economic dependency upon their husbands.[222] Middle-class wives were not expected, even by feminists, to go out to work (although Elizabeth Garrett Anderson, a married feminist doctor, was one obvious exception). But in the early twentieth century a number of feminists, especially the Fabian Women's Group, set up in 1908, were starting to call for married women's economic independence, actual or potential. Disillusioned with the Fabian Society's disinterest in feminism, the Women's Group insisted that 'socialists must recognize that women's economic revolt is not merely against the enslaving economic control of the capitalist, but against the enslaving economic control of the husband'. By 1912 the Fabian Women's Group had 230 members, mostly middle-class and educated, including teachers, journalists, writers, artists and wives and daughters of professional men. Beatrice

Webb, Charlotte Wilson and Emma Brooke were members; so too was Maria Sharpe Pearson and Lina Eckenstein. Maria presented a paper to the group which she had presented to the Men and Women's Club more than twenty years earlier: 'Laws and Regulations relating to Prostitution, AD 800–1500'. She had managed to carve out an independent space within her marriage, even though she may not have had time to embark on new research.[223]

In relation to attempted legal reform, feminists participated in the new national interest in divorce, instigated by the establishment of a Royal Commission on Divorce and Matrimonial Causes in 1909. Although feminists had played little part in pushing for the Commission (a driving force had been the Divorce Law Reform Union, mainly composed of radical male lawyers, with Sir Arthur Conan Doyle as President), a number of feminists gave evidence, and many women's organizations sent resolutions. The central issues facing the Commission, which sat from 1909 to 1912, were whether provisions should be made to enable divorce to be cheaper and more available to a wider section of society, whether to place both sexes on an equal footing with respect to grounds for divorce, and whether to extend those grounds. All feminists, and all the members of the Women's Cooperative Guild (WCG), who were certainly not all feminists, agreed that the change crucially needed was equalization of the divorce law. This, they believed, would raise the moral standards of men. As one WCG member put it: 'A woman has the right to expect from a man the same purity as he demands from her.'[224] A poll of WCG members revealed that most members wanted cheaper and more accessible divorce procedures through the county courts. The great majority also approved of additional grounds for divorce, such as cruelty, insanity, refusal to maintain and desertion. Under cruelty they included abuse of conjugal 'rights'. Some argued for divorce on grounds of incompatibility, a number even wanted divorce by mutual consent.[225] The fact that the WCG took such a radical stand on marriage perhaps shows the depth of female dissatisfaction with marriage, across class. Among the other representatives of women's groups, Helena Swanwick, editor of the National

Union of Women's Suffrage Societies' *The Common Cause*, suggested that to infect one's partner with venereal disease should be a criminal offence as well as grounds for divorce. (The WCG had recommended the latter, as indeed had J.S. Mill back in 1871.)[226]

Rebecca West heralded the Royal Commission's report as a feminist triumph – there was such pressure, the Commission had 'had to concede this demand of the suffragists'.[227] One of its recommendations was the equalization of the divorce law. Another was that communication of venereal disease be included as a grounds for divorce, the Royal Commission's Majority Report commenting that 'no cause . . . more fully justifies an application for divorce than this class of cruelty'.[228] The recent feminist politicization of the issue, as well as years of divorce court cases involving VD, had had an impact. Yet Rebecca West was sure that no political party would bother to introduce the proposed changes. For the time being, she was proved right. None of the recommendations was enacted until years later – the equalization of the divorce law, for example, not being introduced until 1923.

In the early years of the twentieth century, women's role within marriage was being reconceptualized; feminists inevitably responded to, and participated in, this process. The birth rate was steadily falling and many women were clearly playing a part in this fall through the adoption of some kind of fertility control. Yet most feminists were deeply ambivalent about the idea of contraception. This thorny issue of birth control is the subject of the next chapter. Despite, or indeed in a sense partly because of, the falling birth rate, there was a far greater emphasis on a wife's mothering role, particularly its eugenical implications. Feminists either stood in opposition to a eugenical stance, or they adopted such a stance themselves but with a feminist inflection. The feminist take-up of eugenics will be considered in Chapter Six. There were also new ideas concerning the wife as a *sexual* being – ideas to which feminists likewise responded. Feminist debates over sex, marital or otherwise, will be the subject of Chapter Seven.

PART THREE

THE POLITICS OF FERTILITY CONTROL AND SEX

CHAPTER 5

Contraception, Feminism and the Malthusian League

A woman's right to contraception and abortion has been central to the demands of the British Women's Liberation Movement since its beginnings in the late 1960s. While ethical issues render the question of a woman's right to abortion contentious in this country (although not nearly as contentious as in the USA), her right to contraception is largely uncontroversial, except of course for Roman Catholics.[1] This was not the case a hundred years ago.

In the late nineteenth and early twentieth centuries, despite the commitment of all feminists to a woman's right to 'voluntary motherhood', their attitude towards contraception was frequently ambivalent, even hostile. Why? The answer lies partly in the dominant contemporary constructions of sexuality. Some feminists shared the Judaeo–Christian belief that sex was solely for reproduction. Many shared the widely held view that sex was a force in need of constant control – a 'slumbering beast' which once 'awoken' would become unmanageable. Many feminists, indeed many women, were also concerned that contraception would subject them even further to men's carnal desires. With such beliefs and fears, it was hard for women to think of birth control as involving their right to control over their own bodies. It was all the harder given that the whole issue intermeshed not only with questions of morality, but also Malthusianism, health, nation and 'race'. To understand the difficulties women experienced in thinking of birth control as a woman's right, and to show the context in which birth control was discussed and debated, we need to examine the way in which the issue was circumscribed by these various parameters.

Abstinence, withdrawal or coitus interruptus, and various forms of abortifacients were the most widespread methods of birth prevention. Not only was the condom relatively expensive, but it was associated with prostitution and venereal disease and thus unacceptable to many women. Abstinence, withdrawal, use of the 'safe period' (wrongly calculated as mid-month!) and the condom all required male co-operation. But female forms of contraception – sponges, diaphragms, douches – if they were known of at all, had their own disadvantages: they were expensive, difficult to obtain, and douches necessitated access to running water. Quinine pessaries or suppositories were cheaper, and some women made their own pessaries from cocoa butter or glycerine. Abortion, however, despite being illegal since 1803, was the main form of female birth restriction, widely resorted to by women of all classes, although especially working-class women in urban areas. Abortifacients were much cheaper and easier to obtain than contraceptives. In an early twentieth-century survey of the falling birth rate in Northern England, undertaken by Karl Pearson's colleague Ethel Elderton, two 'respectable working women' of York claimed that 70–80% of all women took abortion drugs.[2] Although probably an exaggeration, it appears to be true that among Northern women factory workers, the rate of birth restriction and of resort to abortifacients were amongst the highest in the country.[3] Abortifacients ranged from a pennyworth of various herbs, such as pennyroyal, to gin and salts, castor oil, turpentine and, by the 1890s, lead pills. All such potions were unreliable and many were poisonous, frequently resulting in ill health, even death. More dangerous still were abortions performed with instruments by an abortionist, usually an unqualified female midwife, or sometimes a doctor. Some abortifacients were not so much harmful as completely useless, especially those advertised in newspapers. In such adverts, prosecution was avoided by the use of coded messages such as a particular pill being a 'certain safe and speedy remedy which never fails', or that 'the most OBSTINATE obstruction, irregularities, etc, of the female system are removed in a few doses'.[4] When no miscarriage was forthcoming, the cheated customers had no legal redress, the unhappy victims of a cruel hoax.

To use the term 'birth control' is somewhat anachronistic; the expression was not coined until 1914, by the American feminist Margaret Sanger,[5] although it was subsequently quickly adopted in Britain. Although the word 'contraception' had been coined in 1886 by an American physician E.B. Foote, it was rarely used in Britain until after the First World War. 'Contraceptives' was a term occasionally used in the 1890s, but the more popular terms were 'preventive checks', 'artificial checks' (or simply 'preventives' or 'checks'), 'artificial limitation', 'artificial steriliza-tion' and 'Malthusian appliances'. 'Family limitation' and 'concep-tion control' were also used, but these were broader concepts, including methods of birth prevention other than simply the use of 'appliances', i.e. they also included the withdrawal method, use of the 'safe period', and abstinence. The terms in use give some sense of how contraception was conceptualized: 'artificial' suggests an obvious contrast to what was seen as 'natural', 'Malthusian' speaks of the connection to Malthus's theory. None, however, indicate the *immorality* associated with birth control. I begin by considering this association, followed by birth control's association with Malthusianism and health; issues of nation and 'race', other than within Malthusian discourse, barely informed the discussion of birth control until the growing concern with the falling British birth rate in the late nineteenth century. It was then that the perception of birth control became rapidly re-focused through the lens of eugenics, the subject of the next chapter.

The Immorality of Contraception

Birth control was defined as highly immoral; indeed, prior to the anxiety about the falling birth rate, opposition to contracep-tion usually rested first and foremost on a claim to its immorality. Birth control was in contradiction to the 'true' purpose of sexual intercourse as given by God and Nature. At the trial of Annie Besant and Charles Bradlaugh in 1877 the grounds had been laid for defining contraception as not simply immoral, but obscene. Besant and Bradlaugh's publication and distribution of a birth-control tract called *The Fruits of Philosophy* by an American doctor, Charles Knowlton, led to the charge of obscenity. The book recommended the withdrawal method and the douche or 'female syringe' of home-made spermicide, applied immediately after intercourse. In 1868 Chief Justice Cockburn had laid down that the test for obscenity 'is whether the tendency of the matter charged as obscenity is to deprave and corrupt those whose minds are open to such influences and into whose hands a publication of this sort might fall.'[6] A reading of contemporary debates clearly indicates that it was the working classes, young people and women generally whose minds were assumed to be 'open to such immoral influences' and who therefore needed 'protection' from this 'dangerous' knowledge. The cheapness and literary accessibility of a publication heightened the possibility of it becoming available to these 'suggestible' persons.

Such concerns were explicitly expressed in the Besant–Bradlaugh trial. The Knowlton pamphlet's 'obscenity' rested on what it suggested and to whom. According to the Solicitor-General, prosecuting:

> This is a dirty, filthy book . . . the object of it is to enable persons to have sexual intercourse and not to have that which in the order of Providence is the natural result of that sexual intercourse . . . Is it not calculated to deprave and destroy the morals of persons among whom it is circulated?

The potential 'persons among whom it is circulated' was the nub of the problem, for the pamphlet was cheap and accessible: 'We have here . . . a chapter on restriction published, not written in any learned language, but in plain English, in a facile form, and sold in the public streets for sixpence'. The Solicitor-General was greatly concerned that the pamphlet would

> suggest to the unmarried as well as to the married, and any persons into whose hands this book might get – the boy of 17, and the girl of the same age – that they may gratify their passions without . . . the destruction of character which would be involved if . . . conception followed.

And middle-class women too needed protection from such a publication: 'no decently educated English husband would allow his wife to have it'. He was at pains to emphasize this point: 'I cannot believe that any English jury [all male in this period], having any reverence for the married state; for the chastity and purity of their own wives and daughters' could but condemn this book. Besant and Bradlaugh were sentenced to six months imprisonment and a £200 fine, but on appeal the conviction was quashed on a legal technicality.[7]

One outcome of the trial was that Annie Besant lost custody of her daughter Mabel to her estranged husband Reverend Frank Besant. In the custody case the judge pronounced that 'one cannot expect modest women to associate with her.'[8] She wrote later of the aspersions cast on her by the tarnish of birth control: 'To me it meant the loss of the pure reputation I prized, the good name I had guarded − scandal the most terrible a woman could face'.[9] Those women who stood openly by Besant and Bradlaugh were also heavily castigated, especially by the Press. Florence Fenwick Miller, a young feminist and journalist, wrote a supportive letter to Annie Besant at the time of the trial.[10] Her letter was seized and published in nearly every London newspaper, accompanied by abusive commentary. For example, the *Hackney and Kingsland Gazette* called on her to resign her membership of the London School Board, for 'Miss Florence Fenwick Miller is singularly out of place as a member of a Board charged with the education of the young'.[11] That a woman, especially one associated with children's education, could support such obscenity, was beyond the pale. As for the Knowlton tract itself, to the *Daily Telegraph* it 'suggests vice of a character so abandoned, revolting and unnatural that to see its precepts accepted as "philosophical fruit" could be to witness the first beginnings of a downfall of this nation'.[12] This concern with the promiscuous consequences of contraception was surely predominantly a concern with *women's* potential lasciviousness; it was general knowledge that many men already engaged in pre- and extra-marital sex. If fear of pregnancy was seen as the main barrier to promiscuity, it was presumably recognized as a fear far greater among women than men. Further, it was widely held that frequent sexual intercourse would lead to the loss of a woman's modesty, and given women's supposed lack of will-power, her sexual desires would thereby become wild and untrammelled. If fear of pregnancy 'protected' women against promiscuity, its removal unleashed women's latent, uncontrollable sexuality. As Dr Routh authoritatively informed the British Medical Association:

> If you teach them [women] vicious habits, and a way of sin without detection, how can you assure yourself of their fidelity when assailed by a fascinating seducer? And why may not even the unmarried women taste of the forbidden pleasures also, so that your future wife shall have been defiled ere you know her?[13]

Ten years later the same anxiety about the accessibility of birth-control information to women, the working classes and youth was again apparent in the Allbutt case. In 1887 the General Medical Council (GMC) set up a Committee of Inquiry to consider what procedure to take against Dr Arthur Allbutt, who had included a chapter entitled 'How to Prevent Conception When Advised by the Doctor' in his book *The Wife's Handbook* published the previous year. Allbutt favoured Rendall's quinine pessaries, but he was also the first to recommend the diaphragm or Dutch cap, so named because of its promotion in Holland by feminist Dr Aletta Jacobs. To Allbutt, the cap's advantage, in addition to its reliability, was the possibility of its use 'without inconvenience or knowledge of the husband'.[14] The book had been drawn to the GMC's attention by the 'Leeds Vigilance Association for Enforcing the Criminal Law Amendment Act and the Protection of Girls' (an organization affiliated to The National Vigilance Association). Allbutt intended it as 'a book which could be understood by most women, and at a price which would ensure it a place in even the poorest household.'[15] The book was accordingly priced sixpence. But its cheapness and accessibility led to the GMC finding Allbutt guilty of having published the book 'at so low a price as to bring the work within the reach of the youth of both sexes to the detriment of public morals.'[16] Anxiety about youth was surely only half the story. The fact that *The Wife's Handbook* by its title and content was explicitly addressed to married women meant that the GMC's concern was probably not so much with the likelihood of youthful perusal as with the possibility of a wide readership among working-class women. Allbutt was struck off the Medical Register, and although he was never actually prosecuted for obscenity, those selling his books *were* liable, for example, J. Williamson of Gainsborough was charged soon after the book's publication. Sales of *The Wife's Handbook* spiralled, however; by 1907 it had sold 390,000 copies.[17]

The debate among members of the National Vigilance Association (NVA) about prosecuting birth-control literature throws further light on the construction of contraception's immorality. In the same year as the Allbutt case, on 3 May 1887, a motion approving prosecution 'of persons circulating or selling indecent publications inciting to sexual immoralities' was carried 9 to 4 by the NVA's executive committee.[18] The 'persons' referred to were the medical booksellers Constantine and Jackson. In the preceding discussion, executive members Ralph Thicknesse and Henrietta Muller[19] had spoken in opposition to the motion, Dr Elizabeth Blackwell in its defence. At the next executive meeting a fortnight later, six committee members, including Mrs Laura Chant, noted their desire 'to record our disapproval of such a discussion'. They wished it

> to be understood that our silence did not mean approval. We strongly disapprove of the use of any means ... which in restricting the increase in population, suggests the idea that vice is a necessity ... and ... which tends to relax the incentive for moral restraint.[20]

They supported Constantine and Jackson's prosecution. To hold that contraception suggested the necessity of 'vice' implied that to have sexual intercourse without the potential for reproduction was itself immoral. But the debate indicated a further aspect in the construction of contraception as immoral: the *unspeakability* of the topic. There was the note of disapproval that such a subject was discussed at all, and the references in the Minutes were veiled: the 3 May Minutes gave no indication that the subject under discussion had been contraception, and it was only apparent in the following meeting's minutes because of the reference to means of 'restricting the increase in population'.

Unease with the discussion of birth control reflected not only the wider distaste of the 'respectable' classes for mentioning anything 'sexual', but also a lack of language for such a discussion. Since any reference to sexuality was embarrassing, even shameful, for so many in this period, it is hardly surprising that mention of birth control was literally unspeakable.

Unspeakable or not, it is clear that among the general public there existed a strong desire for the topic to *become* speakable and for contraception to become available. After the Knowlton trial, large crowds attended meetings to hear Besant and Bradlaugh. Prior to the trial, about a thousand copies of *The Fruits of Philosophy* had sold annually; in the four years after the trial, 185,000 copies were purchased (most of the sales taking place in the first year). And Annie Besant received thousands of letters from married women, including clergymen's wives, thanking her 'for showing them how to escape from the veritable hell in which they lived'.[21] In response, she wrote a pamphlet *The Law of Population*[22] to replace *The Fruits of Philosophy* whose physiological details she and Charles Bradlaugh deemed medically outmoded. As for birth-control methods, like Knowlton she recommended withdrawal, but unlike him she favoured the sponge over the douche, viewing the latter as associated with prostitutes. She was careful to differentiate birth control from the criminality of abortion. She withdrew the pamphlet from circulation in 1890 when she became a theosophist: 'Theosophists should sound the note of self-restraint in marriage.'[23] She bought up all existing copies of the pamphlet and had the plates destroyed. By this time it had sold 175,000 copies.[24]

Feminist Opposition to Contraception

Despite this interest from many women in learning about contraception, the majority of feminists appear to have been opposed. No feminist publication mentioned the Besant–Bradlaugh trial despite Annie Besant's explicit support for women's rights. Many feminists spoke the same discourse of moral disapproval witnessed at the trial and the NVA discussion – that in removing the 'safety valve' of possible pregnancy, contraception would encourage promiscuity and sex outside marriage. Many feminists (and indeed non-feminists) were additionally concerned that contraception would dehumanize sexual relations. For example, as we have seen, when the Men and Women's Club discussed contraceptives in May 1887,[25] Maria Sharpe, Lina Eckenstein and Elizabeth Cobb all objected to their use because they believed they would encourage promiscuity and strengthen 'the sexual appetite', and were thus 'brutalising' in their effects, 'vulgarising the emotions'.[26] In other words, these women feared that contraception, in 'encouraging excessive indulgence by removing consequences', would push men and women back to an earlier evolutionary stage of 'brute' existence in which sexual intercourse was devoid of the higher feelings of love and monogamous emotional commitment. As Florence Balgarnie expressed it, preventive checks would lead to 'animalism', and 'whatever tends to animalism is to be condemned'.[27] Here was the widespread idea that the 'beast' of lust lay close below the surface. Twenty-five years later, feminists were still expressing the same disquiet: as Mrs Sherwen informed the feminist journal *The Freewoman*, contraception facilitated 'the indulgence of uncontrolled passions unfortunately *outside* . . . marriage . . . as well as inside'.[28]

As already suggested, many feminists were concerned that contraception would be especially harmful to women, subjecting them more than ever to men's carnal desires. To Maria Sharpe in 1889, reflecting back a couple of years on the Men and Women's Club's discussion: 'It seemed to me one further means of making the woman into an instrument for the use of the man . . . also reducing women to the same irresponsible position as men in these matters.'[29] More than twenty years later, Isabel Leatham, writing to *The Freewoman*, expressed similar sentiments: 'Common Malthusian practices are . . . a gross outrage on the aesthetic sensibilities of women and the final mark of their sexual degradation.'[30] The association of condoms with prostitution was one contributor to this degradation. If feminists were already inclined to view marriage as 'legalized prostitution', use of contraceptives reinforced such a definition.

Contraception, Morality and Malthus

Opposition to contraception on moral grounds was answered by a moral defence. In one argument, contraception was presented not so much as moral, but as less *im*moral than the alternative of overcrowding and poverty. Thus, Annie Besant at her trial passionately declared that 'it is more moral to prevent the birth of children than it is after they are born to murder them ... by want of food, and air, and clothing, and sustenance'.[31] For many years, Britain's leading birth-control paper, the *Malthusian*, flagged a quote from J.S. Mill on its front page: 'Little improvement can be expected in morality until the production of large families is regarded in the same light as drunkenness or any other physical excess.' But birth control was also argued for as morally right in itself, in that it involved prudence, foresight, responsibility and rational control. This argument of responsibility and rationality drew directly on the language of Malthus.

The Reverend Thomas Malthus had written *An Essay on the Principle of Population* in 1798, in which he had claimed that since population expanded geometrically, while food supplies rose only arithmetically, the inevitable result was overpopulation and poverty. Poverty, argued Malthus, was due to the 'reckless over-breeding of the poor'. There were two kinds of checks to this overpopulation: 'positive checks', such as war, disease and famine, which led to premature deaths; and 'preventive checks' which would reduce the number of births. To Malthus, the only acceptable 'preventive checks' were deferred marriage and 'moral restraint': 'The restraint from marriage which is not followed by irregular gratifications.'[32] He was virulently opposed to contraception. Malthus did not seek to abolish population pressure: 'the struggle for existence' (a concept adopted and developed by Darwin)[33] was the basis of progress. Certain post-Malthusians, such as the utilitarians Jeremy Bentham, James Mill, and his son John Stuart Mill, accepted Malthus's basic law, but argued that the 'preventive check' of contraception would not only address the problem of overpopulation, but would also facilitate the greatest happiness of the greatest number through permitting early marriage and 'normal sexual relations'. Contraception also offered the means for couples to determine the size and spacing of their family, thereby countering a key contributor to poverty, and preserving, even improving, the family's standard of living.

Neo-Malthusians, as they called themselves in the latter half of the nineteenth century, deployed Malthus's exact language. When Malthus had written of the temperance and foresight involved in 'preventive checks', he had been referring to the prudence of deferred marriage and 'moral restraint' (sexual absti-nence). To Neo-Malthusians, 'preventive checks' were likewise about temperance, prudence and foresight, but now the term was being used to refer to contraceptives. When they spoke of 'marital prudence', they meant not abstinence but, again, the calculated use of contraception. For example, in Annie Besant's 1877 *Law of Population* she asserted that contraception would not lead to unchastity in women, for 'the means suggested all imply deliberation and foresight. Are these the handmaidens of unchas-tity?'[34] Neo-Malthusians were not simply using the same lan-guage as Malthus; they genuinely shared his wish to inculcate values of prudence, foresight and self-restraint in the working classes. Such sentiments can also be seen as part of a wider middle-class desire to civilize the labouring poor and control their animalistic tendencies. But to the Neo-Malthusians, 'animal-istic tendencies' did not refer to 'sexual indulgence' so much as incessant child-bearing and sex without concern for the conse-quences. They saw birth control as encouraging not promiscuity but 'rational control' of procreation. To sex psychologist Have-lock Ellis, writing in the early twentieth century, family limita-tion was the inevitable result of civilization, since 'all civilization involves an ever-increasing foresight for others, even for others as yet unborn'.[35] Thus, in contrast to those who feared that birth control would encourage 'animalism', Neo-Malthusians held its use to be a mark of developed humanity. And the advocacy of birth control was not, of course, simply about the middle classes wanting to 'civilize' the 'lower orders'. Some of the 'respectable' working classes, faced with the rising infant and child survival rates and the replacement of children's employment by compulsory schooling, sought out birth control as a rational and prudent means of curtailing the cost of offspring. And for *women* to claim rational action in the use of birth control was an implicit, if not explicit, confrontation of the widely held view that women lacked rationality.[36]

Although Malthus had himself been strongly opposed to contraception, throughout the nineteenth century and into the twentieth, the general public continued to associate any discussion of fertility control with his name and ideas. This association acted to deter the acceptance of contraception, especially amongst socialists, for Malthus's ideas appeared to many to entail the attempted manipulation of the working classes. To support birth control suggested support for the theory that poverty was due to over-breeding rather than to capitalism, that welfare and charity would encourage this 'over-breeding', and that economic hardship was the working classes' own fault.[37]

Contraception and Health

Contraception was also believed to have implications for health. Those opposed drew upon medical claims as to the physical and psychological harmfulness of contraceptives. Coitus interruptus was described as 'conjugal onanism' – like masturbation, a form of sexual excess, against 'Nature'. Doctors warned that both the condom and coitus interruptus deprived the male of pleasure and the female of vital fluids, and led to nervous disorders in both sexes. Many feminists were understandably concerned about these risks. For example, in 1912 a *Freewoman* correspondent sent the journal a pamphlet by Dr John Taylor, President of the British Gynaecological Society, called *On the Diminishing Birthrate*, which detailed the damaging effects of contraceptives: neurasthenia, loss of memory and concentration, depression, even madness, symptoms similar to those supposedly caused by 'self-abuse' (masturbation).[38]

Many doctors approved of 'natural' birth-control methods in the form of prolonged nursing, the rhythm method or 'safe period', and abstinence. 'Artificial' limitation stood in opposition to these 'natural' means. However, abstinence was unacceptable to most couples, or at least to most men, lactation possibly reduced the chances of pregnancy but was highly unreliable, while the rhythm method simply did not provide any protection from pregnancy, for the menstrual cycle was totally misunderstood, with the so-called 'safe period' calculated as mid-month. Doctors did not seem to notice the ineffectiveness of these methods! Thus Dr Elizabeth Blackwell, despite all her years working with women, opposed contraception on health and moral grounds but was in favour of the 'safe period', which, in her view, made it possible to 'reconcile marriage with foresight'.[39] To Dr Blackwell, unlike the Neo-Malthusians, 'foresight' referred to 'male periodic continence', which permitted the woman to assume 'her due place as the regulator of sexual intercourse'.[40] Unfortunately, if the 'safe period' allowed a woman to be 'the regulator of sexual intercourse', it did not allow her to be the regulator of her fertility.

Part of doctors' objection to contraception related to its association with 'quacks' and rubber goods suppliers; 'quackery' was perceived as a challenge to the monopoly and professionalism of medicine. And the fact that many people were choosing to buy contraceptives from these lay suppliers, rather than consult the medical profession, demonstrated that birth control was a form of 'self-help'; this would inevitably have been opposed by doctors. Many doctors may genuinely have believed that contraceptives were harmful, but there was clearly some hypocrisy involved, for the 1911 census revealed that the medical profession had the smallest number of children of all occupational categories.[41] The medical profession had made Dr Arthur Allbutt a martyr, and although his book subsequently sold well, other doctors must have been dissuaded from publicly advocating contraceptives, whatever their real views and personal birth-control practices.

Neo-Malthusians did not simply deny contraception's harm, they also claimed its *benefit* to health. Effective birth control enabled women to avoid the ill health resulting from incessant maternity, or from resort to abortion and abortifacients. It also indirectly contributed to children's health through helping families to avoid overcrowding and poverty. And in facilitating early marriage, contraception was championed by Neo-Malthusians as the alternative to the unhealthiness of celibacy, and the diseases caught from prostitution.

The Malthusian League

Until 1877 there was no birth control organization in Britain of any kind. When an organization was set up in the wake of the Besant–Bradlaugh trial, the centrality of Malthus's theory to the whole subject made its title of the Malthusian League almost inevitable.[42] Malthus, of course, would have been horrified that an organization advocating contraception chose to use his name. Annie Besant became the League's honorary secretary (a post she relinquished three years later due to other commitments); the presidency went to Dr Charles Robert Drysdale, who had stood bail for Besant and Bradlaugh at the trial. Within two weeks the League had over 200 members; membership peaked in 1879 at 1,224. It maintained a level of approximately 1,000 members for the next forty years.[43] A journal named the *Malthusian* was launched in 1879, with C.R. Drysdale as editor, a post he held until his death in 1907, when he was succeeded by his son Charles Vickery Drysdale, and Charles V.'s wife Bessie. Charles R.'s presidency of the League was taken over by his common-law wife Dr Alice Vickery; indeed, the Drysdale family dominated the League from the outset.

The Malthusian League presented as its two objectives: 1 'To agitate for the abolition of all penalties in the public discussion of the Population Question . . .'; 2 'To spread among the people, by all practicable means, a knowledge of the law of population, and of the consequences, and of its bearing upon human conduct and morals.' Despite claiming to want to spread knowledge 'among the people', the Malthusian League had no wish to teach the working classes directly. What it believed was needed was the education of public opinion – 'the great censor of public morality' – and this was to be accomplished 'chiefly through the medium of the more educated classes . . . the most effective way of spreading the principle and practice among the less educated masses.'[44] The Malthusian League envisaged the practice somehow *percolating down* to the working classes, with middle-class mediators, doctors and social workers in particular, speeding up this process of percolation. The League made an especial effort to convert doctors to its way of thinking, setting up a medical branch of the League, and engaging in debate with the medical profession. 'Conversion' of the profession was largely unsuccessful, despite Charles Robert Drysdale and Alice Vickery themselves being doctors.

If 'to spread among the people' did not mean to engage directly with the working class, neither did the 'knowledge' the Malthusian League was spreading refer directly to birth control *techniques*. Teaching techniques was not envisaged as part of the League's remit; it existed to teach 'the law of population' – the reason for the *need* for such techniques. The League sought to present a respectable front, seeing itself as heir to radical liberalism and utilitarianism, *not* anarchism and free love. Although in the 1880s the *Malthusian* did carry some adverts for firms selling 'Malthusian appliances', the adverts did not describe, let alone explain, the workings of these appliances. For example, 'Higginson's Syringe' was advertised in 1887, without either a picture or description, but simply giving the supplier's name, and stating that it was 'recommended by Dr Allbutt and others'. In contrast, in Allbutt's book, a picture and details were provided.[45]

The Malthusian League leaders derived their analysis not only from Malthus's work, and the writings of radical liberals such as J.S. Mill, but also from the work of Charles Robert's elder brother George. In 1855, while a medical student, George Drysdale anonymously published the best-selling book *Physical, Sexual and Natural Religion with the Solution of the Social Problem. Containing an Exposition of the True Cause and only Cure of the Three Primary Social Evils – Poverty, Prostitution and Celibacy*. (In the book's second edition, he added as a prefix *The Elements of Social Science* to this already lengthy title! The book was subsequently known by this name.) George Drysdale accepted 'the unanswerable reasonings of Mr Malthus' in all but 'moral restraint'. Over-breeding led to poverty and misery but, argued

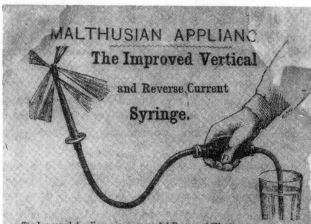

MALTHUSIAN APPLIANC

The Improved Vertical

and Reverse Current

Syringe.

The Improved Appliance is a powerful Enema of Higginson's pattern, fitted with a new receiving and filtering valve for preventing undissolved particles from entering and irritating the person; this is an improvement of great importance, and not obtainable in any other Enema Syringe; also a new Vertical and Reverse Current Vaginal Tube, producing a continual current treble the power of the ordinary tubes used for this purpose, thoroughly cleansing the parts it is applied to. It is to be used with injection of sufficient power to destroy the life properties of the spermatic fluid without injury to the person, and if the instructions are followed it can be used with success and safety.

Complete in Box, with particulars for Injection, and directions for use,
Post free 3s. 6d. and 4s. 6d. each.

IMPROVED CHECK PESSARY.

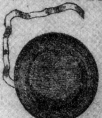

Is a simply devised instrument of pure soft medicated rubber, to be worn by the female (during coition) as a protection against conception. It is constructed on a common-sense principle, and strictly in accordance with the female organisation; can be worn any length of time with ease and comfort; is easily adjusted and removed, adapts itself perfectly, and no apprehension of it going too far or doing the slightest harm need be felt, and with care will last for years.

Post free with directions for use,
2s. 3d. each.

E. LAMBERT & SON, MANUFACTURERS,
38—44 MAYFIELD ROAD, KINGSLAND, LONDON, N.

24 Park Square, Leeds, June 7, 1886.
Dear Sirs,—Your Syringe should be used by every woman for prevention to conception. I should certainly advise you to have the vertical reverse actions in all your future makes.—Yours truly,
To Messrs. E. Lambert and Son.　　　　　H. A. Allbutt, M.R.C.P.

Advert for birth-control appliances in H. Arthur Allbutt's
The Wife's Handbook *1886*

Drysdale, Malthus's 'solutions' of moral restraint and late marriage led to their own miseries, namely prostitution and ill health from celibacy.[46] (Annie Besant quoted *The Elements of Social Science* on the harm of celibacy in her *Law of Population*.) George Drysdale was in favour of early marriage, or better still, free unions – 'the only true mode of sexual union' – although he hoped that they would be stable and longlasting, based on love and commitment. He suggested that contraception represented 'the only cure' to the three evils of poverty, prostitution and celibacy (as mentioned in the book's title). He discussed the various methods of 'preventive intercourse', favouring the vaginal sponge, not simply because of its reliability, but also because it did not interfere with the pleasure of either partner, and it allowed the woman to be in control. This was not the only feminist sentiment expressed in his book. He wanted women to be able to support themselves, necessitating a rise in women's wages – only possible, he argued, when there were fewer workers, and thus a further reason for limiting births. He also argued for better education and more employment opportunities for women.[47]

The Neo-Malthusian Feminists

There was also an explicit feminist commitment and analysis in the Malthusian League, partly because the Neo–Malthusians drew upon the writings of J.S. Mill and George Drysdale, but also because from the beginning there were active feminists in its ranks and its leadership, with about a third of the League's Council being women. In an early issue of the *Malthusian* Annie Besant argued for 'conjugal prudence' (which for the Neo–Malthusians meant contraception) in terms of allowing a woman a fuller life – that being a wife and mother does not 'absorb the whole of the best part of her life'.[48] She and many other Neo–Malthusians claimed that the birth rate was 'a woman's question'. At a discussion on 'Sexual Morality, with specific reference to the limitation of families', held at London's Memorial Hall, Mrs Thornton Smith, a Malthusian League Council member, rhetorically questioned the crowded meeting as to 'what right had men who knew nothing of the pangs of child-bearing to force their wives to endure them?'[49] During the League's 1894 annual general meeting (AGM), in answer to a socialist man who shouted 'No' to her suggestion that socialists should 'inculcate prudence in reproduction', Mrs Thornton Smith was reported to have replied: 'What did men know of women's lives?'[50]

Some of the Malthusian League female members took issue with the League's narrow remit both in relation to the class it addressed, and the 'knowledge' it transmitted. These women, largely freethinkers, appear to have been active in giving working-class people, especially women, practical birth-control information; they also wanted other Neo—Malthusian women to do likewise. They might have been maternalist in their sentiment, but they sound genuinely concerned about working-class women's welfare. For them, contraception was necessary for women's health and protection. For example, Mrs Heatherley, another Council member, who wanted a women's meeting set up to discuss how 'to enlighten poor women' about contraception,[51] suggested to the Malthusian League's 1893 AGM that the 'law of population' (and she was *not* referring simply, if at all, to Malthus's law) be taught to unmarried women, 'since some work-girls had to live in lodgings where they might easily get in trouble.'[52] This was an extremely radical demand,[53] especially when one reflects that contraception was not formally on offer to unmarried women in Britain until the controversial opening of the first Brook Advisory Centre in 1964.[54] Mrs Thornton Smith informed a public meeting at the South Place Institute in 1892 that she had worked with East End working-class women – matchmakers – and 'many of these poor women came to her and asked her advice when they did not wish to have more children'. Like Mrs Heatherley, she knew of the sexual vulnerability of many working women: 'She had heard that the prostitution of [matchgirls] was made a *sine qua non* of their employment.'[55] In rousing the women in the audience – 'Your duty is to speak out' – she was proposing birth-control advice, not 'rescue' work.[56]

Alice Vickery and Birth Control Advice

One woman who consistently addressed the issue of contraception from a feminist viewpoint was prominent League member Alice Vickery, who was born in Devon in 1844 and brought up in South London, daughter of a piano maker and organ builder. In 1868 Alice went to the Ladies Medical College, in 1873 she obtained a certificate from the Obstetrical Society, and in the same year qualified in Pharmacy to become the first British woman chemist. She then went to Paris to study medicine. Here she had her first child, Charles Vickery Drysdale; Alice had met Charles Robert Drysdale at the Ladies Medical College, where he lectured. Miriam Benn's meticulous research has established that Charles Robert and Alice never actually married;[57] they presumably agreed with Charles's brother George that marriage was 'legal prostitution'. But Alice and Charles Robert's contemporaries (and later historians,[58] bar Miriam Benn) appear to have assumed the two were married. For these two doctors' free union to have been generally known about would presumably have greatly affected their livelihood. They both joined the Legitimation League, however, set up in 1893 to secure equal rights for illegitimate children, although prior to the League's advocacy of free love Alice felt that it 'did not go far enough'.[59] Alice kept her name but sometimes added 'Drysdale' to the Vickery, switching between 'Dr Vickery Drysdale' and 'Dr Drysdale Vickery'. In 1877 she returned to Britain to take advantage of the Medical Act 1876 which at last permitted licensing bodies to confer medical degrees to women. She qualified at the London School of Medicine for Women in 1880, one of only five women in Britain with a medical degree. When Alice was called as a witness in the Knowlton trial, her testimony was largely devoted to the dangers of over-lactation as a form of contraception, as well as the harmful effects on women's health from having too many babies too closely spaced.

Despite the Malthusian League's official policy, Alice Vickery was as keen as other Neo-Malthusian feminists for birth-control information to reach working-class women directly. In 1910 she visited the 'Lodge' of the social worker Anna Martin: a house in Rotherhithe used for welfare work, where women gathered for conversation and 'mental improvement'. Here Alice instructed a gathering of women on contraception. According to Anna Martin, some of these women were already using 'preventives', 'picked out on that account, as being most likely to be more convincing missionaries.' Alice herself came from what appears to have been an upper working-class background, although in forming a partnership with Charles Drysdale, a doctor with a private income, and in becoming a doctor herself, she had moved away from her origins. Yet her roots in working-class respectability may have helped the acceptance of her ideas to these women; she was obviously no philanthropist or 'lady bountiful'. Alice Vickery's teaching and the work of the 'missionaries' paid off, for when American birth controller Margaret Sanger spoke to a meeting of over a hundred women at the same Rotherhithe welfare centre ten years later, she was surprised to learn that they all had small families.[60] The explanation was that after Alice Vickery's visit, the information spread and 'some of the more prosperous of these women purchased the necessary contraceptives and furnished them to their poorer neighbours, who reimbursed them on the instalment plan'.[61]

Alice gave birth-control advice to a number of groups of working-class women, including local branches of the Women's Co-operative Guild. Use of birth control and abortifacients by Guild members was apparent from the Women's Co-operative letters published in 1915 under the title *Maternity: Letters from Working Women*. The 160 married women letter-writers, all former or current Guild officers and largely from the skilled and semi-skilled working classes, had filled in a questionnaire for campaign purposes on their experiences of motherhood. For many, the experiences had been highly debilitating. Although the questionnaire had not asked about family limitation, a number of the women volunteered information on use of or support for 'preventives', while a smaller number mentioned abortion drugs. One woman, for example, who had only three children (some had had as many as eight, as well as miscarriages), wrote that 'my husband and myself were quite agreed on the point of restricting our family to our means'. But she added: 'I may say that I have disgusted some of our Guild members by advocating restrictions.'[62]

These women were unlikely to have got information from the Malthusian League directly, for it was not until 1913 that it at last produced its own birth control information: a free pamphlet entitled 'Hygienic Methods of Family Limitation'. Acquiring the pamphlet was not that straightforward, however: applicants had to sign a declaration that they were over 21, married or about to be, and held the 'conscientious belief that family limitation is justifiable on personal as well as national grounds'. The *Malthusian* hoped that members would distribute the pamphlets among the poorest, since they were most in need, but of course all recipients would also have to sign the declaration forms. The pamphlet detailed various kinds of contraceptive, warning against abortion and 'female pills' (abortifacients).

Florence Dixie and Jane Clapperton

Among the Neo-Malthusian feminists, Lady Florence Dixie was considered by the League to be one of its best 'catches': a Scottish, freethinking aristocrat, she was a well-known writer, journalist and adventurer. She was also a suffragist, on the Council of Elizabeth Wolstenholme Elmy's Women's Emancipation Union. She believed ardently that differences between the sexes were made not born: 'Woman is the only animal which shows disproportionate physical strength with the male. Why? ... Boys are given every chance, both in dress and physical exercise, girls none.' In 1890 she wrote her best-known feminist novel, *Gloriana, or the Revolution of 1900*, on this very theme. Set in the near future, the book opens with Gloriana, aged twelve, telling her mother that she wants women of the world to 'rise as one'. Disguised as a boy, s/he goes to Eton then Oxford, under the name of Hector D'Estrange, where s/he sets up establishments for girls and women to learn to ride, shoot, swim, run, and gain an education equal to boys and men. Hector becomes Prime

Minister and introduces a bill for women's full emancipation, linking the need for such a bill with the need to tackle overpopulation:

> There is a problem creeping gradually upon us ... the steady increase in population ... I believe that with the emancipation of women we shall solve this problem now. Fewer children will be born, and those that are born will be of a higher and better physique ...[63]

After exciting adventures on land and sea, Hector's real gender is revealed and all men and women live happily and equally ever after – in a socialist 'new world' of full employment, green parks and food for all. In real life Florence Dixie acted on her conviction that anything a man could do, a woman could do just as well, if not better. She explored Patagonia on horseback in the late 1870s, and in 1880–81, as an anti-imperialist, she travelled to South Africa to cover the first Boer War as correspondent for the *Morning Post*. The *Englishwoman's Review* described her:

> She threw herself eagerly into the Women's Movement ... she carried her views on the equality of the sexes so far as to assert that women were suited for soldiers, and undertook the formation of a Women's Volunteer Corps. She was a good shot, an excellent horsewoman ... she hunted lions in Africa and bears in the Rockies.[64]

Florence Dixie wrote occasionally for the *Malthusian* as well as regularly sending in letters and articles written elsewhere for the journal to reprint. She was the first British woman to join Alice Vickery's Women's Branch; according to Alice, Florence optimistically announced that there would be 100,000 members within the year. Alice later commented: 'Alas! the cowardice of the women of Great Britain in all that relates to really rational moral relations between the sexes is phenomenal!'[65] Florence was seen as the exception. When she died of diphtheria in 1905, aged only 48, the *Englishwoman's Review* felt compelled to remark: 'There was a lack of balance in her mind which interfered with the full development of her literary gifts.'[66] It made no mention of her support for birth control (was *this* her lack of balance?). In contrast, the *Malthusian* waxed lyrically of 'the splendid services she rendered to the cause of Neo–Malthusianism'.[67] It did not add, of course, that despite her radical confrontation of gender roles, she had discussed birth control only within the context of Malthusian ideas; she never mentioned women having a *right* to birth control.

League member Miss Jane Clapperton argued for birth control on rather different grounds to Florence Dixie. Jane Clapperton shared with Florence Dixie a Scottish nationality and the profession of writer, although she was more than twenty years Florence's senior.[68] In 1900 Jane wrote a pamphlet called *What do Women Want?* (regularly advertised in the *Malthusian*) in which she argued for birth control for women on grounds not only of women's health and welfare, but also of women's sexual needs. She suggested that women required 'a healthy animal life', but unfortunately

> sex-intercourse that is voluntary, pleasurable, healthful ... is of comparatively rare occurrence. The common experience of women here is utter failure either from deprivation or excess or compulsion. Until *society* recognizes and honours the sexual function by enabling women to exercise it in purity, dignity and freedom there can be no escape from prostitution, celibacy ... and poverty arising from over-population.'[69]

She was not explicit here as to how women were to be enabled to exercise their 'sexual function' 'in purity, dignity and freedom', but obviously contraception provided one of the key means, not least because she was suggesting that this 'enabling' would lead to the end of prostitution, celibacy and poverty, and it was of course in relation to contraception that the Neo-Malthusians made such a claim.

The Malthusian League and the Women's Movement

By the early twentieth century, the Malthusian League was going out of its way to court the growing Women's Movement. Many Neo-Malthusians had long been feminist sympathizers – indeed, Alice Vickery had set up a women's branch of the

Malthusian League in 1904;[70] it had studied various feminist texts but had disbanded a few years later.[71] By 1911 Neo-Malthusians were increasing their attempts to sell their message to feminists, taking the falling birth rate as point of entry. Statistics were revealing that the British birth rate had been steadily falling since the 1870s; Neo-Malthusians claimed that feminism was indebted to this fall, itself due to the use of contraception. Sometimes the Neo-Malthusians suggested that the Women's Movement would not have reached such heights, other times they suggested that the Women's Movement would not have existed at all, but for the greater freedom women had gained from the fall in fertility. As the birth rate carried on falling, they argued, women's freedom and economic conditions would improve still further. They also hinted that women, including feminists, despite denials to the contrary, had been limiting their births for some time.[72] These associations made between feminism and the falling birth rate led to an angry refutation from Millicent Fawcett in *The Times*. She pointed out that the birth rate in Australia and New Zealand, where women had the vote, was slightly higher than in England, where they did not, whereas in Canada, where women likewise had no vote, fertility was very low.[73]

A different tack of the Neo-Malthusians in their appeal to the Women's Movement was to suggest that feminists were *about* to adopt birth control – that the light would soon dawn upon them – once women had greater freedom, or the vote, or economic independence (different formulations were put forward in different articles). They would then realize that only emancipation from excessive or undesired maternity, through birth control, would make their new rights worth having.[74] There was also an appeal made to women on the basis of their superiority as mothers:

> Women alone can help us to attain such rational birth-rates. Men are too thoughtless in this matter, as they have neither the pains and dangers of parturition, nor the weary, wakeful nights . . .[75]

Some feminists were responsive to Neo-Malthusian arguments. 'Continental women', according to Alice Vickery, were much more aware of the connections between Neo-Malthusianism and feminism than British women, and the speeches given by such women were regularly reprinted in the *Malthusian*. Nevertheless, Alice Vickery and her daughter-in-law Bessie Drysdale persevered with trying to influence British feminists. As committed suffragists, they were members of the Women's Social and Political Union, leaving in 1907 to join the breakaway group the Women's Freedom League (the WFL). The WFL was prepared to listen to occasional talks on the relationship between feminism and family limitation. In July 1911 for example, Bessie Drysdale presented a paper on 'Emancipation and Motherhood' to a weekly WFL meeting held at the Gardinia Restaurant, Drury Lane. In her talk, chaired by Edith How-Martyn (who had recently joined the Malthusian League, despite her hostility to Malthusianism), Bessie differentiated between limitation of families from a 'personal standpoint', for which she stressed the health aspect, and limitation from a 'national standpoint' – its relationship to poverty and unemployment, in other words its place within Malthusian theory. Her paper was followed by 'animated discussion', and all but one speaker agreed with limitation from a personal standpoint. Two or three socialists objected to the Malthusian 'national standpoint' argument, however.[76]

Alice Vickery and Bessie Drysdale might have been occasionally listened to by suffragists, but their contribution to suffrage politics was awarded little or no recognition, presumably due to the embarrassment of their Neo-Malthusianism. Vickery gave generously to the WFL in time and money, but she went virtually unmentioned in the WFL paper the *Vote*, until her death in 1929 forced the paper to acknowledge the 'innumerable suffrage processions [in which] Dr Vickery walked, a striking figure, accompanied by her splendid little grand-daughter [Eva, Bessie's daughter]'.[77]

Feminist Ambivalence

Of those feminists not actually hostile to the idea of contraception many were deeply ambivalent. At the Men and Women's Club, Henrietta Muller and Annie Besant characterized contraceptives

213

as 'the lesser of two evils'.[78] As I have already mentioned, in May 1887 the Club listened to two papers on family limitation, one by Kate Mills, the other by Henrietta Muller. What the women actually said about birth control now needs to be explored further. Kate Mills's paper took the form of a critique of Neo-Malthusianism, in particular the claim that birth control would eradicate prostitution and poverty. In contrast, Kate favoured sexual restraint inside marriage as well as outside. The abstract of Henrietta's paper read: 'Need to consider the question from the *individual* point of view. The right of woman over her own person and the right of the child to be well-born . . .' Like the feminist marriage reformers, she mobilized the language of liberalism. Henrietta wanted birth control to be 'certain in its effect and innocuous', and in the hands of the woman, so that she could use it when she wished, without the man's knowledge.[79] After the meeting she suggested that Maria, Kate and herself go out together one weekend to 'discuss the question more openly than is possible at the club'. She told Maria that she very much liked Kate's paper, and 'the fact of our coming to different conclusions about preventive checks counts for very little because with me it is a mere *pis aller* [a stop-gap] till men have self-control and women have freedom'.[80]

Emma Brooke and Loetitia Sharpe similarly saw contraception as necessary only in the short term. In an anonymous paper (read to the Club by Pearson), Emma argued that birth control 'ought not to be discouraged, but an adequate check to population would probably be found in a free and intelligent womenhood no longer allowing itself to be treated as a machine for the production of superfluous children.'[81] And Loetitia, despite agreeing with her sister Maria that 'the woman will be made more than ever a vehicle of men's pleasure', saw birth control as 'a necessary evil awaiting a better state of self-control and higher relations between the sexes'.[82] Thus even those Club women in favour of contraceptives viewed them as something which would no longer be required once feminism had achieved all its objectives. In the meantime, as a friend of Maria's expressed it, preventive checks, although '*very* odious', were preferable to incessant child-bearing. After all, 'men are only brought up in the tacit understanding that marriage secures sexual intercourse whenever they are the least inclined.'[83] Whatever their position on birth control, most of the Club women would have agreed with Emma Brooke that if women had any say, they would prefer 'self-control and long periods of abstinence'.[84]

Where feminists were in favour of contraception, ambivalently or otherwise, they were not always openly in favour. To be so was to court extreme disapprobation from many quarters. Mona Caird was a case in point. In neither her fiction nor her essays on marriage did she ever explicitly argue for contraception, although like all feminists, she was against enforced maternity. The force of her feeling on this score was illustrated by one of her reflections on feminism: 'If the new movement had no other effect than to raise women to rebellion against the madness of large families, it would confer a priceless benefit to humanity.'[85] However, when she attended the relative privacy of the Men and Women's Club in its discussion of two papers on family limitation, her Malthusian sympathies were explicit: she was minuted as suggesting that 'by limitation of population, pressure of numbers would be relieved and so social misery relieved'.[86] She was, in fact, a member of the Malthusian League. One of her letters to Bessie Drysdale, printed in the *Malthusian* in August 1907, demonstrated the degree of her support for their movement: 'I wish you heartily all success, and enclose a small subscription to your funds. I wish I could subscribe more in proportion to my sympathy with the cause.'[87]

Another surprising Malthusian League member was Ben Elmy, husband of Elizabeth Wolstenholme Elmy. At its annual general conference in 1890 he informed the audience that 'Neo-Malthusianism was the highest of all forms of morality'.[88] But to read his writings under the pseudonym 'Ellis Ethelmer' (which, as I have suggested, could well have been written collaboratively with his wife), and noting the frequent references to the ideal of 'psychic love', one gets the impression that he favoured not contraception but abstinence. For example, in the extended annotated footnotes of his long poem *Woman Free* of 1893 he approvingly quoted 'the advanced biological writers' Patrick Geddes and J. Arthur Thomson:

> We must protest against regarding artificial means of preventing fertilization as adequate solutions of sexual responsibility. After all, the solution is primarily one of temperance ... a large measure of that self-control which must always form the organic basis of the enthusiasm and idealism of lovers.[89]

However, Ethelmer's Malthusianism (as opposed to Neo–Malthusianism) is evident in the same text, where he quoted Florence Dixie's *Gloriana*: 'There is a problem creeping gradually forward upon us ... the steady increase of population'.[90] The *Malthusian* reviewed Ellis Ethelmer's work highly favourably, referring to *The Human Flower* for example as 'a thoroughly sound pamphlet embodying the views held by the Neo–Malthusian party',[91] although at first sight there appears to be nothing in this work that sanctions contraception, or Malthusianism for that matter.

It is possible, however, to read Ethelmer's writings against the grain. Neo–Malthusians deployed the concepts 'temperance', 'foresight' and 'marital prudence' in reference to contraceptive use; Ethelmer's use of these concepts might have had the same implicit reference. Even the Geddes and Thomson quote about 'artificial means of preventing fertility' is not an outright condemnation of contraception, and Geddes and Thomson (who explicitly supported the 'safe period') were themselves unsure of their position, on the one hand fearing that contraception would 'multiply temptations', on the other reflecting that 'it seems probable that the very transition from unconscious animalism to deliberate prevention of fertilization would tend in some to decrease rather than increase sexual appetite'.[92] In his concern with the psychic element in sexual relations, Ethelmer was not necessarily subordinating the physical, and his use of the concept 'reason' has resonances of the Neo–Malthusians' description of fertility control involving the highest 'reason'. In *The Human Flower*, for example, Ethelmer wrote: 'The physical act is only sanctioned ... in so far as it is prompted by pure and mutual psychic love ... Hence in the cultured pair the act is controlled by *reason*.'[93] [Italics are my emphasis.] Whether or not Elmy/ Ethelmer approved of contraceptives, his membership of the Malthusian League was partly to do with his (and his wife's) commitment to sexual openness and the greater availability of sexual knowledge. There were few organizations which stood for such, although, as I've suggested, it was questionable whether the Malthusian League was one of them! There was disparity, however, between what its members did and thought – the likes of Mrs Heatherley and Mrs Thornton-Smith for example – and its official policy.

The Contrariness of Frances Swiney

Perhaps the most surprising Malthusian League member was Frances Swiney. Elizabeth Wolstenholme Elmy got to know Frances Swiney initially in the mid-1890s through their involvement in campaigning for the suffrage. Frances Swiney was President of the Cheltenham branch of the National Union of Women's Suffrage Societies. Elizabeth was enthusiastic: 'Mrs Swiney seems thoroughly in earnest and reliable.'[94] Born in 1847 in India, the daughter of a major, she 'rose' in the military hierarchy by marrying a major-general in 1871 and bore him six children. She began her writing in the late 1890s, starting with *The Awakening of Women, or Women's Part in Evolution* in 1899.[95] Her books and pamphlets included such titles as *The Cosmic Procession or the Feminine Principle in Evolution*, *Women and the Natural Law*, *Alcohol*, *Nicotine* and *The Law of Continence*, the last three being part of her 'Racial Poisons' and 'Racial Problems' series. She was a vice-president of the Cheltenham Food Reform and Health Association. By the early 1900s, if not before, she had become a theosophist, and started her own branch called 'The League of Isis'. She was adamant that 'religion and science by different paths arrive at the same goal – the one by intuition, the other by research.'[96]

Frances Swiney held to the argument that man had transgressed the 'natural laws' through his lasciviousness. According to Frances Swiney, women had not always been oppressed: under the Matriarchate or Matriarchy 'women reigned supreme'. (As mentioned in Chapter 2, many feminists accepted that there was once a Matriarchate.)[97] At some point man had wrested control, and now the inherited effects of his abuse were pervading

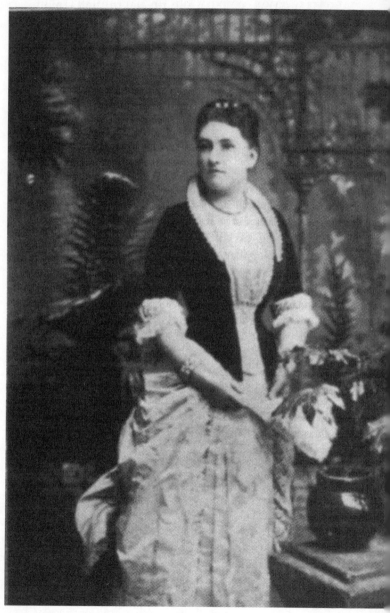

Frances Swiney

the human race. Why had man committed abuse in the first place? In one text she suggested that during the Matriarchate, women had selected the stronger males for their partners – not because of women's weakness but their preciousness. This led, over time, to men becoming stronger and taller than women, but this strength degenerated into force: protection became oppression, love became lust.[98] In another text she presented a different narrative: that man suffered from what sounds very like womb envy: 'The human male, because he falls short of the superior organic functions of the mammalia . . . has, for countless ages, striven to circumscribe woman to the exercise of those functions.'[99] In both narratives, women were reduced to mere breeding machines and sexual servicers, and man was thereby breaking what Swiney termed 'the law of the Mother', namely the 'natural law' of sexual abstinence during pregnancy and lactation. She drew on Dr Nichols for confirmation of this 'law'.

Frances Swiney was first mentioned in the *Malthusian* in August 1904 when she joined the Women's Branch of the Malthusian League; she defined the Women's Branch as 'the greatest reform of the time'.[100] The *Malthusian* started to reprint some of her articles and review her books, but with a marked ambivalence. In her review of *The Bar of Isis* Alice Vickery took issue with Frances Swiney's call for a return to the 'natural law' of 'self-restraint' during and after pregnancy. Alice was in favour of great moderation, even abstinence, through the pre-natal period, but not subsequently, since 'vigorous abstinence . . . is so apt to produce a recoil'. Instead Alice suggested that 'the practice of Neo-Malthusianism supplies a practicable method of approximately regulating the times and frequency and suitability of childbirth, without . . . the severe continence or entire abstinence so forceably advocated by the writer'. She then levelled her fiercest criticism of the implications of Swiney's ideas: 'We suggest to our readers that the so-called Purity Party *unintentionally and unwittingly* aid and abet the Impurity Party. We suggest that asceticism creates profligacy.'[101] The following month Alice's review of *The Bar of Isis* continued, again castigating Swiney for founding 'her theory of life mainly upon the idea of *sex restriction*', yet ending the review as if no word of criticism had ever been raised: 'We sincerely hope that Mrs Swiney's excellent little work will be widely read.'[102]

Despite reservations about Frances Swiney's sexual politics, she was given the front page of the *Malthusian* in November 1909 for an article entitled 'Womanhood vs. Motherhood'. Here she contradictorily admonished the reduction of womanhood to motherhood on the one hand, while on the other, argued that women were superior to men *because of* their mothering capacity. Women were historically and biologically the key sex:

> In every species the female alone initiated the changes, the capacities and the abilities upon which evolution depended ... The science of sociology proves that primitive culture originated with the women of the race, and to their initiative civilization owes ... all ... that has tended to make man human.

As for biology, it 'teaches us that nothing can be innate or inborn except what is transmitted through the germ cell of the mother'.[103] Her assertion that the female of all species was superior to the male was perhaps the most controversial aspect of Frances Swiney's argument. In her articles and books Swiney drew upon various authorities to substantiate her theory. Of these, it was the name of Lester Ward which occurred most frequently, followed by those of Geddes and Thomson. Lester Ward was an American palaeontologist and sociologist who, in 1888, had proposed a 'gynaecocentric' (female–centred) theory of evolution: 'The female is not only the primary and original sex, but continues throughout as the main trunk ... the male is ... a mere afterthought of nature.'[104] This and various references to biologists, allowed Swiney to claim that science gave 'indisputable evidence' that 'life is feminine and organic life begins with the mother cell';[105] 'the male element is simply the vehicle by which new variations are added to the maternal organism'.[106] In total contrast to Darwin and Spencer, she held that 'man on a lower plane is undeveloped woman'.[107] 'On the dustheaps of obsolete dogmas ... are thrown ... Darwin's man, a super-evolved woman, and Spencer's woman, an arrested man.'[108]

The *Malthusian* commented rather uneasily on Swiney's November 1909 article: it 'is a somewhat novel one from our point of view, and we insert it as being a wholesome corrective to the disgusting praise of animal or infra-animal maternity in which our imperialist press ... are indulging'. But the paper added: 'We think that in her zeal for the ennoblement of womanhood, she has somewhat over-stated her case from the biological standpoint.' New discoveries, the *Malthusian* claimed, 'all show absolute equality of the two parents as regards heredity qualities'.[109]

How are we to explain Frances Swiney's membership of the Malthusian League, given that unlike Ethelmer, there appears to be no way one can read her work as advocating contraception in any form? She was certainly a Malthusian, but most of the Malthusians opposed to contraception would not have given the League the time of day. The key to her membership probably lies in her eugenism, for by the early twentieth century, the Malthusian League was at pains to stress its commitment to eugenics. Eugenics had now become central to the whole issue of fertility control.

We have seen that contraception in the nineteenth century was indelibly marked by the Malthusian agenda on the one hand, and associated with immoral, promiscuous sex on the other. It was not viewed by most people, including feminists, as a woman's prerogative. Feminists argued for a woman's right to 'voluntary motherhood', but most were ambivalent, even hostile, towards artificial birth control. Some believed that women would gain not reproductive freedom but sexual slavery – forced into undesired sexual intercourse 'unprotected' by the excuse of potential pregnancy. Of course, not all feminists thought along these lines; Jane Clapperton, for example, linked birth control to a woman's right to sexual pleasure, but in late Victorian England she was one of few. It was not until the interwar years that a woman's right to contraception was more widely voiced, but by then the parameters had shifted and it was partly eugenics that called the tune. It is to eugenics that we now turn.

CHAPTER 6

Eugenics, the Politics of Selective Breeding and Feminist Appropriation

To Frances Swiney, man's violation of 'the cosmic law of the Mother' had led to Nature's retribution:

> Vices ... like curses, come back to roost. In his own enfeebled frame, in his diseased tissues, in his weak will, his gibbering idiocy, his raving insanity and hideous criminality, he reaps the fruit of a dishonoured motherhood, an outraged womanhood, an unnatural abnormally stimulated childbirth, and a starved, poisoned infancy ... The degeneracy we deplore lies at the door of a selfish, lustful, diseased manhood.[1]

Frances Swiney's language may sound extreme but she was drawing on vocabulary, metaphors and fears which were in general circulation, Above all, she drew from the discourse of eugenics. Many other feminists likewise appropriated and subverted eugenical terms in their debates about reproduction and the double moral standard, adopting such terms as ammunition in what they saw as a 'sex war'. Eugenics thus made an important contribution to early twentieth-century feminist discussions of sexual morality.[2] But where had eugenics come from and why had it become so popular?

The Rise of Eugenics

The word 'eugenics' was coined in 1883 by Charles Darwin's first cousin, the scientist and geographer Francis Galton, from a Greek root meaning 'good in birth'. Galton defined eugenics as 'the science of improving stock'.[3] He gave more detailed and slightly varying definitions on several occasions, the one favoured by Karl Pearson being 'the study of social agencies under social control that may improve or impair the racial qualities of future generations either physically or mentally'.[4] Eugenics was the 'science of selective breeding': those deemed 'fit' or 'desirable' were to be encouraged to propagate, while those deemed 'unfit' or 'undesirable' were to be discouraged, even prevented. According to eugenists, encouragement of parenthood by the 'fit' would increase those qualities of fitness in the next generation, for they believed that human characteristics, physical, mental and moral, were predominantly determined by inheritance.

Eugenics blossomed in the late nineteenth and early twentieth centuries in a period in which Germany, the USA and a burgeoning Japan were confronting the economic supremacy of the British Empire. The first serious threat to British Imperialist rule came at the end of the nineteenth century with the struggle with the Boers for control of South Africa's mineral wealth. British governments were also facing one national crisis after another – cyclical economic recessions, organized labour unrest, socialist revival, the demand for Irish Home Rule, the Women's Movement and, above all, the increasingly militant activities of the suffragettes.[5]

The extent of poverty revealed by the late nineteenth-century surveys of Charles Booth and Seebohm Rowntree in London and York respectively,[6] coupled with the high level of rejection of British recruits to the 1899–1902 Boer War on the grounds of ill health, led many commentators to claim that the British population was suffering widespread 'unfitness'.[7] By 'fitness' was generally meant good physical and mental ability, though obviously there was disagreement as to how one might measure these attributes. The physical 'unfitness' of Britain's individual subjects was taken as the basis of Britain's national 'unfitness' *vis-à-vis* other Imperial powers. The concept of 'fitness' was thereby used to apply both to individuals and nations; so too was the concept of 'efficiency'. 'National efficiency' became a central motif in the Imperialist discourse of Conservatives, Liberals and Fabians alike, with the Fabians even attempting to form a 'national efficiency' party.[8] To Karl Pearson, George Bernard Shaw and other Social Darwinist Imperialists, it was simply a matter of the struggle for survival operating on an international level: states struggled with other states over territorial control, the outcome dependent on these states' internal fitness.[9] As part of this attempt to heighten 'national efficiency' there was a growth in militarism, the introduction of physical training for schoolboys, and the formation of the Boy Scouts Movement, and for girls and young women, a development of classes in 'mothercraft' to teach the mothering of fitter babies.[10]

The poor were no longer seen as demoralized by their environmental conditions, but as suffering from degeneracy. This applied particularly to the casual poor or 'residuum', labelled as the 'unemployable'. 'Degeneracy' or 'degeneration' referred originally to the physiological process of the decay of the nervous system, but by the late nineteenth century it was used more loosely to include immoral and deviant attributes and behaviour which were indicative of, possibly even a cause of, a wider social and national decay. The concept of degeneration was frequently used as an equivalent to atavism – the reversion to an earlier stage of evolution.[11] Reverend Andrew Mearns's pamphlet *The Bitter Cry of Outcast London* shone a spotlight on one aspect of this 'decay': the immoral, including incestuous, relations of London's urban poor.[12] To eugenists, such degeneracy was the result of the violation, even reversal, of natural selection. Such violation was due to environmentalism – the distortions of philanthropy, state aid and modern medicine facilitating an artificial lifespan of the 'unfit' and undesirable. Eugenists conceded that environmental factors had some influence on an individual's capacities, but they believed that the effects of heredity were five to ten times greater.[13] They did not call for a return to untrammelled natural selection, however, but for *rational* selection through positive and negative methods of 'regeneration': 'race building' and 'race cleansing'. The former entailed encouragement of 'fit' procreation through both education of the public, and financial incentives, such as tax relief for the genetically 'sound'; the latter entailed the discouragement and prevention of 'unfit' procreation, again through education and state legislation, with proposals for sterilization and segregation.

To eugenists, degeneracy was hereditary, and it was spreading ever further with the prolific breeding of the poor (or 'tabid' and 'wilted') stock, with their 'feeble and tainted' constitutions, at the expense of the more 'desirable' types – the 'fit' artisans and middle classes, especially professionals. Statistics on fertility revealed that the birth rate had been falling since the mid-1870s. Up until this period, with the growth of industrial capitalism, Britain had experienced a high birth rate and a rapidly rising population. The birth rate peaked in 1876 at 36.3 births per 1,000 of the population before beginning to fall. The British *population* was not falling, since births continued to exceed deaths, but it was rising more slowly than almost every other European country except France. By 1901 the birth rate had fallen to 28.5 per 1,000 of the population; in 1914 the figure was 24 per 1,000. Until the 1880s, families averaged six children; by 1914 the average was less than three. What so concerned eugenists was the differential nature of this decrease, with the highest reductions in fertility taking place among the upper and middle classes.[14] The birth rate was also believed to be differential in terms of race. Fabian Sidney Webb, for example, feared that while the British birth rate generally was falling, 'children are being freely born to the Irish Catholics and the Polish, Russian and German Jews on the one hand, and to the thriftless and irresponsible . . . on the other'. One outcome might be 'this country gradually falling to the Irish and Jews'. He was not alone in his racist sentiments.[15]

Why was this fall in the birth rate taking place? Initially, many assumed a reduction in fecundity (the capacity to bear children) rather than simply in fertility (the actual bearing of children). The degenerating effects of urbanism was one theory;[16] there was also Herbert Spencer's thesis on the conflict between 'genesis' and 'individuation'. In 1867, before any decrease in the birth rate, Spencer had argued that diminished fertility was inevitable in advanced societies, since the complexity and differentiation of highly evolved individuals required a greater 'expenditure of force, and this supposes consumption of . . . food, which might otherwise have gone to make new organisms or germs of them.'[17] I have mentioned earlier how a variation of this theory was posed in opposition to women's entry into higher education: that the energy expended in brain work would leave women short for the work of motherhood. Women's higher education was thus seen as a contributor to the falling birth rate.

By the early twentieth century it was generally established that the decline in the birth rate was a decline not in fecundity but in fertility. The question was accordingly revised: why were women and men *choosing* to limit their offspring? The middle classes were accused of selfishly opting for luxury rather than the expense of children. Middle-class women were castigated for entering careers or higher education rather than motherhood – it was now women's volition, rather than deformed biology, which was the reason for their childlessness. They were 'shirking' their 'racial' duty to breed, 'sinning against nature'. The invidious effects of feminism were often cited. More sympathetic explanations blamed the high cost of living and level of taxes, leading to the deferment of marriage, while the expense of children's education deterred from parenthood. But such arguments tended to be drowned in the wild prediction of 'race suicide'.[18]

Eugenics Institutionalized

The concept of 'eugenics' may have been coined in 1883, yet it had little impact on social thought for another twenty years. In the early twentieth century, the growing interest of academic and intellectual circles in eugenics was manifest in the lengthy discussions of the subject at the newly founded Sociological Society. Eugenics drew upon, and was to contribute to, a number of other new disciplines – clinical psychology, psychiatry, community medicine and social work. The Eugenics Record Office, later renamed the Francis Galton Eugenics Laboratory, was set up in 1904 at University College, London University. The first Fellowship in National Eugenics was created the following year with money donated by Galton, a post that passed to Karl Pearson in October 1906. With zoologist Walter F.R. Weldon, Pearson had also recently formed a small team of researchers to focus on what Pearson termed 'biometry' – the application of mathematics to biology. On Galton's death in 1911 a legacy was left in his will for Pearson to become the first

Professor in Eugenics. The 'Biometry Laboratory' and the 'Eugenics Laboratory' remained under the direction of Pearson until
his retirement in 1933.[19]

In November 1907 the Eugenics Education Society (the EES)
was founded by a number of members of the Sociological
Society and a section of the Moral Education League (an organization committed to the promotion of moral education in
schools).[20] While the Eugenics Laboratory saw its role as entirely
one of research, the Eugenics Education Society, as its name
suggested, defined itself as educative and popularizing. To Pearson, the EES's work was rank propaganda, not science,[21] and
the Society's founders were 'high-strung enthusiastic quacks'.[22]
The two organizations were also divided over theories of
heredity: the Eugenics Laboratory staff were all biometricians,
following Galton's theory of ancestral heredity (inheritance occurring through continuous blending and variation); the EES embraced Mendelianism, the theory of particulate inheritance, in
which discrete genetic factors (later called genes) passed through
random distribution from parent to offspring, but with no
blending. Some of these genetic factors were dominant, others
recessive.[23]

Francis Galton was persuaded to become Honorary President
of the Eugenics Education Society and, in 1909, was knighted
for his contribution to science. In the same year the EES
launched its journal, the *Eugenics Review*, and, in 1912, organized
an International Eugenics Congress, with 700 representatives
from various European countries and the USA. One feminist
delegate who attended, Barbara Low from the *Freewoman*, was
bored stiff: 'When one had done surmising what these mild and
dull-looking professional persons, and the sprinklings of fashion-
ably dressed Ladies (whose motto seems to be "when in doubt,
try theosophy or Eugenics") thought they were doing, there was
little to do but sleep.'[24] The Women's Freedom League representative was less dismissive, but she did not think eugenics would get
very far without addressing women's suffrage. For 'the whole
question of Eugenics is obviously one for women to determine'
– impossible while women still held a 'degraded position'.[25] In
1914 former Prime Minister A.J. Balfour became Honorary

Vice-President of the now highly respectable Eugenics Society. Membership of the EES London branch reached a peak in 1913, with a total of 713 members. There were, additionally, several hundred members in provincial branches (the biggest being in Birmingham) as well as five branches in New Zealand and one in Australia. Daniel Kevles estimates the top nominal membership figure for the British Eugenics Society to have been 1,700.[26]

Male eugenists were predominantly professional middle class (precisely the category they deemed the fittest!), in particular scientists, doctors and lecturers – indeed, many of those were from the new 'scientific' disciplines upon which eugenics drew and to which it contributed.[27] Female eugenists likewise included many professionals, such as teachers, social workers, civil servants and a few doctors, but also a number of titled ladies, including Society hostess Lady Ottoline Morrell, temperance campaigner and social purist feminist Lady Isabel Somerset and theosophist Lady Emily Lutyens. Eugenists included many leading politicians, clerics and intellectuals, such as Neville Chamberlain, Winston Churchill, the Dean of St Paul's and Maynard Keynes. There were radicals, socialists and Fabians who were also attracted to eugenical ideas, including G.B. Shaw, H.G. Wells, Beatrice and Sidney Webb and Havelock Ellis. The Eugenics Education Society was asked for evidence by the Home Office Inebriates Enquiry 1908, the Royal Commission on Divorce and Matrimonial Causes 1909–13, and the National Birth-rate Commission 1913; it was central to the establishment of a Royal Commission on Venereal Diseases in 1913, and importantly influenced the Royal Commission on the Care and Control of the Feeble-Minded 1908, and the Minority Report of the Royal Commission on the Poor Law 1910. It was indeed an established Edwardian institution. In 1907 Pearson wrote to Galton:

> You would be amused to hear how general is now the use of your *Eugenics*! . . . I hear most respectable middle-class matrons saying if children are weakly: 'Ah that was not a eugenic marriage!'[28]

Eugenics' Appeal to Women

Many women (including a fair number of feminists) were attracted to eugenics; indeed, there was a majority of women in the EES's London branch (the parent Society). Women were also in the majority of official EES visiting lecturers sent out to numerous and varied organizations which themselves included many women's groups. At its foundation, nearly half of the EES Council were women.[29] Women were presumably encouraged by the formal commitment made in the Society's Constitution:

> Women shall be eligible for election as members of the Society and no expression herein after shall be held to debar them from exercising any right or privilege of the Society, or from filling any office to which they may be elected.[30]

The vast majority of eugenists appeared to have agreed with Mrs Alec Tweedie that 'it is to the women of the country we must look in this great eugenic movement'.[31] Eugenists realized that they needed women's active support if they were to succeed. To some eugenists, it was not simply women in general whom they wished to win to eugenics, but feminists in particular. EES member Dr Caleb Saleeby noted that 'the best woman' was 'largely found in the ranks of feminism', and it was precisely such a woman who needed convincing of her 'true' role as wife and mother. He called for a 'Eugenic Feminism' to lure these 'incomplete and aberrant women' (feminists) back to their natural roles.[32]

Why were women attracted to eugenics? In part the appeal related to eugenics' promise of a new morality. As expressed by the EES's first President Montague Crackanthorpe: 'Eugenics . . . is a great moral question founded on a scientific basis.'[33] The 'great moral question' of eugenics was not so much sexual morality but moral ('fit') breeding; as a concomitant, immorality according to eugenics referred first and foremost to the production of 'unfit' offspring. In Chapter Two I described feminists' attempts to unite scientific and religious ideas into an overarching epistemology and moral philosophy. With similar intent, a number of feminist social purists saw in eugenics the potential of scientific validation and reinforcement of moral purity beliefs. Within such a framework, genetic purity and moral purity became equivalents, mutually reinforcing. Eugenics was also defined as philanthropic; as one female eugenist rhetorically inquired, in her praise of eugenic policies: 'Could anything be more moral than to stop immorality? Could anything be more philanthropic than to stamp out degeneracy?'[34]

A second aspect of the appeal of eugenics to women related to the subject position on offer. The 'rational control' of the nation's reproduction required intervention at the level of the individual; it was woman as reproducer who was the main object of this intervention. But within the Eugenic Programme women were not simply the objects of eugenical direction, they were also the subjects of eugenical didactics – the educators of other women and girls in their reproductive duties. Women were to be at the forefront of pronouncing on 'responsible motherhood'. It was a subject position with the potential of substantial power – power to dictate to others – not dissimilar from that exercised within philanthropy. Eugenists shared the widespread middle-class belief that the moral instruction of 'subordinates', be they the working classes, other races, women or children, could be best accomplished by women.[35]

While middle-class women pedagogically had the responsibility to educate other women, adolescents and children into eugenical practices, biologically they had their own 'sacred duty' to procreate – they were the regenerators of the 'race'. The claim that women were morally superior, which women had exploited for all its worth in the arena of philanthropy, could now coalesce with the claim that women, in their role as mothers, were also evolutionarily superior, a position developed above all by Frances Swiney. Eugenics offered 'fit' women great social esteem as mothers of the 'nation' and 'race'. 'The breeding of man lies largely in the hands of women', declared Havelock Ellis.[36] Women were the link to the future: as educators of children, as genetic transmitters of their offspring's qualities, and as 'carriers of the race'.

Following the convention of the time, feminists in this period used the concept of 'race' incessantly. 'Race' might mean the 'human race', the 'Anglo-Saxon race', 'the British race', etc., depending on the context. The ambiguity of meaning allowed a slippage between the different usages.[37] Yet when feminists wrote or spoke of being mothers of the 'race', they were implicitly referring to several meanings simultaneously: women were the mothers, the creators indeed, of humankind (their evolutionary role), but they were also mothers of a 'superior' race, be it white, Anglo-Saxon or British (their national role). When feminists adopted the eugenical terms which spoke of women as reproducers of 'fit' offspring and moral saviours who would thus 'purify' the 'race', they were drawing on criteria of 'fitness' and 'purity' which although usually more explicitly about class than race, assumed the 'whiteness' of purity. Where the issue of miscegenation came to the fore, this assumption was made explicit. To Frances Swiney, for example, with her colonial upbringing in India, 'the Aryan male has never failed to have relations with the lowest and most disgusting females of the most degraded races'. The result was:

> The half-caste, who ... literally born of sin, inherits usually the vices of both parents ... it is to the influence of the white woman in the future that we must look for the enforcement of that high and pure morality ... Our modern civilization counts for nothing if the great Anglo-Saxon nation cannot keep its blood-royal pure and undefiled.

Women must 'transmit untainted the purity and nobility of racial characteristics'. It makes disturbing reading for feminists today. But Swiney was no aberrant exception; she spoke the language of maternalist Imperialism, held in common by many, if not most, English middle-class feminists of her time.[38]

Positive Eugenics and Motherhood

Eugenics had what were termed the 'positive' and 'negative' sides to its policies. 'Positive' eugenics referred to the encouragement of 'fit' procreation, 'negative' eugenics to the discouragement of procreation deemed 'unfit'. Women were the main objects of intervention on both sides of eugenic policy; as the eugenist couple the Whethams declared: 'The chief burden of maintaining a sound hereditary stock of the national assets of good health, good ability and good character falls on the women.'[39] Positive eugenics included ideas of tax incentives, scholarships for the children of the middle classes,[40] old-age pensions based on the number of children raised, and 'endowment of motherhood'. The central positive eugenic strategy, however, was educational. Several women doctors were to the forefront in this propaganda war for 'fit' mothering, Mary Scharlieb and Elizabeth Sloan Chesser being the most prolific. They combined a stress on hereditary factors (the orthodox eugenic line) with an emphasis on the need for environmental influence in the form of education in mothercraft and healthy 'pure' living.[41] Suffragist Dr Mary Scharlieb was a well-known gynaecologist at the London School of Medicine for Women (later its President) and the first woman medical graduate from the University of London. As a Catholic, she was adamantly opposed to birth control; she was also deeply disturbed by the falling birth rate.[42] Her writings presented mothers as 'race regenerators': 'It is no exaggeration to say that on woman depends the welfare of the race . . . the race will be whatever the women of the race make it.'[43] But women needed motherhood training, not least the inculcation of their 'racial duty' to breed eugenically to counter the Empire's physical and moral deterioration.[44] Dr Elizabeth Sloan Chesser, a lecturer in hygiene with the Women's Imperial Health Association, was likewise concerned with 'preparation for motherhood' – motherhood that was 'healthy and efficient'.[45] She addressed the adolescent girl directly: 'By your conduct you can help to keep the life stream pure, help to uplift the race.' Like many eugenists, she termed the sexual instinct the 'racial instinct'.[46]

Constance Hartley also wrote emotively about motherhood. Unlike Scharlieb and Sloan Chesser, Hartley was not a doctor but a writer and journalist. She was an active feminist – a member of the Women's Freedom League, contributing regularly to the *Vote*. She shared with the two doctors the stress on a woman's 'racial duty' to breed: 'Woman's Duty to society is paramount. She is the Guardian of the Race-body and the Race-soul.' Where she perhaps differed was in the presentation of a more active role for women:

> Just as at the dawn of civilisation society was moulded ... by women ... so, in the future our society will be carried on and humanised by women, deliberately working for the race, their creative energy having become self-conscious and organized.[47]

Most, if not all, eugenist feminists (and many non-eugenist feminists besides) believed that women as sexual selectors could and should be to the fore in evolutionary development. Constance Hartley, for example, declared that 'as woman's right of selection is given back to her to exercise without restraint ... her choice will be guided by the man's fitness alone, not, as now it is, by his capacity and power for work and protection'.[48] But for women to have their 'right of selection' restored, they needed economic independence. Neo-Malthusian Alice Vickery, a member of the Eugenics Education Society, agreed. Women's sexual selection was inherently eugenic, she asserted, but 'matrimonial social selection determined by the economic dependence of women' had undermined this natural eugenism.[49] Both Hartley and Vickery, along with many other feminists, believed that evolution was moving from natural selection towards conscious, moral selection, with women's selective power 'a main factor in the spiritual evolution of the race'.[50] They did not, however, quite accept Frances Swiney's claim that the world was moving from 'the masculine state of being' towards 'the Divine Feminine Consciousness ... the Eternal Motherhood'.[51]

If some feminists embraced the eugenical message on motherhood, others used a language of racialized motherhood without being eugenists as such, an indication of the wide currency of eugenical concepts and metaphors. Eugenics defined the parameters within which debate about reproduction took place. Elizabeth Wolstenholme Elmy, for example, argued that 'motherhood, *in its largest sense*, is the highest function of women ... the mother risks her life for the perpetuation and progress of the race'.[52] There were also feminists who, though not dismissive of eugenics *per se*, took issue with the accusation that 'race suicide' was largely due to women's selfish restriction of offspring. Some argued that, on the contrary, if there was a decline in the birth rate it was based on sound eugenics. For example, in reply to a Mr Percy Cohen in the *Standard*, who blamed feminists for the decline in fertility: 'In proportion as the door of "equality of opportunity" opens, the door of maternity closes', feminist birth-controller Edith How-Martyn declared: 'Some of us are exceedingly anxious to close the door of maternity in some candidates', namely 'all the babies ... not desired by their mothers, the offspring of parents ... with hereditary diseases.' It was a eugenical argument for the restriction in the birth rate, but combined with the assumption of a woman's right to choose.[53]

It is perhaps surprising that there was little feminist opposition to eugenical pronouncements on motherhood, given that the role offered to women was so circumscribed. In many cases eugenists were explicitly anti-feminist in their accusations against the women's movement as the promoters of sterility. And even so-called feminist sympathizer Karl Pearson had stated, in his 'The Woman's Question' paper for the Men and Women's Club, that 'we have first to settle what is the physical capacity of woman, what would be the effect of her emancipation on her function of race-reproduction, before we can talk about her "rights"'.[54] Other eugenists made many similar assertions. There were, however, a few feminist voices stressing the rights of the individual woman. One, for example, angrily declared:

> We are often warned that nothing but disaster can result if the good of the individual is placed before the good of the race. But what other than disaster can result if the good of the individual is sacrificed to the good of the race? The individual is more real than the species. If the welfare of the species is inimical to the welfare of the individual then the species had far better die out.[55]

Another feminist declared: 'As a Freewoman ... I care nothing for the continuance of the race nor the reproduction of any man; my desire is to continue *myself*.'[56]

Many feminists objected to the self-sacrifice which was being demanded of women – the idea, propagated by, among others, Elizabeth Sloan Chesser, that 'the sacrifice of self ... is the crown of woman's destiny. The eternal law of womanhood is the suffering for the sake of the race.'[57] Mary Knight, for example, declared that such self-sacrifice was no longer acceptable to women. She and others were sick of being treated as child-bearing machines; in response they were scorning matrimony and rejecting motherhood.[58] *Votes for Women* suggested tongue-in-cheek that 'if we are to learn from the animal kingdom' rather than Dr Saleeby's celebrated queen bee, who does nothing but breed, 'we will produce the lady spider – she eats her husband. Would this not be a simple solution to the whole question?'[59] There was also an indirect criticism of the eugenists' pronouncements on maternity from the Fabian Women's Group. They argued the need for married women's economic independence, so that a woman's life would not be confined solely to the role of wife and mother.[60]

The relatively low volume of feminist criticism of eugenics related partly to one of the reasons for its appeal: the centrality and validation accorded women as mothers within the eugenic discourse. Such validation was echoed in the pronouncements of organized labour, which espoused the ideal of homekeeping wife and mother, both as a defence of men's jobs and wage rates, and as a view of harmonious family life. In truth, for most women, motherhood was the only dignified and rewarding work open to them.[61] The application of *negative* eugenic policy to women, however, could not be looked upon so benignly.

The Negative Eugenics Programme

For eugenists, more hope lay with negative eugenics than positive eugenics on the grounds that it was easier to determine who should not breed than who should. The 'undesirables' were easier to identify; their fertility also appeared easier to control. As H.G. Wells expressed it:

> I believe that now and always the conscious selection of the best for reproduction will be impossible ... It is in the sterilisation of

failures, and not in the selection of successes for breeding, that the possibility of an improvement of the human stock lies.[62]

There were four main policy areas within the negative eugenic programme: marriage regulation, birth control, sterilization and segregation.[63] In relation to marriage regulation, there is evidence that doctors in this period were playing a part in giving advice as to whether a young man or woman should marry – and/or whether their desired-to-be was eugenically sound. Although most doctors were far from open about the dangers to women of catching venereal diseases from their husbands, there were exceptions. Dr Arthur Allbutt not only advised women on birth control, he did so too on the risk of VD. In *The Wife's Handbook*, in a language free from euphemism, he warned women against marriage to men with syphilis:

> A young woman may be ruined in health for life, and have her innocent offspring diseased, if she is allied to a man who had disease lurking in his system. I refer to what is called syphilis. I should like to see it a custom for women or their parents to demand a recent certificate of freedom from syphilis from all men proposing marriage. In this matter false delicacy should be dropped.[64]

More typically, doctors had a quiet word with the prospective husband rather than his fiancée. Medical witnesses to the 1913–16 Royal Commission on Venereal Disease testified that middle- and upper-class men commonly sought their doctors' assurance before marriage that they were free from disease.[65] And Pat Jalland suggests that at least amongst the English upper classes, many families investigated the health of future spouses.[66] Feminist Ellen Gaskell confidently wrote to the *Freewoman* in 1912 that 'it will simply become impossible for any man to face a woman with suggestion of marriage without a positive assurance of a good bill of health'.[67] Working-class men and women, however, were unlikely to have been able to contemplate the luxury of a doctor's 'assurance'. Not all the upper classes were so conscientious either, if the case of Rosie Potter, youngest sister of Beatrice Webb, is anything to go by. The Potters, a wealthy upper-class family with nine daughters, were only too relieved when Dyson Williams, a barrister, proposed to Rosie in the late

1880s, thereby taking their 'difficult' daughter/sister off their hands. Unbeknown to them, Williams had syphilis, and soon after his marriage he became very ill, dying in 1896. Fortunately it appears that he did not pass the disease on to Rosie, although many wives were not so lucky.[68] One of the most infamous divorce cases of the period was that of Lady Colin Campbell, whose petition cited the cruelty of contraction of venereal disease from her husband as grounds for divorce.[69]

Doctors did not advise prospective partners simply on VD. In 1904, for example, Scottish psychiatrist T.S. Clouston was recommending that a neurotic man should preferably marry 'a fat phlegmatic young woman', but every effort should be made to prevent the marriage of 'the neurotic, thin, hysterical young women with insanity in their ancestry . . . we know they will not make safe or good mothers'.[70] (Clearly he assumed the restriction on women should be greater than on men.) A letter to the *Daily Telegraph* during the 'marriage debate' also focused solely on the woman's ancestry: '. . . more attention should be given to the immediate relatives of the intended wife. Why should a husband be surprised if his wife's beauty soon fades, if in so doing she merely becomes more like her plain and wrinkled mother?'[71] The advantage of choosing a eugenically fit partner was also depicted fictionally. In 'new woman' writing it was the prospective husband's health which was of concern. For example, in her novel *Gallia*, Menie Muriel Dowie has her eponymous heroine decide to marry a man not for love, but because 'I have wanted the father of my child to be a fine, strong manly man, full of health and strength. A man who is a man, whose faults are manly'. In what is clearly a didactic text (like many of the 'new woman' novels), the author appears to support Gallia's eugenic intent.[72]

Other than agreeing with the advisability of acquiring a 'clean bill of health' for the fiancé(e) and his/her ancestors, most eugenists did not argue very seriously for actual certificates to forbid the 'unfit' or dysgenic from marrying.[73] Lack of such a certificate would in no way prevent parenthood. As the *British Medical Journal* regretfully expressed it, marriage regulation would simply mean that 'the unfit would propagate degenerates with the added stigma of illegitimacy'.[74]

Negative Eugenics and Birth Control

The option of birth control as a negative eugenical strategy did not appeal to most eugenists. The opposition was partly on moral grounds and partly on grounds of eugenics. The moral objections to birth control in the nineteenth century still held in the early twentieth and were subscribed to by many eugenists. The eugenic argument concerned the differential nature of the falling birth rate. By the early twentieth century it was widely accepted that the fall was due to the use of birth control,[75] not least because it could not but be noted that the onset of the fall coincided with the 1877 Besant–Bradlaugh trial and its surrounding publicity. Most eugenists thus unsurprisingly opposed the current practice of Neo-Malthusianism on the grounds of its dysgenic consequences. Karl Pearson was a case in point. When C.R. Drysdale requested Pearson's co-operation in 1899, Pearson reprimanded him:

> Until your Association takes the view that limitation is nationally disastrous, until it starts with the bad stock and not with the good ... I cannot aid it ... Your teaching reaches only the thoughtful and prudent, and leaves the task of reproducing the community more and more to the bad stock.[76]

By this time Pearson was predicting that half of the next generation in England would be produced by a quarter of the present generation, and that among 'civilized' man, natural selection had been replaced by 'reproductive selection'.[77]

The Neo-Malthusians were highly defensive, denying that their propaganda was working dysgenically. They argued that if it was true that the 'lower orders' had a higher birth rate, this did not indicate higher survival, since a high birth rate meant a high death rate. And anyway the poor wanted birth-control information, they suggested, citing the widespread use of abortifacients. The Malthusian League obviously opposed positive eugenics since it opposed any encouragement of human procreation, but its objection was also to the class nature of the eugenic project: 'The fault of positive eugenics is that it is essentially aristocratic; that it aims at concentrating the best stock instead of obtaining a uniform and democratic but gradual improvement of the whole of society.'[78] It declared that although opposed to positive eugenics, it was the originator of *negative* eugenics, and the apparent contradiction

> is bound to automatically settle itself if Neo–Malthusianism is consciously and openly prescribed ... There are few women indeed who would continue to bear sickly and diseased children if easy means of prevention were known to them.[79]

Whatever their misgivings, most Neo–Malthusians saw in eugenics the potential for the recognition of birth control. Despite hostility from many eugenists, prominent EES member Dr Caleb Saleeby supported their cause[80] and this encouraged the Neo–Malthusians to pronounce enthusiastically that 'with the aid of eugenics and Neo–Malthusianism a reconstruction [of religion] will commence which, while dealing a death blow to theological superstition, will ... reanimate the world with faith and hope'.[81] But it was not until well after the First World War that the eugenics movement gave official support to contraception. By this time eugenical ideas had superseded Malthusian theory and the emphasis was on the 'racial' duty for 'healthy and efficient' mothering; mothering other than this needed to be restrained.[82]

Eugenics and the Feeble-Minded Woman

If positive eugenics was primarily directed at women, so too was negative eugenics. Through proposals of segregation and sterilization rather than marriage regulation and birth control, eugenists sought to curb the civil liberties and fertility of the 'unfit' woman. To one female eugenist, any woman less than five foot high was deemed dysgenic: 'No one can wish to perpetuate a race of dwarfs.'[83] While some eugenists wanted all 'undesirables' segregated, others argued for sterilization.[84] The idea of 'segregation' was nothing new; since the 1880s there had been widespread proposals for labour colonies for the 'casual poor' and the residuum from, among others, philanthropist Canon Barnett, economist Alfred Marshall, social investigator Charles Booth and Salvation Army leader William Booth.[85] A number of eugenists were keener on sterilization,[86] ideally offered to *all* the 'unfit'. Dr Caleb Saleeby, for example, advocated voluntary sterilization for 'persons somatically normal but liable to a genetic defect'.[87]

One sub-section of 'unfit' or dysgenic women was the object of immediate attention at the Eugenics Society's first general meeting in February 1908. The London County Council had recently closed the homes for inebriate women in London; the Society was concerned that 'some hundreds of chronic inebriate women will be set adrift in London, with an inevitable detrimental result to the race'.[88] By 'detrimental result to the race' the EES was referring to these women's potential offspring. Why this was such an issue was due to the belief that inebriety was a sign of feeble-mindedness,[89] that feeble-mindedness was an hereditary condition and that the feeble-minded bred more prolifically than other people. Thus, it was claimed that alcoholics, as largely feeble-minded, contributed to the degeneracy of the next generation. And according to one authority, alcoholism in women precipitated a descent 'even more rapid and terrible' than in men.[90] The feeble-minded bred more prolifically, according to Havelock Ellis and other eugenists, because they lacked foresight and self-restraint.[91] This growth of the feeble-minded, coupled, as Winston Churchill informed the Prime Minister Herbert Asquith, with a 'restriction of progeny among all the thrifty, energetic and superior stock', represented a 'very terrible danger to the race'.[92]

The feeble-minded were not simply well-represented among alcoholics, they were also thought to make up a sizeable proportion of criminals, vagrants, prostitutes and other 'undesirables'[93] – indeed all those categories lumped together as the 'residuum'. While the 'residuum' and the 'feeble-minded' were not equivalents as such, those deemed part of the residuum in their poverty and their anti-social behaviour were frequently assumed to be feeble-minded by virtue of being poor and anti-social. In other words, the psychological state of feeble-mindedness was knowable only on the basis of the anti-social behaviour it induced.[94] To the eugenist, the feeble-minded person became the archetypal representation of a deteriorating, degenerate race, and it was the feeble-minded woman who was the greatest threat – the most dysgenic of the lot.

Concern about the feeble-minded and their multiplying progeny led to the formation in 1896 of the National Association for
the Care of the Feeble-Minded. The Association was central to
the establishment in 1904 of a Royal Commission. On the basis
of the Royal Commission's recommendations, a joint committee
of the Eugenics Society and the Association formulated a Mental
Deficiency Bill, enacted in 1913. Only when the feeble-minded
were unable to be cared for by relatives or guardians did they
become open to incarceration in mental-defective establishments.
Such people generally came to a local authority's attention
because they were on the streets 'without visible means of
support', or were already in institutions. Those in workhouses
who were deemed feeble-minded included women 'in receipt of
poor relief at the time of giving birth to an illegitimate child or
when pregnant of such child'.[95] As Mary Dendy, leading campaigner in this area, informed the Royal Commission: 'The first
test [of feeble-mindedness] I think is that if a woman comes into
the workhouse with an illegitimate child, it should be considered
evidence of weakness of mind; there is certainly evidence of lack
of moral fibre.'[96] This equation of women's 'immorality' and
feeble-mindedness clearly informed the decision as to who was
in need of incarceration. Parents or guardians of a defective
under twenty-one could petition the local authority; there were
cases of young women engaging in underage sex, possibly
becoming pregnant, being disowned by their parents, turned out
or handed over to the local authority, and defined as feeble-
minded by virtue of their immoral activities. In one of Steve
Humphries's recent BBC TV programmes for his series *A Secret
World of Sex*, two women were interviewed who, when young,
were sent to mental hospitals under the 1913 Act. Both women
had been raped but not believed, and for one of them, Ruth
Neale, this had resulted in her bearing an illegitimate child. She
is still in mental hospital today. By the time her plight had been
discovered years later, after the repeal of the 1913 Act in 1959,
she had become institutionalized.[97] There may well have been
many such cases, but exact figures are hard to ascertain.

Incarceration for 'moral deficiency' was nothing new. So-
called 'wayward girls' had been locked away in 'Magdalene

Homes' in Ireland and Scotland for many years, and made to work unpaid in the laundry 'washing away their sins'. These Homes were run predominantly by Catholic nuns. Lockburn House, the Magdalen Institute in Glasgow, welcomed the Mental Deficiency Act 1913; according to the Institute, many of the young women admitted were 'hardly responsible for their actions'.[98] Moral deficiency was now being recast in medical terms – the scientific gloss of feeble-mindedness – and eugenics had enabled the transition to a new way of defining 'waywardness'.

Negative Eugenics, Feminism and the Blaming of Men

Although the eugenical definition of the feeble-minded 'problem' was widely accepted, there were a few voices of opposition. Dora Marsden, editor of the anarchist feminist journal the *Freewoman*, was one such voice, calling the Eugenics Society 'a danger to the community', and accusing not the poor but the rich of being unfit and workshy. And she claimed that the 'defective' was so '*because* of the demands the rich wastrel and workshy made upon his forebears'.[99] The Women's Freedom League paper the *Vote* also warned against the eugenical desire to control feeble-minded women, and the ignoring of 'the heavy responsibility of alcoholic, criminal, diseased and viciously inclined men'.[100] These remarks aside, most feminists, however, appear to have been silent, at least publicly, on the question of negative eugenic policy in relation to women. Yet a number of them were far from silent about negative eugenics in relation to *men*.

Some negative eugenical arguments could be applied straightforwardly by feminists to their advantage; others were appropriated and subverted. The link made between degeneracy and alcoholism, in men at least, was a straightforward application: it vindicated women temperance workers, feminist and non-feminist, in their role as moral arbiters. Drink was bad not simply for the individual, the family, and the safety of women on the streets, but also for the future of the 'race'. A blind eye appears to have been turned on eugenic proposals in relation to female alcoholics, however.

The discourse most amenable to feminist appropriation and subversion was that surrounding venereal disease. While Britain's 'deterioration' and its falling birth rate were frequently blamed on women, with accusations of irresponsible mothering, selfish 'shirking' of maternity or degenerate sterility, a number of feminists shifted the blame from women on to men. It was men, through their sexual licentiousness and their spreading of venereal disease, who were the ones really responsible for the nation's deterioration. Feminists were not, of course, alone in being concerned about VD, but they were the first to speak openly and loudly on the subject and to place the blame squarely on men. Eugenics in particular, as Claire Williams perceptively notes,

> strengthened women's arguments against venereal disease, alcohol, prostitution and the double standard by elevating the issues from the private realm into the realm of 'race' with its social, national and international parameters.[101]

A focus on venereal disease indexed all the contemporary fears of national deterioration, degeneracy and 'race suicide'. VD clearly debilitated its sufferers, not least because treatment was largely ineffective. In the nineteenth century there was no real cure for syphilis; mercury was a so-called 'heroic' cure that was likely to lead to illness, if not death, by mercury poisoning. In the early twentieth century a new treatment, an arsenic derivative (initially referred to as '606', later as 'salvarsan')[102] was seen as the new 'magic bullet', but it was expensive and not widely available. Treatment of gonorrhoea was also inadequate. Within medical circles there was recognition of venereal diseases' contribution to sterility on the one hand,[103] and infant mortality, morbidity and blindness on the other. (They went on blaming mothers nevertheless.) Medical statistics showed no actual increase in VD, but various serious illnesses, particularly dementia paralytica, were being revealed to be manifestations of the tertiary stage of syphilis. Since syphilis was transmittable to the next generation, Dr Saleeby labelled it a 'racial poison': a substance acting 'through the individual upon the race'.[104] To eugenists, tackling VD was crucial – it was 'nothing less than the cleansing of the portals of life'.[105]

The VD rate could also be read as an index of the country's sexual immorality. VD was known to be transmitted principally through 'promiscuous sex', and to be experienced as painful and potentially deforming. Yet ignorance and taboo encircled the subject; it represented a lurking, undefined threat to stability, the family, the British race, the Empire. It was caught from that 'other' woman, the prostitute – the conduit of infection between classes.[106] For feminists, however, venereal disease indicated not simply the 'perils of promiscuity' and the extent of prostitution, but also the horrific consequences of male sexual hypocrisy. For trusting, 'innocent' wives were the unsuspecting victims of a disease imposed by licentious, lying husbands. The feminist focus on VD became a way of 'speaking out' about sexual immorality and the double moral standard.

In the 1870s and 1880s, feminists had indirectly raised the VD issue in their campaign against the Contagious Diseases Acts. Yet their concern had been not so much with the effects of *disease* as the effects on prostitutes of state regulation. In the 1890s, the 'new woman' novelist spoke out on venereal disease in fictional form. By the early twentieth century, feminists moved from fiction to the presentation of 'facts'. Such feminists were arguing that the syphilis and gonorrhoea brought by men into the home were the main causes of sterility in women and death in infants. Although they were simply speaking openly of what the medical profession was discussing within closed ranks, they were up against male assumptions about the allocation of blame. While the medical profession recognized that men were by far the most likely spreaders of venereal disease within the home (indeed, there were doctors known to be complicit in obscuring the true nature of many so-called 'women's diseases'), it still managed to place the blame on women: the prostitute as the originator, and the wife whose venereal diseases were 'more fatal' to offspring than the diseases of her husband.[107]

In 1908 Dr Louisa Martindale, commissioned by the National Union of Women's Suffrage Societies, produced the first feminist text devoted solely to VD, *Under the Surface*.[108] The pamphlet detailed the diseases' various horrific effects as well as quoting eminent physicians on the harmlessness of male celibacy. It also linked prostitution and VD with the demand for the suffrage: only when women had the vote could they gain the economic independence necessary to rid the world of prostitution. The text 'was the occasion for a furious onslaught on the National Union [of Women's Suffrage Societies] in the House of Commons by a member who held it to be injurious to morals. This proved a great advertisement.' The NUWSS sent the pamphlet to every member of both Houses.[109]

The most (in)famous text, however, came a few years later with Christabel Pankhurst's *The Great Scourge and How to End It*, one of the period's most hard-hitting attacks on the double moral standard. Published in 1913, it was a compilation of articles which had first appeared in the *Suffragette*, and drew on various sets of medical statistics which, she claimed, proved that 75–80 per cent of all men were infected with gonorrhoea and 'a considerable percentage' with syphilis. She was adamant that women should know the dangers of marriage. Although she was accused of great exaggeration, it was the medical profession's figures upon which she drew. Several doctors, including male doctors, actually congratulated her on her plain speaking. To Christabel Pankhurst, breaking the conspiracy of silence was essential, for venereal diseases were 'the great cause of physical, mental and moral degeneracy and of race suicide ... ravaging the community'.[110] Cicely Hamilton, actress and writer, likewise voiced warnings of the marital dangers of disease and male sexual excess. In her witty, biting polemic *Marriage as a Trade*, she explained how marital sexual intercourse and motherhood not only involved frequent lack of female consent, but also grave dangers to women's health – the dangers of VD. 'If marriage is a trade, we ought to know its risks', she remarked laconically.[111] And Louise Bulley, feminist writer of sex education pamphlets, warned 'young men and girls of 18' that VD was the chief cause of sterility: 'The diseases of the streets ... are conducted to innocent wives ... and no-one is honest enough to tell them the cause of their disease.'[112]

Frances Swiney was even more condemning of men than Christabel Pankhurst: man was life's 'destroyer'. His sexual 'excessiveness' had generated venereal disease and had also turned his own sperm into a 'racial poison' (and here she was drawing on Saleeby's term): if 'limited, its power is for good; in excess it is a virulent poison'. Woman was being widely accused of 'sinning against nature', but to Swiney it was man who sinned, and his violation of the 'cosmic law of the Mother' had led to retribution: 'Vices . . . like curses, come back to roost . . .'[113]

Swiney, Pankhurst and Hamilton all objected to men's reduction of women to mere physicality – this was at the heart of women's subordination and the basic reason for the spread of VD. To Swiney, 'men have sought in women only a body. They have possessed that body. They have made it the refuse-heap of sexual pathology'. To Hamilton, women were seen by men merely as bodies to service another, be it man or child. And to Christabel Pankhurst:

> Sexual disease . . . is due . . . to the doctrine that woman is sex and beyond that nothing . . . or that . . . women are mothers and beyond that nothing. What a man . . . really means is that women are created primarily for the sex gratification of men and secondly for the bearing of children.[114]

We have seen that most feminists were in favour of sex education as one important element in the long-term solution to male sexual behaviour, but how was a more immediate change to be realized? The answer for these feminists did not include birth control. Although Frances Swiney was a member of the Malthusian League, her writings advocated chastity rather than contraception as a solution to the relation between the sexes. Christabel Pankhurst was likewise no supporter of birth control. Hamilton, Pankhurst and Lucy Re-Bartlett, among others, all declared that women were already forcing a change in men by refusing either to marry, to cater sexually to men, or to bear their children; the falling birth rate was partly due to these women's acts of defiance, they claimed. Told that they had a duty to breed, women were now responding that this same duty forbade their cohabitation with potentially diseased men. Lucy Re-Bartlett, ardent supporter of the Pankhursts' Women's Social and Political Union, was certain that:

> In the hearts of many women today is rising a cry . . . *I will know no man and bear no child until this apathy be broken through – these wrongs be righted* . . . it is the 'silent strike' and it is going on all over the world.[115]

Many feminists spoke of this 'birth strike', whether to advocate it or claim its actual existence. The WFL debated it as a possible strategy at their 1914 annual conference. One proposal was that

> a definite threat be made, embodied in letters directed to the Prime Minister, the Archbishop of Canterbury, and other authorities, that should women's suffrage be denied beyond a certain date, a campaign to assist working women to limit the birth rate be commenced.[116]

While this involved giving contraceptive advice to working-class women, other WFL members, opposed to birth control, preferred the advocacy of chastity instead. This was a view similar to Christabel Pankhurst: until men reformed she was convinced that 'there can be no mating between the spiritually developed women of this new day and men who in thought and conduct with regard to sex matters are their inferiors'. If the race was not to be exterminated altogether, the only solution was 'Votes for Women, Chastity for Men'.[117]

Woman as Chaste versus Woman as Sexual

Not all feminists received Christabel Pankhurst's *The Great Scourge* with enthusiasm. The *Shield* (journal of the repealers of the former Contagious Diseases Acts), although finding the book 'courageous', believed her claims to be misleading. It disliked the tone of 'sex antagonism' and the implication that all men were bad and all women good.[118] Rebecca West's response was more acidic: 'I say that her remarks are utterly valueless and likely to discredit the cause in which we believe.' Further, 'this scolding attitude . . . is also a positive incentive to keep these diseases the secret, spreading things they are.'[119] Stella Browne would have agreed.

Stella Browne, a Canadian socialist feminist living in England, was a supporter of eugenics, although she kept a sharp eye out for the 'class-bias and sex-bias' of the Eugenics Education Society.[120] Despite responding positively to eugenics' validation of maternity, she was insistent that a woman's absolute right to choose or refuse motherhood should be to the fore; she was adamant that 'motherhood as social duty' should not eclipse 'motherhood as woman's individual right':

> We must see to it that the Woman who is passionately and pre-eminently maternal shall not be condemned to childlessness through economic pressure and medieval conventions, yet our right to refuse maternity is also an invaluable right. Our wills are our own, our persons are ours.[121]

A few years later she was pondering 'whether maternity can ever be a duty towards an outside entity – state, individual or deity. I deny that it can'.[122] Given the Eugenics Society's distress at 'the multiplication of the less fortunate classes', she wondered why they 'persistently refused to give help towards extending the knowledge of contraceptives'.[123] The Malthusian League, of which she was a member, was barely better on this score; it was inert in the spreading of birth-control information, and unsupportive of abortion.[124] She was one of very few feminists in this period to argue for abortion as a woman's 'fundamental' right – an 'indispensable second line of defence, pending the invention and circulation of an absolutely reliable preventive'.[125]

Stella Browne was encouraged by the 'birth strike', which by 1917 she was describing as 'already, and increasingly, practical politics'.[126] But to her it was more indicative of women's use of contraceptives than their insistence on celibacy. As a confrontation to the double moral standard and as a politics of resistance, Christabel Pankhurst, Frances Swiney, Cecily Hamilton and other like-minded women advocated women's withdrawal from sexual engagement with men until men had changed. The crucial requirement was that men live by the same standard demanded of women, namely chastity. But for those feminists such as Stella Browne, who strove for freedom in women's sexual self-expression, the emphasis on chastity was anathema.[127] Feminist debate over sexuality and its discontents was at times acrimonious; the nature of this debate and the languages deployed by women seeking a sexual identity are the concern of the next chapter.

CHAPTER 7

Speaking of Sex

> It is often alleged that female sexuality is a more complex matter
> than male, and if so, a major reason is that sex spells potential
> danger as well as pleasure for women. A feminist politics about sex,
> therefore, if it is to be credible as well as hopeful, must seek both to
> protect women from sexual danger and to encourage their pursuit
> of sexual pleasure.

After opening their thought-provoking article 'Seeking Ecstasy
on the Battlefield' with the above statement (which today needs
amending in the light of Aids – sex is dangerous for men too),
Linda Gordon and Ellen DuBois go on to suggest that American
and British feminists in the late nineteenth and early twentieth
centuries did not manage to combine these concerns. Feminists
polarized into two opposing tendencies: a mainstream emphasis
on sexual danger and a minority emphasis on sexual pleasure.[1]
While it is certainly true that a number of feminists were clearly
of one or other tendency, I would suggest that, in Britain at
least, the majority cannot be allocated to opposing camps in this
way. Many feminists worked on *both* fronts, addressing questions
of danger *and* pleasure, even if they might have prioritized one
set of issues at any point in time. Elizabeth Wolstenholme Elmy,
for example, campaigned and wrote widely on male abuse of
women, but she was simultaneously committed to the development of ideal male–female sexual relations. And the fact that she
initially chose to enter a free union in preference to marriage
assigns her, according to the criteria of Gordon and DuBois, to
the sexual pleasure camp, although her choice was more about
personal autonomy generally than sexual freedom.

To feminists, the transformation of sexual relations between
men and women necessitated changes in the law on the one
hand, and in cultural representations and social behaviour on the
other. The law was seen as having the potential to be both
empowering and protective, although to date its application in

relation to women had been experienced as largely restrictive. Feminists had always wanted legal change in relation to marriage, economic conditions, education, suffrage, etc., but as I have suggested earlier, by the turn of the century some were also campaigning for it in relation to sexual morality. The vote was seen as a panacea for most of women's ills, but in the meantime, immediate *protective* legislation of women and children was also in demand, especially that which addressed the dangers of sex.

Concern with the potential *pleasures* of sex was an aspect of the attempts to change cultural representations and social behaviour, although the problem of sexual danger featured prominently here as well. Through sex education men were to learn 'self-control' and women were to be armed with knowledge of the risks and hazards of encounters with men. But although late nineteenth-century sex education focused more on protection than sexual exploration, feminists saw it as a way of informing women not simply of the risks but also the potential joys, even if descriptions of the latter were somewhat oblique. The birth-control movement too is another example of this combination of concern with danger *and* pleasure. While birth control was seen primarily as a means to protect women from unwanted pregnancy, it was also viewed by many birth controllers as facilitating sex that was free from anxiety.

In the early twentieth century, while male sexual abuse continued to concern most feminists, there also developed a more *explicit* engagement with questions of sexual pleasure, witnessed above all on the pages of a new journal called the *Freewoman*. Whatever its radicalism, however, the journal still implicitly assumed the norm of heterosexuality. Yet certain feminists were beginning to identify as lesbian, adopting the labels provided by sexology without necessarily accepting the sexological definitions. Therefore, to examine feminists' engagement with sexual issues in this period, one needs to study at least three different arenas of debate: the campaign around sexual danger, the discussion of (heterosexual) pleasure, and the development of a new lesbian identity.

Feminism, the Courts, and Sexual Danger

The feminist campaign against venereal disease, which began as fictional portrayals in didactic novels and culminated in Christabel Pankhurst's *The Great Scourge*, was a key part of the feminist attempt at sexual protection. Women were to be educated into a knowledge of risk. But feminists wished women to know not simply the sexual dangers, but the absence of legal recognition of such dangers. It was thus that in February 1912, in the Women's Freedom League's paper the *Vote*, Edith Watson started a weekly column entitled, with irony, 'How Men Protect Women'.[2] It was devoted to the giving of information on current court cases of male abuse. Such details were sought not simply to alert women to the widespread existence of male abuse, but to demonstrate the complete lack of legal protection offered women and children by their supposed 'protectors'. The light sentences given for men's assault of women and children were compared with the much heavier sentences handed out for property crimes or crimes committed by women. *Votes for Women* soon followed suit with its own column, 'Man-made Law', later entitled 'In the Courts'. (*Votes for Women* was originally the paper of the WSPU, but became independent in October 1912 on the expulsion from the Union of its proprietors, Emmeline and Frederick Pethick-Lawrence. They had opposed the Pankhursts' autocracy.)

This feminist concern with disparity in sentence was not new. In the late 1870s, Frances Power Cobbe and others had written articles in the *Women's Suffrage Journal* on the injustice of low sentences given for male attacks on women.[3] One of the more positive effects of the Maiden Tribute articles of 1885 was the encouragement of feminists to 'speak out' on sexual violence. (The more negative effects included the extension not of protection but coercion, as witnessed, for example, in certain feminists' attempts to 'rescue' prostitutes from brothels against their will.) Mrs Laura Chant and several others wrote to the *Pall Mall Gazette* about the 'male pests' bothering women on the streets of London.[4] A number of feminists went further and became involved in individual cases of sexual abuse. In 1887, for example,

Henrietta Muller intervened in the case of a fifteen-year-old working-class girl who had been raped and made pregnant by her uncle. Henrietta Muller managed to get the man charged (with rape, not incest. Incest was not a criminal offence until 1908, and feminists as well as the NVA were involved in getting it on to the statute books).[5] At the magistrates' court there were a few women present, but when the clerk ordered 'all females leave the court', Henrietta was the only one who refused to move. The Moral Reform Union's paper the *Pioneer* described what happened next:

> The constable looked at Miss Muller, and she looked at him, at the same time determining that if she left the court she would have to be carried out. The constable, however, desisted, and the case proceeded, with the result that as much assistance as the court could award was given to the girl.[6]

Generally though, the outcome of such cases left much to be desired. A couple of years later Henrietta Muller's brother-in-law, the MP Walter McLaren, presented a Home Office report to Parliament entitled 'Assault on Females', which gave the figures for males convicted in 1889 of murder, manslaughter, and assault on females. Of 8,075 assaults on women, only 43 had been punished with a prison sentence of more than two years. The report made no difference to subsequent sentencing, for when Matilda Blake investigated the issue three years later, she found numerous cases of similarly low penalties for male abuse. For example, a man who knocked a woman down three times without provocation was simply fined forty shillings, and a man who killed his wife with a poker only got nine months, but a man who pickpocketed two guineas received five years' penal servitude.[7]

In 1912 Edith Watson (who became full-time court correspondent for the Women's Freedom League (the WFL) the following year) invited League branches 'to find members who have some knowledge of legal procedure, and who will undertake to watch the police and other courts two or three times a week'.[8] Volunteers came forward, and despite magistrates and judges regularly calling for all females to leave the court each time there was a case of sexual assault, these women, like Henrietta Muller, refused to move. Such cases were considered unfit for the ears of 'respectable' women; female victims consequently, whatever their age, were generally left on their own to give evidence to a room full of men. Unsurprisingly, feminists were calling for female magistrates, judges, jurors and police. (The NVA too had been making such demands since the 1890s.) Feminists explained their grievance: 'Men say, in reference to lenient cases, "magistrates are only human". It is our complaint not that magistrates are only human but that magistrates are only men.'[9] The comparison of cases was as shocking as those of the 1880s and 1890s. One, for example, of indecent assault on three children, resulted in two months' imprisonment,[10] compared with fifteen months given to a man for stealing a suitcase.[11] On the same day, in the same court where Teresa Billington–Greig was charged with breaking the window of a car she believed to be Churchill's and received fourteen days' imprisonment, a man convicted of persistently molesting women and girls on the streets was 'admonished' and discharged; he had pleaded 'drunkenness'.[12] When on trial at the Old Bailey in April 1913, Emmeline Pankhurst told the court that one of the key reasons for feminist militancy was this disparity in sentencing:

> Women are revolted when they compare [property] law [with maximum penalty of 14 years] with the law which makes the maximum punishment for certain injuries to the moral and physical well-being of a little girl two years' imprisonment.[13]

Magistrates and judges were not averse to explicitly justifying their low sentencing. One magistrate, when trying a case of the sexual abuse of a girl aged three, remarked that crimes of that kind were 'sometimes committed by the *very best-conducted men* and just one of those things that *the very best people* in every class of life were apt, in an unguarded moment, to commit'. [Italics of the feminist reporter.] To prolific novelist and WFL member Gertrude Colmore, in these magistratic words: 'You have the mark of the beast ... it is a mark which will never be wiped away save by women ... fight they must, till the beast is driven back'. The 'beast' would be 'driven back' once

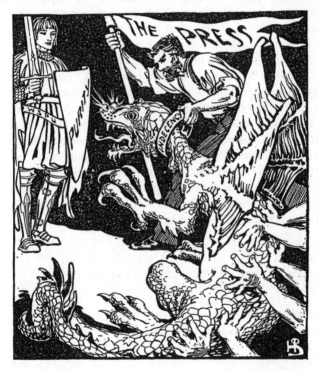

An example of the suffragettes' visual depiction of the 'beast'

women had acquired positions of authority – as judges, magistrates, police, jurors – and, most essential of all, had acquired the vote.[14] In the meantime, feminists were determined to break the 'conspiracy of silence' surrounding male sexual abuse.

If the beast of lust was male, where did that leave those women who wished to claim a sexuality; could they be sexual beings without manifesting 'the mark of the beast'? It was becoming an issue for debate in certain feminist circles.

PLEASURES AND IDENTITIES

In the early twentieth century, a woman's right to sexual protection remained a central feminist demand, but there were now a few feminists beginning to claim the right to *be sexual*. This was indeed a radical development given that, for most of the Victorian period, a sexual identity for a woman implied the identity of a prostitute. How was such a shift conceivable? The new openings for women in public life and on the job market, and thus the increasing possibility of economic and social independence, contributed to the development in young women of a self-identity separate from marital status or familial obligation.[15] But for this younger generation to think about claiming a *sexual* identity, whether heterosexual or lesbian, required the appearance of new ideas about sexuality. The crucial contributor was the body of work being generated by sex theorists and reformers – the ideas of the new 'science' of sex, namely 'sexology'.[16]

The Rise of Sexology

As the French philosopher Michel Foucault has pointed out in his ground-breaking work,[17] from the late eighteenth century onwards, Europe, Britain and America witnessed a proliferation of discourses concerning population and the body. By the mid to late nineteenth century, this concern with the labelling of acts and conditions of the body had extended to the classification of multiple aspects of sexuality, including a pathologizing of women's physiology and sexuality. Not only was there now the specification of fantasies, fetishes and numerous pleasures of the body, but also new pathologized individual identities, such as the homosexual, the lesbian, the pervert, the sado-masochist, the nymphomaniac, the frigid woman.

To Sheila Jeffreys, in *The Spinster and Her Enemies*, the development of what was becoming known as sexology was a direct and negative response to the impact of feminism.[18] Sexology, Jeffreys argues, attacked feminism via an assault upon the spinster. The difficulty with this claim is that many sex theorists, certainly the early sexologists, were both explicitly pro feminist and also in favour of chastity. But if the growth of sexology was not first and foremost a response to feminism, sexologists certainly engaged with feminist ideas, and a number of them writing later, in the interwar years, *were* explicitly anti-feminist.[19] Further, Ellis's version of feminism, in its exaggerated emphasis on motherhood, had negative implications for those women who could not or chose not to mother.

Sexologists also engaged with ideas and practices being developed by homosexuals themselves; the sexological stereotypes were not simply imposed on a passive community. The leading sexologists, such as Havelock Ellis and Krafft-Ebing, were supporters of homosexual rights and observed and listened to members of these (predominantly male) sub-cultures; further, a number of sex theorists were themselves homosexual, such as Karl Ulrichs, John Addington Symonds (who had, before his death, collaborated with Ellis on the first version of *Sexual Inversion*) and Edward Carpenter. As Alison Hennegan suggests, the work of sexologists was a fusion between heterosexual observations and homosexual information – a 'two-way traffic' between sexologists' theorizing and inverts' lifestyle.[20]

The power and influence of these sexological writings in the pre-war years must not be over-emphasized; their impact on ideas about sexuality did not come into full effect until the 1920s and 1930s. This new 'science' (which incidentally fought long and hard to be recognized as a 'science' at all) had marginal status within the British medical establishment, and the work was often difficult to obtain, frequently being subjected to various forms of censorship. The books were either banned outright, as in the case of Havelock Ellis's *Sexual Inversion* in 1898, or, in relation to bookshops and libraries, their readership was restricted to members of the medical and legal professions. Yet where the texts were available, they clearly made it easier for women to think and talk about issues formerly taboo. Readers did not need to accept the work wholesale; indeed, many feminists made *selective* use of these writings. To Margaret Rhondda, for example, Ellis's work 'opened up a whole new world of thought' but she 'was far from accepting it all'.[21] These sexological concepts, however, did not start from women's experience. As Carroll Smith-Rosenberg perceives it: 'Women's assumption of men's symbolic constructs [the language of sexology] involved women in a fundamental act of alienation.'[22] What this meant in practice will become apparent.

So what did these sexologists have to say about women's sexuality? Sexual theorists were not an homogeneous grouping, but one view which was becoming prominent at the time of the *Freewoman* journal was that women, whether heterosexual or lesbian, were, and should be, sexual beings. The crucial factor in relation to married women was the legitimization of their heterosexual desire – so long as it was passive and responsive rather than initiating. The other side of such legitimizing was the assumption that married women who were not sexually 'responsive' to men were 'frigid', and thereby pathological. As for relations between women, these were now sexualized and the 'romantic friendship' discredited, but the effects cannot be seen to have been always wholly negative. Women who loved other women became defined as 'unnatural', but many were simultaneously empowered through their ability to name themselves and their feelings, and through the help that 'naming' gave them in identifying other lesbians, even if the 'naming' was within the sexological terms.[23]

In pre-war Britain, the most influential of these sexological thinkers were Iwan Bloch, August Forel and Britain's leading sex theorist of the time, Havelock Ellis. Indeed, they were the theorists most frequently referred to by *Freewoman* contributors.[24]

(Sigmund Freud's writings had little impact in Britain until the First World War.) Havelock Ellis wrote numerous texts on sexuality, including his six volume 'Studies in the Psychology of Sex', the first volume of which appeared in 1897[25] (although it was to be banned almost immediately). According to one enthusiast, Ellis's work 'established the basic moral categories for nearly all subsequent sexual theorizing, including . . . Masters and Johnson.'[26] Be that as it may, it certainly established certain views about female sexuality which have been replicated in numerous texts right up until the present. Ellis has been heralded as a progressive sexual radical because of his stress on the importance of sexual pleasure for both sexes and his call for toleration of sexual deviancy, homosexuality in particular. However, it could be argued that his views on the nature of female sexuality, the limitation of his ideas on lesbianism (of which, more below), and his conviction that motherhood was essential for women (and the nation), amounted in all to a stance which was clearly less than progressive for women.

Ellis argued that women's modesty was central to courtship (seen by him as a prerequisite to every sexual act between the sexes) and reflected the 'primordial urge' of the female to be conquered. This urge − still with us today − was the mirror-image of the urge of the male to conquer.[27] He was thus arguing that male sexual domination and female sexual submission were rooted in our earliest evolution and thereby inevitable. Ellis extended the argument to claim that women required some element of pain to gain sexual pleasure and their resistance was simply part of the 'game' of courtship.[28] In addition to modesty, Ellis believed that the other main sexual difference took the form of women's sexuality being 'more complex, less apt to appear spontaneously, and more often needing to be aroused, while the sexual orgasm develops more slowly than in men'.[29] Although he thought that women's 'sexual appetite' was as great as men's, women were naturally more passive. In his discussion of women's need for arousal, he used the analogy (favoured by Balzac among others) of woman as a musical instrument which man must learn to play: 'It must be his hand and his bow which evoke the music'.[30] Many women had an apparent aversion to sexual intercourse, suggested Ellis, partly because their husbands, ignorant of the complexity of women's sexuality, failed to arouse them, and partly because women had not gone beyond the initial shock of pain, normal to sexual intercourse, to discover its inherent pleasure. Learning 'the art of love' was to be an important task for all newly-weds – the husband, once informed, teaching his wife. Ellis also fervently believed that women's true destiny lay with motherhood, his (in)famous statement that women's brains are 'in a sense . . . in their wombs'[31] reflecting this belief, as well as replicating the nineteenth-century dichotomy between the woman ruled by her body, the man ruled by his mind.

Dr Iwan Bloch of Germany, writing in 1908, also believed women to be as sexual as men:

> I have myself asked a great many cultured women about the matter. *Without exception* they declared the theory of the lesser sexual sensibility of women to be erroneous; many were even of opinion that sexual sensibility was greater and more enduring in woman than in man.

Women's apparent sexual frigidity was due, claimed Bloch, either to conventional morality or the man's inability to arouse the woman's 'complicated and difficult' sexuality. Despite Bloch's awareness of women's 'erotic sensibility',[32] it was the familiar story of woman being a mysterious and difficult animal that man must learn to handle.

The vast majority of sexologists gave some recognition to female sexuality, but there were exceptions. The Swiss professor August Forel, writing at the same time as Ellis and Bloch, assumed that 'in a considerable number of women the sexual appetite is completely absent'. Instead, 'the most profound and most natural irradiation of the sexual appetite in woman is *maternal love*. A mother who does not love her children is an unnatural being'.[33] So, although Forel was in some ways located in the nineteenth century with his view of women's virtual sexlessness, his stress on maternal love was in accord with Ellis, and, as we saw in the last chapter, was part of a wider early twentieth-century concern.

Sexologists did not agree either about the effects of chastity. Of the three men, only Ellis thought that chastity in women was harmful, instigating a host of problems from general atrophy to irregular menstruation. Bloch assumed that women bore abstinence far better than men, while Forel believed that single women could compensate for lack of 'sexual love' and maternity through work such as philanthropy, art and nursing. Writing in this same period was an influential French sex theorist, the pacifist and anti-racist Jean Finot, who favoured both chastity outside marriage and continence within. To Finot:

> The external chastity of former days is tending in our own times to become inward purity. Nay, we are striving to extend the purity of woman to man himself . . . A new sexual morality is on the eve of being born.[34]

It should now be apparent that the early twentieth-century sexologists cannot be lumped together as an homogenous group bent on the destruction of spinsterhood.

Sexology and 'Inversion'

As Martha Vicinus points out, feminist historians today are divided over the question of 'whether the famous sexologists of the late nineteenth and early twentieth centuries were detrimental or helpful to women's single sex friendships'.[35] One grouping of historians, including Lillian Faderman and Sheila Jeffreys, claim that sexology pathologized and 'morbidified' women's romantic friendships, thereby forcing previously 'innocent', in the sense of non-sexual and 'normal', relationships to be seen as deviant and sexually perverse. Women in such relationships thus became the passive victims of sexological labelling.[36] Another grouping of feminist historians, including Carroll Smith-Rosenberg, Esther Newton and Liz Stanley, while aware of sexology's imposition, point also to its more positive effects, namely the provision of a language of identification and a means of communicating one's identity with other like-minded women.[37] Clearly there is truth in both interpretations. Women who loved other women were now singled out and labelled, but many, as I have suggested, gained a new ability to name themselves and their feelings, although it was, of course, within the limitations of sexological language.

So what did the sex theorists have to say about the female 'invert'? Havelock Ellis's book *Sexual Inversion* in 1897 gave some publicity to homosexuality and lesbianism, not so much because of its circulation, which was minimal, but its prosecution the following year. Ellis himself was not very keen for the subject to reach a lay readership, and he addressed the book exclusively to doctors and lawyers. Nevertheless, a reader for the first publishing house approached by Ellis, Dr Hack Tuke (whose son was homosexual), rejected the book because he feared it might contaminate the wider public. By late 1897 Ellis had found a publisher in the little-known Watford University Press; the Press also published the *Adult*. The *Adult*'s office displayed *Sexual Inversion* for sale among other books and magazines. *Sexual Inversion* had been out only a short while when the *Adult*'s editor George Bedborough was arrested and tried for selling 'a certain lewd, wicked, bawdy, scandalous libel', namely *Sexual Inversion* and various issues of the *Adult*. It appears that the police were primarily concerned not so much with the banning of Ellis's book as finding a means by which to destroy 'a growing evil in the shape of a vigorous campaign of free love and Anarchism', namely the Legitimation League.[38] They succeeded. And since Bedborough pleaded guilty, the book, undefended, was labelled scandalous and obscene.

The publicity over the trial led to hundreds of letters to Ellis from lesbians and homosexuals,[39] although few people could have had access to the limited copies of the book. Three years later, however, *Sexual Inversion* was republished in the United States, and presumably imported. Ellis was the first to write a book in English which treated homosexuality as neither a disease nor a crime. According to his definition: 'Sexual inversion . . . means sexual instinct turned by inborn constitutional abnormality towards persons of the same sex.'[40] He claimed that this 'abnormality' was widespread among animals and among different cultures in all historical periods. He was insistent that one needed to distinguish the 'true' invert, for whom inversion was congenital and thus inevitable, from the 'artificial' invert or 'pseudosexual', who was basically heterosexual in inclination.[41] Ellis challenged the stereotype of homosexual men as effeminate, unhealthy and sexually obsessed. On the contrary, he argued, homosexuals were respectable, frequently intellectual, artistic and generally healthy.[42]

Although Ellis might have challenged preconceptions about the male homosexual, he did not exend the challenge to the stereotype of the lesbian. He presented her as mannish. This was partly related to Ellis's (and others') belief that a woman was generally sexually passive; thus, if a woman was witnessed as taking the sexual initiative, she must possess a degree of 'maleness'. Assuming that only opposites attract, the 'masculine' aspect of the female invert compelled her attraction to a 'feminine' woman – not to another (mannish) 'true' female invert, but an 'artificial' homosexual, 'a class in which homosexuality . . . is only slightly marked'. Although 'womanly', such women were 'the pick of the women whom the average man would pass by'.[43] Because such women could equally well turn to heterosexuality, congenital female inverts were presented as both predatory and the sexual rivals of men. Again, in contrast to his view of male homosexuality, Ellis claimed that the 'female invert' had some hereditary taint. For example, of his six case studies of the 'female invert', he announced that four had family histories of neurosis.[44]

Edward Carpenter's writings on homosexuality in this period were at least as influential as those of Ellis. An anarchist socialist and sex reformer, Carpenter lived openly as a homosexual in a village outside Sheffield, offering hospitality to like-minded men and women. He numbered many feminists among his friends, including Olive Schreiner, Edith Lees, Isabella Ford, Constance Lytton and Henrietta Muller. In 1908 Edward Carpenter's *The Intermediate Sex* was published, a revision of several of his earlier essays. 'The number of persons occupying an intermediate position between the two sexes is very great', Carpenter asserted.[45] He called this group 'Uranians' or 'Urnings' (from *Ouranos*, Greek for heaven; 'Urning' was the German form), a term coined in the 1860s by Karl Ulrichs, who championed the congenital theory of homosexuality and the idea of the 'female soul in a male body' and vice versa. In contrast to Ellis, Carpenter, wishing to convey the respectability, even superiority, of the Uranian, did not present *sexual* orientation as the key to homosexuality:

> I use the word Uranians to indicate simply those whose lives and activities are inspired by a genuine friendship or love for their own sex ... Some Intermediates ... are physically very reserved and continent; others are sensual.[46]

Like Ellis, Carpenter claimed that some of the world's greatest leaders and artists had been Uranians, but, unlike Ellis, he saw this as an indication of their superiority and a sign of the unique role that Uranians had to play:

> As the ordinary love has a special function in the propagation of the race, so the other has a special function in social and heroic work, and in the generation – not of bodily children – but of those children of the mind, the philosophical conceptions of our lives and those of society.[47]

The medical profession was even less keen on Carpenter's book than Ellis's. The *British Medical Journal* wrote a hostile and ridiculing review, complaining that it was 'a low price book of no scientific or literary merit advocating the culture of unnatural and criminal practices'. It was also 'pernicious'. In other words the book's cheapness, accessibility and encouraging tone would be sure to incite this 'odious' orientation.[48]

By 1908, in addition to *Sexual Inversion* and *The Intermediate Sex*, there were several other publications in English which dealt with homosexuality, including texts by Iwan Bloch and August Forel. While Ellis, Carpenter, Bloch and Forel all subscribed to a congenital view of homosexuality, up until at least the early 1900s, the official British medical profession held to the degeneracy theory: homosexuality was 'an acquired and depraved manifestation of the sexual passions'.[49] Ellis, Carpenter and Bloch believed that the Women's Movement was encouraging female inversion, Ellis being the most concerned, fearing that it was encouraging not true inversion but its 'spurious imitation'.[50] As for the question of what sexual practice female inverts engaged in, Ellis asserted that the clitoris generally played no part, their sexual interaction taking the form of kissing and caressing (which, as I have already suggested, had been seen as a normal part of nineteenth-century 'romantic friendships'), and also the use of dildos (although his case studies made no mention of the latter practice!).[51] In contrast, Forel saw kissing and caressing between young women as normal and unrelated to inversion. And, again in contrast to Ellis, he mentioned cunnilingus as a 'dangerous' activity practised by women lovers.[52]

The Shock of the Freewoman

In August 1912 Olive Schreiner wrote disgustedly to Havelock Ellis about a new weekly feminist journal called the *Freewoman*:

> I think it ought to be called the *Licentious Male*. Almost all the articles are by men and *not* by women, and the whole tone is unlike even the most licentious females or prostitutes. It is the tone of the brutal self-indulgent selfish male. There is something that makes one sick, as if one were on board ship. It is unclean. And sex is so beautiful! It can be discussed scientifically ... philosophically ... from the poetic standpoint ... from the matter-of-fact standpoint ... from the personal standpoint ... and it is all beautifully clean and natural and healthy.[53]

She was not alone in her outrage. Suffragist Maude Royden called it a 'nauseous publication',[54] while Millicent Fawcett, President of the National Union of Women's Suffrage Societies (NUWSS), was so appalled by the copy she read that 'she tore it up into small pieces'.[55]

Why did these feminists react so strongly? Opposition to the paper was partly due to the editorial assault on the politics of women's suffrage. The editors, Dora Marsden and Mary Gawthorpe, had both been active members of the Women's Social and Political Union (WSPU), but had recently left, Dora, far more than Mary, having become virulently opposed to a feminism which concentrated solely on the vote. She reserved her greatest hostility, however, for the Pankhursts and the WSPU.

Indeed, Mary's early resignation from joint editorship, although partly due to poor health, was also due to her anger at Dora's continual attacks on the politics of former colleagues.[56] But opposition to the paper, from Olive Schreiner's point of view at least, was also, if not centrally, to do with its explicit discussions of sex.

Olive Schreiner was wrong on one point at least: not more than about half the articles and letters in the journal were by men, with Dora Marsden writing at least one or two long articles each week. And a number of the articles, and certainly many of the letters, did at least think they were discussing sex either scientifically or philosophically, if not poetically and personally as well. The paper printed a range of positions, from those which Olive might well have seen as licentious, through to those with which she is unlikely to have disagreed. She would certainly have objected to an article by a Dr Wrench (male), which suggested that prostitution was a social necessity. Yet this (and many other articles) did not go uncontested; Dr Wrench, for example, was roundly attacked in the following weeks by several irate correspondents. Indeed, early on in the life of the journal, Dora Marsden stressed its openness to a range of views:

> We do not endeavour merely to secure opinions which support our own. We give direct encouragement to those who disagree with our views to state their case as openly as possible.[57]

She repeated this point on a number of occasions.

From the *Freewoman*'s beginnings, sex, among other things, was a subject which it was keen to discuss. The week before its first issue in November 1911, an advert for the paper appeared in the WSPU's *Votes for Women* (at this stage happy to publicize the new feminist venture). Part of it read:

> An effort will be made to treat the subject of sexual morality in a spirit free from bias. Holding the view that conventional sex is open to question, the entire subject will be dealt with in an unreservedly fair and straightforward way.[58]

It was also announced that the paper would be open to male contributors and readers, claiming that the interests of men as

266

well as women were implicated in any theory of feminism.
Once the *Freewoman* had been out a couple of months, several
correspondents wrote to congratulate the paper for providing a
public forum in which to discuss sex. One of these was S.
Skelhorn (gender unspecified; quite a few of the paper's female
correspondents signed only with their initials, so we cannot
assume the writer to be male). S. Skelhorn claimed:

> Men and women have *never* had an opportunity of discussing the
> sex question. The subject had been shirked by the 'respectable',
> defiled by the prurient, and unwholesomely approached by the
> morbidly curious ... the *Freewoman* is doing incalculable service
> by throwing open its columns to sane, serious, searching
> discussion.[59]

Dora Marsden was in full agreement; displaying no false modesty, she asserted:

> We make bold to say that never before the advent of the *Freewoman*
> has the opportunity [to study sex], either for men or women, in
> England or elsewhere, been at hand. That is the reason why the
> *Freewoman*'s advent is phenomenal.[60]

The Freewoman *and its Discussion Circle*

The *Freewoman* first appeared in November 1911 and ran weekly
up until October 1912, when it closed through lack of funds. Its
insolvency had been exacerbated by W.H. Smith withdrawing
the paper from its shops the previous month – ostensibly because
of the paper's discussion of sex, although Dora Marsden, the
editor, thought the ban politically motivated. The paper re-
appeared in June 1913 as the *New Freewoman*, now irrevocably a
literary journal, but it again folded at the end of the year. In its
third and last incarnation the following year it took the name
the *Egoist*; by this time under the control of Ezra Pound, its
original feminist concerns were nowhere in sight. The *Freewoman*'s circulation was always small, but its influence upon
feminists and sex radicals in Britain and the United States was far
greater than its low print run might suggest. Years later, Rebecca

West's verdict was that the *Freewoman* had had 'an immense effect on its time'.[61]

Dora Marsden, born in 1882, was the main force behind the original paper.[62] She came from an impoverished middle-class one-parent family (her father, a mill owner, had been affected by the recession, and deserted his wife and five children when Dora was eight). She had become a pupil teacher at thirteen, a university student in Manchester at eighteen, and later the head of a teacher-training college. She had been a suffragette, indeed a paid organizer of the WSPU, but at the paper's opening she saw herself as a feminist anarchist individualist. Politically she had much in common with the feminist members of the Legitimation League; the League had long disbanded (in 1898), but several of its former members occasionally wrote for the new journal. Contributors of articles and letters included many types of feminist, socialist and anarchist, such as socialist and radical suffragist Ada Nield Chew,[63] Teresa Billington-Greig (another ex-WSPU paid organizer), Rebecca West and Stella Browne (both of whom were socialist feminists), Fabian novelist H.G. Wells, homosexual activist Edward Carpenter, and anarchists Guy Aldred and Rose Witcop.

Dora's dissatisfaction with suffrage politics was forcefully conveyed in a number of scathing attacks on the militancy of the WSPU and the autocracy of the Pankhursts. To Dora, the paper was concerned with *real* emancipation: '. . . what [woman] may become. Our interest is in the Freewoman herself, her psychology, philosophy, morality and achievements.'[64] She saw women *themselves* as responsible for their emancipation – an emancipation held back in part by women's own cowardice. Women must give up the protection of men and take their place in the world as breadwinners; with the re-design of housing, the introduction of nurseries, the collectivization of cooking and cleaning, even those with children would be able to go out to work.

The journal published various articles on women's waged work, housework, motherhood, the suffrage movement and theories of art and literature, but it was soon devoting more and more space, especially in its lengthy correspondence, to the discussion of sex, morality and marriage. The advent of the

Freewoman might have been 'phenomenal' (to quote Dora Marsden) in relation to the discussion of sex, but the nature of debate was a mixture of old and new, rooted in past feminist concerns and explanations but developing new ideas and formulations, especially in the esoteric writings of Dora Marsden. Sex as 'naturally' heterosexual was still implicitly assumed and lesbianism was barely mentioned. Contributors continued to raise many of the same problems that had concerned feminists over the past thirty years. There were arguments over birth control, the inevitability or otherwise of prostitution, the problems with the present marriage system, the possible weapon of a birth strike by women to force the granting of the vote, the demand for male purity. Most contributors agreed that, ideally, sex was not an uncontrollable physical urge, indiscriminate in its object; most were opposed to promiscuity. All upheld a woman's right to control her body and fertility.

In February 1912 *The Freewoman* announced that 'Freewoman discussion circles', as they came to be called, had been proposed by several members. Within a few months they were springing up around the country.[65] The first meeting of London's 'Freewoman discussion circle' was held in April at the International Suffrage shop in the Strand. Dora Marsden expected twelve to fifteen people, but nearly a hundred turned up, squeezing themselves into a room meant for a meeting half the size. Dora addressed the second meeting, a fortnight later, on 'the Evolutionary Meaning of the Freewoman'. At the third meeting, which continued to be very crowded, ten rules were drawn up by which the discussion circle was to abide. The Circle was to meet fortnightly, with annual membership at five shillings paid in two instalments.[66] At the close of each session (a session seems to have been about three months), members were to elect a working committee, including a secretary, treasurer and programme committee. The meeting voted in Barbara Low, a well-known psychologist, as the circle's first secretary.

Other meetings included talks from the anarchist Guy Aldred on 'Sex Oppression and the Way Out'; the 'way out' was through an overturning of the existing social system, including the family. The subsequent debate was so animated that a follow-up meeting was arranged. Another speaker was Mrs Havelock Ellis (Edith Lees) who discussed 'Eugenics and Ideals'; 'ideals' including women's eugenical breeding, upon which the health of the nation depended, a position strongly opposed by the anti-eugenists present. In September 1912 Dr Charles Drysdale discussed 'Neo-Malthusianism' and in October Miss Rona Robinson and Mrs Alice Melvin (Secretary for the Promotion of Co-operative Housekeeping and House Service) argued for 'The Abolition of Domestic Drudgery' through the setting up of 'Co-operative Colonies'. Other meetings included papers on 'Freedom', 'Some Problems of Celibacy', 'Prostitution' and 'Reform of the Divorce Laws'.

Rebecca West was also a contributor to the Freewoman circle. She read a paper on 'Interpretation of Life' about duality between men and women, God and man. Rebecca West was born Cicely Fairfield in 1892, the youngest daughter of an unsuccessful Irish journalist.[67] Her father left her mother when Cicely was eight (in this and her impoverished middle-class background Rebecca West was similar to Dora Marsden). The Fairfields – Scottish mother and three daughters – moved to Edinburgh, where all three daughters became socialists and suffragists. Cicely ('Cissie') wrote a letter to the *Scotsman* on women's suffrage when only fourteen, and sold *Votes for Women*. The Fairfields moved back to London and bought a house in Hampstead Garden Suburb. Cicely, at nineteen, started reviewing books for the *Freewoman*, but took the pen-name 'Rebecca West' (from Ibsen's play *Rosmersholm*) to spare her mother: the *Freewoman* 'had such a bad name for its candour that I was forbidden to read it by my family'.[68]

Rebecca West's biographer Victoria Glendinning mentions that she was 'much preoccupied by the plight of a penniless pregnant unmarried friend in the Freewoman Circle'.[69] This is likely to have been Françoise Lafitte, a regular circle attender. Françoise, born in France in 1886, was the daughter of an architect fallen on hard times. She taught at a school in England from 1906 to 1910, returned to France, but came back the following year to escape her mother's attempts to marry her off. She was a feminist and pacifist and lived briefly in a Tolstoyan colony, set up by two *Freewoman* contributors.[70] In September 1912 she met American Syndicalist John Collier, fell in love and went to live with him in a free union. The relationship quickly proved disastrous and she left, but not before becoming pregnant.[71]

By this time Françoise was attending the Freewoman discussion circle, which she described later as

carried on in a manner befitting human beings rather than hooligans. These meetings were naturally opened to both sexes, and . . . one felt there was a more fundamental equality between men and women than in the world at large, or in the ranks of the Socialists and the Suffragettes.[72]

She seems to have enjoyed the discussion circle more than Rebecca West who described it as 'too like being in church'.[73] At one meeting Barbara Low gave a paper on 'What Women Want'; this generated such lively discussion that a follow-up talk on the same subject was proposed. Françoise volunteered to speak, giving a passionate plea for the endowment of motherhood by the State:

Women may claim children without a man, in spite of man, apart from his so-called chivalry, which feeds her and her little children only to keep her enslaved.[74]

The talk was all the more heartfelt given Françoise's predicament as a single pregnant woman. Françoise made great friends with Ruth Slate who she met at the Freewoman circle. Ruth thought her 'a second Olive Schreiner', partly because she was 'less bound by sense of female propriety and "humility"'.[75] In 1913 Françoise and Ruth got a flat together in Notting Hill and Françoise's son was born in August. After the war, Françoise became the partner of Havelock Ellis.

Sex and Reproduction

Françoise Lafitte may have been keen to talk about the practicality of surviving as an unmarried mother, but generally the debate about reproduction in the pages of the *Freewoman* was more abstract. *Freewoman* contributors, many concerned for sexual relationships to become more spiritual and more *meaningful*, sought to understand the 'true' purpose of human sexuality. This inevitably included a consideration of the relationship of sex to reproduction. Some assumed that the sexual instinct for *both* sexes was a 'reproductive instinct', and that any other deployment of sex was unnatural and immoral. This position was rooted, of course, in the Judaeo–Christian formulation that sex must be 'purposive': for procreation alone. Yet this view was presented with a new dimension, namely as an argument against the imposition of male sexual demands on women other than when they both desired a child. It was also a view which sanctified sex as sacred and consensual. Jane Craig, for example, announced that

> the Freewoman . . . with a clear understanding of sex . . . will rescue the marvel of creation in the continuance of the race from the plane of the present general sensuality to that of reverence.[76]

To many of the *Freewoman* feminists, however, sex was more than simply reproductive.[77] (This did not prompt a discussion of sex between women, however.) To socialist and feminist Isabel Leatham, sex needed to be *conceptually* separated from reproduction:

> I certainly hope that Freewomen will not enter upon their sex relationship for any such conscious purpose as that of reproduction, but rather that they will find in passionate love between man and woman, even if that be transient, the only sanction for sex intimacy.[78]

Dora Marsden took an extreme position:

> It is surely a fallacy to hold that sex is primarily experienced with the motive of continuing the race. From the first protozoa up through the scale of life, it has been experienced for its own satisfaction.[79]

Indeed, she saw reproduction as purely incidental! a position quite at variance to the Darwinian functional view of sex. 'A Grandmother' saw the non-reproductive aspect of sex, which she termed the human 'love problem', as superior to its reproductive aspect, the animal 'parenthood problem'. She warned: 'Let us beware of allowing [the] more prosaic animal side of the sex-relationship to eclipse the other, which is human and spiritual'.[80] Thus, in stark contrast to those who saw procreative sex as its only moral (as well as natural) function, she characterized it as the 'animal' and baser side of sex. This also implicitly entailed viewing sex as working on two different *levels*: the physical and the mental, moral or spiritual (different feminists used different terms). One correspondent suggested that there were three possible levels, with women first attaining 'the material sexual level, with children of the flesh'; while most women remained at this level, some attained the second and third levels – the levels of the 'psychic' and the 'spiritual' – the levels of 'passion'.[81]

Constructing a Language

What was meant by 'passion'? Feminists had for a long time perceived that one of the difficulties in talking about sex, indeed in *understanding* sex, was the lack of an adequate language. (One could add that things are not much better today.) In 1897, an article by 'Ess Tee' in the *Adult* entitled 'Wanted: A New Dictionary', had complained that

> there are only two forms of speech or language in connection with sex matters: the seriously scientific, as used by the medical profession, anatomists and lawyers – technical terms and Latin phrases; and . . . the bald, rugged phrases of the gutter and the market-place . . . To raise the discussion of sex matters to a higher plane, a pressing necessity is the formulation of a vocabulary which shall enable ordinary people to discuss in set, clear cut and clean phrases the sexual thoughts, doubts and desires which arise in the mind of almost every human being.[82]

Fifteen years later, the lack of an adequate language to discuss sex was similarly bemoaned in the *Freewoman*; as Dora Marsden expressed it: 'The failure of language to advance parallel with the new differentiations of thought.'[83] Stella Browne felt that a lack of language was a greater problem for women:

> The realities of women's sexual life have been greatly obscured by the lack of any sexual vocabulary. While her brother has often learned all the slang of the street before adolescence, the conventionally 'decently brought-up' girl, of the upper and middle classes, has no terms to define many of her sensations and experiences.[84]

Presumably she did not think that the conventionally 'decently brought-up' girl knew anything of 'the seriously scientific' language mentioned by 'Ess Tee'.

Dora Marsden pointed to another difficulty: even with the inadequate language available to discuss sex, there was disagreement over meanings. This very problem had arisen in the Freewoman discussion circle:

> We are met with misunderstanding and fruitless argument, for a word, as one man uses it, means a thing different from that which it connotes to another. The value of words is not constant.

She proposed 'the gradual compiling of a "Select Glossary"'.[85] To Nora Kiernan, differences of meaning were contingent upon one's sex. Rather than discuss religion (which had been the 'utterly irrelevant' issue brought up at the Freewoman discussion circle she had just attended):

> We need to discuss . . . questions that we, as men and women, are as yet at variance, such as, for instance, the questions of love, passion and sex, which so many of us women do not conceive of in the same sense as men do.[86]

This concern that men and women did not speak the same language had arisen twenty-five years earlier, in the Men and Women's Club. Maria Sharpe had commented to Pearson: 'How many different languages we all talk',[87] while Emma Brooke had informed him that he had misunderstood her paper: 'The misunderstanding lies where, between men and women, it always does lie – in the use of the same words with different meanings.'[88]

That Nora Kiernan noted variance on the question of sex did not relate simply to a gender difference but also to a linguistic confusion. An examination of various kinds of writing by feminists, sexologists and others which touched on sexuality in the period 1885–1918, indicates that the meaning of sex as 'sexual

274

intercourse'/'penetration' was only just starting to be used. Indeed, the early twentieth-century equivalent of the Oxford English Dictionary, edited by Sir James Murray[89] (the volume for Q–Sh having been compiled in 1912–14) does not register 'sexual intercourse' as one of the meanings of sex, the primary meaning being the distinction between males and females. I would suggest that the exploration of sex as something other than simply physical and reproductive was easier before the *fixing* in popular speech of 'sex' as 'sexual intercourse' (and 'sexual intercourse' as 'penetration'). Logically, sex as other than heterosexual should also have been conceivable, but for many feminists, this does not seem to have been the case. Interestingly, the term 'heterosexuality', and of course 'homosexuality', had only relatively recently entered the language, both invented in 1869.[90] But the term 'heterosexuality' was simply not used in popular speech before the First World War. This did not mean, however, that it was any the less assumed.

The different meanings of the word 'passion' may also have helped in thinking about sex as non-physical. Nora Kiernan gave the *Freewoman* examples of these different meanings:

> As a child I learnt of the 'passion' of Jesus Christ, and nearly in the same breath was told my 'passions' would lead me to hell ... I have heard men describe themselves as 'passionate', meaning thereby that they were susceptible to the solicitations of the average prostitute. Another man ... described 'passion' as the feeling he would have for a woman with whom he was in perfect agreement – mentally and physically.[91]

Sir James Murray's dictionary confirmed there were many different and contrasting meanings to the noun 'passion', including 'the sufferings of Jesus Christ on the Cross'; 'a vehement, commanding or overpowering emotion'; 'amorous feeling; strong sexual affection; love'; 'sexual desire or impulse'.[92] I would suggest that, although the dictionary definitions today are almost identical, passion as 'sexual desire' is a far more common, everyday usage than it was in the early twentieth century. Indeed, some feminists saw the concept 'passion' as standing in opposition to 'sexual desire', or at least in opposition to lust and sensuality.

Thus, Dora Marsden, for example, saw passion as largely a spiritual experience, not

> the bare counterfeit of passion [which] betrays passion – sensuality, lust, the tippling with sensation, the snacking at sex, the dreary, monotonous sound of one note in sex.

Passion was nothing to do with promiscuity, and '[t]o anyone who had ever got anything out of sexual passion, the aggravated emphasis ... bestowed on physical sexual intercourse is more absurd than wicked'.[93]

Writing elsewhere at approximately the same time, Lucy Re-Bartlett expressed similar views:

> In the minds of many people there reigns a great confusion regarding sensuality and passion; all too often ... considered as one thing ... While sensuality is the force which ... degrades humanity, passion in its nobler forms is, at this stage of evolution, the force which best can elevate it ... While sensuality is of the body only, passion is also of the mind and soul.[94]

The similarity of ideas is striking, yet other aspects of the two women's feminism were very different. While Dora Marsden was an anarchist, pro 'free love', and by this time highly critical of feminism's concentration on the vote, Lucy Re-Bartlett was opposed to 'free love' and an ardent supporter of the WSPU.

Most feminists had a positive definition of passion.[95] They tended to use the concept and its ambiguity of meaning to talk about ideal feelings and experiences which were 'above' the purely physical. Slippage between meanings facilitated the exploration of new ideas concerning sex – new possibilities and imaginings. Feminists used the concept of passion to explore the potential for other states of being – states of *pleasure* – which were not inevitably rooted in *physical* sensation.

Dora Marsden's definition of 'passion' was not only primarily non-physical, but it also included the non-sexual. She described the experiences of 'a feminist rebel' (herself?) imprisoned for her beliefs (Dora was herself imprisoned when a member of the WSPU):

Shut up for the night in the cell, suffering acute physical pain, with the quiet came an extraordinary sense of 'spirit' expansion . . . The whole was suffused with the consciousness of calm, radiant, *abiding* joy. The entire experience *lasted*, how long cannot be stated, but it was extended enough to appear 'long' . . . The incident described, although arising from passion inspired by a Cause, is not in our opinion in any essential feature different from what might be inspired by human 'love'. It has, indeed, features which immediately suggest similarities with the exaltation of momentary semi-physical sex-experience. The chief difference would lie in the prolongation of time length of the experience given, as compared with that of sex.[96]

A correspondent to the *Freewoman* signing herself 'M.S.', and declaring that she had been in a very happy free union for the past seventeen years, described a similar experience, although with her it was 'inspired by passionate love – not sexual, though tinged with sexual desire'. She continued:

I was in rather a nervous condition, having been unable to take food or to sleep for several days, when one night . . . I flung myself across my bed and . . . the expansion suddenly began. I not only *saw* the vibration of the atmosphere, but, in it, the ethereal form of the beloved.

She was certain that 'no sexual act can be compared with it'.[97] The pleasure and joy described by both writers were presented as experiences superior to the pleasures not simply of sexual intercourse, but, it seems, of any kind of sex at all; to 'M.S.' the experience was simply incomparable, to Dora its superiority lay in its 'abiding' quality, as opposed to the relative brevity of sex.

The fluidity of language surrounding sexuality, especially the richness of the concept 'passion', allowed these feminists freely to describe and discuss pleasurable feelings and sensations without feeling compelled to label them as orgasmic, hallucinogenic, or simply mad. Such feelings were not only vindicated, but viewed as of a higher order than the 'baseness' of pure physicality, lust and 'snacking at sex'. Yet for a woman to feel able to value the *physical* side of sexuality, and to claim the *right* to be sexual in all its physicality as well as its sublimity, many of the younger generation of feminists turned to the new sexology.

Using Sexology

The two polarized groupings of feminists discussed by Linda Gordon and Ellen DuBois – the sexual protectors and the sexual explorers – are, according to Sheila Jeffreys in her *The Spinster and Her Enemies*, present on the pages of the *Freewoman*, although her political sympathies differ from Gordon and DuBois in viewing the 'true' feminists as those who were critical of male sexuality, as opposed to 'that small group of feminists who had recently embraced sex reform'.[98] She sees the latter as betraying feminism in their use of sexology. But this is to ignore the fact that all kinds of feminists in this period, including those highly critical of male sexuality, drew on sexology. They did so selectively as part of their *own* project: the exploration of what sex meant and could mean for women and men.

What was this selective use of sexology? One example was the citing of sexological writings by a number of *Freewoman* contributors in their disavowal of female sexual passivity. For example, 'A Would-be Freewoman' (a clergyman's wife, who wanted to leave her husband) approvingly quoted the idea of sex reformer Iwan Bloch that women were sexually different from men, but their 'sexual sensibility' was at least as great. She was also adamant, as was Stella Browne, that there was enormous sexual variation among women. But her concern with a woman's right to be sexual did not blind her to sexual danger, especially 'the husband [who] may insist on his "rights", no matter what her feelings of repugnance or distaste may be'.[99] Feminists also drew on sexology in their discussion of what constituted *legitimate* sex. Masturbation, for example, was discussed in the *Freewoman* in two contexts: as a valid practice for single women, and as an alternative to prostitution for men. Stella Browne wondered how many single women entirely abstained from those 'various forms of onanism' which Havelock Ellis termed 'auto-eroticism'. She believed that 'without having recourse to their aid, many women would find abstinence from normal sexual relations impossible'. In other words, she was claiming that most of those women who saw themselves as chaste were in fact engaged in practices which 'constitute sexual indulgence just as truly as do normal sexual relations'.[100]

Masturbation was also raised by a respondent to Dr Wrench's article on Japanese prostitution – the one which I suggested would have so outraged Olive Schreiner – in which he claimed that sex in brothels was turned into 'an art'. One of the furious responses was from E.M. Watson (who declared herself a woman). She lamented:

> Oh, how sick we are of men's 'necessity', and all his disloyal excuses for the exploiting of womanhood! . . . Is purity really impossible to men? . . . And to those to whom sex is an obsession, is there no possibility of their indulging it alone, without obtruding their 'necessities' upon women?[101]

The debate continued along two tracks. On the one hand, there was an attack on, and defence of, state-regulated prostitution, with Amy Stovgaard-Pedersen and Stella Browne putting the case against (drawing on sexologist Forel's book, *The Sexual Question*), and Dr Wrench for.[102] On the other hand, there was a discussion of 'self-abuse' (masturbation) as an alternative to prostitution for men. Dr Wrench accused E.M. Watson of recommending this practice (her reference to 'indulging it [sex obsession] alone').[103] She replied that she did not 'recommend' it, but thought it far preferable to male abuse of others. She also referred to Professor Forel, in particular to his claim that masturbation was harmless.[104] There were many other examples of feminists who, though drawing on sexology, were, like E.M. Watson, critical of male sexual practices.

Reading letters in the *Freewoman* one senses a great thirst for 'knowledge' about sexual issues. Readers wrote in with information concerning where to buy the works of Ellis, Forel, Bloch and others, and offers to lend their copies (often in the original German) to anyone interested, although they had frequent difficulties in getting hold of these works.[105] In their keenness to discuss sex, its role and potential, many *Freewoman* contributors appear to have read as much sexology as they were able to lay their hands on. It was the only current discourse offering a set of ideas with which women could explore the possibility of being sexual *agents* as opposed to eternal victims. They may not have agreed with all they read, but many of them were determined to take from it anything which appeared useful in their pursuit of sexual self-expression. As we shall see, this could unfortunately be at the expense of other feminists.

Differences within the Freewoman

It might appear from the discussion so far that there was much agreement among feminist contributors to the *Freewoman* over the question of sex. Most of them shared a common ideal of spiritualized sexual relations between men and women, drawing upon a notion of passion to describe a form of sexual encounter in which the physical aspect was minimal, if not non-existent. This ideal relationship between the sexes was envisaged as being based on love, commitment, monogamy and mutual respect. But although there was no straightforward feminist polarity, there were certainly one or two issues which radically divided the *Freewoman*'s female contributors. The issues arose in relation to what constituted the desired feminist morality. Early on in the life of the *Freewoman*, Dora Marsden declared herself an advocate of the 'New Morality' as opposed to the 'Old Morality' of 'Indissoluble Monogamy'. The 'New Morality' of the 'free-woman' favoured 'limited monogamy' and 'free unions': monogamous relationships that could be freely entered and freely left. The 'Indissoluble Monogamy' of current marriage had 'maintained itself by means of the support of men's hypocrisy, the spinster's dumb resignation, the prostitute's unsightly degradation and the married woman's monopoly and satisfaction'.[106] No *Freewoman* contributor favoured the 'Old Morality' of 'Indissoluble Monogamy', but many disagreed on the definition of the 'freewoman', the implications of 'limited monogamy' and the negative portrayal conveyed in Dora's mention of the 'spinster's dumb resignation'. They also disagreed on the acceptability of birth control. These issues of dispute related in essence to the question of the desirability of *physical* relations and their frequency on the one hand, and the exercise of sexual self-control on the other.

Debating Chastity and the Spinster in the Freewoman

Probably one of the greatest disagreements between feminist contributors to the *Freewoman*, and indeed feminists generally, related to the evaluation of chastity. As in the late nineteenth century, the debate over chastity in the *Freewoman* was frequently linked to reflections – positive and negative – on the spinster and her sexual status. What had changed was a tightening up of the battle lines: a joust between chastity as morally superior versus chastity as sexually deficient. The journal's first issue contained a savage, ironic? and anonymous attack: ' "The Spinster" by One':

> I write of the High Priestess of Society. Not of the mothers of sons, but of her barren sister, the withered tree, the acidulous vestal under whose pale shadow we chill and whiten, of the spinster I write.

The writer went on to introduce the now familiar spectre of the sexually frustrated and sickening celibate:

> The Spinster does not overcome Sex as a saint overcomes Sin . . . Driven inward, denied its rightful, ordained fulfilment, the instinct becomes defused . . . If prurience has slain its thousands, chastity has slain its tens of thousands.[107]

By the following week the article had elicited a couple of responses,[108] but the debate on chastity got truly underway (and was to continue weekly over a period of three months) when the American socialist Upton Sinclair asserted that it was among celibate women 'that modern psychologists discover the greatest proportion of nervous disorders, anaemics and insanities.'[109] In reply, women wrote of the value of sexual self-control. E.M. Watson, unlike many advocates of celibacy, did not assume women to be less sexual than men – merely better at controlling their desires. But she thought the so-called 'suffering' of male celibates was simply an argument to force married women to 'sacrifice themselves . . . daily'.[110] Miss Kathlyn Oliver, suffragist and ex-secretary of the Domestic Workers Union, declared: 'I am neither a prude nor a Puritan, but I am an apostle of self-restraint in sex matters. What is it that raises us above the brute level but the exercise of self-restraint?' She wrote that she was nearly thirty, unmarried, had always practised abstinence, and, challenging the health aspect, said she enjoyed the best of health: 'My married women friends, on the contrary, have always some complaint.'[111]

In the next issue of the *Freewoman*, E.M. Watson and Kathlyn Oliver were sharply rebuked by 'a New Subscriber', adamant that they should not 'make their temperamental coldness into a rigid standard for others'.[112] Kathlyn Oliver was indignant; wrongly assuming 'a New Subscriber' to be male (she later revealed herself to be Stella Browne), Kathlyn claimed to speak for most women in declaring

> until they love, the idea of the sexual relationship seldom enters their thoughts. Personally, I never desired the sex relationship until I 'fell in love' at about 20 . . . We couldn't marry and from then till now I have had to crush and subdue the sex feeling.[113]

'A New Subscriber' was scathing. Refusing the claims of moral worth, she dismissively replied: 'It will be an unspeakable catastrophe if our richly complex Feminist Movement . . . falls under the domination of sexually deficient and disappointed women.'[114] Kathlyn Oliver replied in fury,[115] but 'New Subscriber' finally silenced her with an accusation of cowardice:

> Let those women who . . . will not try to enjoy their elemental human rights, refrain from unmeasured public attacks on the others who have the courage of their desires as well as their convictions.[116]

The struggle over the moral status of the spinster being waged in the *Freewoman* reflected a wider feminist debate. On the one hand, there were those such as Christabel Pankhurst and Cicely Hamilton for whom the chaste spinster, seen as superior in health and morals to her married counterpart, was the key to women's liberation. On the other hand, in opposition to this claim of superiority was mobilized the view of the spinster as 'sexually deficient and disappointed'. Stella Browne and others deployed sexological ideas to assert their right to be sexual, or rather heterosexual, but they did so via the condemnation of those women who wished to disavow such a right.

Self-Control in Marriage, the 'freewoman', and 'artificial sterilization'

While the concept of self-control was central to the defence of chastity, it was also applied to the discussion of ideal marital relations. Self-control within marriage was referred to as 'continence': infrequent sexual intercourse with lengthy periods of abstinence. Unsurprisingly, those who advocated chastity for single people tended to advocate continence for the married. To quote E.M. Watson:

> The free woman ... will seek to teach the man the restraint that Nature has taught her to impose upon herself ... To this end she will seek to tame in herself as well as her lover the mere mating instinct ... she will seek to raise marriage to the standard of a spiritual and intellectual as well as a physical union.[117]

If a 'freewoman' was defined by Dora Marsden as a feminist in favour of limited monogamy and free unions, there were many who took issue with this definition and claimed her as an advocate of self-control. For example, E.M. Watson assumed that teaching man 'restraint' was central to what being a 'free-woman' meant, and Kathlyn Oliver, in asking rhetorically: 'How can we possibly be Free Women if, like the majority of men, we become the slaves of our lower appetites?'[118] clearly saw the *freedom* of the 'freewoman' as a freedom not only from unsolicited sexual advances, but also from the 'bestial' lower instinct of sexual excess – freedom from the 'beast in man'. There were other feminist contributors who thought like-wise.[119]

Self-control in marriage was also seen as a 'natural' method of birth control: infrequent sexual intercourse except when a child was desired. As I have suggested, many women, including feminists, were opposed to contraception because they feared that the use of such appliances reduced a woman to the status of a prostitute, was possibly harmful (which is what most doctors claimed), and, as Mrs Sherwen expressed it, facilitated 'the indulgence of uncontrolled passions'.[120] In addition to total abstinence, 'natural' methods of fertility control included partial abstinence, in the sense of intercourse only during the so-called 'safe period' (which I have mentioned was wrongly calculated as mid-month). Although there was disagreement as to whether coitus interruptus and coitus reservatus (intercourse without ejaculation) were 'natural' methods, there was one kind of coitus reservatus declared to be a spiritualized form of sexual intercourse, entailing heightened self-control. Developed by John Humphrey Noyes at his nineteenth-century American Oneida Colony, the method involved the man supposedly reabsorbing the sperm back into the urethra, thereby retaining the 'vital fluid'.[121] American feminist physician and spiritualist Alicé B. Stockham called her own version of this technique 'Karezza', writing a book on the subject in 1896. She argued that this method was of special benefit to women in that it both avoided unwanted pregnancy, and, through the prolonging of intercourse and its experience at a *spiritual* plane, it satisfied women's sexual and emotional needs. In contrast, the 'ordinary' method of sexual intercourse was hasty and spasmodic and left the woman unsatisfied. With Karezza, the husband needed to improve his powers of self-control, so that

> through the power of the will, and loving thoughts, the final crisis is not reached ... During a lengthy period of perfect control, the whole being of each is merged into the other, an exquisite exaltation experienced ... the thrill of passion for either party will go beyond a pleasurable exchange ... In a course of an hour the physical tension subsides, the spiritual exaltation increases.

She held that women should dictate the timing of intercourse and that they would be likely to prefer it only at intervals of a few weeks. She believed that the method 'removed all vestiges of the old idea of man's dominion over woman'.[122]

'Free union' couple Mary and Stanley Randolph wrote enthusiastically to the *Freewoman* about this technique.[123] The method was widely publicized in the United States, but it is impossible to know how many people actually attempted it either there or in this country. As Linda Gordon points out, however, whatever the obvious advantages for the woman, a technique which 'demanded a suppression of gratification by the male would not seem destined for great popularity'.[124] This method was possibly used by the *Freewoman* feminist correspondent E.M. Watson and her partner, however; her references to 'self-control' may refer not simply to abstinence, but also to the practice of Karezza. It all depends on whether or not E.M. Watson (who, as I have noted, declared herself a woman) was in fact Edith M. Watson, Women's Freedom League court correspondent. When Edith Watson wrote for the *Vote* and other papers she signed herself 'Edith M. Watson' or 'E.M.W.'. I have no direct evidence of her familiarity with the *Freewoman*, but she was a close friend of Nina Boyle, who certainly knew the *Freewoman* because she sent it a letter on one occasion; Edith was also an acquaintance of Rebecca West, a regular contributor to the paper. Edith married Ernest Watson, a socialist, on 1 February 1912 (the date, incidentally, of E.M. Watson's first letter to the *Freewoman*) but had been living with him beforehand. In her unpublished autobiography, she reflects back on their early sex life, referring to Ernest as 'Eustace':

> Eustace's lovemaking was as lengthy as many of his arguments. Indeed . . . I was still, at 22, [she was 23 when E.M. Watson's first letter appeared in the *Freewoman*] ignorant of the exact nature of the sex act and the feelings it could engender, of its ordinary course and completion. I had no idea that Eustace's long lovemaking without any culmination was anything but what he said it was, self-control. He prided himself on keeping his feelings under control – a Yogi had nothing on him.

It does sound as if Ernest/Eustace had been engaging in the Karezza practice, although she gives no name to his method of birth control. She continued:

> One reason he gave for this self-control was that we could not have children, not being married, and that in any case he was not going to bring a child INTO THE WORLD [sic] to be cannon fodder for the next war.

(He conceded on the child issue. He married Edith and they had one child, Bernard.) The 'prolonged loveplay' made her 'blissfully happy', but in the end it wore her out: 'I lost my health and had no energy.'[125]

The Place of Physical Sex

While what one might call the 'old school' of feminism prioritized freedom *from* undesired sex, and from lustfulness in both men and themselves as women, the 'new school' – those embracing the idea of the 'new morality' – were more concerned to gain women's freedom *to have* sexual relations, for women to develop their sexual potential. But there were also important similarities between the two schools. Not only did both tend to hold spiritualized sex as the ideal, but ambivalence towards *physical* sex was also evident among some, possibly many, of the 'new moralists'. Although in one article Dora Marsden argued for the importance for women of satisfying 'the hunger of the body',[126] in another she wrote:

> It is the prolongation of the mental experience which is desired . . . the physical desire . . . was the whole of sex in the sub-human sphere, and . . . will be eliminated in the super-human . . . we have it only in the form of a remnant in the human.[127]

In her description of the imprisoned feminist whose 'acute physical pain' turned to 'calm, radiant, *abiding* joy', she suggests that the sensation was essentially the *same* as that inspired by human love. Despite her growing hostility towards militant suffragism, she did not deny that bodily sacrifice in the form of the suffragette's hunger strike could be a rewarding, 'spiritual' experience. Neither did she reduce the experience to being simply sexual. On the contrary, she pointed to similarity not equivalence. She was as yet uncertain as to how sex was to be defined, let alone experienced. She did, however, believe in variation, for although claiming that 'with passion sex-satisfaction is primarily mental', she added that it 'depends upon opportunity and temperament' as to whether it is also physical.[128]

Even Stella Browne was not as clear-cut on the need for

physical sex as her attack on the spinster suggests. She did not write about sex as 'spiritual' but she did see it as 'largely mental and imaginative'. She validated the role of fantasy over actual physical contact:

> Any direct external stimulation is much rarer among young girls than among boys . . . But day-dreaming, the production of a higher degree of enjoyment, by means of vague yet delightful imaginings, is the most exquisite pleasure, and deepest secret of many imaginative and sensitive girls.[129]

Yet this was about *girls*; on older women she had this to say: 'After twenty-five, the woman who has neither husband nor lover . . . is suffering mentally and bodily.' More than Dora Marsden she insisted on a woman's right to *be sexual*:

> The sexual experience is the right of every human being not hopelessly afflicted in mind or body and should be entirely a matter of free choice and personal preference, untainted by bargain or compulsion.[130]

Three years later she was demanding: 'Let [women] set their own requirements, and boldly claim a share of life and erotic experience, as perfectly consistent with their own self-respect.'[131]

In the nineteenth century the chief ideological polarity between women had been between the married woman and the prostitute – the respectable and the despised. Now a new and additional configuration was being born between the *sexualized* married woman and the *sexless* spinster. It was a configuration instigated by sexology, medicine and the heightened concern with 'breeding'. But in their attempt to claim a new identity, it was also drawn upon by some of the 'new moralist' feminists. That these feminists appeared only able to claim their right to be sexual through distancing from – even condemning – that which they were not (the 'sexless' spinster), constituted part of the 'act of alienation' mentioned by Carroll Smith-Rosenberg in her analysis of the effects of using sexological ideas. This new claim to a female sexual identity implicitly assumed the norm of heterosexuality. Yet there were also women in this period drawing on sexology in order to develop an identity as lesbian.

A LESBIAN IDENTITY IN THE MAKING

Feminism, Homosexuality and Lesbianism

Many feminists appear to have had limited knowledge of homo-sexuality and lesbianism – they were familiar with neither the terms nor the practices and identities to which the terms referred. The feminist Evelyn Sharp, although a contributor to the 'Yellow Book' and acquainted with Aubrey Beardsley and his circle, confessed that homosexuality was 'something of which I, in common, I believe, with numbers of my contempor-aries, were entirely ignorant until the Oscar Wilde trial set everybody talking about it in corners'.[132] They might have talked in corners, but feminists were silent in public – as silent as they had been in 1885 about the Labouchère Amendment which had criminalized male homosexuality. Why? There is no indica-tion that feminists either supported or opposed the Labou-chère Amendment, although their silence, along with the silence of social purists such as W.T. Stead, could be read as *tacit* support.

Josephine Butler's response to the trials of Oscar Wilde in 1895 gives a sense of what might have been a widely held position among social purity feminists. She wrote to her son Stanley during the trials:

> Yes, I have heard . . . that the Oscar Wilde madness is spread like a plague through London's fashionable and artistic society . . . I am sorry for sensitive youths with some principle . . . [who are] so corrupted . . . London upper society is simply *rotten* with this vice. What fools people are who worship art and performers and poetry and nonsense in place of God. I think there was more excuse for the Greeks. They had never heard of the pure ethics of Christ.[133]

Butler saw herself as an outsider from the provinces, looking in on corrupt Metropolitan life.[134] Her remarks drew on a wide gamut of definitions and understandings of homosexuality: the older tradition of seeing it as a vice, a mark of Godlessness and as a sign of upper-class decadence; the more recent 'explanation' of homosexuality as a contagious and corrupting disease. It is

possible that many of those involved in the social purity movement saw male homosexuality as simply another aspect of male
bestiality and indiscriminate lust, which, along with a resort to
prostitution, was thought to be especially prevalent among the
upper classes. With Wilde's conviction, however, Josephine
Butler's attitude changed: he became a victim in her eyes and her
Christian compassion took precedence. She wrote to Stanley
again:

> I am so sorry for Oscar Wilde. I dare confess it to you. Most people
> are shocked at one feeling for him. It is such a complete rush down
> to perdition. What must solitary confinement be to such a man? . . .
> I long to be allowed to write him a letter in prison . . . I pray for
> him constantly.[135]

Where was the lesbian in the discussions of homosexuality and
Wilde? The Wilde trials were important in creating a public
image of and for the homosexual: as decadent, artistic, white,
upper class – and male. Soon after the Wilde trials, W.T. Stead
informed Edward Carpenter that 'the existence of Oscar Wildes
and its counterparts in the female sex is very low'. However, in
the next sentence he was contradicting himself:

> The law is absolutely indifferent to any amount of indecent familiar-
> ity taking place between two women . . . the result is that many
> women give themselves up to this kind of thing without any
> consciousness of being wrong.[136]

He may have been right on the latter point, although 'giving
themselves up' hardly seems the appropriate way of putting
it.
Where feminists wrote publicly on lesbianism, which was
extremely rare, they were not usually sympathetic. In 1909 Dr
Mary Scharlieb warned that in adolescence

> girls were apt to form overwhelming and most unhealthy attach-
> ments to each other, or to women of maturer years. Not infre-
> quently, these absorbing friendships are carried beyond the bounds
> of sanity, and form one of the most serious . . . dangers to young
> people.[137]

It was a warning that was to become more and more widespread in the interwar years.[138] Stella Browne, clearly a feminist and a good and supportive friend of 'real' invert Edith Lees Ellis,[139] declared in 1915 that 'I repudiate all wish to slight or deprecate the love-life of the real homosexual'.[140] She was, however, very concerned by the growth of female 'artificial' inversion. It was due, she was sure (unsurprisingly, given her views on chastity) to 'the repression of normal gratification and the segregation of the sexes'. Although condemning of this 'pseudosexuality', she seemed rather unsure of its identification:

> Sometimes its only direct manifestations are quite noncommittal and platonic; but even this incomplete and timid homosexuality can always be distinguished from true affectionate friendship between women, by its jealous, exacting and extravagant tone.[141]

The reason for her extreme hostility is unclear.

Lesbian Feminists, Love and the Language of Sexology: Kathlyn Oliver, Amy Tasker and Edith Lees Ellis

If the majority of feminists did not mention lesbians, while a few did so contemptuously, there were others who were beginning to claim the label of 'invert', 'Uranian' or 'lesbian' for themselves. Ellis argued that many women did not recognize their inversion because they did not see their attraction as sexual.[142] I would suggest that the women who did identify as 'inverts' or 'Uranians' did so for a variety of reasons (including being familiar with the concept), but seeing their attraction as *sexual* was not necessarily the key element in their identification. I have already pointed out how for a woman in the Victorian period to be labelled 'sexual' was to be labelled deviant. By the early twentieth century such an idea was shifting, as is obvious in the ability of the *Freewoman* to talk openly about sex, although the paper's daring was condemned from all sides. It is likely that many lesbians, especially those of the older generation, would still have felt deep ambivalence about accepting a sexual label for their lesbianism, not least because what constituted the 'sexual' was still seen as essentially heterosexual. Clearly there was a great disparity of relationships between women in the past (as, of course, there is in the present), but for many of the women starting to identify as inverts, the one common element was that their attraction was first and foremost one of love and commitment. In this they were similar to women in nineteenth-century romantic friendships; the difference lay with the adoption of a label of identity. Among the Edward Carpenter archives there are several letters written to Carpenter from lesbians about their feelings concerning sex, love and identity. I want to consider here the letters of three feminists who defined themselves as Uranians or inverts: Kathlyn Oliver, Amy Tasker and Edith Lees Ellis.

Kathlyn Oliver, who had regularly written to the *Freewoman* in 1912, wrote to Carpenter three years later with the declaration that she had recently read his book *The Intermediate Sex* 'and it has lately dawned on me that I myself belong to that class'. She wanted his help in getting in touch 'with others of the same temperament'.[143] She wrote that she had never been in love with men, but many times with women. However, she had never experienced sexual desire for either sex until two years ago (1913), when she felt it towards a woman she fell in love with. She had been engaged in her early twenties:

> I liked the man a great deal and I suppose I thought I loved him but when the time came for him to talk of furniture and marriage I backed out. The thought of marriage and all it meant repelled and disgusted me.[144]

As we have seen, in correspondence to the *Freewoman* three years earlier, Kathlyn Oliver had given a very different account to 'A New Subscriber', namely that she had never had sexual desire until she had fallen in love with a man when she was about twenty, but that 'we couldn't marry and from then till now I have had to crush and subdue the sex feeling'. She had also defensively added: 'Perhaps "A New Subscriber" will now concede that I am at least fairly normal.'[145] Presumably her experience the following year of feeling sexual desire for the woman she fell in love with led her to reassess her former view of herself. But she did not yet have an explanation or theory with which to make sense of her experience:

> I couldn't quite understand my feeling towards her. I just concluded that I had a dash of the masculine (I have been told more than once that I have a masculine mind).[146]

She told Carpenter that everything had become clear when she had been introduced to his book a few months ago by the woman with whom she was currently in love. (Kathlyn had met this woman through advertising in 'a little pacifist and socialist paper' for correspondence with 'any lonely woman rebel'. Unfortunately I have been unable to trace this paper.) Carpenter's book 'somehow made me realize that I was more closely related to the intermediate sex than I had hitherto imagined'.[147] This implies that she had heard of the 'intermediate sex' before, but had not seen herself in that light. (Carpenter mentions the 'intermediate sex' in other writings, and Kathlyn told him that she had long been an admirer of his work.) Her lack of 'recognition' is perhaps unsurprising, given that Carpenter presented Uranians as predominantly male.

Amy Tasker, another feminist and self-defined Uranian, wrote Carpenter a heart-rending account of her desperate situation. She had, she said, always felt different from other girls, dressing in boys' clothes and following boys' pursuits. But longing to be like other girls, she became engaged at eighteen although, like Kathlyn Oliver, 'the thought of marriage was mental and physical torture, all my being told me that marriage with a man would be a heinous crime'. Her plea for higher education had been denied to her by her parents and she was now trapped, aged forty-five, looking after her aged mother. The two women she had loved had left her in the end for men, the 'woman of her dreams' having become engaged a month ago. If she had had her own home and income, 'my Love she would have been mine to her life's end', but 'terror of the future has taken her from me', and Amy Tasker was left with 'unspeakable pain'.[148]

Kathlyn Oliver and Amy Tasker had similar attitudes towards their feelings of sexual desire. They both felt it was acceptable because it was never *merely* physical. To Amy:

My sense of Love . . . is a soul-Love, the highest and best in me . . . and passion is but an attribute, passion exists owing to earthly environment and the yearning to be one life . . . I know nothing of mere physical attraction.[149]

When Kathlyn thought of the woman she loved:

I have physical desire . . . I don't feel that this desire is at all immoral or degrading. It is not merely or chiefly physical desire, I can't bear the idea of losing her friendship, even if the physical desire is never gratified.

She feared that this was likely because 'I am afraid that the attachment is one sided'. The world might see a physical relationship between two of the same sex as an 'unspeakable crime', wrote Kathlyn, but until women ceased to be 'in economic slavery to man', it could never be as degrading as 'normal' sexual relationships. Yet Kathlyn was contradictory about her sexual feelings. She had said she first felt sexual desire two years ago and that

when alone with [this woman she loved] I had a strong desire to caress and fondle her, but I am naturally reserved . . . and we never advanced further than the formal handshake.

But her next sentence read: 'I had no sexual desire in connection with her',[150] which both contradicts her statement that this was the woman for whom she first felt sexual desire, as well as implying that a desire to caress and fondle was *not* sexual. Until she had a way of understanding and naming herself (as a Uranian), which two years ago she had not yet possessed, it was only in seeing herself as having 'a dash of the masculine' that she could permit her feelings to be seen as *sexual*. Having 'a dash of the masculine' was unlikely to have been experienced as a fixed and totalizing identity, so possessing *sexual* desire might have felt similarly unstable.

Maybe Edith Lees Ellis was an exception in this period in apparently having no ambivalence about the sexual side of her love for women. Edith was a feminist and socialist, active since 1887 in the utopian socialist 'Fellowship of the New Life'.[151] The 'Fellowship' founded a 'Fellowship House' in Doughty Street,

London, in which various Fellowship members, including Edith (and future Labour Prime Minister Ramsay MacDonald), attempted to live collectively. (Later, in her novel *Attainment*, she presented an account of this period of which she remarked: 'Fellowship is Hell.') She was married to Havelock Ellis for twenty-five years, until her death in 1916 from diabetes. For over half of each year they chose to live separately, although were regularly in touch; they both had other sexual relationships. Ellis included Edith in his case studies of female inverts, admitting that he had been largely dependent on her friendship network for his five other cases. When he wrote up his study of Edith (as Miss H) he gave her age as 30, and recounted that although she found the idea of marriage repugnant, she could imagine a man she could love and marry.[152] Edith was 30 in 1891 and she married Ellis in December of that year. Less than a year after marrying Ellis, Edith started an affair with an old friend, referred to as 'Clare' in Ellis's autobiography. Edith subsequently had a succession of passionate relationships with women, the love of her life being Lily, an artist in St Ives, who died suddenly in 1903 from Bright's disease.

Edith felt that the sexual side of loving women was not only morally right but physically *good* for her. Here, in contrast to Kathlyn Oliver and Amy Tasker (or indeed Ellis's other five case studies), she had adopted the new medical emphasis on sexual expression being healthy and necessary; she differed from the vast majority of the medical profession in claiming that where the sexual desire 'naturally' took an 'inverted' form, its expression was equally necessary to health. In *Sexual Inversion*, Ellis reported on Miss H [Edith]: 'The effects of her loving women is distinctly good, she asserts, both spiritually and physically, while repression leads to morbidity and hysteria.'[153] (This is, of course, *Ellis's* account of what Edith said, although the argument is similar to that expressed elsewhere by Edith herself.) Edith was a close friend of Edward Carpenter and in 1905 she told him how much she liked his 'gospel of . . . the joy and the glory of the flesh *as well* as the other'.[154] In a letter to him the following month she reflected: 'I wondered *why* I got headaches . . . and began to think the need of the lusts of the flesh – like wine – was the reason!'[155]

Edith felt that 'homosexual love is morally right when it is really part of a person's nature'.[156] The implication was that if it was not 'really part of a person's nature', it was morally wrong. Here she was following Ellis and others in differentiating true and artificial inversion. In a paper given to the Eugenics Education Society in 1911 (and revised for a woman-only talk in the USA in 1915) she again made the distinction. The appeal for homosexuals and lesbians of such a distinction related to the appeal of the congenital argument: stressing the congenital basis to inversion absolved homosexuals of all guilt (homosexuality was no longer a 'sin') and from pressure to change (homosexuality was inborn and thus inevitable). In the same American talk she expounded on 'the place in the great scheme of things' for the 'true' invert, namely 'spiritual parenthood'. (Here was the influence of Carpenter rather than Ellis.) 'Some of the best men and women I have ever known belong to the "peculiar people"', she declared.[157] Understandably perhaps, she did not admit her own inclusion. There are indications, however, that Edith in some contexts boldly admitted her lesbianism. After Lily died she became a believer in spiritualism, convinced that Lily guided her from 'the other side'. Sometime after giving her talk in America in 1915, she told Carpenter how in the face of gossip about her 'inversion':

> I came home ... and felt my dead woman [Lily] by my side ... Now I've decided I'm not going ever again to be afraid – not if they spit at me, they can't kill the woman I love again ... I shall just be true and try to be calm.[158]

Concepts from sexology gave women who loved women a language with which to name themselves. In so doing, they opened themselves up to the pathologizing label of 'pervert'. But for those women, like Kathlyn Oliver, who had always had a sense of themselves as *different*, the 'recognition' of an identity must have brought relief, even as it brought danger. The women who adopted the term 'invert' as their own did not necessarily take the term as a *sexual* identity in the way defined by sexologists, preferring to stress the emotional as opposed to the physical side of their relationship with women. In contrast, sexological concepts enabled heterosexual women to claim a right to the physicality of sex, although what many feminists desired was the uniting of the physical and spiritual, rather than the subordination of one to the other. The dominant assumptions of women's sexual passivity, 'natural' monogamy, and the double standards around female reputation, precluded the possibility of women being sexual on the same terms as men, even had they wished to be.

This brief moment in which a space was opened up for feminists to discuss sex (and lesbians to adopt a non-sexualized self-definition) was soon to evaporate with the increasing eugenical emphasis on 'fit' motherhood and the tightening up of the definition of 'sex'. In the early twentieth century and into the inter-war years, while sexologists (including Freudians) *extended* the definition of the 'sexual', the definition of 'sex' itself was narrowed down into 'penetration' (and 'normal sex' into 'heterosexual penetration'). This emphasis on penetration related centrally to the stress on *reproductive* sex, itself the product of the fears in circulation about the declining birth rate (an anxiety which continued in Britain right up until the Second World War).[159] The eugenics movement was to the forefront in orchestrating a 'moral panic' around the differential nature of this decline. Eugenists' concern with 'fit' reproduction led to their renaming the 'sexual instinct' the '*racial* instinct',[160] thereby constructing legitimate sexual desire in terms of desire to procreate 'for the race'. The simultaneous meanings of 'race' in use – a race which was human, white, Anglo–Saxon and/or British – operated consecutively to present 'racial' breeding as not simply a human endeavour, but an endeavour only to be undertaken by those able to reproduce a British race along eugenical lines. With the sexual instinct racialized (and implicitly 'nationalized'), the sexual activity of the so-called dysgenic, be they working class, 'feeble-minded', 'feckless' or non-white, was by definition deviant. As for non-penetrative sexual activity, it was simply not 'real' sex. I am referring here in particular to the common-sense assumption, still in circulation today, that lesbians cannot be having 'real' sex unless some kind of penetration is involved, and that non-penetrative sex between men and women is simply 'foreplay' for the 'real thing'.

Conclusion

The Return of 'White Slavery'

In 1912 there was a renewed public interest in the phenomenon of 'white slavery'. The term 'white slavery' had been used from at least the mid-nineteenth century to refer not simply to the plight of victimized women, but sometimes more broadly to the harsh conditions of industrial workers. Not only did the term imply a parallel with victimized black peoples, but the movement against white slavery saw itself on a par with the great reform movement for abolition. Although on occasion used by Josephine Butler to refer to prostitution in general (for she and many of her co-workers could not think of the prostitute as anything other than coerced by economic circumstance or vicious men), from the 1880s the term 'white slavery' connoted abduction of girls and women by deception or force to brothels, including brothels abroad.[1] Social reformers were somewhat vague as to whether this included the taking abroad of women already working as prostitutes. While public sympathy was forthcoming to the image of 'innocent' girls compelled into the 'social evil', it was unlikely to extend to what was, in fact, the far more likely occurrence – the prostitute who fell for a false offer of lucrative work. The predominant representation, however, was that of helpless victims preyed upon by evil procurers.[2]

There had been attempts to bring in a 'White Slave Traffic' Bill since 1907 on the initiative of a joint committee of the Jewish Association for the Protection of Women and Girls, the Jewish Board of Deputies, the London Council for the Promotion of Public Morality (run by the Bishop of London) and the National Vigilance Association (NVA). While the actions of W.T. Stead had propelled the 1885 Criminal Law Amendment Act on to the statute book, he again was instrumental, if only from his watery grave, in the success of this new Bill. For when Stead drowned in the *Titanic* disaster in April 1912, it was proposed that the Bill should stand as a memorial to his memory – to 'the man who has striven with such courage and determination on behalf of the "maidens of Babylon"'.[3] Parallels were made between the two Bills; in the July edition of the *Review of Reviews* (which had been Stead's journal) the headline ran 'As it was in 1885; so it is in 1912'. Stead was eulogized from many quarters. Elizabeth Cobb, for example, was one of many who wrote in support of the memorial proposal.[4] To his feminist friend, the actress and novelist Elizabeth Robins:

> He saw the women and children into the boats. And he seems to have left some silent charge behind, that other lifeboats should be sent out to save the women who are launched on angrier seas in a blacker night.[5]

Feminists quickly became involved in campaigning for this new Criminal Law Amendment Bill. They bombarded the Prime Minister, Asquith, with petitions and helped the NVA to form a 'Pass the Bill' Committee. They pointed to the inadequacy of existing legislation in halting the white slave traffic: 'The law made by men renders men's vices very easy of satisfaction by punishing lightly the traders who control and purvey the victims'.[6] Suddenly, after all its past rejections, the Bill was taken up by the Government. Elizabeth Robins explained why: 'What all of a sudden brought the need for the Bill sharply home to men? Not the abiding horror of those women's lives . . . but the death of a man.'[7] But it was more than that. The extra push had come in early June when the Women's Liberal Federation resolved that if the (Liberal) Government's Reform Bill became law without the inclusion of women's suffrage, it would be impossible for the Federation to sustain its good relations with the Liberal Party. In response, according to *The Times*, the Government 'regarded the threatened loss of the support of the Liberal ladies rather seriously'.[8] To appease them it adopted the 'White Slave Traffic' Bill. The Bill passed its second reading on 10 June.

As with the 1885 Act, the 1912 Act had been substantially helped on its way by the power of sensational narratives. Neither the narratives of 1885 nor 1912 were of women's making, and girls and women were portrayed in both as passive victims. No feminist in 1885 openly attacked Stead's 'Maiden Tribute' articles, but in 1912 Teresa Billington-Greig (former member of the Women's Freedom League, and, before that, the WSPU) was publicly scathing about the contemporary equivalent. She objected to the portrayal of female passivity:

> Just as these neuropaths [the Bill's advocates] hold that man is vicious, so do they hold that women are impotent and imbecile weaklings, incapable of resisting him.

She also pointed to 'several remarkable features of this epidemic of terrible rumours', namely the frequency of such stories which 'strained credulity', the 'incredible' nature of such stories, and the repetition of the same story 'again and again in various forms':

> The tales of drugged hankerchiefs, sweets and flowers had so many variants as to create the impression that the country must be decimated of their daughters by drugging.[9]

(She would have been horrified by the advice of an American suffragist to her female audience that 'it is more important to be aroused than to be accurate. Apathy is more of a crime than exaggeration in dealing with this subject'.[10] In the years 1911–15 America too was going through a nationwide panic over white slavery.) In Britain the white slave stories were always offered second- or third-hand. Teresa Billington-Greig conducted her own inquiry, talking to the police, social workers and white slavery campaigners, but no one could verify even one story. She concluded that it was a 'campaign of sedulously calculated sexual hysterics', which

> fed on flattery, the silly notion of the perfection of women and dangerous fellow notion of the indescribable imperfection of men ... The Fathers of the old Church made a mess of the world by teaching the Adam story and classing women as unclean; the Mothers

of the new Church are threatening the future by the whitewashing of women and the doctrine of the uncleanliness of men.[11]

Teresa Billington-Greig may have treated the white slavery narratives as nothing but 'terrible rumours', but most other feminists appear to have believed such tales, or at least believed that there was *something* which one could call white slavery – a lurking, threatening phenomenon which remained disconcertingly vague. Rebecca West, for example, writing in the socialist paper the *Clarion*, wondered aloud:

> Is there a White Slave Traffic? I think so, you think so, and so does the House of Commons. But where it is carried on and to what extent, none of us really knows.[12]

Elizabeth Robins' best-selling novel *Where are You Going to . . .?*[13] made its own contribution to white slavery myth-making. It is a story of two young sisters who live in the country with their mother in fairly idyllic middle-class surroundings, save for the lack of a father and the sense of some undefined threat. Indeed, throughout the narrative there runs as an undercurrent the as-yet-unspecified horror of what is to come. The young sisters go up to London, supposedly to be met by their aunt Josephine, but instead are taken under false pretences to 'one of the most infamous houses in Europe'. The older sister manages to escape but her beloved Bettina, aged sixteen, disappears into the underworld of 'vice' with no hope of recovery. This cautionary tale concludes: 'Not in vain her innocence has borne the burden of sin.'[14]

This representation of white slavery as a threat to middle-class country girls, and not solely to impoverished girls of the slums (as in the earlier 'Maiden Tribute' articles) was in congruence with the feminist campaign against sexual innocence-cum-ignorance. The representation was also another exposure of the dangers of middle-class family life: while wives risked catching venereal diseases from their husbands, their daughters risked entrapment into white slavery. The message ran: nowhere was safe for girls and young women, regardless of class. If the 1912 campaign differed from that of 1885 in terms of its representation of class, it also differed in its representation of race. Throughout the

'Maiden Tribute' articles Stead emphasized the danger to *English* girls, but although some of those that threatened them might have been other than English, their race was not a key definer. In 1912, however, the racial classification of the abductors and pimps was central. There were claims that many of them were 'foreign', especially Jewish. This was one of the reasons why Jewish organizations were involved in the campaign, although it was also because Jewish women were believed to represent a large percentage of the trade's victims.[15]

Why did this moral panic over white slavery take place? As Mariana Valverde points out, moral panics are by definition multi-dimensional, and 'the social anxiety associated with them is probably rooted in the unconscious coming together or condensation of different discourses, different fears, in a single image'.[16] For women, fear of white slavery was fed by their fear of male sexuality, presented culturally as rampant and excessive and experienced by many as oppressive. The fear of white slavery was also fed by the dread of prostitution; Maria Sharpe was not alone among middle-class women in feeling that prostitution 'haunted' relations between the sexes. Feminists in the 1912 campaign tended to cast men generically in the role of potential abductors of any woman; white slavery was another item in the inventory of sins committed by males against all females.

To the *male* campaigners in 1912, the abductors and pimps were not men in general but 'foreign' men in particular. Immigration into Britain of foreigners, especially Jews, became the basis for another fear – that of the racial Other. In addition, the old anxiety over the dangers of urban life took not simply a racial and class form, but a gendered one too, as young women moved into cities to take up new occupations, with new freedoms, away from the traditional networks of support and control.[17] And given the rise of feminist militancy, the representation of women as helpless victims in need of male protection was a satisfying reflection for those, such as Asquith, up against the suffragettes, or indeed for any man fearful of feminism. As Nina Boyle of the Women's Freedom League perceptively suggested: 'There is a strong desire on the part of the Government to wrest from women's hands a dangerous and effective weapon, and subsequently to pose as benefactors to those disarmed.'[18] Indeed, the Bill's promoter Arthur Lee MP, who was explicitly opposed to women's franchise, told the House of Commons:

> The attitude of the anti-Suffragist would be inexcusable . . . if it could be said . . . that men were callous to the sufferings of women, and not willing to accord them an elementary measure of protection.[19]

In his eyes at least (and the Government's?), for men to be seen to be 'protecting' women undermined the feminist rationale for the vote, for what need was there for a female voice in Parliament when men were addressing women's concerns? These combined conditions laid the basis for a large-scale moral panic which in one form or another reverberated on through the first half of the twentieth century. This is not to deny the existence of enforced prostitution, but the representation of its nature and extent in early twentieth-century England has to be seen in this wider context.

The new Criminal Law Amendment Bill became law in December 1912. Its first clause permitted the arrest of suspected procurers without the delay of obtaining a warrant. Some MPs objected on the grounds that innocent people might be wrongly arrested, with injury to reputation. But many feminists believed that the risks of this clause were outweighed by the gains.[20] And they also pointed to the double standard at play: the civil liberties of *women* arrested without a warrant on suspicion of soliciting had never been a parliamentary concern.[21] Yet there were other clauses of the Bill with which some feminists were less than happy. The law was strengthened in relation to brothel-keeping, including requiring a landlord to evict a tenant who had been convicted of using her room for prostitution. If the landlord did not evict, he/she would be 'deemed to have know-ingly aided or abetted'. It was feared that this would lead both to raised rents for prostitutes, and to more prostitutes becoming homeless or forced to live with pimps.[22]

Feminists had had high expectations of the Criminal Law Amendment Act 1885. While a few subsequently contributed to the increased surveillance of prostitutes in the name of women's

safety, many came to recognize that the Act's *application* was of
no advantage to women. With the 1912 Act, hopes were once
again raised, although many women were more cautious. The
Common Cause (the paper of the National Union of Women's
Suffrage Societies) gave general support to the Bill, but urged
that the extended police powers be carefully monitored, 'lest
they should lead to further harrying of the unfortunate women'.[23]
Yet, as Sylvia Pankhurst observed two years later, harrying
women was precisely what the new Act accomplished: 'It is a
strange thing that the latest Criminal Law Amendment Act,
which was passed ostensibly to protect women, is being used
almost exclusively to punish women.' She related a recent case
of a woman sentenced to pay £7 or a month's imprisonment
because one of her lodgers was using her bedroom 'for immoral
purposes'. The landlady went to prison since she could not pay
the fine; her husband went untouched.[24]

Sylvia Pankhurst's sister Christabel and her mother Emmeline
had been wholeheartedly committed to the enactment of the
'White Slave Traffic' Bill. Once it was on the statute book,
Christabel turned her attention from man as abductor to man as
polluter.[25] As we have seen, her focus now became the contribution of venereal disease to 'the downfall of the nation'. In
venereal disease, Nature had 'decreed a punishment for sexual
immorality such as she imposes in respect of no other sin'. *The
Great Scourge* was published in 1913. In August the following
year, she ominously declared:

> As I write a dreadful war-cloud seems about to burst and deluge the
> people of Europe with fire, slaughter, ruin – this then is the World
> as men have made it . . . This great war . . . is Nature's vengeance –
> is God's vengeance upon the people who held women in
> subjection . . .[26]

While men were still to blame, the form of Nature's revenge
had shifted from VD to war. A month later, a public notice
announced that Miss Christabel Pankhurst would speak at the
London Opera House 'on the great need of vigorous national
defence against the *GERMAN PERIL*'.[27] The 'doctrine of the
uncleanliness of men', to which Teresa Billington-Greig had so

objected, had become racialized – the enemy was no longer within the nation but without: the racial Other.

In this book I have set out to discover the ways in which feminists debated and campaigned around issues of sexual morality in England at the turn of the century. Given the taboos on respectable women speaking about such things, I wanted to know how feminists were *able* to speak, what languages and ideas they drew upon and what difficulties or otherwise feminists may have had drawing upon concepts and representations which were not in any real sense their 'own'. Were the contradictions too great, or did feminists manage to subvert these discourses to their advantage?

I have suggested that it was aspects of religion, medicine and, above all, evolutionary theory, that late nineteenth-century feminists managed to appropriate. In the process, they attempted to construct a feminist epistemology for the understanding of women's subordination and the means for its eradication. In contrast to the dominant representation of woman as 'Other' and equivalent to uncivilized 'savages', feminists constructed man, in his sexual 'excessiveness', as the *real* 'primitive' 'Other', lacking the true mark of civilization (self-control). In this obvious case of what Michel Foucault calls a 'reverse discourse',[28] feminists subverted the notion of Eve's role in original sin by replacing it with a narrative in which man was the initial transgressor. As a theory for women's empowerment, the appeal was obvious. The problems arose, however, in the *application* of such ideas to the politics of sexuality.

Feminists drew on the ideology of female moral superiority and altruistic maternity to claim a subject position from which to enter the public world as 'moral' 'missionaries', and to insist, on the basis of their 'civilizing capacities', on a right to political status. In their concern with 'purifying' public space, including the promotion of safer streets for women, feminists combined the idea of civil liberties (women's right to walk the streets without fear and curtailment) with a stress on women's 'moralizing' attributes. In their zeal for the abolition of prostitution, a number of feminists focused more on the policing of the prostitute than her male client, operating a form of 'protective surveil-lance'. Through their differentiation between the reclaimable prostitute (passive victim of male lust and/or economic hardship) and the unreclaimable (vicious agent of her own immorality), these feminists inadvertently mobilized the virgin/whore dichotomy to which they were supposedly so opposed. For in claiming moral superiority (the one 'positive' attribute of femininity found within Christian religion), some feminists became caught in the contradiction on which this notion was based, namely that those women who fell short on the 'purity' stakes were not 'real' women – they had become quite 'other', ruled by the 'beast' within.

In relation to marriage and the home, feminists again drew on liberal principles of freedom, liberty and bodily autonomy in order to demand a right of control over their own person. And again they combined this stress on freedom with an emphasis on women's purifying role. Feminists insisted that the marital iniquities of involuntary childbearing, rape and imposed VD, should cease, demanding that men live by the same sexual ethics required of women, namely chastity outside marriage and continence (sexual moderation) within. Rather than calling for the abolition of marriage, however, most feminists feared their vulnerability within non-marital relations, seeking marital reform as the preferred option. In this strategy to purify marriage and reconstruct it as a site of true liberty for women (impossible, they recognized, without simultaneous political equality), feminists campaigned on three fronts: a legislative tactic to reform divorce law, the law of coverture, and lack of recognition of marital rape: a protective and educative tactic to provide basic sex education for girls and young women – more to protect them from undesired sexual advances than to lay the foundation for sexual pleasure; and a utopian, imaginative tactic to inspire women in their struggle towards the ideal marital relationship of spiritual unity and harmony – the embodiment of the equal moral standard.

It is difficult to measure feminists' success in reforming marriage. Clearly they made no gains on the legal front around sexual morality, not managing to win changes in either divorce law or marital rape. Feminists had great hopes for enlightened sex education as the way forward: boys would learn respect for girls and the sanctity of sex; girls would be empowered by sexual knowledge and the encouragement of a view of their bodies as inviolable. Although individual women may have been empowered to some extent by such writings, the widespread public and private silence, as Ellen Ross points out, made it impossible for 'wives to develop a collective sense of where their "rights" lay and what their interests were'.[29] Further, feminist optimism in relation to sex education was largely dependent on the Lamarckian belief that habits learned in one's lifetime became part of the (genetic) inheritance passed down to future generations. Such wild optimism was short-lived. In the early twentieth century, Lamarckianism was discredited, and sex education, what little there was of it, focused almost exclusively on the dangers of sex, namely venereal diseases and pregnancy outside marriage. When it was not stressing dangers, sex education entailed the propagation of eugenical preparation for motherhood.

In speaking of women's right to bodily autonomy, feminists included the right to refuse involuntary childbearing. Yet most feminists were ambivalent, at the very least, about contraception, fearing its use would increase the inequalities between the sexes and reduce the woman to the status of prostitute. When the politics of fertility control became dominated by eugenics, many feminists, if not actually becoming eugenists as such, deployed the language of eugenism as an extra dimension to their claim of moral superiority. Genetic purity and moral purity converged in their construction of a new moral standard, and motherhood gained new dignity as a 'duty for the race'. The co-existence of different meanings of race (the human race, the white race, the Anglo-Saxon race, the British race) allowed those feminists whose politics rested on a self-designation as 'mothers of the race' to gain the additional kudos of being not simply the mothers of humankind (their evolutionary role), but mothers too of a 'superior' race (their national(ist) role). The double-edged maternalism of female philanthropists, feminist or otherwise, took on an additional aspect to give Imperialist maternalism. Yet whatever the racist (and classist) contradictions of women's use of eugenics, those feminists who deployed eugenical categories were also able to subvert the terms and add to their construction of man as the 'Other'. Drawing on current fears about VD, a number of feminists cast man as the source of pollution – the originator of sin/ill health/genetic decay. Rather than promiscuous and prostitute women, it was the sexual practices of men which were held accountable for the spread of disease and degeneration.

While eugenics fed into the politics of fertility control, sexology, the 'new science of sex', had begun to categorize different sexual behaviours and identities. As Foucault has suggested, the 'medicine of perversions' (sexology) and the programme of eugenics were the two great innovations in the late nineteenth-century technology of sex.[30] Yet the language of sexology gave women a means to *name*. For women who loved other women, the ability to claim an identity as an 'invert' or Uranian was sometimes positive and empowering, even as it courted the danger of a deviant labelling. For some heterosexual women, to be able to validate the physicality of sex felt like a step towards sexual self-determination. Such women appear to have been able to claim a positive sexualized identity, however, only within the terms set, terms which included the vilification of those women deemed sexless – the celibate spinsters.

While the claim to moral superiority of the chaste spinster rested on her purity and social (not, of course, literal) motherliness, a new representation of a *sexualized* mother began to emerge. Feminist contributors to the *Freewoman* may have discussed sensual and sexual experiences unrelated to reproduction, but in the writings of Scharlieb, Chesser and other eugenist sex educators, a woman's sexual and maternal instincts converged – a woman was sexualized *in terms of* her maternity. Thus, as Dr Elizabeth Sloan Chesser expressed it:

> The longing of every normal woman to find happiness in sex union and to exercise her functions physically and psychically in marriage and motherhood is an ineradicable instinct.

Since ideal motherhood already stood as the embodiment of selfless love, love, sex and maternity were inextricably bound within the ideology of motherhood, all to be subsumed to the interests of the 'race' – all indeed constituting the female 'racial instinct'. This new kind of nationalist maternity-focused sex education was organized to guide the girl and young woman towards motherhood and away from promiscuity, seen as the two competing courses for the development of a girl's sexuality.[31] A girl's sexual expression outside marriage and motherhood was deemed not only immoral, but unhealthy, for she faced the exorbitant risk of the 'racial poison' VD.

Sheila Jeffreys argues that the downfall of the women's movement after 1918 was largely due to the anti-feminism of sexology.[32] Whether there was indeed a 'downfall' is, in fact, contested,[33] but it is clear that the sense of an enormous energizing movement disappeared, and with it went the biting critique of male sexuality. I would suggest that a host of factors contributed to the decline of the women's movement: the anti-climactic effect of gaining the suffrage in 1918; the devastating outcome of the First World War, the human carnage of which resulted in many erstwhile feminists redefining themselves as 'humanists', feminism seeming too divisive;[34] and last but not least the influence of eugenic discourse in constructing women's ideal role as that of mother. By the 1930s, the rise of fascism in Europe significantly contributed to a mood of anti-feminism. Women over thirty may have gained the vote in 1918 (extended to women of twenty-one years or over in 1928), but ideologically they were still located within domesticity, not simply as wives, but first and foremost as mothers. If sexology played a part in feminism's demise, its contribution was more in terms of collaboration with eugenism than any single-handed crusade. One stream of feminism, in the celebration of the evolutionary power of maternity, made its own contribution to the ideological location of women within motherhood. Yet there were some advantages for women: what became known as 'New Feminism' (which stressed the particularity of women as against the 'Old Feminism' of equality) demanded *material* back-up to motherhood in the form of family allowances, ('endowment of motherhood').[35]

The feminist contributors to the *Freewoman* had debated the sexualizing of women, but their hopes for fluidity of expression and bodily autonomy gained no realization. Instead, there was the widespread assumption of a 'natural' maternal instinct and a 'natural' heterosexuality. Although the new literature gave recognition to female sexual desire, and a woman was no longer viewed as the asexual being assumed by Dr Acton and others, her sexuality was to be channelled into pleasurable, reproductive and marital heterosexuality. Stella Browne's demand that women 'set their own requirement, and boldly claim a share of life and erotic experience'[36] was sadly nowhere on the agenda. It would take until the late 1960s and the rise of the women's liberation movement for its reinstatement as a crucial feminist aspiration. This time, the assumed heterosexuality would be challenged and the racialized 'common-sense' of white feminists taken to task.[37] What still remains, however, are some of the same problems and contradictions faced by our foremothers.

Echoing of Problems and Contradictions

> We have something women have never enjoyed before – a feminist past, a history of 150 years of feminist theory and praxis in the area of sexuality. This is a resource too precious to squander, by not learning from it, in all its complexity.[38]

So what can we learn from the account of feminist sexual politics given in this book? Given that expectations in relation to sexuality have shifted significantly, it could be thought inadvisable (and ahistorical) to attempt to draw connections, let alone parallels, between feminists then and now. Yet I cannot help but note the resonances of earlier problems and contradictions in the sexual politics of today.

There have, of course, been enormous changes in how women live out their sexual relationships, due in part to greater physiological understanding of sexual feeling and a vision of sexuality that is neither exclusively heterosexual nor tied to reproduction. Yet one of the remaining problems faced by women is the threat of sexual violence. It has been suggested that contemporary feminists who concentrate on the harm of pornography and the horrors of rape are replicating the politics of those earlier feminists who focused exclusively on sexual danger.[39] This replication of politics includes the impact on sex workers. The contradiction facing feminists then and now is how to *protect* women and children without it inevitably entailing surveillance and control. As we have seen, the prostitution campaigns of certain late nineteenth-century feminists had detrimental effects on the lives of prostitutes. In attempting to protect one group of women from danger and discomfort in the public arena, another group of women were subjected to surveillance. Eighty years later, prostitutes were again being affected negatively by the campaigns of feminists, although this time it was feminists' confrontation not of prostitution but of male violence and pornography via 'Reclaim the Night' marches.

These marches first took place in Britain in November 1977, in eleven major towns simultaneously.[40] Four hundred women took to the streets in Manchester, several hundred invaded Soho and hundreds more walked through city centres across the country. The initiative had come from Leeds feminists who, like other women in the North of England, lived in daily fear of the 'Yorkshire Ripper'.[41] Yorkshire police had effectively advised a curfew on women at night: for their own 'safety' they were told to stay behind closed doors, only venturing out under the protection of a known man. (That women were also at risk of violence from 'known men' was not acknowledged.) But feminists, reasonably enough, wanted the streets to be *safe* for women. To 'reclaim' the streets (which have never, of course, been ours *to* reclaim) seemed a radical – and celebratory – form of politics. It all depended however, on *where* you decided to do your 'reclaiming'.

According to one account, women who marched through Soho found it exhilarating; they charged down the streets, slapping stickers on windows which read 'THIS EXPLOITS WOMEN', laughing in the face of irate male proprietors. The reporter did mention, however, that an ex-prostitute disagreed with the march because it would be bad for the Soho prostitutes' business.[42] In the late 1970s I went on a Reclaim the Night demonstration through Balsall Heath, a well-known 'red light' district in South Birmingham. I can remember the subsequent anger expressed by PROS, the Birmingham prostitutes' group:[43]

in spotlighting one of their sites of work, we had given the police an additional excuse to 'clean-up' the area, i.e. to arrest prostitutes. I am shocked now by how unthinking we were; were we that different from those late nineteenth-century feminists who wanted the streets cleared of prostitutes in order to enhance the safety of the 'ordinary' woman? The marches also had racist implications. The women marchers, who were mainly white, sometimes chose to march through areas with a largely black population, as in the case of a Reclaim the Night demonstration in 1979 in Chapeltown, Leeds, where a young woman had been murdered earlier that year. As Pratibha Parmar points out, such marches reinforced the racist idea that black men are the perpetrators of sexual crimes against white women. It also legitimated the selective policing of such areas.[44] In seeking to protect women from male violence on the streets, feminists inadvertently ended up increasing the surveillance of prostitutes and black men.

Feminists object not only to sexual violence but also, of course, to certain sexual representations. For feminists past and present, this has raised the question of whether censorship is ever a desirable option. A number of nineteenth-century feminists attempted to censor music-hall entertainment (concerned about 'the revealing of too much flesh'), although others were strongly opposed. Feminists today are also divided over the issue. While the feminist Campaign Against Pornography (CAP)[45] has backed bills for the prohibition of 'Page 3' of the *Sun* and its equivalents in other papers (bills drawn up on the initiative of Clare Short MP), Feminists Against Censorship (FAC) stresses the danger of greater powers leading to the censoring of gay and lesbian porn and erotica.[46] Related to this issue of censorship is the question of what causal role, if any, pornography plays in the subordination of women. While nineteenth-century prostitution stood, as Walkowitz expresses it, as 'a paradigm for the female condition, a symbol of women's powerlessness and sexual victimization', for some feminists pornography has now replaced prostitution as the quintessential site of women's degradation.[47] Yet whatever feminists' dislike and fear of pornography – or at least of heterosexual pornogra-

phy, with its representation of submissive and available femininity, and its reduction of women to bodily parts – the majority
probably do not support a feminism which reduces women's
oppression to one key factor.

Resonances from the past are also heard in the feminist anti-
porn representation of sexuality, and its differentiation according
to gender. While many turn-of-the-century feminists saw prostitutes (and potentially all women, in the face of white slavery) as
passive victims, the prey of lustful, coercive male sexuality,
today's anti-porn feminists tend likewise to construct women as
passive receptors of undifferentiated male lust. The irony here is
that in presenting women as in essence passive objects of a
monolithic lustful male sexuality (man as the 'beast'), contemporary campaigners recreate the fantasy world of porn and all its
misinformation about sexuality. As Elizabeth Wilson describes
it, this is a world 'where men are always ready to perform,
erections are repeatable, and ejaculation is never premature'.[48]
And in their huge sexual powerfulness and threat lies men's
bestiality; the spectre of the 'beast in man' still haunts debates on
sex.

A number of early twentieth-century feminists called on
women to disengage from sexual relations with men; late
twentieth-century radical feminists do likewise: sex with men is
'sleeping with the enemy'.[49] To Christabel Pankhurst: 'There can
be no mating between the spiritually developed women of this
day and men who in thought and conduct with regard to sex
matters are their inferiors.'[50] In calling for the cessation of sex
between men and women, Christabel effectively called for
women to renounce *all* sexual activity, given that relations
between women were generally not yet thought of in sexual
terms. Today, to British radical feminist Sheila Jeffreys, the
answer is not so much 'no sex' (though certainly no sex with
men), but no 'heterosexual desire', which she defines as 'the
eroticizing of otherness and power difference'. Not only should
feminists be lesbians, she argues, but they should be lesbians with
true 'homosexual desire', namely 'the eroticizing of sameness, a
sameness of power, equality and mutuality'.[51] Lesbians involved
in role-playing or sadomasochistic practices are, according to

Sheila, still caught within a desire that is basically heterosexual. Apart from the sanctimoniousnness of this position (of which more below), where does this leave the *celebration* of difference, including that of race?[52] Is there an implicit racist logic to this stress on 'sameness'?

To a small number of radical feminists, the only valid political position on sexuality is one of total '*de*sexualization'. Thus, one American group, calling themselves 'Women against Sex', assert that:

> There is no way out of the practice of sexuality except *out* ... *We know of no exception to male supremacist sex* ... We name orgasm as the epistemological mark of the sexual, and we therefore criticize it too, as oppressive to women.

Their political agenda? 'Sex has to stop before male supremacy will be defeated.'[53] What I find disturbing about these pronouncements on what sex, if any, is appropriate for feminists to engage in, is the moralism: feminists are policed in terms of their sexual practices and desires.[54] And here again we find resonances between feminists past and present: a shared view of their role as redeemers of other women as well as an assumption of their moral superiority versus all men, and versus women who disagree with their political analysis (who by definition cannot be 'real' feminists), or who follow an 'undesirable' sexual practice. The latter were labelled as 'immoral' by feminists of the nineteenth century, and as engaging in 'the eroticization of women's subordination' (to use the terms of Sheila Jeffreys) in the twentieth.

Whatever feminists may think is or is not acceptable sexual practice, the problem of how women can control their reproduction has not gone away. Like our foremothers, we still face the question of how best, within heterosexual practice, to separate sex from procreation, given the inadequacies of most, if not all, means of contraception. The fears of nineteenth-century feminists that birth control would render women more susceptible to male sexual demands as well as adversely affect their health seems to some extent to have been confirmed. The advent of the contraceptive pill in the 1960s, while highly liberating for women in its removal of the fear of possible pregnancy, also removed women's ability to refuse intercourse on the grounds of this possibility. It was simply assumed that women would be taking the pill, and thereby taking all responsibility for contraception. Further, women could no longer persuade men to enter the old terms of the sexual contract whereby men promised financial support and commitment in return for sex.[55] In conjunction with the 60s 'permissive' dictate that sex was not only 'good' for you, but essential for one's liberation, women's avoidance of heterosexual intercourse, should they wish such avoidance, was all the harder.[56] In addition, links between the pill and a variety of health problems began to be revealed; it is now generally acknowledged that women on the pill are at higher risk of contracting breast cancer and thrombosis, for example.[57] And to suggest that heterosexuality (indeed any sexuality) need not involve penetrative sex, is still as difficult today, if not more so, given the dominant culture's equation of sex and penetration.

One obvious way of attempting to shift and widen the definition of sex is through sex education. While feminists are as dissatisfied with the blatantly inadequate nature of existing sex education as our foremothers, unlike them we are not on the whole attempting to produce alternative material.[58] Pornography, prostitution, birth control and sex education have been of concern to feminists past and present because they all, though in very different ways, raise the thorny and ongoing question of how to balance women's protection and autonomy, their safety and pleasure. All feminists wish women to be protected from male sexual violence, from unwanted pregnancy and from sexual disease. What we are less clear about and less agreed upon is how to combine such wishes with the active encouragement of an environment in which women can explore and define our sexuality freely, with all its potentialities and pleasures. Rather than a censoring of sexual images, such an endeavour requires both open debate and the production of sexually explicit material produced by and for women.

NOTES

Where both surname and short title only are used in the notes for both books and articles, full references will be found, under either Primary or Secondary sources, in the Bibliography. Unpublished material will be followed by the initials of the collection containing it: Josephine Butler Collection (JBC); Edward Carpenter Collection (ECC); Pearson Collection (PC); Sharpe Collection (SC); Elizabeth Wolstenholme Elmy Collection (EWEC).

INTRODUCTION

1 Re-Bartlett, *The Coming Order*, pp. ix-xii.
2 Snowden, *The Feminist Movement*, p. 249. The classic article on the double standard is by Thomas, 'The Double Standard', pp. 195–216.
3 See Walkowitz, *Prostitution and Victorian Society*.
4 Hansard Parliamentary debates [Lords] 24 June 1884, quoted in Gorham, 'The "Maiden Tribute of Modern Babylon" Re-examined', p. 366.
5 Walkowitz, *City of Dreadful Delight*, p. 84.
6 Stout, 'W.T. Stead: a Character Sketch', in Stead, *A Journalist on Journalism*, p. 11.
7 *Pall Mall Gazette*, 6 July 1885. On the 'Maiden Tribute' generally see Gorham, 'The "Maiden Tribute of Modern Babylon" Re-examined'; Walkowitz, *City of Dreadful Delight*.
8 *Pall Mall Gazette*, 4, 6, 7, 8 and 9 July 1885.
9 Walkowitz, *City of Dreadful Delight*, pp. 106–7.
10 *Pall Mall Gazette*, 8 August 1885.
11 Pearson, *The Age of Consent*, p. 164; *The Times*, 31 July 1885.
12 *Pall Mall Gazette*, 22 August 1885.
13 On this Amendment see Smith, 'Labouchère's Amendment to the Criminal Law Amendment Bill'; Weeks, *Coming Out*; Bristow, 'Wilde, Dorian Grey, and Gross Indecency', in Bristow (ed.), *Sexual Sameness*.
14 Sharpe, 'Autobiographical History', 1889 (PC).

CHAPTER 1 The Men and Women's Club

Unless otherwise indicated, all the references below are to unpublished material in the Pearson Collection (PC).

1 1. Clemes to K. Pearson, 15 November 1885.
2 Minutes of the Men and Women's Club, 9 July 1885. For other discussions of the Men and Women's Club, see First and Scott, *Olive Schreiner*, pp. 144–75; Walkowitz, 'Science, Feminism and Romance'; Walkowitz, *City of Dreadful Delight*.

An earlier, shorter version of this chapter appeared as Bland, 'Rational Sex or Spiritual Love? The Men and Women's Club of the 1880s'. For the Fabian Society see MacKenzie and MacKenzie, *The First Fabians*. For the Hampstead Marx Circle see Pierson, *Marxism and the Origins of British Socialism*, p. 119.

3 Carol Dyhouse quotes a woman's memoir of a Victorian childhood: as a pupil at Cheltenham Ladies' College, when a friend 'smuggled in *The Story of an African Farm*, just out, the whole sky aflame, and many of us became violent feminists' (Dyhouse, *Feminism and the Family in England*, p. 15).

4 Dr Kate Mitchell was a supporter of birth control and one of the few doctors to defend it at the trial of Annie Besant and Charles Bradlaugh in 1877 (see Chapter Five for details of the trial). After the trial she joined a newly formed organization, the Malthusian League. At the inaugural meeting of the Women's Franchise League in 1889, she made a speech against marriage (see Benn, *Predicaments of Love*, p. 150). Her heterodoxy may have contributed to the verdict by Elizabeth Cobb of her being 'unrefined'.

5 K. Pearson to M. Sharpe, 30 March 1885, and Minutes, 9 July 1885.

Stallybrass and White, *The Politics and Poetics of Transgression*, p. 174, argue that 'science only emerged as an autonomous set of discursive values after a prolonged struggle against ritual, and it marked out its own identity by the distance which it established from "mere superstition"'.

6 K. Pearson, 'The Woman's Question', July 1885. See An English Anarchist, *The Criminal Law Amendment Act*, London, International Publishing Co., 1885, p. 3, which in criticism of the Act proposed other means of countering the existence of prostitution. One proposal was 'social intercourse, contempt for all conventional restraints preventing free and open friendship between men and women, and hindering all true knowledge of one another's character, views and feelings. Formations of association for such communication. One such club has

been started in London.' This is very likely to have been the Men and Women's Club. See Priscilla Moulder, 'Friendship between the Sexes', *Westminster Review* 151, June 1899; Schonfield, *The Precariously Privileged* and Davidoff, *The Best Circles* for discussion of Victorian middle-class etiquette.

7 M. Sharpe, 'Autobiographical History', 1889.
8 M. Sharpe, 'Conclusion', 5 July 1889.
9 K. Pearson to M. Sharpe, 14 February 1888.
10 M. Sharpe to K. Pearson, 19 July 1885.
11 E. Cobb to K. Pearson, 4 September 1885.
12 O. Schreiner to W.T. Stead, July 1885.
13 E. Cobb to K. Pearson, 18 September 1885.
14 K. Pearson to M. Sharpe, 6 July 1885.
15 R. Parker to K. Pearson, 13 August 1885.
16 R. Thicknesse to K. Pearson, 6 August 1885; on Thicknesse see Janet E. Courtney, *An Oxford Portrait Gallery*.
17 L.G. Wickham Legg (ed.), *Dictionary of National Biography, 1931–49*, p. 683; and see E. Pearson, *Karl Pearson, an Appreciation*.
18 M. Sharpe, 'Conclusion', 5 July 1889.
19 K. Pearson, 'The Woman's Question', July 1885.
20 K. Pearson, 'The Woman's Question', July 1885.
21 K. Pearson, 'The Woman's Question', July 1885.
22 K. Pearson, 'The Woman's Question', July 1885.
23 E. Cobb to K. Pearson, 19 May 1885; 4 September 1885.
24 M. Sharpe to K. Pearson, 18 July 1886.
25 H. Muller, 'The Other Side of the Question', October 1885.
26 O. Schreiner to K. Pearson, 5 November 1885.
27 H. Muller to M. Sharpe, 12 November 1885.
28 Mrs Walters, 'What Hope?', see Minutes, November 1885.
29 But see R. Thicknesse to K. Pearson, 6 August 1885: 'Mrs Cobb ... seemed to think that the sexual instinct can only be healthily exercised with a strict regard to the procreation of children and nothing else'.
30 O. Schreiner to E. Cobb, 25 March 1885.
31 K. Mills to M. Sharpe, quoting M. Sharpe, 13 May 1885.
32 E. Brooke to K. Pearson, 14 March 1886.
33 E. Cobb to K. Pearson, 12 December 1885.
34 E. Cobb to K. Pearson, 12 December 1885.
35 Minutes, 14 December 1885.
36 M. Sharpe, 'Autobiographical History', 1889.
37 Minutes, 14 December 1885.
38 Minutes, 9 May 1887.

39 Minutes, 9 May 1887.

40 See L. Sharpe, 'Comments on papers on artificial checks on population', June 1887; M. Sharpe, 'On Karl Pearson's Paper', 2 June 1887; F. Balgarnie, 'On Karl Pearson's Paper' n.d. (c. summer/autumn 1887). For a study of nineteenth-century 'romantic' friendships see Faderman, *Surpassing the Love of Men*.

41 E. Brooke to K. Pearson, 13 February 1886.

42 H. Muller to M. Sharpe, May 1887.

43 See K. Pearson, 'Thoughts suggested by the papers and discussion . . .', May 1887; L. Sharpe, 'Comments on Papers on Artificial Checks on Population', June 1887; H. Muller, 'Limitation of the Family', May 1887. Maria later changed her mind on birth control, 'discovering how many people in our class and the respectable working classes do use checks, but fear to speak from natural modesty', 'Autobiograpical History', 1889.

44 H. Muller to M. Sharpe, May 1887.

45 M. Sharpe, 'On Karl Pearson's Paper', 2 June 1887; on Olive's sexual experience see First and Scott, *Olive Schreiner*, p. 63.

46 Carpenter, *My Days and Dreams*, p. 227; on Olive Schreiner see First and Scott, *Olive Schreiner*; Berkman, *The Healing Imagination of Olive Schreiner*.

47 E. Cobb to K. Pearson, 15 December 1886.

48 O. Schreiner to K. Pearson, 10 June 1886.

49 O. Schreiner to K. Pearson, 12 June 1886.

50 O. Schreiner to K. Pearson, 2 July 1886.

51 K. Pearson, 'Thoughts suggested by the papers and discussion . . .', May 1887.

52 M. Sharpe, 'On Karl Pearson's Paper', 2 June 1887.

53 E. Brooke to K. Pearson, 14 March 1886.

54 E. Cobb to K. Pearson, 23 December 1885.

55 Minutes, 9 November 1885.

56 A. Eastty, 'The Meaning of the Word "Morality"', Minutes, 11 January 1886.

57 I. Clemes, 'The Measures of the Science of Morality', Minutes, 11 January 1886.

58 R. Parker to K. Pearson, 14 August 1885.

59 K. Pearson, 'The Ethics of the Market Place and of the Study', 29 November 1885.

60 R. Parker to M. Sharpe, 18 March 1888.

61 Minutes, 11 January 1886.

62 R. Parker to M. Sharpe, 19 January 1886.

63 M. Sharpe to R. Parker, 20 January 1886.

64 Minutes, 10 May 1886.

65 K. Pearson, 'Notes on Thicknesse's Paper', December 1886 [basis for 'Socialism and Sex', in *Today*, February 1887].

66 M. Sharpe, 'Conclusion', 5 July 1889.

67 M. Sharpe, 'Autobiographical History', 1889.

68 M. Sharpe to R. Parker, 10 November 1885.

69 A. Eastty to M. Sharpe, 26 February 1888.

70 M. Sharpe to K. Pearson, 2 February 1889.

71 M. Sharpe, 'Autobiographical History', 1889.

72 M. Sharpe, 'Conclusion', 5 July 1889.

73 M. Sharpe, 'Autobiographical History', 1889. Judith Walkowitz discusses how female readers entered the male preserve of the British Museum Reading Room, and how men complained about their presence, *City of Dreadful Delight*, p. 69.

74 In 'What Women are Fitted For', *Westminster Review*, January 1887, p. 72, Henrietta Muller also suggested that 'mothers stunt their own humanity in their children's service, and in revenge the children are stunted too'.

75 E. Brooke, 'Notes on Pearson's "The Woman's Question"', February 1886.

76 E. Brooke, 'Notes on Pearson's "The Woman's Question"', February 1886. No woman present at the club seems to have challenged Pearson's eugenical ideas about motherhood, but Olive Schreiner wrote an allegory, 'A Dream of Wild Bees', originally written as a letter to Pearson, which represented just such a challenge. In the poem the foetus's fate is chosen by the mother, not determined by genetics. See Chrisman, 'Allegory, Feminist Thought and the *Dreams* of Olive Schreiner'.

77 E. Brooke, 'Notes on Pearson's "The Woman's Question"', February 1886.

78 F. Balgarnic to K. Pearson, 24 July 1888.

79 R. Parker to M. Sharpe, 26 February 1888.

80 Ware, *Beyond the Pale*, pp. 173, 183.

81 H. Muller to K. Pearson, 14 May 1887.

82 H. Muller to K. Pearson, 29 March 1888.

83 M. Sharpe, 'Autobiographical History', 1889.

84 Minutes, 12 December 1887 and 9 January 1888.

85 M. Sharpe, 'Autobiographical History', 1889.

86 O. Schreiner to M. Sharpe, 24 November 1887.

87 M. Sharpe to K. Pearson, 24 November 1886.

88 A. Eastty to M. Sharpe, 26 February 1888.

89 M. Sharpe, 'Autobiographical History', 1889.

90 Walkowitz, *City of Dreadful Delight*, p. 159.

91 Minutes, 12 March 1888.

92 Minutes, 9 January 1888.

93 Minutes, 12 March 1888.

94 K. Pearson to M. Sharpe, 13 March 1888.

95 K. Pearson to M. Sharpe, 13 March 1888.

96 A. Eastty to M. Sharpe, 18 March 1888.

97 Schreiner, *From Man to Man*.

98 O. Schreiner to K. Pearson, 9 July 1886.

99 C. Wilson to K. Pearson, 14 May 1889.

100 C. Wilson to K. Pearson, 17 May 1889.

101 K. Pearson, '*The Positive Creed of Freethought*'.

102 K. Pearson, 'On Foregoing Notes', 27 March 1888; see R. Coward, *Patriarchal Precedents*, for discussion of the anthropological debates on early family forms.

103 Minutes, 28 March 1888.

104 Minutes, 15 October 1888.

105 R. Parker, 'Emancipation of Women', Minutes, 13 November 1888.

106 R. Parker, Minutes, 10 December 1888.

107 R. Thicknesse, 'Claims of Children', Minutes, 13 November 1888.

108 Minutes, 13 November 1888.

109 K. Pearson, 'The Woman's Question', *The Ethic of Freethought*.

110 M. Sharpe, 'Note on the Women's Movement', Minutes, 10 December 1888.

111 L. Sharpe, 'Note', Minutes, 10 December 1888.

112 Minutes, 10 December 1888.

113 E. Cobb to K. Pearson, 3 November 1885.

114 E. Cobb to K. Pearson, 6 July 1885.

115 O. Schreiner to K. Pearson, 11 October 1886.

116 K. Pearson to M. Sharpe, 14 June 1887.

117 M. Sharpe to K. Pearson, 30 May 1889.

118 On the limitations of the 'new man' see Beatrice Webb's 1892 letter to fellow Fabian Edward Pease explaining why she could not speak at a Fabian meeting: 'The hidden masculinity of Sydney's view of women are [sic] incurable in his decided objection to my figuring among the speakers. See how skindeep are these professions of advanced opinion, with regard to women among your leaders of the forward party!' Quoted in B. Caine, 'Beatrice Webb and the Woman Question', p. 35.

119 K. Pearson to M. Sharpe, 17 April 1889.

120 L. Sharpe, 'Comments on papers on artificial checks on population', June 1887.
121 H. Muller to K. Pearson, 29 April 1887.
122 K. Mills to M. Sharpe, 24 April 1889.
123 R. Parker to M. Sharpe, 25 April 1889.
124 R. Parker, 'Work of the Club during the Past Four Years', Minutes, 19 June 1889.
125 K. Pearson to M. Sharpe, 14 February 1888.
126 E. Brooke, 'Notes on Pearson's "The Woman's Question"', February 1886.
127 H. Muller to O. Schreiner, [nd] 1888.
128 I. Clemes to M. Sharpe, 10 November 1885.
129 See First and Scott, *Olive Schreiner*, Chapter 4; Summers, 'The Correspondence of Havelock Ellis'.
130 F. Balgarnie to M. Sharpe, 8 April 1888.
131 *Woman's Penny Paper*, 16 March 1889.
132 See First and Scott, *Olive Schreiner*, Chapter 4.
133 O. Schreiner to H. Ellis, 14 February 1887. Many thanks to Liz Stanley for generously sharing this letter with me, which she read at the Humanities Research Center, University of Texas at Austin.
134 O. Schreiner to K. Pearson, 14 December 1886.
135 O. Schreiner to H. Ellis, 17 February 1887, Humanities Research Center, Austin. Again thanks to Liz Stanley.
136 Schreiner, 'The Buddhist Priest's Wife'.
137 M. Sharpe to K. Pearson, 27 April 1889.
138 E. Brooke to K. Pearson, 14 March 1886.
139 H. Muller to O. Schreiner, [nd] 1888.
140 H. Muller to K. Pearson, 29 March 1888.

CHAPTER 2 Women Defined

1 Blackwell, *Essays in Medical Sociology*.
2 Quoted in Collini, *Liberalism and Sociology*, p. 190.
3 Quoted in Davidoff and Hall, *Family Fortunes*, p. 108.
4 Cott, 'Passionlessness'.
5 Davidoff and Hall, *Family Fortunes*, p. 114; and see Harris, *Sexual Ideology and Religion*.
6 Davidoff and Hall, *Family Fortunes*, p. 225.
7 Simcox, 'The Capacity of Women', pp. 392, 402.
8 Philippa Levine has managed to establish the religion at birth of nearly half of her sample of 194 English Victorian feminists. Of these, 9%

were Quakers and 11% were Unitarians. See Levine, *Feminist Lives in Victorian England*, p. 32.

9 See Banks, *Faces of Feminism*; Rendall, *The Origins of Modern Feminism*.

10 See Watts, 'Knowledge is Power – Unitarians, Gender and Education in The Eighteenth and Nineteenth Centuries'.

11 See Strachey, *The Cause*, pp. 212–16; Walkowitz, *City of Dreadful Delight*, pp. 73–6; Walker, '"I Live but not yet I for Christ liveth in me": Men and Masculinity in the Salvation Army, 1865–90', in Roper and Tosh (eds.), *Manful Assertions*; Samuel, 'The Discovery of Puritanism, 1820–1914', in Garnett and Matthew (eds.), *Revival and Religions since 1700*.

12 See Davidoff and Hall, *Family Fortunes*; Rendall, *The Origins of Modern Feminism*; Cott, 'Passionlessness', p. 233.

13 See Foucault, *The Birth of the Clinic*; Jordanova, *Sexual Visions*.

14 See Parry and Parry, *The Rise of the Medical Profession*; see Mort, *Dangerous Sexualities* for discussion of the relation of the medical profession to the State, and see George Eliot, *Middlemarch*, London, 1871–2, Penguin 1965, for an example, in Dr Lydgate, of the precarious social standing of doctors in the early nineteenth century. For women and healing see Oakley, 'Wisewomen and Medicine Men', in Mitchell and Oakley (eds.), *The Rights and Wrongs of Women*.

15 Jordanova, *Sexual Visions*, Chapter 5.

16 In November 1887 there were 54 registered medical women in Britain, in November 1888 there were 72 – *Englishwoman's Review*, 15 February 1889. By 1901 there were only 212 women doctors in Britain, compared to 22,698 men – Tickner, *The Spectacle of Women*, p. 315, footnote 179.

17 Laqueur, *Making Sex*.

18 On the assumption of heterosexuality, see Weeks, *Sex, Politics and Society*.

19 See Marcus, *The Other Victorians*. Acton was not, in fact, a 'doctor' as such since he never gained the MD degree. See Peterson, *The Medical Profession in Mid-Victorian London*, pp. 233–4 for discussion of how the use of the title 'Doctor' was debated.

20 Acton, *The Functions and Disorders of the Reproductive Organs*, 3rd edition, p. 101.

21 See Mort, *Dangerous Sexualities*, p. 78; Hall, *Hidden Anxieties*, pp. 16–17.

22 Acton, *The Functions and Disorders of the Reproductive Organs*, 6th edition, p. 209, quoting Professor Newman, who in turn was quoting 'an eminent London physician'.

23 Acton, *The Functions and Disorders of the Reproductive Organs*, 5th edition, p. 115.

24 Acton, *The Functions and Disorders of the Reproductive Organs*, 5th edition, p. 196.

25 Acton, *The Functions and Disorders of the Reproductive Organs*, 6th edition, p. 214.

26 Acton, *The Functions and Disorders of the Reproductive Organs*, 3rd edition, pp. 102–6.

27 On the response to Acton, see Peterson, 'Dr Acton's Enemy', p. 578; Gay, *Education of the Senses*; Smith, 'Sexuality in Britain, 1800–1900: Some Suggested Revisions', in Vicinus (ed.), *A Widening Sphere*; Stearns and Stearns, 'Victorian Sexuality: Can Historians Do Better?'. See Ellis, *Studies in the Psychology of Sex Vol. 3*, for discussion of the different medical opinions on female sexuality.

28 Tait, *Diseases of Women and Abdominal Surgery*, vol. 1, p. 57.

29 Mercier, 'Vice, Crime and Insanity', in Allbutt and Rolleston (eds.), *A System of Medicine*, p. 276.

30 Matthews Duncan, *On Sterility in Women*, p. 96.

31 Wade, 'Some Functional Disorders of Females', p. 1057.

32 Nichols, *Esoteric Anthropology*, p. 98.

33 Tait, *Diseases of Women and Abdominal Surgery*, p. 151.

34 Nichols, *Human Physiology: the Basis of Sanitary and Social Science*, p. 269.

35 Nichols was an atypical doctor in other respects – he was an American living in England, who ran a water-cure establishment with his wife in the Malvern hills. His wife, Mary Gove Nichols, was one of the period's most influential alternative healers. See Owen, *The Darkened Room: Women, Power and Spiritualism in Late Victorian England*; Nichols and Nichols, *Marriage: Its History, Character and Results*. Nichols was one of the few Victorian doctors who openly discussed birth-control methods, although he simultaneously condemned them. In the Old Bailey trial of the poisoner Adelaide Bartlett in 1886, the presence of Nichols's *Esoteric Anthropology* among her possessions was one of the factors which so shocked the court. See Hartman, *Victorian Murderesses*, pp. 185–6.

36 Murray, *A New English Dictionary on Historical Principles*, vol. VI L-M, p. 575. While modesty was generally assumed to be an attribute of women, the gender ascription was, on occasion, reversed for pragmatic reasons. Thus, under the Contagious Diseases Acts, the soldier, rather than the prostitute, was protected from examination for venereal disease on the grounds of *male* modesty. See Levine, 'Venereal Disease, Prostitution and the Politics of the Empire', p. 597.

37 See, for example, the Moral Reform Union, *The Fallen Woman!* leaflet, n.d.
38 *Pall Mall Gazette*, 8 July 1885.
39 See Bachofen, *Myth, Religion and Mother Right*; and McLennan, *Studies in Ancient History*. Compare with Tylor, *Anthropology*.
40 Karl Pearson's paper circulated May/June 1887 (PC), compare with Ellis, *Man and Woman: a Study of Human Secondary Sex Characters*, p. 67, who argues that there is 'considerable evidence ... that their [the "lower races"] sexual instincts are not very intense', and Westermarck, *The History of Human Marriage*, p. 539, who suggests that there is no evidence of promiscuity among 'lower' races except where 'contact with "higher culture" had proved pernicious to the morality of savage peoples'.
41 On the 'atavist' prostitute, see Ellis, *The Criminal*; Lombroso and Ferrero, *The Female Offender*.
42 See Stepan, 'Biological Degeneration: Race and Proper Places', in Chamberlin and Sander Gilman (eds.), *Degeneration*.
43 Mercier, 'Vice, Crime and Insanity', in Allbutt and Rolleston (eds.), *A System of Medicine*, pp. 258, 279.
44 *Lancet*, 22 August 1885, p. 350.
45 *British Medical Journal*, 11 July 1885, p. 70; information on Hart from Dr Peter Bartup (personal communication).
46 *Lancet*, 22 August 1885, p. 350.
47 *British Medical Journal*, 15 August 1885, p. 304.
48 See Mercier, 'Vice, Crime and Insanity', in Allbutt and Rolleston (eds.), *A System of Medicine*.
49 See Poovey, *Uneven Developments*, Chapter 2, for a fascinating discussion of the contradictory medical representation of female nature in the mid-Victorian period.
50 Blackwell, *Counsel to Parents on the Moral Education of Their Children in Relation to Sex*, 8th edition, p. 69, quotes 'one of our ablest surgeons' that the only safeguard lies in keeping even the thoughts pure, and that it is *far* harder to be continent once having been incontinent.
51 See Acton, *The Functions and Disorders of the Reproductive Organs*, 6th edition, p. 209, who quotes Professor Newman, who in turn is quoting 'an eminent London physician'.
52 Nichols, *Esoteric Anthropology*, p. 114.
53 Nichols, *Human Physiology: The Basis of Sanitary and Social Science*, p. 304.
54 Nichols, *Esoteric Anthropology*, p. 102.

55 Acton, *The Functions and Disorders of the Reproductive Organs*, 6th edition, p. 215.

56 This argument was not new but had become much more prominent; in the early nineteenth century a few doctors held chastity to be bad for women. See McLaren, *Birth Control in Nineteenth-Century England*, p. 96.

57 Campbell, *Differences in the Nervous Organism of Man and Woman*, p. 200.

58 Maudsley, *Pathology of Mind*, p. 164.

59 Maudsley, *Body and Mind*, p. 84.

60 Maudsley, *Pathology of Mind*, p. 164. And see Owen, *The Darkened Room*, p. 145.

61 Clouston, *Clinical Lectures on Mental Diseases*, p. 478; and see Mortimer, *Chapters on Human Love*, pp. 52-3, for a similar statement on 'Old Maids' Mania', and also Mercier, *Textbook of Insanity*, p. 157.

62 Ware, *Beyond the Pale*, pp. 190-95.

63 Quoted in Ware, *Beyond the Pale*, p 194.

64 Ware, *Beyond the Pale*, p. 192.

65 Moscucci, *The Science of Women*, p. 28.

66 Barnes and Barnes, *A System of Obstetric Medicine and Surgery*, pp. 202-3.

67 For example, see Wilson, 'A Theory of Sex', pp. 713-14; Walter K. Sibley, letter in the *Lancet*, 3 October 1891, pp. 787-8; Charles R. Straton, letter in the *Lancet*, 10 October 1891, pp. 841-2. For discussion of medical debates on menstruation in mid-Victorian period, see Shuttleworth, 'Female Circulation: Medical Discourse and Popular Advertising in Mid-Victorian Era', in Jacobus *et al*, *Body/ Politics*.

68 Clouston, *Clinical Lectures on Mental Diseases*, 5th edition, p. 582.

69 This was to change in the early twentieth century. See Showalter, *The Female Malady*. James Paget was one of the few Victorian doctors to reject the gender identification of hysteria and the claim that it was caused by reproductive disorders. See Peterson, 'Dr Acton's Enemy: Medicine, Sex and Society in Victorian England', p. 578.

70 Nichols, *Human Physiology*, p. 2.

71 *Edinburgh Medical Journal*, June 1883, p. 1123.

72 Campbell, *Differences in the Nervous Organism of Man and Woman*, p. 166, and see Showalter, *The Female Malady*.

73 See Tickner, *The Spectacle of Women*, pp. 192-205. And see Dr Almroth Wright's letter, 'On Militant Hysteria', to *The Times*, 28 March 1912.

74 See Showalter, *The Female Malady*, Chapter 7.

75 Bryan Donkin, 'Hysteria', in Tuke (ed.), *A Dictionary of Psychological Medicine: Volume 1*, pp. 619, 620.

76 See Maudsley, 'Sex in Mind and in Education'; T.S. Clouston, *Popular Science Monthly*, 1883/4; Withers Moore, *British Medical Journal*, 7 August 1886; Crichton-Browne, 'Sex in Education', *Lancet*, 7 May 1892; and see Dyhouse, 'Social Darwinistic Ideas and the Development of Women's Education in England, 1880–1920'.

77 Showalter, *The Female Malady*, p. 129.

78 Tait, *Diseases of Women and Abdominal Surgery*, p. 344.

79 See Tait, *Diseases of Women and Abdominal Surgery*, p. 622; Moscucci, *The Science of Woman*. See Showalter, *The Female Malady*, p. 130, on the view that the clitoris was threatening. The operation is still performed in Britain today; see *Rites*, the Channel 4 programme by Penny Deadman, transmitted in 1990. The medical profession's concern with accusations of non-consensual operations needs to be seen in the context of other accusations of medical misconduct, e.g. bodysnatching and vivisection. See Richardson, *Death, Dissection and the Destitute*; Elston, 'Women and Anti-vivisection in Victorian England, 1870–1900', in Rupke (ed.), *Vivisection in Historical Perspective*, p. 249. On the traditional division between physicians and surgeons, see Parry and Parry, *The Rise of the Medical Profession*.

80 *Lancet*, 14 August 1886, and see *Lancet*, 22 February 1890.

81 See Elston, 'Women and Anti-vivisection in Victorian England, 1870–1900', in Rupke (ed.), *Vivisection in Historical Perspective*, p. 249. A feminist commentator noted: 'Literary and scientific men have invented a new form of vivisection . . . its victim is Woman with a capital W' (Mrs Alfred Osler, 'Moral Vivisection', *Woman's Penny Paper*, 8 December 1888).

82 Lawson Tait, *Lancet*, 21 August 1886, p. 375; in contrast to the *Lancet*, the *British Medical Journal* gave much favourable coverage to, and reproduction of, talks by Tait on his surgical achievements. There is still medical debate today as to whether oophorectomy (removal of both ovaries) leads to loss of sexual desire. Thanks to Dr Helen Massil for this information.

83 *British Medical Journal*, 30 June 1888, p. 1387.

84 See *British Medical Journal*, vol. 2, 1897, pp. 769–70; Moscucci, *The Science of Woman*, p. 81.

85 Part of the feminist distrust of the medical profession related to the profession's support for the Contagious Diseases Acts. Feminists did draw on medical statistics for their own uses, however. See, for

example, Pankhurst, *The Great Scourge and How to End It*, discussed in Chapter 6.

86 Kent, *Sex and Suffrage in Britain, 1860–1914*, pp. 114–15.

87 Blackwell, 'Influence of Women in the Profession of Medicine', in Blackwell, *Essays in Medical Sociology*, vol. 2. Mary Ann Elston, however, argues that from the 1880s onwards the majority of the female medical teachers did not endorse Blackwell's vision of women's special spiritual role in medicine, in 'Women and Anti-vivisection in Victorian England, 1870–1900', in Rupke (ed.), *Vivisection in Historical Perspective*, p. 285.

88 See Nancy Ann Sahli, 'Elizabeth Blackwell, MD, (1821–1910): a Biography', unpublished PhD, University of Pennsylvania, 1974; Forster, *Significant Sisters*, Chapter 2; Jackson, *The Real Facts of Life*, Chapter 3.

89 The Christo-Theosophical Society stood in opposition to the Blavatsky Theosophical Society's subordination of Christianity to Eastern religions. See Chapter 4 for brief discussion of theosophy.

90 Laqueur, *Making Sex*, pp. 205–6.

91 See Blackwell, 'Scientific Method in Biology', in Blackwell, *Essays in Medical Sociology*, vol. 2.

92 See Elston, 'Women and Anti-vivisection in Victorian England, 1870–1900', in Rupke (ed.), *Vivisection in Historical Perspective*; Moscucci, *The Science of Woman*, p. 124; Blackwell, 'Scientific Method in Biology', in Blackwell, *Essays in Medical Sociology*, vol. 2, pp. 119–20.

93 Blackwell, *The Human Element in Sex*, 4th edition, pp. 45, 46.

94 See Valverde, 'The Concept of "Race" in First-wave Feminist Sexual and Reproductive Politics', in Iacovetta and Valverde (eds.), *Expanding Boundaries: New Essays in Women's History*.

95 See Burton, 'The Feminist Quest for Identity: British Imperialist Suffragism and "Global Sisterhood", 1900–1915'. There were exceptions in the form of British women working against racism. See Ware, *Beyond the Pale*, Part 4, for the example of women involved in the Anti-Lynching Committee.

96 Young, 'The Impact of Darwin on Conventional Thought', in Symondson (ed.), *The Victorian Crisis in Faith*.

97 Webb, *My Apprenticeship*, p. 83.

98 See Peel, *Herbert Spencer: The Evolution of a Sociologist*.

99 Darwin, *The Descent of Man*, 1901 edition, p. 939.

100 See, for example, Ellis, *Studies in the Psychology of Sex Vol. 3*, pp. 19–20. Westermarck, *The History of Human Marriage*, pp. 542–3; Russett, *Sexual Science*, pp. 89–92; Stepan, *The Idea of Race in Science*, p. 61.

101 Darwin, *The Descent of Man*, 1901 edition, p. 858.

102 Darwin, *The Descent of Man*, 1901 edition, p. 861.

103 Darwin, *The Descent of Man*, 1901 edition, p. 858.

104 Darwin, *The Descent of Man*, 1901 edition, pp. 857, 858. In response to this remark, the feminist writer Ellis Ethelmer commented: 'In even so sedate and usually dispassionate a physiologist and philosopher as Charles Darwin, the masculine sex-bias is so engrained ... that he strives to disparage and condemn the notorious mental quickness or intuition of women' (*Woman Free*, pp. 64–5).

105 See Stepan, *The Idea of Race in Science*; Semmel, *Imperialism and Social Reform*, compare with Freeden, *The New Liberalism*.

106 Ellis, *Man and Woman*, 6th edition, p. 98. See Stepan, 'Race and Gender: the Role of Analogy in Science', in Goldberg (ed.), *The Anatomy of Racism*.

107 Ellis, *Man and Woman*.

108 Campbell, *Differences in the Nervous Organism of Man and Woman*, p. 612; see Spencer, 'The Comparative Psychology of Man', pp. 257–89; see Biddis (ed.), *Images of the Race*, for discussion of Spencer's ideas on the parallels between the child's and the savage's minds.

109 Stepan, 'Race and Gender: the Role of Analogy in Science', in Goldberg (ed.), *The Anatomy of Racism*, p. 40.

110 See Sulloway, *Freud, Biologist of the Mind*.

111 See Gilman, 'Black Bodies, White Bodies: Towards an Iconography of Female Sexuality in Late Nineteenth-Century Art'.

112 See Siegel, 'Literature: the Representation of "Decadence"', in Chamberlin and Gilman (eds.), *Degeneration*.

113 See Lorimer, *Colour, Class and the Victorians*; Irvine *et al* (eds.), *Demystifying Social Statistics*; Gould, *The Mismeasure of Man*; Tagg, 'Power and Photography: a Means of Surveillance'.

114 Stepan, 'Race and Gender: the Role of Analogy in Science', in Goldberg (ed.), *The Anatomy of Racism*, pp. 40–41.

115 See Said, *Culture and Imperialism*; on the Governor Eyre case, see Hall, *White, Male and Middle Class*.

116 Stepan, 'Race and Gender: the Role of Analogy in Science', in Goldberg (ed.), *The Anatomy of Racism*, p. 40.

117 See *The Descent of Man*, p. 861, where Darwin quotes naturalist Carl Vogt on this subject. See Ritchie, *Darwinism and Politics*, for critique of this argument. Also see Forel, *The Sexual Question*, p. 190; Bloch, *The Sexual Life of Our Time in Its Relation to Modern Civilization*, p. 58.

118 Ellis, *Man and Woman*, p. 53.

119 Tait, *Diseases of Women and Abdominal Surgery*, p. 4; and see Ellis, *Man and Woman*, p. 66.

120 See Talbot, *Degeneracy*; Stepan, 'Biological Degeneration: Race and Proper Places', in Chamberlin and Gilman (eds.), *Degeneration*, pp. 98, 113; Gilman, 'Black Bodies, White Bodies: Towards an Iconography of Female Sexuality in Late Nineteenth-Century Art'.

121 Jordanova, *Sexual Visions*, p. 105.

122 Stepan, 'Biological Degeneration: Race and Proper Places', in Chamberlin and Gilman, *Degeneration*, p. 105. And see Stanley (ed.), *The Diaries of Hannah Cullwick*, for an example of the erotic obsession of an English middle-class man, Arthur Munby, with working-class women.

123 Romanes, 'The Mental Differences between Men and Women'.

124 *British Medical Journal*, 20 July 1887. One of the most convincing critiques of the intelligence and brain-size relationship came in 1901 from research of Karl Pearson and his assistant Alice Lee. See Love, 'Alice in Eugenics Land'. On craniology see Fee, 'Nineteenth-Century Craniology'. See also Pearson, 'Variation in Man and Woman', and Havelock Ellis's reply in *Popular Science Monthly*, January 1903.

125 Romanes, 'The Mental Differences between Men and Women', pp. 657-9.

126 Geddes and Thomson, *The Evolution of Sex*; and see Conway, 'Stereotypes of Femininity in a Theory of Sexual Evolution', in Vicinus (ed.), *Suffer and be Still*; Russett, *Sexual Science*.

127 Geddes and Thomson, *The Evolution of Sex*, p. 270.

128 Ellis, *Man and Woman*, p. 491.

129 Geddes and Thomson, *The Evolution of Sex*, p. 267.

130 Clapperton, *Scientific Meliorism and the Evolution of Happiness*, p. 27.

131 Ritchie, *Darwinism and Politics*, p. 2.

132 Maria Sharpe to editor of *Woman's Penny Paper*, 23 March 1889.

133 See Coward, *Patriarchal Precedents*, for discussion of nineteenth-century theories of Matriarchy.

134 See Besant, *Theosophy and the Law of Population*; Blackwell, *Essays in Medical Sociology*; Ethelmer, *Life to Woman*; Ethelmer, *Phases of Love*; Anon. (see under Henrietta Muller), 'The Future of Single Women'; Anon. (see under Henrietta Muller), 'What Woman is Fitted for'.

135 Jordanova, '"Natural Facts": An Historical Perspective on Science and Sexuality', in MacCormack and Strathern (eds.), *Nature, Culture and Gender*, p. 47.

136 See Gould, *The Panda's Thumb*, pp. 65-71.

137 Ethelmer, *Life to Woman*, p. 30.

138 Feminists were not alone in holding such a position. The famous German psychologist Richard Krafft-Ebing, for example, believed that culture and civilization emerged through the refinement and suppression of the human sexual instinct; see Sulloway, *Freud: Biologist of the Mind*. See Raymond Williams for a discussion of the different meanings of nature, *Keywords*, p. 184.

139 K. Mills, Minutes, May 1887 (PC); and see Swiney, *The Bar of Isis*.

140 See Ellis, *Studies in the Psychology of Sex Vol. 3*, Appendix A, p. 239, for a discussion of the different views of the 'savage' sexuality. Ellis himself, citing Westermarck, Frazer and Crawley, claimed that the romantic view and the licentious view were both incorrect, although he believed that there was evidence of a weaker sexual instinct among 'savages'.

141 Ethelmer, *Life to Woman*, p. 39.

142 See Jeffreys, *The Spinster and Her Enemies*, for a discussion of the work of Ellice Hopkins in educating men into chastity.

143 On Spencer, see Peel, *Herbert Spencer: the Evolution of a Sociologist*, and Wiltshire, *The Social and Political Thought of Herbert Spencer*; on Wallace, see Wallace, 'Human Selection', and see Durant, 'Scientific Naturalism and Social Reform in the Thought of Alfred Russel Wallace'; on J.A. Hobson's belief that with the advance of civilization, the struggle for existence is transmuted, see Collini, *Liberalism and Sociology*, pp. 178–9.

144 See review of H. and M. Bernard, 'Women and Evolution', in *Votes for Women*, 14 January 1910, p. 246.

145 H. Muller, 'The Other Side of the Question', October 1885 (PC).

146 See Beer, *Darwin's Plots* and '"The Face of Nature": Anthropomorphic Elements in the Language of *The Origins of Species*', in Jordanova (ed.), *Languages of Nature*.

147 Beer, *Darwin's Plots*, p. 8

148 See Olroyd, *Darwinian Impacts*.

149 R. Parker, 'Note on Emancipation of Women', November 1888 (PC).

150 See Heyck, *The Transformation of Intellectual Life in Victorian England*.

151 On altruism, see Collini, *Public Moralists*.

152 Darwin, *The Descent of Man*, 1871 edition, p. 933.

153 Mercier, 'Vice, Crime and Insanity', in Allbutt and Rolleston (eds.), *A System of Medicine*, vol. 8, p. 248.

154 Men and Women's Club Minutes, October 1885 (PC).

155 See Carpenter, *Principles of Mental Physiology*, first published in 1874.

156 Blackwell, *Counsel to Parents on the Moral Education of Their Children in Relation to Sex*, 8th edition, p. 78.
157 Darwin, *The Descent of Man*, 1871 edition, pp. 148, 934.
158 Annie Eastty, Men and Women's Club Minutes, January 1886.
159 Maria Sharpe's letter to the *Inquirer*, 1 June 1889.
160 See Davidoff and Hall, *Family Fortunes*.
161 Spencer, *The Principles of Ethics*, vol. 2, p. 196.
162 See Jones, *Social Darwinism and English Thought*, p. 23.
163 Semmel, *Imperialism and Social Reform*.
164 Stephen and Pollock (eds.), *Lectures and Essays by the late William Kingdon Clifford*, p. 42.
165 Clifford, 'On the Scientific Basis of Morals', *Contemporary Review*, 1875, reprinted in Stephen and Pollock (eds.), *Lectures and Essays by the late William Kingdon Clifford*, p. 81.
166 Robert Parker's notes on 'Emancipation of Women', November 1888 (PC).

CHAPTER 3 'Purifying' the Public World: Feminist Vigilantes, Prostitution and 'Protective Surveillance'

1 An earlier and shorter version of this chapter appears as Bland, 'Purifying the Public World: Feminist vigilantes in late Victorian England'.
2 Laura Chant, *Woman's Signal*, 1 November 1894; and see Chant, *Why We Attacked the Empire*.
3 *Vigilance Record*, October 1894.
4 Laura Chant, *Woman's Signal*, 1 November 1894; and see Chant, *Why We Attacked the Empire*.
5 Josephine Butler to Mary Priestman, 5 November 1894 (JBC).
6 Stedman Jones, 'Working-Class Culture and Working-Class Politics in London, 1870–1900'.
7 Harrison, 'State Intervention and Moral Reform in Nineteenth-Century England', in Hollis (ed.), *Pressure from Without*; see Valverde, *The Age of Light, Soap and Water*, p. 29, who points out that in the North American context: 'What has been described as imposing values on another class is simultaneously a process of creating and reaffirming one's own class.' The same analysis would be applicable to Britain.
8 See Stedman Jones, *Outcast London*, p. 224.
9 Walkowitz, *Prostitution and Victorian Society*, p. 251.
10 See Wilson, *The Sphinx in the City*.

11 As Brian Harrison points out, moral reformers, feminist or not, cannot be understood in simple class terms anyway. Not all the middle classes supported them, nor did all the aristocracy. And they had the support of some of the working class (Harrison, 'State Intervention and Moral Reform in Nineteenth-Century England', in Hollis (ed.), *Pressure from Without*, pp. 297–8).

12 See Walkowitz, *Prostitution and Victorian Society*; McHugh, *Prostitution and Victorian Social Reform*.

13 Josephine Butler, speech at Exeter Hall, reported in *The Shield*, 11 April 1885.

14 On repealers in the NVA, see *The Sentinel*, April 1887.

15 On law as 'schoolmaster to the nation' see Harrison, 'State Intervention and Moral Reform in Nineteenth-Century England', in Hollis (ed.), *Pressure from Without*; see Jeffreys, *The Spinster and Her Enemies* for a positive portrayal of the NVA's activities. Thanks to Walter McLaughlin for discussion of the NVA.

16 Elizabeth Wolstenholme Elmy, *Journal of the Personal Rights Association*, May 1887.

17 Josephine Butler, 1897, quoted in Higson, *The Story of a Beginning*.

18 The *Journal of the Vigilance Association*, 15 October 1885.

19 Bristow, *Vice and Vigilance*, p. 154. Judith Walkowitz points out that the Jack the Ripper murders of 1888 led to increased coercion of brothels and prostitutes. Further, the slum clearance response as a way of 'cleaning up' Whitechapel heightened the homelessness of prostitutes and their fellow lodgers (*City of Dreadful Delight*, pp. 224–6).

20 The London Council for the Promotion of Public Morality (LCPPM) drafted a bill in 1902 to cover prostitutes living in flats and single rooms. It did not become law. See LCPPM Annual Report, 23 February 1903.

21 Lucy Wilson, editorial, *Journal of the Personal Rights Association*, 15 January 1886.

22 Henrietta Muller quoted in *Personal Rights Journal*, 1 October 1886.

23 Elizabeth Wolstenholme Elmy, *Journal of the Personal Rights Association*, May 1886.

24 William Coote, *The Vigilance Record*, 15 April 1887.

25 *Vigilance Record*, 15 April 1887.

26 *Vigilance Record*, July 1888.

27 *Personal Rights Journal*, January 1889.

28 On Millicent Fawcett's work for the NVA see Rubinstein, *A Different World for Women*, p. 90. Twenty-three years later, many feminists were still concerned about Mrs Fawcett's membership of the NVA.

For example, 'Fatum' wrote to *The Freewoman*, 20 June 1912, pp. 96– 7: 'There are many cultured and educated suffragists who would like to see Mrs H. Fawcett resign from her position as a member of the [NVA].'

29 The *Hants and Surrey Times*, 30 June 1888, quoted in the *Vigilance Record*, July 1888, p. 68.

30 The *Aldershot Gazette*, 23 June 1888; quoted in the *Vigilance Record*, July 1888, p. 68.

31 *Woman's Penny Paper*, 1 December 1888.

32 Arthur Collier, 'Two Purity Societies', *The Adult*, vol. 2, no. 7, August 1898, p. 207.

33 Chant, 'Woman and the Streets', in Marchant (ed.), *Public Morals*.

34 Stedman Jones, 'Working-class Culture and Working-class Politics in London, 1870–1900', p. 77.

35 Laura Chant, *Vigilance Record*, April 1889, January 1888; on music-halls in general in this period, see Bailey (ed.), *Music Hall: the Business of Pleasure*.

36 Laura Chant, *Vigilance Record*, July 1888.

37 Laura Chant, *Woman's Signal*, 1 November 1894.

38 Chant, *Why We Attacked the Empire*, p. 30.

39 Blackwell, *Right and Wrong Methods with Dealing with the Social Evil*, pp. 12, 29. Elizabeth Blackwell was so committed to strong local government because she saw it in terms of a defence of community autonomy and an alternative to strong central government. This was reflective of her earlier interest in co-operation, communitarianism and Christian socialism. Thanks to Sandra Holton for this insight.

40 London Council for the Promotion of Public Morality Annual Report, February 1902. A number of London borough councils were appointing their own officials to monitor prostitution and to work with the NVA and other morality groups, see Coote, *A Romance of Philanthropy*; Mort, *Dangerous Sexualities*, p. 135.

41 On Elizabeth Blackwell's objections see NVA Executive Minutes, 8 March 1887.

42 See William Coote's evidence to the Royal Commission on the Police, reported in *Vigilance Record*, October 1906; Storch, 'Police Control of Street Prostitution in Victorian London', in Bayley (ed.), *Police and Society*.

43 The Aliens Act 1905 forbade 'undesirable and destitute aliens' to enter as steerage passengers in ships containing twenty or more aliens. See Foot, *Immigrants and Race in British Politics*.

44 London Council for the Promotion of Public Morality Annual Report 28 February 1903, and see annual reports for 31 December 1905 and 31

December 1906. Also see Coote, *A Romance of Philanthropy*. Coote informed the Royal Commission on Metropolitan Police that London was now 'an open-air Cathedral' compared to forty years ago, when it was 'vicious in every particular' (*Royal Commission on the Duties of the Metropolitan Police* 1908, p. 686, quoted in Mort, *Dangerous Sexualities*, p. 136).

45 Walkowitz, *Prostitution and Victorian Society*, pp. 247, 251–2.

46 *Journal of the Vigilance Association*, 15 October 1885.

47 Chant, *Why We Attacked the Empire*, p. 5.

48 Hollis (ed.), *Ladies Elect*, p. 48; and see Shiman, ' "Changes are Dangerous": Women and Temperance in Victorian England', in Malmgreen (ed.), *Religion in the Lives of English Women, 1760–1930*; Amanda Sebestyen, 'Women against the Demon Drink', *Spare Rib*, no. 100, 1980; Bordin, *Women and Temperance*.

49 Levine, *Feminist Lives in Victorian England*, p. 87.

50 See Prochaska, *Women and Philanthropy in Nineteenth-Century England*; Summers, 'A Home from Home – Women's Philanthropic Work in the Nineteenth Century', in Burman, *Fit Work for Women*.

51 Nead, *Myths of Sexuality*, pp. 196–7.

52 Donzelot, *The Policing of Families*.

53 Walkowitz, 'Male Vice and Female Virtue: Feminism and the Politics of Prostitution in Nineteenth-Century Britain', in Snitow *et al* (eds.), *Desire: the Politics of Sexuality*.

54 Riley, *Am I that Name? Feminism and the Category of 'Woman' in History*, pp. 49, 51. By the late nineteenth century there were at least 20,000 salaried and half a million voluntary women 'charity workers' (Walkowitz, *City of Dreadful Delight*, p. 53).

55 See Hollis, *Ladies Elect*; Summers, 'A Home from Home – Women's Philanthropic Work in the Nineteenth Century', in Burman, *Fit Work for Women*.

56 Hollis, *Ladies Elect*.

57 Feminists campaigned for entry into the police force in the late nineteenth and early twentieth centuries. See Bland, 'In the Name of Protection: the Policing of Women in the First World War', in Smart and Brophy (eds.), *Women in Law*; Levine, ' "Walking the Streets in a Way No Decent Woman Should": Women Police in World War I'.

58 On women's attempts to be councillors see Hollis, *Ladies Elect*.

59 *Vigilance Record*, April 1889. With the decrease in aristocratic power and the rise of a middle-class professional state bureaucracy, classic Liberal hostility to the 'corrupt' aristocratic state appeared outdated. In the face of an increasingly organized working class, and rising evidence of widespread poverty, a number of Liberals – 'New Liberals' – felt

the need to redefine Liberalism's attitude toward the state and its '*laissez-faire*' individualism. The 'New Liberals' were a group of liberal intellectuals who, from the 1880s on, developed a new political ideology which argued that individual liberties and true 'equality of opportunity' could only be realized through greater state intervention. The state should act *ethically*, for the 'collective will' of society. See Clarke *et al*, *Ideologies of Welfare*, and Langan and Schwarz (eds.), *Crises in the British State, 1880–1930*. Many social purity feminists were Liberal in their politics. It is worth noting that New Liberals' changing views of the state, especially the idea of an ethical state, were in congruence with the feminist demand that government and the law should act as agents of moral reform.

60 See Summerfield, 'The Effingham Arms and the Empire: Deliberate Selection in the Evolution of Music Hall in London', in Yeo and Yeo (eds.), *Popular Culture and Class Conflict, 1590–1914*.

61 See Samuel, 'The Discovery of Puritanism, 1820–1914: a Preliminary Sketch', in Garnett and Matthew (eds.), *Revival and Religion since 1700*. Of Progressive members Beatrice Webb reflected in her Diary: 'The ordinary Progressive member is either a bounder, a narrow-minded fanatic or a mere piece of putty' (23 January 1895, quoted in MacKenzie and MacKenzie, *The First Fabians*, p. 304).

62 Theatre and Music Halls Committee of the LCC, 31 July 1890, quoted in Pennybacker, '"It was not what she said, but the way in which she said it": The London County Council and the Music Halls', in Bailey (ed.), *Music Hall: The Business of Pleasure*.

63 For example, see Booth, *London Town*, p. 142.

64 See, for example, *Daily Telegraph*, 18 October 1894, p. 3; see Stokes, *In the Nineties*, p. 58.

65 See Churchill, *My Early Life*; Turner, *Roads to Ruin*, Chapter 9.

66 Sec Stokes, *In the Nineties*, p. 57.

67 Walkowitz, *Prostitution and Victorian Society*, p. 249.

68 *Vigilance Record*, 15 January 1888. On the widespread view that the prostitute was characterized by idleness see Levine, 'Venereal Disease, Prostitution and the Politics of Empire'.

69 Moral Reform Union, *The Fallen Woman!* leaflet, n.d.

70 Moral Reform Union, *The Fallen Woman!* leaflet, n.d.

71 Blackwell, *Purchase of Women: the Great Economic Blunder*.

72 On the distinction between the deserving and undeserving poor – part of the classification being widely employed by philanthropic organizations and state institutions from the 1880s on – see Stedman Jones, *Outcast London*.

73 See Tomalin, *The Invisible Woman*; Davis, *Actresses as Working Women*.

74 Laura Chant, *Woman's Signal*, 1 November 1894.

75 Chant, 'Women and the Streets', in Marchant (ed.), *Public Morals*.

76 On the nature of prostitution, see Walkowitz, *Prostitution and Victorian Society*, Chapter 1. See Tickner, *The Spectacle of Women*, p.225, for a discussion of the iconography of the prostitute in suffrage politics.

77 Walkowitz, *City of Dreadful Delight*.

78 Judith Walkowitz, 'Jack the Ripper and the Myth of Male Violence', p 544.

79 Showalter, *Sexual Anarchy*, p.118.

80 A contemporary observer noted of the Empire: 'The Promenade was, except for its main attraction, a male preserve' (W.M. Queen-Pope, *Twenty Shillings in the Pound*, quoted in Turner, *Roads to Ruin*, p 211). See Sennett, *The Fall of Public Man*.

81 Levine, *Feminist Lives*, p 84.

82 Walkowitz, *City of Dreadful Delight*, pp. 24, 45, 52. See Bowlby, *Just Looking*, Chapter 2.

83 See Valverde, 'The Love of Finery: Fashion and the Fallen Woman in Nineteenth-Century Social Discourse', pp. 168–88.

84 Olive Schreiner to the editor of *Daily News*, 28 December 1885, reprinted in Rive (ed.), *Olive Schreiner Letters: vol. 1, 1871–1899*, pp. 70–71.

85 On the Cass case see *The Pioneer*, 1 August 1887; Walkowitz, *City of Dreadful Delight*, p 218. There were many other cases of false arrest, but most did not become *causes célèbres*. See, for example, 'How Men Protect Women', *The Vote*, 17 February 1912, p 197.

86 *The Pioneer*, 1 August 1887.

87 Josephine Butler to Anon., 5 November 1896 (JBC).

88 Chant, 'Women and the Streets', in Marchant (ed.), *Public Morals*, p. 129.

89 Millicent Fawcett, *Vigilance Record*, June 1893.

90 *Personal Rights Journal*, January 1889.

91 Paper given to the National Union of Women Workers, October 1895, reproduced in *Vigilance Record*, December 1895.

92 Gorham, 'The "Maiden Tribute of Modern Babylon" Reexamined', pp. 366–7.

CHAPTER 4 Marriage: Its Iniquities and Its Alternatives

1 Quilter (ed.), *Is Marriage a Failure?*. Also see Rubenstein, *Before the Suffragettes*. The letters were discussed by the fictitious Pooters of Holloway. Charles Pooter recorded in his diary: 'Nov 2. I spent the

evening quietly with Carrie . . . We had a most pleasant chat *re* the letters on "Is Marriage a Failure?"' (G. and W. Grossmith, *The Diary of a Nobody*, Bristol, J.W. Arrowsmith, 1892; London, Penguin, 1965).

2 See Shanley, *Feminism, Marriage and the Law in Victorian England, 1850–1895*. In 1895 the Summary Jurisdiction (Married Women's) Act extended maintenance and separation allowances to women who had already left their husbands because of assault, neglect or 'persistent cruelty'.

3 Shanley, *Feminism, Marriage and the Law in Victorian England, 1850–1895*, p. 187.

4 This is pointed out by Clarke, 'Feminism and the Popular Novel of the 1890s'.

5 Caird, 'Marriage'.

6 Quilter, *Is Marriage a Failure?*, p. 1.

7 See interview with Mona Caird in *The Woman's Penny Paper*, 28 June 1890. Her marriage articles were collected together in *The Morality of Marriage and Other Essays*.

8 O. Schreiner to R. Parker, 30 September 1885 (PC).

9 See O. Schreiner to E. Carpenter, 11 November 1888 (ECC).

10 M. Sharpe, 'Autobiographical History', 1889, p. 72 (PC).

11 Caird, 'Marriage', p. 189.

12 Caird, 'Phases of Human Development', p. 229.

13 Caird, 'Ideal Marriage', p. 635.

14 Caird, 'Marriage', p. 191.

15 Caird, 'Marriage', p. 198.

16 Caird, 'Phases of Human Development', p. 169.

17 Caird, 'Ideal Marriage'.

18 Caird, 'Marriage', p. 188.

19 Hammerton, *Cruelty and Companionship*, pp. 1–2; and see Munday, 'Women's Attitudes to Womanhood and Marriage in the Periodical Press, 1885–95'; Stedman Jones, 'Working-Class Culture and Working-Class Politics in London, 1870–1900', pp. 491–2.

20 Shanley, *Feminism, Marriage and the Law*, p. 7.

21 Cobbe, 'Wife Torture in England'.

22 Cobbe, 'Celibacy v. Marriage', p. 233.

23 Thompson and Wheeler, *Appeal of One Half of the Human Race, Women, Against the Pretensions of the Other Half, Men*, and see Ware, *Beyond the Pale*, pp. 102–4 for a discussion of this book.

24 Ignota, 'Judicial Sex Bias', p. 285. 'Ignota' was the pseudonym of Elizabeth Wolstenholme Elmy.

25 Brooke, *A Superfluous Woman*, pp. 202 and 12. On Orientalism, see de Groot, '"Sex" and "Race": the Construction of Language and Image in the Nineteenth Century', in Mendus and Rendall (eds.), *Sexuality and Subordination*; Kabbani, *Europe's Myths of Orient*.

26 See Fawcett, 'The Emancipation of Women'; according to her biographer Claire Tomalin, Mary Wollstonecraft was the first to refer to marriage as 'legalized prostitution'. This was in her *A Vindication of the Rights of Woman*.

27 Ker, *Motherhood*, p. 29. And see Besant, 'The Economic Position of Women', p. 99.

28 Egerton, 'Virgin Soil' in *Discords*, p. 155.

29 Alma Gillen, *Shafts*, March 1894.

30 Hewitt, 'Woman's Duty', p. 83. Some men were making the same argument, for example, see Professor A. Posoda in Sociological Society, *Sociological Papers*, vol. 2.

31 Black, 'The Organization of Working Women', p. 695.

32 See Dyhouse, *Feminism and the Family in England, 1880–1939*.

33 Chapman, *Marriage Questions in Modern Fiction*, p. 205.

34 Fawcett, 'The Emancipation of Women', p. 675; and see Grand, 'Marriage Questions in Fiction: the Standpoint of a Typical Modern Woman', pp. 385–9; see Black, 'On Marriage: a Criticism', for a feminist demand for incompatibility as grounds for divorce.

35 Besant, *Marriage as it was, as it is, and as it should be*.

36 J.S. Mill quoted in Ignota, 'Judicial Sex Bias', p. 283.

37 Besant, *Marriage as it is, as it was, and as it should be*; paper read by Elizabeth Wolstenholme Elmy before the Dialectical Society in 1880, quoted in Ignota, 'Judicial Sex Bias', pp. 283–4.

38 Ignota, 'Judicial Sex Bias', p. 285; and see Ethelmer, *Woman Free*, p. 101. On 23 October 1991 the House of Lords upheld the Court of Appeal's decision, as handed down in the case of *Regina* v. *R.*, abolishing a husband's immunity from prosecution for the rape of his wife, effectively ending Hale's law on marital rights. See Harrison, 'No means No – that's final', p. 1489.

39 *R.* v. *Jackson*, *Law Reports*, 1 Q.B., 1891, p. 671; and see Rubinstein, *Before the Suffragettes*.

40 *The Times* and the *Law Times* quoted in Pankhurst, *The Suffragette Movement*, p. 95.

41 E. Wolstenholme Elmy to H. McIlquaham, 26 April 1891, *British Library Add. Mss*, 47, 449.

42 Blake, 'The Lady and the Law', p. 367.

43 Shanley, *Marriage and the Law in Victorian England*, p. 184.

44 Wolstenholme Elmy, 'Suffrage', p. 365; and see *WEU 1891–1899: an Epitome of 8 Years' Effort for Justice to Women*, Congleton, 1899.

45 E. Wolstenholme Elmy to H. McIlquaham, 26 November 1895, *British Library Add. Mss* 47, 450.

46 Hemory, 'The Revolt of the Daughters – an answer by one of them', p. 680.

47 Ethelmer, *The Human Flower*, p. 43.

48 Cameron, 'How We Marry', p. 690.

49 Elizabeth Blackwell, 'Pioneer', *The Vote*, 7 August 1914, p. 266.

50 Blackwell, *Counsel to Parents on the Moral Education of Their Children in Relation to Sex*.

51 Blackwell, *Counsel to Parents on the Moral Education of Their Children in Relation to Sex*, p. 88.

52 Valverde, *The Age of Soap, Light and Water*, p. 68.

53 Blackwell, *Counsel to Parents on the Moral Education of Their Children in Relation to Sex*, p. 95.

54 Blackwell, *Counsel to Parents on the Moral Education of Their Children in Relation to Sex*, p. 104.

55 Blackwell, 'The Human Element in Relation to Sex', in Blackwell, *Essays in Medical Sociology*, vol. 1, pp. 22–3.

56 Quoted in K. Pearson to M. Sharpe, 5 March 1887 (PC).

57 Historians disagree as to whether Ethelmer was the pseudonym for Elizabeth Wolstenholme Elmy, her husband, or a shared name. Pankhurst, *The Suffragette Movement*, p. 31, while claiming Ellis Ethelmer to be Ben Elmy's 'habitual pseudonym', then wrote that 'he co-operated with his wife in efforts to advance the study of sex and maternity . . . Together and severally they produced works on sex education . . .' Jeffreys, *The Spinster and Her Enemies*, believes that Ellis Ethelmer is a pseudonym for Elizabeth Wolstenholme Elmy; Levine, '"So Few Prizes and So Many Blanks"', p. 157, states that Ethelmer is Ben Elmy; Shanley, *Feminism, Marriage and the Law*, p. 186, claims that they wrote jointly under the pseudonym, as does Kent, *Sex and Suffrage in Britain, 1860–1914*, p. 110. Evidence seems to substantiate the claim of the pseudonym being that of Ben Elmy, for Elizabeth wrote an obituary of her husband for the *Westminster Review*, recounting how he came to take the name Ellis Ethelmer. See Ignota, 'Pioneers! O Pioneers!'. Many thanks to Muriel Fielding for this reference. There are also several references in Wolstenholme Elmy's letters to her close friend Harriett McIlquaham which indicate that her husband and Ellis Ethelmer are one and the same. It is, however, likely that Elizabeth collaborated with her husband; she certainly was involved in the

publication of the texts, for it is her name which is listed as publisher. She did not write any of the verses, however, for in 1897 she sent Harriett McIlquaham 'some old verses of mine, the very last I ever wrote, early in 1856', E. Wolstenholme Elmy to H. McIlquaham, 18 October 1897.

58 Ethelmer: *Woman Free, Phases of Love, Life to Woman, The Human Flower, Baby Buds*. The outcome of reading Ethelmer's sex education material was not always as Ethelmer intended. Havelock Ellis refers to a woman who was about to be married and was lent *The Human Flower* by her cousin. 'She learnt from this that men desired the body of a woman, and this so appalled her that she was quite ill for several days. The next time her lover attempted a caress she told him it was "lust"' (Ellis, *Studies in the Psychology of Sex Volume 6: Sex in Relation to Society*, pp. 521-2). The *British Medical Journal* praised *Baby Buds*: 'A very difficult and delicate subject is treated with considerable skill.' It added, however: 'Many will think that it [the delicate and difficult matter] had better have been left alone' (*British Medical Journal*, 1896, p. 28).

59 Ethelmer, *Woman Free*, Stanzas 23, 6.

60 Ethelmer, *Life to Woman*, p. 30.

61 Ethelmer, *The Human Flower*, pp. 43, 37.

62 Ker, *Motherhood*, p. 29.

63 *Shafts*, January and February 1895.

64 The 'New Woman' was widely caricatured in the Press. See examples in Gilbert and Gubar, *No Man's Land*, vol. 2: *Sexchanges*, p. 49. Sarah Grand claimed that she invented the term in an article she wrote for the *North American Review* in 1894 (see *Lady's World*, June 1900, p. 883). However, she used the term earlier: a character in her novel *The Heavenly Twins* in 1893 speaks of Evadne as 'the new woman'.

65 Mary Haweis in her 1894 address to the Women's Writers Dinner in Rev. H.R. Haweis (ed.), *Words to Women: Addresses and Essays*, 1909, p. 71, quoted in Showalter, *A Literature of Their Own*, p. 183.

66 For example, see *Shafts*, 1, 25 February 1893, p. 268, for a review of Sarah Grand, *The Heavenly Twins*, and *Shafts* III, April, June and July 1895, for a lengthy and highly praising review of Caird, *The Daughters of Danaus*; see the interview with Mona Caird in *The Woman's Penny Paper* 11, 28 June 1890. Many 'new women' novelists quoted each other, for example, Caird approvingly quoted Grand's 'Ideala' in *The Morality of Marriage and Other Essays*.

67 Elaine Showalter suggests that once the Victorian three-volume novel disappeared, which had been designed for family reading and was thus

340

'an aesthetic straitjacket', the single book of the *fin de siècle*, and not simply those by the 'new woman' writers, took sex as its subject, *Sexual Anarchy*, pp. 15–16. On Thomas Hardy see Boumelha, *Thomas Hardy and Women*.

68 Stutfield, 'Tommyrotics', p. 836.

69 Grand, *The Beth Book*, pp. 424–5.

70 Egerton, *Discords*, p. 157.

71 Brooke, *A Superfluous Woman*, p. 87.

72 Leppington, 'Debrutalisation of Man', p. 742.

73 See Savage, '"The Wilful Communication of a Loathsome Sore"'.

74 Showalter, 'Syphilis, Sexuality and the Fiction of the *Fin de Siècle*', in Yeazell, *Sex, Politics and Science in the Nineteenth-Century Novel*, p. 105.

75 See Shaw, *The Quintessence of Ibsenism*.

76 Kersley, *Darling Madame*, p. 47. And see Clarke, 'Feminism and the Popular Novel of the 1890s'.

77 Kersley, *Darling Madame*, pp. 70, 91.

78 Grand, *The Heavenly Twins*, pp. 103, 79, 159, 292.

79 See Talbot, *Degeneracy*; Ellis, *Studies in the Psychology of Sex Volume 6*; Gilman, 'Black Bodies, White Bodies'.

80 Grand, *The Heavenly Twins*, p. 178.

81 Oppenheim, *The Face and How to Read It*, p. 165.

82 Brooke, *A Superfluous Woman*, p. 20.

83 Grand, *The Heavenly Twins*, p. 80.

84 Letitia Fairfield, quoted in Kersley, *Darling Madame*, p. 15.

85 Interview in *The Humanitarian*, March 1896, quoted in Kersley, *Darling Madame*.

86 Besant, *Marriage as it was, as it is, and as it should be*, p. 51.

87 Aveling and Aveling, *The Woman Question*, p. 15.

88 See Kapp, *Eleanor Marx: the Crowded Years 1884–1898*; Brandon, *The New Women and the Old Men*.

89 Ross, 'Fierce Questions and Taunts', pp. 578–80. See Sally Alexander's Introduction to Pember Reeves, *Round about a Pound a Week*; Jane Lewis, 'The Working-Class Wife and Mother and State Intervention, 1870–1918', in Lewis (ed.), *Labour and Love*.

90 The parallel today is with a woman saying that she supports women's equality but is not a feminist. Thanks to Judy Greenway for this suggestion.

91 Besant, *An Autobiography*, pp. 90, 81.

92 See Wittinger, *Annie Besant and Progressive Messianism, 1847–1933*; Taylor, *Annie Besant*.

93 Beatrice Webb, 1887, quoted in Taylor, *Annie Besant*, p. 35.
94 Walkowitz, *City of Dreadful Delight*, p. 97.
95 Taylor, *Annie Besant*.
96 Besant, *Marriage*, pp. 30–31.
97 Club Minutes, January 1887 (PC).
98 Moral Reform Union, *4th Annual Report*, London, MRU, 1886, p. 3.
99 Quilter, *Is Marriage a Failure?*, p. 142.
100 Eleanor Keeting, *Shafts*, July 1895, p. 61.
101 Mary Reed, *The Adult*, vol. 2, no. 7, August 1898, p. 204.
102 See Johnson, 'Marriage or Free Love', pp. 91–8.
103 Quilter, *Is Marriage a Failure?*, p. 267.
104 See Greenway, 'Uneasy Bedfellows'.
105 See Stallybrass and White, *The Politics and Poetics of Transgression*.
106 Cook, 'Virtue', pp. 19–20.
107 It was also for reasons of impropriety that many feminists kept separate
    the sexual campaign against the Contagious Diseases Acts from other
    feminist campaigns.
108 Pankhurst, *The Suffragette Movement*, p. 31.
109 Some feminists, on marriage, kept their own names – for example,
    Florence Fenwick Miller – while others joined their names with those
    of their husbands, such as Elizabeth Garrett Anderson. Sometimes,
    both partners took on new hyphenated names – for example, Teresa
    Billington and Frederick Greig became Teresa and Frederick
    Billington-Greig. When Olive Schreiner married Cron Cronwright,
    he became Cron Cronwright-Schreiner while she remained simply
    Olive Schreiner. All such feminists kept their names to indicate their
    rejection of the marital law of coverture.
110 M. Fawcett to E. Wolstenholme Elmy, 10 December 1875 Fawcett
    Library.
111 Shanley, *Marriage and the Law*, p. 116.
112 Dawson (ed.), *The Bar Sinister and Licit Love*, p. 1.
113 Gerald Moore, *The Adult*, September 1898.
114 W.T. Stead, quoted in the second Biennial proceedings reported in
    The Adult, 1898.
115 *The Adult*, October 1897.
116 *Shafts*, April 1897, p. 125.
117 *The Adult*, June 1897. See also Dawson, 'Legitimation and Licit
    Love'.
118 Sweeney, *At Scotland Yard*, pp. 178, 182.
119 *The Adult*, August 1898.
120 Dawson (ed.), *The Bar Sinister and Licit Love*, pp. 228–9.

121 J.C. Spence: letter to the Legitimation League's second annual meeting 1895, reprinted in Dawson (ed.), *The Bar Sinister and Licit Love*, p. 237.

122 Lillian Harman, 'Eve and Her Eden', *The Adult*, vol. 2, no. 2, 1898, p. 32.

123 *British Medical Journal*, 2 November 1895. Dr Blandford argued that if she had been contemplating ordinary suicide, a certificate would have been signed without delay, and that social suicide was no different. The *Lancet* disagreed, pointing out that while an attempt at suicide was a penal offence, 'living together' was not. See Dawson (ed.), *Bar Sinister and Licit Love*, pp. 368–9, 378–9. In 1871, spiritualist Louisa Lowe owed her *release* from mental asylum to Dr Blandford. Louisa Lowe had been certified 'insane' on account of her spiritualism. See Owen, *The Darkened Room*, p. 192. Indeed, Dr Blandford had cautioned the medical practitioner to be concerned with insanity, not immorality, in *Insanity and Its Treatment*, p. 489.

124 See Lanchester, *Elsa Lanchester Herself*, pp. 1–5.

125 But see Collette, 'Socialism and Scandal', for discussion of a more sympathetic response of the SDF to the scandal surrounding upper-class Dora Montefiore's relationship with a working-class married man in 1899.

126 *The Woman's Signal*, 31 October 1895, p. 280.

127 Levine, '"So Few Prizes and So Many Blanks"'.

128 Collet, 'Prospects of Marriage for Women', pp. 540, 542.

129 Dyhouse, *Girls Growing Up in Late Victorian and Edwardian England*.

130 See Steedman, *Childhood, Culture and Class in Britain*, p. 141, for discussion of journalism as a new field of employment for women.

131 Vicinus, *Independent Women*, p. 5.

132 Anon. (see under Henrietta Muller), 'The Future of the Single Woman', p. 162.

133 Grand, 'At What Age Should Girls Marry?', p. 163. In Roman Catholic countries, of course, entering a convent was always a respectable alternative to marriage.

134 Besant, 'The Economic Position of Women', p. 99.

135 Hamilton, *Marriage as a Trade*, p. 21.

136 Allen, 'Plain Words on the Woman Question', p. 455.

137 Martin, 'The Glorified Spinster', p. 374. And see Minerva, 'Why Men do not Marry', p. 422.

138 'A Glorified Spinster', correspondence to the *Daily Telegraph*, 11 November 1888, reprinted in Quilter, *Is Marriage a Failure?*.

139 M.A.B., 'Normal or Abnormal?'.

140 Anon. (see under Henrietta Muller), 'The Future of the Single Woman', p. 152.

141 H. Muller to O. Schreiner, 25 June 1886 (PC).

142 Hollis, *Ladies Elect*, p. 100. On Muller at the London School Board see Turnbull, '"So Extremely Like Parliament"'.

143 E. Cobb to K. Pearson, 26 June 1885 (PC).

144 See Burton, 'The White Woman's Burden'; Doughan and Sanchez (eds.), *Feminist Periodicals, 1855–1984*.

145 Anon. (see under Henrietta Muller), 'What Woman is Fitted For', p. 65.

146 Muller, 'The Other Side of the Question', p. 65 (PC).

147 Muller, 'The Other Side of the Question', p. 158 (PC).

148 Anon. (see under Henrietta Muller), 'What Woman is Fitted For', p. 71.

149 Muller, 'The Other Side of the Question', pp. 160, 162 (PC).

150 M. Sharpe to K. Pearson, 26 March 1885 (PC).

151 K. Mills to M. Sharpe, 21 April 1889 (PC).

152 K. Mills to M. Sharpe, 24 April 1889 (PC).

153 K. Mills to M. Sharpe, 21 April 1889 (PC).

154 Personal communication from Joy Dixon, who has done research into the Theosophical Society, and has generously shared some of her findings.

155 See Burfield, 'Theosophy and Feminism: some explorations in Nineteenth-Century Biography', in Holden (ed.), *Women's Religious Experience*.

156 Dixon, '"Spiritual Androgynes"'.

157 *Theosophist*, vol. XVI, February 1895, p. 344. Thanks to Joy Dixon for this reference and also for information on Kate Mills's membership of the Inner Section.

158 K. Mills to M. Sharpe, 24 April 1889, 29 March 1891 (PC).

159 Faderman, *Surpassing the Love of Men*; Smith-Rosenberg, *Disorderly Conduct*; Vicinus, '"One Life to Stand beside Me"'; Vicinus, *Independent Women*.

160 Constance Maynard, unpublished Autobiography, 1887, quoted in Vicinus, *Independent Women*. In contrast, early nineteenth-century aristocrat Anne Lister was quite clear about the sexual nature of her relations with women. Her ability to define herself as 'sapphic' was probably a survival of the more open eighteenth-century libertine tradition. See Whitbread (ed.), *I Know My Own Heart*.

161 L. Eckenstein to M. Sharpe, 3 February 1886 (SC).

162 L. Eckenstein to K. Pearson, 24 April 1890 (PC).

163 L. Eckenstein to M. Sharpe Pearson, 27 August 1893 (PC).

164 Eva's diary, 22 February 1914, quoted in Thompson, *Dear Girl*, p. 199.

165 Eva's diary, 2 July 1913, quoted in Thompson, *Dear Girl*, p. 176.

166 Thompson, *Dear Girl*, p. 211.

167 Ackland, *For Sylvia*, pp. 64, 67–8. Thanks to Anna Davin for this reference.

168 See Faderman, *Surpassing the Love of Men*; also Chapter Seven of this book.

169 Dora Kerr, *The Adult*, October 1897, p. 40.

170 Aveling and Aveling, *The Woman Question*.

171 Clapperton, *Scientific Meliorism and the Evolution of Happiness*.

172 Clapperton, *A Vision of the Future*, p. 111.

173 Clare, 'Stagnant Virginity', p. 413.

174 M. Sharpe to K. Pearson, 27 April 1889 (PC).

175 M. Sharpe to K. Pearson, 11 February 1886 (PC).

176 O. Schreiner to K. Pearson, 26 September 1885 (PC).

177 K. Pearson to M. Sharpe, 6 July 1885 (PC).

178 M. Sharpe to K. Pearson, 21 March 1889 (PC).

179 K. Pearson to M. Sharpe, 24 March 1889 (PC).

180 M. Sharpe to K. Pearson, 26 March 1889 (PC).

181 O. Schreiner to K. Pearson, 26 September 1885 (PC).

182 A. Besant to K. Pearson, 26 March 1889 (PC).

183 M. Sharpe to editor of the *Inquirer*, 1 June 1889.

184 Walkowitz, *City of Dreadful Delight*, p. 161

185 M. Sharpe to K. Pearson, 27 April 1889 (PC).

186 Clarke, 'Feminism and the Popular Novel of the 1890s', p. 93.

187 MacKenzie and MacKenzie, *The First Fabians*, p. 168.

188 O. Schreiner to H. Ellis, 28 March 1884, in Rive (ed.), *Olive Schreiner Letters*, p. 36.

189 See E. Pearson, *Karl Pearson*; Kevles, *In the Name of Eugenics*.

190 K. Pearson to M. Sharpe, 14 August 1889 (PC).

191 Mrs Ellis (Edith Lees), 'A Noviciate for Marriage', reprinted in Ellis, *The New Horizon of Love and Life*.

192 E. Cobb to K. Pearson, 28 September 1889 (PC).

193 L. Sharpe quoted in E. Cobb to K. Pearson, 28 September 1889 (PC).

194 L. Eckenstein to K. Pearson, 11 October 1889 (PC).

195 E. Cobb to K. Pearson, 28 September 1889 (PC).

196 E. Cobb to K. Pearson, 24 October 1889 (PC).

197 M. Sharpe to K. Pearson, 30 May 1889 (PC).

198 See Broughton, 'Women's Autobiography: the Self at Stake?'.

199 M. Sharpe, 'Autobiographical History', 1889 (PC).

200 Maria Sharpe, 'Henrik Ibsen's Women or "Noblesse Oblige"', The Woman's Penny Paper, 28 June 1889.

201 MacKenzie and MacKenzie (eds.), The Diary of Beatrice Webb Vol. 1, 22 April 1884, p. 116.

202 MacKenzie and MacKenzie (eds.), The Diary of Beatrice Webb Vol. 1, 16 March 1884, p. 111.

203 MacKenzie and MacKenzie (eds.). The Diary of Beatrice Webb Vol. 1, 12 January 1884, p. 102; and see Caine, Destined to be Wives, pp. 78–80.

204 K. Pearson to M. Sharpe, 30 July 1889 (PC).

205 M. Sharpe to K. Pearson, 30 May 1889 (PC); and see Walkowitz, City of Dreadful Delight, Chapter 5.

206 K. Pearson to M. Sharpe, 10 July 1889 (PC).

207 M. Sharpe to K. Pearson, 19 October 1889 (PC).

208 M. Sharpe to K. Pearson, 22 October 1889 (PC).

209 M. Sharpe to K. Pearson, 5 April 1890 (PC).

210 M. Sharpe to K. Pearson, 1 April 1890 (PC).

211 E. Cobb to K. Pearson, 10 October 1889 (PC).

212 E. Cobb to K. Pearson, 18 October 1889 (PC).

213 M. Sharpe to K. Pearson, 23 March 1890 (PC).

214 M. Sharpe to K. Pearson, 15 November 1885 (PC).

215 M. Sharpe to K. Pearson, 12 April 1890 (PC).

216 K. Pearson to E. Cobb, 2 April 1927 (PC).

217 Tosh, 'Domesticity and Manliness in the Victorian Middle Class', in Roper and Tosh (eds.), Manful Assertions.

218 R. Parker to E. Cobb, 28 October 1889 (PC).

219 Walkowitz, City of Dreadful Delight, p. 139.

220 Dictionary of National Biography 1931–40, p. 683.

221 On Pearson's female assistants see Love, 'Alice in Eugenics Land'.

222 Shanley, Feminism, Marriage and the Law, p. 190.

223 The Fabian Women's Group, Three Years' Work of the Women's Group; see Sally Alexander's Introduction to Pember Reeves, Round about a Pound a Week, pp. xiv, xvii–xviii.

224 Women's Co-operative Guild, Working Women and Divorce, p. 6.

225 Women's Co-operative Guild's evidence to the Royal Commission on Divorce and Matrimonial Causes, discussed in Savage, 'The Wilful Communication of a Loathsome Sore', p. 39.

226 Shanley, Feminism, Marriage and the Law, p. 85.

227 Rebecca West, 'The Divorce Commission', The Clarion, 29 November 1912, reprinted in Marcus, The Young Rebecca.

228 Royal Commission on Divorce and Matrimonial Causes: Majority Report, London, HMSO, 1912, p. 99.

CHAPTER 5 Contraception, Feminism and the Malthusian League

1 On the abortion debate in the USA see Petchesky, *Abortion and Woman's Choice*; Luker, *Abortion and the Politics of Motherhood*; Durham, *Sex and Politics*; Durham, 'USA: Abortion and Politics of Morality'; on abortion in Ireland, see *Feminist Review*, no. 29, Spring 1988. The Pope's 1968 encyclical *Humanae Vitae* condemned contraception, although use of the natural rhythm method (the 'safe period') to space births was declared acceptable. The Pope's 1993 encyclical *Veritas Splendor* declared that contraception was 'intrinsically evil'. There is also the controversy over Depo-Provera. The offer of this injectable long-term contraceptive to certain black and working-class women without their informed consent was taken up by the Organization of Women of Asian and African Descent (OWAAD) in the 1980s. The contraceptive has harmful side-effects – OWAAD, 'Black Women and Health', 1979, reprinted in the Feminist Anthology Collective, *No Turning Back*, London, Women's Press, 1981.

2 Elderton, *Report of the English Birth Rate, Part 1. England north of the Humber*.

3 Knight, 'Women and Abortion in Victorian and Edwardian England', p. 61.

4 McLaren, *Birth Control in Nineteenth-Century England*, p. 233; on birth control generally see McLaren and also Soloway, *Birth Control and the Population Question in England, 1877–1930*.

5 Burchfield (ed.), *The Oxford English Dictionary*. But How-Martyn and Breed, *The Birth Control Movement in England*, p. 14, date it as 1913.

6 Chief Justice Cockburn, quoted in St John Stevas, *Obscenity and the Law*, p. 126. See Nead, *The Female Nude*, for a useful discussion of obscenity.

7 Manvell, *The Trial of Annie Besant and Charles Bradlaugh*, pp. 65, 66, 147, 148; Annie Besant's remarkable two-day defence greatly impressed the jury, and contributed to their ambivalent verdict: 'We find the book is calculated to corrupt public morals, but we entirely exonerate the defendants from any corrupt motive in publishing it' (quoted in St John Stevas, *Obscenity and the Law*, p. 73). Judge Cockburn defined this as a guilty verdict.

8 Quoted in Taylor, *Annie Besant*, p. 132.

9 Besant, *An Autobiography*, p. 208.

10 See VanArsdel, 'Florence Fenwick Miller 1854–1935', p. 114.

11 *The Hackney and Kingsland Gazette*, 11 April 1877, quoted in Van-Arsdel, 'Florence Fenwick Miller 1854–1935'. Florence presented her defence in the *Eastern Argus and Bethnal Green Times*, in which she argued that in matters unrelated to the School Board, she had a right to her own opinion. She also described and defended Knowlton's book. Such was the demand for her article that it was published two weeks running – VanArsdel, 'Florence Fenwick Miller 1854–1935', p. 114.

12 *Daily Telegraph*, 22 June 1877, quoted in Banks and Banks, 'The Bradlaugh-Besant Trial and the English Newspapers', pp. 27–8. Only *Reynolds* of the national press did not condemn the pamphlet. See Royle, *Radicals, Secularists and Republicans*, p. 256.

13 C.H. Routh, *The Moral and Physical Evils Likely To Follow if Practices Intended To Act as Checks to Population be not Strongly Discouraged and Condemned*, 1879, quoted in McLaren, *Birth Control in Nineteenth-Century England*, p. 131. Charles Darwin expressed concern that birth control might pose the danger of 'extreme profligacy among unmarried women', C. Darwin to G.A. Gaskell, 15 November 1878, quoted in McLaren, *Birth Control in Nineteenth-Century England*, p. 155.

14 Allbutt, *The Wife's Handbook*, p. 49.

15 Allbutt, *The Wife's Handbook*, pp. ii.

16 *Minutes of the General Medical Council for 1887*, 1888, pp. 316–17, quoted in Fryer, *The Birth Controllers*, p. 170.

17 On Williamson's prosecution see Royle, *Radicals, Secularists and Republicans*, p. 276; on the sales of *The Wife's Handbook* see Fryer, *The Birth Controllers*, p. 171; Soloway, *Birth Control and the Population Question in England, 1877–1930*, p. 57, says that it sold more than 250,000 copies by the end of the nineteenth century.

18 National Vigilance Association (NVA) Minutes, 3 May 1887, unpublished, Fawcett Library.

19 Henrietta Muller was unhappy with censorship; she appears to have supported the anti-censorship position of the Moral Reform Union, of which she was a member. See *The Pioneer*, April 1887.

20 NVA Executive Minutes, 17 May 1887.

21 Besant, *An Autobiography*, pp. 223–4.

22 Besant, *The Law of Population*.

23 Annie Besant quoted in Taylor, *Annie Besant*.

24 See Soloway, *Birth Control and the Population Question*, p. 57.

25 Men and Women's Club Minutes, May 1887 (PC).

26 Maria Sharpe, 'Autobiographical History', 1889, p. 44 (PC).

27 Florence Balgarnie, late summer/early autumn 1887 (PC).

28 Mrs Sherwen, *The Freewoman*, 25 January 1912, p. 192. And see Coralie Boord, *The Freewoman*, 8 February 1912, p. 232; W.B. Esson, *The Freewoman*, 1 February 1912, p. 209; A. Herage Edwards, *The Freewoman*, 8 February 1912, pp. 231–2.

29 Maria Sharpe, 'Autobiographical History', 1889 (PC).

30 Isabel Leatham, *The Freewoman*, 7 December 1912, pp. 51–2, and see W.B. Esson, *The Freewoman*, 8 February 1912, p. 209.

31 Quoted in Manvell, *The Trial of Annie Besant and Charles Bradlaugh*, p. 91.

32 Quoted in Benn, *Predicaments of Love*, p. 5.

33 See Young, 'Malthus and the Evolutionists'.

34 Besant, *The Law of Population*, p. 39.

35 Ellis, *The Problem of Race-Regeneration*, p. 51.

36 One defender of birth control signed herself 'Rationalist', and described herself as a very happily married woman who 'found deplorable the assumption that if married people regulate their family, their lives are one long orgy!' She had healthy children whose births had been 'deliberate', i.e. planned through the use of birth control, and 'to say . . . a child is not a "love" child because its birth is deliberated on . . . is to have a degraded idea of "love"', 'Rationalist', *The Freewoman*, 22 February 1912, p. 271.

37 Suspicions were in some ways well founded, for in the name of Malthusianism people around the world have indeed been manipulated and controlled. In the early nineteenth century, Malthus's theory was evoked as the Scottish enclosures forced 'excess' people off the land to make way for profits from sheep. See Prebble, *The Highland Clearances*. In the twentieth century, Malthusianism fuelled Indian population policy in which men underwent enforced vasectomies in the 1970s, and women were, in the 1980s – and still are, in the 1990s – administered dangerous sterilizing drugs. See *Something Like a War*, Parminder Var, Channel 4, 1990.

38 For examples of the medical debate on the dangers of contraception, see J.W. Taylor, *British Medical Journal*, 20 February 1904; F.E. Fremantle, *Lancet*, 22 April 1911; O.A.R. Berkeley-Hill, *Lancet*, 8 July 1911; F.E. Fremantle, *Lancet*, 22 July 1911. And see McLaren, *Birth Control in Nineteenth-Century England*, Chapter 7, and Soloway, *Birth Control and the Population Question in England, 1877–1930*, Chapter 6; 'A Truth-Seeker', *The Freewoman*, 22 February 1912, p. 271; and see Coralie Boord, *The Freewoman*, 1 February 1912, p. 213.

39 Blackwell, 'The Moral Education of the Young in Relation to Sex', in Blackwell, *Essays in Medical Sociology*, p. 293.

40 Blackwell, *The Human Element in Sex*, p. 78; and see Newman, *The Corruption Called Neo–Malthusianism*, with notes by Elizabeth Blackwell.

41 McLaren, *Birth Control in Nineteenth-Century England*, p. 134.

42 Annie Besant suggested that their Defence Committee become the nucleus of a Malthusian League. Ledbetter, *A History of the Malthusian League 1877–1927*, p. 49; Bradlaugh had suggested such a League back in 1861 but the idea had not caught on.

43 Soloway, *Birth Control and the Population Question in England, 1877–1930*, Chapter 3.

44 *The Malthusian*, 15 May 1909, p. 37.

45 Allbutt, *The Wife's Handbook*. The suppliers, E. Lambert and Son of Dalston, were to become the leading suppliers of contraceptives of the twentieth century. See McLaren, *Birth Control in Nineteenth-Century England*, p. 225.

46 Quoted in Benn, *Predicaments of Love*, p. 6. Drysdale's book contained a case history of a young male patient whose seven-year enforced celibacy had led to intense mental and physical suffering. Miriam Benn has established that the patient was George Drysdale himself – *The Predicaments of Love*, p. 38.

47 Benn, *The Predicaments of Love*, pp. 72, 76, 75.

48 *The Malthusian*, April 1879, p. 18.

49 *The Malthusian*, March 1891, p. 21.

50 *The Malthusian*, July 1894, p. 51.

51 *The Malthusian*, July 1890, p. 49.

52 *The Malthusian*, July 1893, p. 50.

53 Mrs Heatherley also proposed that 'in the Board Schools a knowledge of physiology ought to be taught instead of the Bible'! and hypothesized that 'the marriage of the future would consist of the registration of children by persons about to become parents'. And see Summers, *Angels and Citizens*, p. 185, on Mrs Heatherley as Chair of the Women's Volunteer Medical Staff Corps.

54 See Leathard, *The Fight for Family Planning*, pp. 140–41.

55 *The Malthusian*, July 1894, p. 51.

56 *The Malthusian*, July 1892, p. 50. It would be incorrect to imply that it was only women who took issue with the League's limited approach; a few men also challenged the League's remit. For example, R.B. Kerr, a lawyer, correspondent of *The Freewoman*, and a member of the Malthusian League, wrote with irritation to *The Malthusian*: 'We must show that incessant pregnancy is utterly destructive of the lives of women . . . If we carry on this sort of propaganda and stop wrangling

over the dry bones of Malthusianism, we shall at last awaken some real human interest in the movement' (October 1907, pp. 74–5). He wanted the State to provide free birth control, free literature and numerous lectures.

57 Benn, *Predicaments of Love*, pp. 106–7, 147–8.

58 See Ledbetter, *A History of the Malthusian League 1877–1927*, p. 81, who hypothesizes that lack of a record of their marriage suggests that they married in the early 1870s but kept it a secret because of prejudice against married women in the professions.

59 They were present at the Legitimation League's annual meeting, March 1894, reported in Dawson (ed.), *The Bar Sinister and Licit Love*, p. 49. And see Chapter 4.

60 Anna Martin, *The Malthusian*, 15 November 1920, recalling the occasion. Thanks to Hilary Frances for drawing my attention to this reference.

61 Margaret Sanger, *American Birth Control Review*, September 1920, quoted in *The Malthusian*, 15 October 1920, and see Benn, *The Predicaments of Love*, p. 204.

62 Llewelyn Davies (ed.), *Maternity*, p.115; on abortion see Knight, 'Women and Abortion in Victorian and Edwardian England'.

63 Dixie, *Gloriana, or the Glorious Revolution of 1900*, p. 137.

64 *The Englishwoman's Review*, 15 January 1906, pp. 69–70.

65 *The Malthusian*, December 1905, p. 94.

66 *The Englishwoman's Review*, 15 January 1906, pp. 69–70.

67 *The Malthusian*, December 1905, p. 92.

68 Jane Clapperton was born in 1832, Florence Dixie in 1857. See interview with Jane Clapperton in *The Woman's Penny Paper*, 22 June 1889.

69 Clapperton, *What Do Women Want?*, p. 4.

70 See *The Malthusian*, September 1904.

71 *The Malthusian*, 15 August 1914, p. 60, explains its demise. And see Bland, 'Banishing the Beast', pp. 201–3.

72 See C.V. Drysdale, *The Malthusian*, 15 August 1911, and C.V. Drysdale, *The Freewoman*, 30 November 1911. See Gordon, *Woman's Body, Woman's Right*, pp. 151–7, for a discussion, in the American context, of the relation between feminism and the falling birth rate. She suggests that 'smaller families were both cause and effect of feminism'. The analysis might be applicable to Britain. However, Banks and Banks, *Feminism and Family Planning in Victorian England*, argue that there is no evidence of a causal link between feminism and the falling birth rate.

73 Mrs Fawcett, *The Times*, 5 November 1910, reference in Soloway, *Birth Control and the Population Question in England, 1877–1930*, p. 152.

74 See Marie Fisher, 'Ought Women be Punished for Having Too Many Children?', *The Malthusian*, August 1888, pp. 58–60; September 1888, pp. 68–9; October 1888, pp. 75–6; and see C.R. Drysdale, *The Malthusian*, March 1907, pp. 20–21; Bessie Drysdale, *The Malthusian*, July 1907, p. 54; Bessie Drysdale, *The Malthusian*, 15 August 1910, pp. 63–4.

75 C.R. Drysdale, *The Malthusian*, March 1907, pp. 20–21.

76 *The Malthusian*, 15 August 1911, p. 64; on the Women's Freedom League see Newsome, *The Women's Freedom League 1907–1957*.

77 *The Vote*, 25 January 1919, quoted in Benn, *Predicaments of Love*, p. 195.

78 Maria Sharpe, 'Autobiographical History', 1889, p. 44 (PC).

79 Henrietta Muller, Men and Women's Club Minutes, May 1887.

80 H. Muller to M. Sharpe, May 1887 (PC).

81 Anon. [Emma Brooke], 'The Woman's Sphere in Modern Society', 14 March 1887 (PC).

82 Loetitia Sharpe, 'Comments on Papers in Artificial Checks on Population', June 1887 (PC).

83 Letter quoted in Maria Sharpe's 'Note on Karl Pearson's Paper', Men and Women's Club Minutes, 2 June 1887 (PC).

84 E. Brooke to K. Pearson, February 1886 (PC).

85 Caird, 'A Defence of the so-called "Wild Woman"'.

86 Men and Women's Club Minutes, 9 May 1887 (PC).

87 Mona Caird to Bessie Drysdale, *The Malthusian*, August 1907, p. 61.

88 *The Malthusian*, July 1890, p. 49.

89 Geddes and Thomson, *The Evolution of Sex*, quoted in Ethelmer, *Woman Free*, pp. 175–7; Ethelmer also quoted Geddes and Thomson in *Human Flower*, pp. 44–5.

90 Ethelmer, *Woman Free*, pp. 173–4.

91 *The Malthusian*, October 1894, pp. 69–70.

92 Geddes and Thomson, *The Evolution of Sex*, p. 294.

93 Ethelmer, *Human Flower*, p. 40. In *Life to Woman* a similar position was presented: 'The fuller human being – man or woman – ... is striving to raise the impulses and feelings physical to a higher level; and is applying to emotions and to actions hitherto deemed involuntary and uncontrollable, the guiding and ruling powers of *reason* and purity of intent' [italics are my emphasis] (*Life to Woman*, p. 63 and *Phases of Love*, p. 17).

94 E. Wolstenholme Elmy to H. McIlquaham, 13 December 1897. On Frances Swiney see Jeffreys, *The Spinster and Her Enemies*, pp. 35–9.

95 For an enthusiastic review by Elizabeth Wolstenholme Elmy see Ignota, 'The Awakening of Women'.

96 Swiney, *The Awakening of Women or Women's Part in Evolution*, p. 102.

97 Swiney, *The Awakening of Women or Women's Part in Evolution*, p. 86; and see Alice Vickery, *The Malthusian*, March, May, July, 1904, on Matriarchy theory.

98 Swiney, *The Cosmic Procession or the Feminine Principle in Evolution*, pp. 77–8, 216.

99 Swiney, *Woman and the Natural Law*, p. 40.

100 *The Malthusian*, August 1904, p. 58. Dutch historian Petra de Vries informs me that Frances Swiney was very popular in Holland with feminists opposed to Neo-Malthusianism.

101 *The Malthusian*, March 1908, pp. 22, 23.

102 *The Malthusian*, April 1908, pp. 27, 28.

103 *The Malthusian*, 15 November 1909, p. 81.

104 Ward, *Pure Sociology*, p. 314.

105 Swiney, *The Awakening of Women or Women's Part in Evolution*, p. 19.

106 Swiney, *Woman and the Natural Law*, pp. 13–14.

107 Swiney, *The Cosmic Procession or the Feminine Principle in Evolution*, p. 221.

108 Swiney, *Woman and the Natural Law*, p. 40

109 *The Malthusian*, 15 November 1909, p. 84.

CHAPTER 6 Eugenics, the Politics of Selective Breeding and Feminist Appropriation

1 Swiney, *The Bar of Isis*, pp. 38–9.

2 This had usually been ignored by historians. Exceptions include Anna Davin's seminal article 'Imperialism and Motherhood' and Claire Williams's 'The Destiny of the Race'.

3 See Galton, *Hereditary Genius*. On Galton see Forrest, *Francis Galton*.

4 F. Galton to K. Pearson, 15 November 1906 (PC). This definition was used as a masthead on publications of the Galton Eugenics Laboratory. See Galton, *Inquiries into Human Faculty*, pp. 24–5; Sociological Society, *Sociological Papers*, p. 45, for other definitions.

5 The 1880s saw the foundation of the General Unions, and in the late nineteenth century several socialist parties were formed: the ILP, SDF, the Socialist League. See Cole and Postgate, *The Common People, 1746–1946*. On Ireland see Wilson, 'Imperialism in Crisis: the "Irish Dimension"', in Langan and Schwarz (eds.), *Crises in the British*

State, *1880–1930*. On the suffragettes see Pankhurst, *The Suffragette Movement*; Strachey, *The Cause*.

6 Charles Booth's study, *Life and Labour of People in London*, was issued in 17 volumes, 1889–1903; Seebohm Rowntree, *Poverty, a Study of Town Life*, 1901. See Stedman Jones, *Outcast London*.

7 There was a 37% rejection rate of Boer War recruits. See Taylor, 'The Medical Profession in Relation to the Army'. Caleb Saleeby rejected 'fit' and 'unfit' as eugenical terms because, he said, they referred to the fit of a species to its environment in non-moral terms. He preferred the concepts 'worthy' and 'unworthy' (*The Methods of Race-Regeneration*, p. 18). Although the idea of correlation between physical health and intellectual ability was held by many eugenists, it was challenged by the investigations of Karl Pearson's Biometry Laboratory (Searle, *Eugenics and Politics in Britain 1900–1914*, p. 77). Galton wrote of 'civic worth', by which he meant an average share of 'at least goodness in constitution, of physique, and of mental capacity' (Galton, *Essays in Eugenics*, 1909, quoted in Searle, *Eugenics and Politics in Britain, 1900–1914*, p. 76).

8 See Searle, *The Quest for National Efficiency*.

9 See Semmel, *Imperialism and Social Reform, 1895–1914*.

10 On mothercraft, see Davin, 'Imperialism and Motherhood'; Lewis, *The Politics of Motherhood*.

11 See Stedman Jones, *Outcast London*, p. 287. On degeneracy see Nordau, *Degeneration*; Chamberlin and Gilman (eds), *Degeneration*; Mosse, *Nationalism and Sexuality*.

12 Mearns, *The Bitter Cry of Outcast London*. See Valverde, *The Age of Light, Soap and Water*, p. 139, on how the slum as site of incest functioned symbolically as the demonic opposite of the spacious bourgeois home.

13 Pearson, *The Problem of Practical Eugenics*, p. 8.

14 On birth-rate statistics, see Soloway, *Birth Control and the Population Question in England 1877–1930*, p. xi.

15 Webb, *The Decline in the Birth-Rate*, p. 17. On anti-semitism, see also White, *Efficiency and Empire*.

16 See Stedman Jones, *Outcast London*, Chapter 6.

17 Spencer, *Principles of Biology*, vol. 2. 1867, p. 427, quoted in Soloway, *Birth Control and the Population Question in England 1877–1930*, p. 14.

18 On 'shirking' motherhood see Leonard Darwin's Presidential Address in *Third Annual Report 1910–11*, London, EES, 1911, p. 17; the Bishop of London, *The Times*, 20 October 1903; Leslie, 'Woman's Progress in Relation to Eugenics'; Whetham, 'The Extinction of the Upper-

classes', pp. 105–6. As Mariana Valverde points out: ' "Race suicide" did not refer to the physical extinction of humanity as a whole, but rather the effects on humanity of middle-class women's low fertility rates' (Valverde, 'A Passion for Purity', p. 6). On 'race suicide' see Rentoul, *Race Culture; or, Race Suicide? (A Plea for the Unborn)*; Barclay, 'The Suicide Scare', pp. 895–99; Soloway, *Birth Control and the Population Question in England 1877–1930*; Mrs Edward Francis, 'Race Suicide', *The Vote*, 21 January 1911. To Havelock Ellis 'the wild outcry of many unbalanced persons today that a falling birth rate means degeneration and disaster is so altogether removed from … reason' that it paralleled the 'ancient outcry against witches' (Ellis, *The Task of Social Hygiene*, p. 173).

19 See Searle, *Eugenics and Politics in Britain, 1900–1914*; Farrall, *The Origins and Growth of the English Eugenics Movement, 1865–1915*; Kevles, *In the Name of Eugenics*.

20 On the EES's foundation, see *First Annual Report*, EES, 1908; Schenk and Parker, 'The Activities of the Eugenics Society', p. 142. Officially the foundation of the Society occurred at Caxton Hall, London, but according to social worker Mrs Sybil Gotto, its formation was planned and launched in her bedsitting-room in a residential women's club (Neville-Rolfe, *Social Biology and Welfare*, p. 17). Mrs Gotto became the Eugenics Society's Honorary Secretary, a post she held for many years.

21 On Pearson's view of the EES see Kevles, *In the Name of Eugenics*, p. 104.

22 Pearson, quoted in Soloway, *Birth Control and the Population Question in England 1877–1930*, p. 30.

23 On the two theories of heredity see Froggart and Nevin, 'The "Law of Ancestral Heredity" in the Mendelian-Ancestrian Controversy in England, 1889–1906', pp. 1–36; Farrall, 'Controversy and Conflict in Science: a Case Study – the English Biometric School and Mendel's Laws', pp. 269–301; McKenzie, 'Sociobiologists in Competition: the Biometrician-Mendelian Debate', in Webster (ed.), *Biology, Medicine and Society, 1840–1940*. Biometry was attacked on many occasions by fellow eugenist Saleeby.

24 B.L., *The Freewoman*, 1 August 1912, p. 204.

25 *The Vote*, 10 August 1912.

26 Kevles, *In the Name of Eugenics*, p. 59; as Soloway rightly suggests, 'unlike the Neo-Malthusians whose radical-secularist roots were highly suspect, the eugenists, mostly successful, well-educated and middle-class scientists, physicians, academicians, churchmen and other profes-

sionals, brought to the population question both social and scientific credibility' (*Birth Control and the Population Question in England, 1877–1930*, p. xv).

27 Despite doctors being one of the largest groups in the EES, with Sir James Barr among their number, they represented only a small minority in their profession. Genetics was not even accepted on the medical syllabus until 1938. Searle, *Eugenics and Politics in Britain, 1900–1914*, p. 100.

28 K. Pearson to F. Galton, 20 June 1907, quoted in Kevles, *In the Name of Eugenics*, p. 57.

29 In 1909, of 112 ordinary and life members, 51 were women, while of 229 associate members, 139 were women; in 1913, of 406 ordinary and life members, 139 were women, while of 307 associate members, 209 were women (EES Annual Reports, 1909–13). See Annual Reports 1908–14 with details of programmed meetings. Organizations lectured to included Paddington and Kensington Women's Socialist Circle, various branches of the Women's Liberal Association, Berkhamsted National Union of Women Workers, the Fabian Women's Group, the Women's Institute, the Westminster branch of Conservative and Unionist Women, Croydon's Women's Debating Society, Walton-on-Thames Women's Club. In 1909, of 24 Council members, 11 were women. In 1913, of 39 Council members, only 7 were women, improving marginally by 1916: 38 Council members, of which 8 were women (*Minutes of Eugenics Education Society, 1907–1916*, London, EES).

30 EES, *First Annual Report*, 1909.

31 Mrs Alec Tweedie, 'Eugenics', *Eugenics Review*, p. 857.

32 Saleeby, *Woman and Womanhood*, pp. 14, 262.

33 Presidential Address, *Third Annual Report*, EES, 1911, p. 17; and see Leonard Darwin (second EES President), Presidential Address, *Problems in Eugenics: Papers of 1st International Eugenics Congress July 1912*, EES, 1912.

34 Mrs Alec Tweedie, 'Eugenics', *Eugenics Review*, p. 855.

35 McLaren, *Birth Control in Nineteenth-Century England*, p. 47, makes this point in relation to the role of women in popularizing fertility control.

36 Ellis, *Task of Social Hygiene*, p. 46.

37 See Valverde, 'The Concept of "Race" in First-wave Feminist Sexual and Reproductive Politics', in Iacovetta and Valverde (eds.), *Expanding Boundaries*.

38 Swiney, *The Awakening of Women*, p. 120. Dr Elizabeth Blackwell similarly disapproved of the 'congress of different races', and trumpeted

Anglo–Saxon chauvinism. See Valverde, 'The Concept of "Race"';
Burton, 'The Feminist Quest for Identity'. On Olive Schreiner's fear
of miscegenation, see Krebs, 'Interpreting South Africa to Britain'.

39 W.C.D. Whetham and C.D. Whetham, *Heredity and Society*, quoted
in Duffin, 'Prisoners of Progress: Women and Evolution', in Durant
and Duffin, *The Nineteenth-Century Woman*, p. 79.

40 For example, see McDougall, 'A Practicable Eugenic Suggestion'.

41 See Davin, 'Imperialism and Motherhood', and Lewis, *The Politics of
Motherhood*. Various other eugenists also emphasized the need to look
at environment as well as inheritance, for example, Dr Saleeby and
Havelock Ellis. For the debate over 'endowment of motherhood' see
Dora Marsden, 'Women Endowed or Free?', *The Freewoman*, 29
February 1912, pp. 281–3; 7 March 1912, pp. 301–2; 14 March 1912,
pp. 321–2; and 21 March 1912, pp. 341–2.

42 See Mary Scharlieb's evidence to the National Birth-Rate Commission:
National Council of Public Morals, *The Declining Birth Rate*, London,
Chapman and Hall, 1916.

43 Scharlieb, *Womanhood and Race Regeneration*, p. 7.

44 See Davin, 'Imperialism and Motherhood', for discussion of how it
was maternal, not medical, ignorance which always received the
blame.

45 Chesser, *Perfect Health for Women and Children*.

46 Chesser, *From Girlhood to Womanhood*, p. 126.

47 Hartley, *The Truth about Women*, p. 283.

48 Hartley, *The Truth about Women*, p. 255.

49 Vickery, 'Response to Galton's "Studies in National Eugenics"', p. 22.
And see Isabel Leatham, *The Freewoman*, 4 January 1912, p. 132.

50 Vickery, 'Response to Galton's "Studies in National Eugenics"', pp.
21–2. See Margaret Hill, *The Freewoman*, 30 November 1911, p. 31.
Many men held to the idea that women should regain their former
power of sexual selection. See C.V. Drysdale, *The Freewoman*, 21
November 1911, p. 194 and 25 January 1912, p. 194; Pearson, 'Woman
and Labour', in *The Chances of Death and Other Studies in Evolution*, p.
254; Wallace, 'Human Selection'; Ellis, *Woman and Marriage*.

51 Swincy, *The Cosmic Procession or the Feminine Principle in Evolution*, p.
xi, and see *The Ancient Road or the Development of the Soul*, p. 37.

52 Wolstenholme Elmy, *Woman and the Law*, p. 6; and see Ignota, 'The
Awakening of Women', p. 69; Ethelmer, *The Human Flower*, p. 47.

53 *The Standard* chose not to publish Edith How-Martyn's letter, but *The
Malthusian*, 15 September 1912, p. 69, reprinted both letters.

54 Pearson, 'The Woman's Question', *The Ethic of Freethought*, p. 371.

55 M. Taylor, 'College Women and Marriage', *The Englishwoman*, 1913, quoted in Williams, 'The Destiny of the Race', p. 60.

56 Helen Winter, *The Freewoman*, 7 March 1912, p. 312.

57 Chesser, *Woman, Marriage and Motherhood*, p. 274, and see Saleeby, *Woman and Womanhood*, p. 12: 'Women must indeed give themselves up for the community and the future; ... the right fulfilment of Nature's purpose is one with the right fulfilment of their own destiny.'

58 Knight, 'Woman v. the State', pp. 39, 38, 36.

59 *Votes for Women*, 25 October 1912.

60 Atkinson, *The Economic Foundations of the Women's Movement*.

61 See Gordon, 'Why Nineteenth-Century Feminists did not support "Birth Control" and Twentieth-Century Feminists do', in Thorne and Yalom (eds.), *Rethinking the Family*.

62 H.G. Wells at meeting of the Sociological Society, *Sociological Papers*, vol. 1, p. 60.

63 See Barker, 'How to Curb the Fertility of the Unfit: the Feeble-minded in Edwardian Britain'. Thanks to Pat Devine for drawing my attention to this article.

64 Allbutt, *The Wife's Handbook*, quoted in Jalland, *Women, Marriage and Politics, 1860–1914*, p. 85.

65 See Savage, '"The Wilful Communication of a Loathsome Sore"'.

66 Jalland, *Women, Marriage and Politics*, p. 85.

67 Ellen Gaskell, *The Freewoman*, 18 January 1912, p. 176.

68 Caine, *Destined to be Wives*.

69 Fleming, *Victorian 'Sex Goddess'*.

70 T.S. Clouston, *Mental Disease*, 1904, p. 693, quoted in Barker, 'How to Curb the Fertility of the Unfit', p. 198.

71 Letter quoted in Quilter (ed.), *Is Marriage a Failure?*, p. 223.

72 Dowie, *Gallia*, p. 231.

73 Frances Galton made a proposal for marriage certificates, however. See Galton, 'Restrictions in Marriage'.

74 *British Medical Journal*, vol. 2, 1913, pp. 508–9, quoted in Barker, 'How to Curb the Fertility of the Unfit'. And see Saleeby, *The Progress of Eugenics*.

75 See Webb, *The Decline in the Birth-Rate*. Soloway, *Birth Control and the Population Question in England, 1877–1930*, p. 34, suggests that this tract was probably the most widely read of the pre-census inquiries into differential fertility. There was a 'Fertility of Marriage' census in 1911.

76 Letter from Karl Pearson published in *The Malthusian*, January 1900, p. 4.

77 Pearson, 'Reproductive Selection', *The Chances of Death and Other Studies in Evolution*, p. 101. Pearson's predictions were pronounced

confirmed in 1906 with the results of Pearson's assistant David Heron, whose research was on the degree to which the reduced fertility of married women in a number of London districts was associated with social status. In 1903, Pearson announced dramatically: 'We stand . . . at the commencement of an epoch, which will be marked by a great dearth of ability' (Pearson, 'On the Inheritance of the Mental and Moral Charactérs', *Journal of the Anthropological Institute of Great Britain and Ireland*, 33, 1903, quoted in Soloway, *Birth Control and the Population Question in England, 1877–1930*, p. 28).

78   *The Malthusian*, 15 December 1909, p. 90.

79   *The Malthusian*, 15 September 1918, p. 66.

80   See Saleeby's Eugenic Programme and letter to the Malthusian League, *The Malthusian*, 15 May 1910, p. 35.

81   *The Malthusian*, 15 May 1910, p. 34.

82   On the inter-war eugenical birth-control movement see Hall, *Marie Stopes*; Rose, *Marie Stopes and the Sexual Revolution*. Compare with Cohen's 'Private Lives in Public Spaces: Marie Stopes, the Mothers' Clinics and the Practice of Contraception', on how Stopes subordinated her eugenical views to her concern for the individual woman's health and happiness.

83   Julia Bromos, in Mond (ed.), *The Burden of Woman*, p. 130. And see Campbell, 'Eugenics from the Physician's Standpoint', pp. 225–7.

84   On the disagreements between the segregationists and the sterilizers see Barker, 'How to Curb the Fertility of the Unfit', pp. 203–4.

85   On segregationist proposals see Stedman Jones, *Outcast London*, Chapter 16.

86   See Ellis, 'Sterilization of the Unfit', and 'Birth Control and Eugenics', p. 41. Some asylum officers approved of sterilization. See C.T. Ewart, 'Eugenics and Degeneracy', p. 687. And see Rentoul, *Proposed Sterilization of Certain Mental and Physical Degenerates*. He proposed sterilization of, among others, all prostitutes, tramps and those with VD.

87   Saleeby, *The Progress of Eugenics*, pp. 208–9; and see Ellis, *The Problem of Race Regeneration*, p. 67. The book suggests the refusal of relief to second, third and subsequent generations unless they 'voluntarily' submitted to sterilization, pp. 68–9.

88   *First Annual Report*, EES, 1908, p. 16.

89   See Simmons, 'Explaining Social Policy', p. 388. Thanks to Matthew Thomson for drawing my attention to this article.

90   See Strahan, *Marriage and Disease*, p. 128. The research of eugenist Karl Pearson and his assistant Ethel Elderton on the children of alcoholic parents challenged this assumed relationship between alcoholism and

genetic degeneracy (Elderton and Pearson *A First Study of the Influence of Parental Alcoholism on the Physique and Ability of the Offspring*).

91 Ellis, *The Problem of Race Regeneration*, p. 46.

92 Churchill to Asquith, 'The Asquith Papers', quoted in Freeden, *The New Liberalism*, p. 189.

93 See Saleeby, *The Methods of Race Regeneration*, p. 48; Schuster, *Eugenics*, p. 172.

94 There was still no psychological 'measure' of feeble-mindedness. See Rose, *The Psychological Complex*, p. 108.

95 Quoted in Simmons, 'Explaining Social Policy', p. 399.

96 Quoted in Simmons, 'Explaining Social Policy', p. 392.

97 *A Secret World of Sex*, No. 5, 'Acts of Violence', directed by Steve Humphries, and see his book, *A Secret World of Sex*; see Thomson, 'The Problem of Mental Deficiency in England and Wales, c. 1913–1946', pp. 229–30, for the details of two similar cases. Thomson points out (p. 225) that national statistics on the certification of mental defectives were not differentiated according to sex and age until the 1950s.

98 Quoted in Mahood, *The Magdalenes*, p. 153.

99 Dora Marsden, *The Freewoman*, 25 July 1912, pp. 181–2.

100 *The Vote*, 3 August 1912.

101 Williams, 'The Destiny of Race', p. 82.

102 On salvarsan see *Lancet*, 1911 and 1912 passim.

103 On VD's contribution to sterility, etc., see Allbutt and Rolleston (eds.), *A System of Medicine*.

104 Lane, 'Racial Poisons 1: Venereal Disease'; see also Pfeffer, *The Stork and the Syringe*, Chapters 1 and 2.

105 White, 'Eugenics and Venereal Disease', p. 270. See Bland, '"The Cleansing of the Portals of Life"' in Langan and Schwarz (eds), *Crises in the British State, 1880–1930*.

106 See Nead, *Myths of Sexuality* and Walkowitz, *Prostitution and Victorian Society* for discussion of representations of the prostitute.

107 See Strahan, *Marriage and Disease*; Dr A. Mjoen, 'Legal Certificates of Health before Marriage'. For doctors' complicity see Dr William Sinclair, *On Gonorrhoeal Infection*, 1888, cited in Walkowitz, *Prostitution and Victorian Society*, p. 55.

108 Martindale, *Under the Surface*.

109 Committee of Inquiry, *The State and Sexual Morality*.

110 Pankhurst, *The Great Scourge and How to End It*. And see Richardson, 'The Outcasts', p. 187. Several letters of response from doctors are reprinted in *The Suffragette*, 2 January and 6 February 1914.

111 Hamilton, *Marriage as a Trade*, p. 34.

112 Bulley, *A Talk on Questions of Sex. For Young Men and Girls of 18.*

113 Swiney, *The Bar of Isis*, pp. 19, 38–9, 43. Swiney was nominated to the Eugenics Education Society's Council, but certain Council members, including Lady Emily Lutyens (a fellow Theosophist, but of a different school), 'thought her views might prejudice the Society', so her nomination was rejected (Council Minutes, 12 February 1906, unpublished, London, EES).

114 Swiney, *The Bar of Isis*, p. 43; Pankhurst, *The Great Scourge*, pp. 19–20.

115 Re-Bartlett, *Sex and Sanctity*, pp. 25–6.

116 WFL 9th Annual Conference, 28 March 1914; and see Coralie Boord, *The Freewoman*, 4 January 1912, p. 130; Minerva, 'Why Men do not Marry'.

117 Pankhurst, *The Great Scourge*, pp. 78–9, 100. For examples of anti-feminist reactions to this 'birth-strike' see 'Decadence and Civilisation', *The Hibbert Journal*, October 1911; Heape, *Sex Antagonism*, p. 4.

118 *The Shield*, April 1914. And see Creighton, *The Social Disease and How to Fight It: a Rejoinder*. Although her 'rejoinder' is not explicitly a response to Pankhurst's *The Great Scourge*, it is clear that she had the tract in mind.

119 Rebecca West in *The Clarion*, 26 September 1913, reprinted in Marcus, *The Young Rebecca*.

120 Browne, 'Women and Birth-Control', in Paul and Paul (eds.), *Population and Birth-Control*, p. 251, and see Rowbotham, *A New World for Women*.

121 Stella Browne, *The Freewoman*, 1 August 1912, pp. 217–18.

122 Browne, 'Women and Birth-Control', in Paul and Paul (eds.), *Population and Birth-Control*, p. 152.

123 Browne, 'Women and Birth-Control', in Paul and Paul (eds.), *Population and Birth-Control*, p. 251.

124 *The Malthusian*, 15 March 1915, pp. 21–2.

125 Browne, 'Women and Birth-Control', in Paul and Paul (eds.), *Population and Birth-Control*, p. 255; and see Stella Browne in *The Malthusian*, 15 March 1915, p. 22.

126 Browne, 'Women and Birth-Control', in Paul and Paul (eds.), *Population and Birth-Control*, p. 257.

127 See Browne, 'The Sexual Variety and Variability among Women and Their Bearing upon Social Reconstruction', 1916, reprinted in Rowbotham, *A New World for Women*; Browne, 'Some Problems of Sex'; see Hartley, *Truth about Women*, p. 326.

CHAPTER 7 Speaking of Sex

1 Gordon and DuBois, 'Seeking Ecstasy on the Battlefield', p. 42. .

2 Edith Watson, 'How Men Protect Women', *The Vote*, 10 February 1912.

3 Hammerton, *Cruelty and Companionship*, pp. 64–5.

4 Walkowitz, *City of Dreadful Delight*, p. 129.

5 On the feminist campaign against incest and sexual abuse of children generally see Jeffreys, *The Spinster and Her Enemies*.

6 *The Pioneer*, 1 June 1887.

7 Blake, 'Are Women Protected?', pp. 47, 45, 43; and see Libra, 'The Legal Value of the Unrepresented', *Shafts*, 25 February 1893, pp. 259–60.

8 Edith Watson, 'How Men Protect Women', *The Vote*, 10 February 1912, p. 185.

9 *The Vote*, 19 June 1914.

10 *The Vote*, 9 March 1912, p. 237.

11 *The Vote*, 3 July 1914, p. 178.

12 *The Vote*, 9 March 1912, p. 237.

13 Emmeline Pankhurst reported in *The Suffragette*, 11 April 1913.

14 Gertrude Colmore, *The Vote*, 15 August 1913.

15 See Vicinus, *Independent Women*.

16 In 1885 Karl Pearson coined the word 'sexualogy', meaning the science of sexual relations, but the word did not catch on, and in the early twentieth century the American term 'sexology' was adopted.

17 Foucault, *The History of Sexuality. Volume 1*.

18 Jeffreys, *The Spinster and Her Enemies*; compare with Birken, *Consuming Desire*, who suggests that this science of sex, with its decoupling of sexual desire from reproduction, facilitated the coterminous shift in the West from a productionist to a consumerist ideology, in which the channelling of desire was essential.

19 See Jeffreys, *The Spinster and Her Enemies*, Chapters 8–10.

20 Alison Hennegan's Introduction to Radclyffe Hall, *The Well of Loneliness*, pp. ix–x. And see Stanley, *The Auto/biographical I*, Chapter 8.

21 Rhondda, *This was My World*, p. 126.

22 Smith-Rosenberg, 'The New Woman as Androgyne: Social Disorder and Gender Crisis, 1870–1936', in Smith-Rosenberg, *Disorderly Conduct*, pp. 265–6.

23 Smith-Rosenberg, 'A Richer and Gentler Sex', p. 288.

24 And Jeffreys, *The Spinster and Her Enemies*, p. 108, points out that Ellis,

Block and Forel were cited at the 1929 Sex Reform Congress in London as the founding fathers of sexology.

25 Ellis, *Studies in the Psychology of Sex Volume 2* (originally *Volume 1*).

26 Robinson, *The Modernisation of Sex*. And see Weeks, *Sex, Politics and Society*, Chapter 8; Jackson, 'Sexology and the Construction of Male Sexuality (Havelock Ellis)', in Coveney *et al*, *The Sexuality Papers*.

27 Ellis, *Studies in the Psychology of Sex Volume 3*, p. 33.

28 Ellis, *Studies in the Psychology of Sex Volume 3*, pp. 68–9.

29 Ellis, *Studies in the Psychology of Sex Volume 3*, p. 256.

30 Ellis, *Studies in the Psychology of Sex Volume 6*, p. 539.

31 Ellis, *Studies in the Psychology of Sex Volume 3*, p. 253.

32 Bloch, *The Sexual Life of Our Time*, pp. 83, 86.

33 Forel, *The Sexual Question*, pp. 93, 48.

34 Finot, *The Problems of the Sexes*, pp. 338–9; see *The Vote*, 24 December 1910, praising the work of Finot. And see Féré, *The Evolution and Dissolution of the Sexual Instinct*.

35 Vicinus, 'Distance and Desire: English Boarding School Friendships, 1870–1920', in Duberman *et al* (eds.), *Hidden from History*, pp. 212–13.

36 Faderman, *Surpassing the Love of Men*; Jeffreys, *The Spinster and Her Enemies*. And see Faderman, *Odd Girls and Twilight Lovers*, in which she revises her views on sexology to some extent, pointing to some of its more positive aspects.

37 Smith-Rosenberg, *Disorderly Conduct*; Newton, 'The Mythic Mannish Lesbian'; Stanley, *The Auto/biographical I*; and see Smith-Rosenberg's highly perceptive discussion in 'A Richer and Gentler Sex'.

38 Sweeney, *At Scotland Yard*, p. 186.

39 See Weeks, *Coming Out*, p. 61.

40 Ellis, *Studies in the Psychology of Sex Volume 2*, p. 1.

41 Ellis, *Studies in the Psychology of Sex Volume 2*, p. 83.

42 Ellis, *Studies in the Psychology of Sex Volume 2*, Chapter 5.

43 Ellis, *Studies in the Psychology of Sex Volume 2*, p. 222.

44 Miss S's family had 'a marked neuropathic element', similarly with Miss M; Miss H's maternal relatives were eccentric and prone to 'nervous disease', while one of Miss B's siblings was neurotic and another also inverted (Ellis, *Studies in the Psychology of Sex Volume 2*). See Smith-Rosenberg, 'The New Woman as Androgyne' for an illuminating discussion of Ellis.

45 Carpenter, *The Intermediate Sex*, p. 9.

46 Carpenter, *The Intermediate Sex*, p. 108.

47 Carpenter, *The Intermediate Sex*, p. 70.

48 *British Medical Journal*, 26 June 1909, pp. 1546–7. On Carpenter, see Rowbotham and Weeks, *Socialism and the New Life*.

49 *Lancet*, 19 November 1898, p. 1344; and see the *British Medical Journal*, 1 June 1895, p. 1225.

50 Ellis, *Studies in the Psychology of Sex Volume 2*, p. 262.

51 Ellis, *Studies in the Psychology of Sex Volume 2*, pp. 257–8.

52 Forel, *The Sexual Question*, pp. 94, 230.

53 O. Schreiner to H. Ellis, 7 August 1912, in Cronwright-Schreiner (ed.), *The Letters of Olive Schreiner 1876–1920*, p. 312.

54 Maude Royden, *The Times*, 22 June 1912, and see *The Freewoman*, 11 July 1912, pp. 142–3.

55 Strachey, *Millicent Garrett Fawcett*, p. 235.

56 See Garner, *A Brave and Beautiful Spirit*, pp. 71–2. Teresa Billington-Greig was also highly critical of the WSPU. See Billington-Greig, *The Militant Suffrage Movement – Emancipation in a Hurry*. On Mary Gawthorpe see Holton, 'The Suffragist and the "Average Woman"', *Women's History Review*, vol. 1, no. 1, 1992.

57 *The Freewoman*, 7 December 1911, p. 55.

58 *Votes for Women*, 17 November 1911 (*The Common Cause* and *The Vote* also carried the advert).

59 S. Skelhorn, *The Freewoman*, 28 March 1912, p. 376; and see R. C. Fletcher Woods, *The Freewoman*, 4 July 1912, p. 132, and Coralie Boord, *The Freewoman*, 14 March 1912, p. 331.

60 Dora Marsden, *The Freewoman*, 14 March 1912, p. 332.

61 Rebecca West, 'The Freewoman'. Les Garner points to the interest in the USA and, to a lesser extent, France (*A Brave and Beautiful Spirit*, pp. 94–5).

62 On Dora Marsden see Garner, *A Brave and Beautiful Spirit*.

63 See *The Life and Writings of Ada Nield Chew*, remembered and collected by Doris Nield Chew; and see Ada Nield Chew to *The Freewoman*, 13 April and 18 April 1912, reprinted in *The Life and Writings of Ada Nield Chew*, pp. 235–8. Realizing that '*The Freewoman* is too poor to pay', she offered her work for free (Garner, *A Brave and Beautiful Spirit*, p. 76).

64 Dora Marsden, *The Freewoman*, 23 November 1911, p. 3.

65 In March a 'Freewoman discussion circle' was formed in Bristol by the Bristol Fabian Women's Group (Ethel Bradshaw, *The Freewoman*, 7 March 1912, p. 315); in May, a circle was formed in Dover, and in June a demand was put for an 'actionist group' (Barbara Low, *The Freewoman*, 11 July 1912, p. 153).

66 The circle met every other Wednesday, 8–10 p.m. All administration

was to be dealt with in the first quarter of an hour, followed by half an hour for the introduction of the subject, with all subsequent speakers confining their comments to five minutes. Formal discussion was to close at 10 p.m., with another half- hour for general conversation. One reader subsequently wrote to *The Freewoman* to complain that the high fee 'seems to make Freewomen appear snobs' (O. Ricks, *The Freewoman*, 30 May 1912, p. 38).

67 Glendinning, *Rebecca West*.

68 Rebecca West, 'The Freewoman'.

69 Glendinning, *Rebecca West*, p. 51.

70 Allen and Helen McDonald, who wrote a number of articles for *The Freewoman* on 'The New Order' had set up the Tolstoyan colony. On Tolstoyan colonies see Hardy, *Alternative Communities in Nineteenth-Century England*; Greenway, 'Sex, Politics and Housework', in Coates *et al*, *Diggers and Dreamers*, p. 48.

71 Delisle, *Friendship's Odyssey*, p. 187.

72 Delisle, *Friendship's Odyssey*, p. 181.

73 Glendinning, *Rebecca West*, p. 37.

74 Quoted in Thompson (ed.), *Dear Girl*, p. 160.

75 Thompson, *Dear Girl*, p. 160.

76 Jane Craig, *The Freewoman*, 25 January 1912, p. 192. In the same issue of the paper, Mrs P. Sherwen reflected that 'surely the ideal should be that sex relationship and sex organs should be held absolutely sacred to the production of children, and never be degraded to minister to a lustful pleasure' (*The Freewoman*, 25 January 1912, p. 192).

77 This was not a new idea, of course. For example, in the 1880s, Olive Schreiner had suggested to Karl Pearson: 'May not the sex nature far from being simple have become complex and have 2 functions?' These two functions were the reproductive and the 'aesthetic' (O. Schreiner to K. Pearson, 2 July 1886 (PC)).

78 Isabel Leatham, *The Freewoman*, 11 January 1912, p. 151; and see the response of 'A.B.' to Mrs Sherwen's letter with the claim that 'the sex instinct flows into aesthetic expression, which is by no means connected with the production of children' (*The Freewoman*, 1 February 1912, p. 213).

79 Dora Marsden, *The Freewoman*, 2 May 1912, p. 461; and note the parallel to Karl Pearson's ideas, as presented in Chapter One. Feminists in the United States were making a similar distinction: between the 'amative' and 'propagative' function. See Gordon, *Woman's Body, Woman's Right*, p. 86.

80 'A Grandmother', *The Freewoman*, 22 February 1912, p. 270.

81 W.H.A., *The Freewoman*, 15 August 1912, p. 259.

82 'Ess Tee', 'Wanted: a New Dictionary', *The Adult*, vol. 1, no. 4, November 1897, p. 58.

83 Dora Marsden, *The Freewoman*, 16 May 1912, p. 503.

84 Browne, 'The Sexual Variety and Variability among Women and Their Bearing upon Social Reconstruction', given to the British Society for the Study of Sex Psychology in 1915, reprinted in Rowbotham, *A New World for Women*, pp. 103–4.

85 Dora Marsden, *The Freewoman*, 16 May 1912, p. 503.

86 Nora Kiernan, *The Freewoman*, 20 June 1912, p. 66.

87 M. Sharpe to K. Pearson, 2 February 1889 (PC).

88 E. Brooke to K. Pearson, 14 March 1886 (PC).

89 Murray (ed.), *A New English Dictionary on Historical Principles*.

90 Karl Kertbeny (pseudonym for Benkert) coined the terms. See Katz, 'The Invention of Heterosexuality'. Elaine Showalter points out that the word 'homosexual' did not enter the English vocabulary until the translation of Krafft–Ebing's *Psychopathia Sexualis* in the 1890s (Showalter, *Sexual Anarchy*, p. 171).

91 Nora Kiernan, *The Freewoman*, 20 June 1912, p. 99.

92 Murray, *A New English Dictionary on Historical Principles*, vol. VII: O-P.

93 Dora Marsden, *The Freewoman*, 28 December 1911, p. 102.

94 Re-Bartlett, *The Coming Order*, pp. 33–4.

95 Because most feminists did not equate carnality and passion, I would suggest that Nancy Cott's claim – that nineteenth-century feminists took 'passionlessness' as a self-definition (Cott, 'Passionlessness') – is misleading. It was non-carnality by which they defined themselves.

96 Dora Marsden, *The Freewoman*, 9 May 1912, p. 482.

97 M.S., *The Freewoman*, 4 July 1912, p. 138; and see E. Noel Morgan, *The Freewoman*, 8 August 1912, p. 234, and Hibernian, *The Freewoman*, 7 May 1912, p. 313, for other examples of non-physical passion.

98 Jeffreys, *The Spinster and Her Enemies*, p. 51

99 'A Would-Be Freewoman', *The Freewoman*, 21 March 1912, p. 353.

100 'A New Subscriber', *The Freewoman*, 22 February 1912, p. 270.

101 E.M. Watson, *The Freewoman*, 20 June 1912, p. 95, responding to Dr Wrench, 'Shall the Yoshiwara be Rebuilt?', *The Freewoman*, 30 May 1912, pp. 25–6.

102 Amy Stovgaard-Pedersen, *The Freewoman*, 27 June 1912, pp. 116–17; 'A New Subscriber', *The Freewoman*, 4 July 1912, p. 136; E.O. Wrench, *The Freewoman*, 1 July 1912 p. 139.

103 E.O. Wrench, *The Freewoman*, 27 June 1912, p. 116.

104 E.M. Watson, *The Freewoman*, 4 July 1912, p. 139, and see Browne, 'The Sexual Variety and Variability among Women and Their Bearing upon Social Reconstruction', 1915, in Rowbotham, *A New World for Women*, pp. 100–101, who also argued that masturbation was preferable to prostitution. And see A.B., *The Freewoman*, 18 July 1912, p. 177.

105 See P.T.T., *The Freewoman*, 1 August 1912, p. 219; W.H.A., *The Freewoman*, 15 August 1912, p. 259: W.H.A. was refused Forel's *The Sexual Question* from Lewis's Science and Medical Library on the grounds that it was only available to doctors and lawyers.

106 Dora Marsden, *The Freewoman*, 4 January 1912, p. 121.

107 '"The Spinster": by One', *The Freewoman*, 23 November 1911, p. 10.

108 Margaret Hill, *The Freewoman*, 30 November 1911, p. 31; 'A Spinster', *The Freewoman*, 7 December 1911, pp. 53–4. And see the response to the article in *The Common Cause*, 30 November 1911: 'To harp on the one string of sex will jar the nerves of readers in the long run. One article of the type of "The Spinster" would be stimulating; but 5 or 6 gives the impression of an obsession.' Quoted in Oldfield, *Spinsters of Our Parish*, p. 163.

109 Upton Sinclair, *The Freewoman*, 18 January 1912, p. 165.

110 E.M. Watson, *The Freewoman*, 8 February 1912, p. 231.

111 Kathlyn Oliver, *The Freewoman*, 15 February 1912, p. 252.

112 'A New Subscriber', *The Freewoman*, 22 February 1912, p. 270.

113 Kathlyn Oliver, *The Freewoman*, 29 February 1912, p. 290.

114 'A New Subscriber', *The Freewoman*, 7 March 1912, p. 313.

115 Kathlyn Oliver, *The Freewoman*, 4 April 1912, p. 398.

116 'A New Subscriber', *The Freewoman*, 18 April 1912, p. 437.

117 E.M. Watson, *The Freewoman*, 8 February 1912, p. 231.

118 Kathlyn Oliver, *The Freewoman*, 15 February 1912, p. 252.

119 See Isabel Leatham, *The Freewoman*, 11 January 1912, p. 151, and Jane Craig, *The Freewoman*, 25 January 1912, p. 192.

120 Mrs Sherwen, *The Freewoman*, 25 January 1912, p. 192.

121 See Gordon, *Woman's Body, Woman's Right*, p 85.

122 Stockham, *Karezza*, pp. 22–3, 67; and see Miller, *The Strike of a Sex: a Novel* and *After the Strike of a Sex, or Zugassent's Discovery*. Edward Carpenter recommended Karezza's provision of 'a more complete *soul union*, a strange and intoxicating exchange of life and transmutation of elements', (*Love's Coming of Age*, Fifth edition, pp. 173–4). Stockham's book was highly recommended by the Canadian Women's Christian Temperance Union's Purity Superintendent in 1897 (Valverde, *The Age of Light, Soap and Water*, p 70). See Smith-Rosenberg, 'A Richer and Gentler Sex' for a discussion of the technique.

123 Mary and Stanley Randolph, *The Freewoman*, 13 June 1912, p 79 and *The Freewoman*, 27 June 1912, p 118.

124 Gordon, *Woman's Body, Woman's Right*, p 62.

125 Unpublished autobiography of Edith Watson. I am indebted to Hilary Frances's generosity in sharing this and other details of Edith Watson's life.

126 Dora Marsden, *The New Freewoman*, 1 August 1913, p 64.

127 Dora Marsden, *The Freewoman*, 9 May 1912, p 482; see Vicinus, *Independent Women*, Chapter 7, for a wonderful analysis of suffragette sacrifice of the body.

128 Dora Marsden, *The Freewoman*, 2 May 1912, p 241.

129 Browne, 'The Sexual Variety and Variability among Women and Their Bearing upon Social Reconstruction', 1915, in Rowbotham, *A New World for Women*, p 101.

130 'A New Subscriber', *The Freewoman*, 21 March 1912, p 354.

131 Browne, 'The Sexual Variety and Variability among Women and Their Bearing upon social Reconstruction', 1915, in Rowbotham, *A New World for Women*, p 96.

132 Sharp, *Unfinished Adventure*, p 58.

133 J. Butler to S. Butler, 24 April 1895 (JBC).

134 Thanks to Frank Mort for this insight.

135 J. Butler to S. Butler, 4 June 1895 (JBC).

136 W.T. Stead to E. Carpenter, 22 June 1895 (ECC).

137 Scharlieb, 'Adolescent Girlhood under Modern Conditions, with Special Reference to Motherhood', pp. 175–6.

138 See Auchmuty, *A World of Girls*, and Jeffreys, *The Spinster and Her Enemies*.

139 See Stella Browne's letter to Edward Carpenter concerning her helping Edith Lees when Lees was very ill, 7 September 1916 (ECC).

140 Browne, 'The Sexual Variety and Variability among Women and Their Bearing upon Social Reconstruction', 1915, reprinted in Rowbotham, *A New World for Women*, p 103.

141 Browne, 'The Sexual Variety and Variability among Women and Their Bearing upon Social Reconstruction', 1915, reprinted in Rowbotham, *A New World for Women*, p 102.

142 Ellis, *Studies in the Psychology of Sex Volume 2*, p 204.

143 K. Oliver to E. Carpenter, 25 October 1915 (ECC).

144 K. Oliver to E. Carpenter, 25 October 1915 (ECC).

145 Kathlyn Oliver, *The Freewoman*, 29 February 1912, p 290.

146 K. Oliver to E. Carpenter, 25 October 1915 (ECC).

147 K. Oliver to E. Carpenter, 25 October 1915 (ECC).

148 A. Tasker to E. Carpenter, 21 July 1913 (ECC).

149 A. Tasker to E. Carpenter, 21 July 1913 (ECC).

150 K. Oliver to E. Carpenter, 25 October 1915 (ECC).

151 On 'Fellowship of the New Life' see Smith, *The London Heretics, 1870–1914*, pp. 134–40.

152 Ellis, *Studies in the Psychology of Sex Volume 2*, pp. 224–6.

153 Ellis, *Studies in the Psychology of Sex Volume 2*, p. 226.

154 E. Lees Ellis to E. Carpenter, 6 November 1905 (ECC).

155 E. Lees Ellis to E. Carpenter, 5 December 1905 (ECC).

156 Edith Lees quoted in Ellis, *Studies in the Psychology of Sex Volume 2*, p. 226.

157 Edith Lees Ellis, 'Eugenics and Spiritual Parenthood', reprinted in Mrs Havelock Ellis, *The New Horizon in Love and Life*, p. 62.

158 E. Lees Ellis to E. Carpenter, no date (*c.* late 1915/early 1916) (ECC).

159 See Soloway, *Birth Control and the Population Question in England, 1877–1930*; see Bland, McCabe and Mort, 'Sexuality and Reproduction: Three Official Instances' in Barrett *et al* (eds.), *Ideology and Cultural Production*, for a discussion of the Beveridge Report 1942 and the continuing concern with the falling birth rate.

160 See, for example, Chesser, *From Girlhood to Womanhood*, p. 22.

Conclusion

1 See Bristow, *Vice and Vigilance*, p. 86.

2 Walkowitz, 'Male Vice and Feminist Virtue', p. 83.

3 Bunting, 'The White Slave Traffic Crusade', p. 31.

4 Elizabeth Cobb, *Common Cause*, 16 May 1912.

5 Elizabeth Robins, 10 June 1912, reported in Robins, *Way Stations*, p. 329. Thanks to Angela V. John for this reference. And see Millicent Fawcett quoted in *The Shield*, 19 May 1912, and Dr Saleeby's tribute to Stead, reported in *The Vote*, 4 May 1912.

6 *Votes for Women*, 30 August 1912.

7 Robins, *Way Stations*, p. 328.

8 *The Times*, 10 June 1912.

9 Billington-Greig, 'The Truth about White Slavery', pp. 445, 450, 443, 445.

10 Harriet Laidlaw quoted in Rosen, *The Lost Sisterhood*, p. 114.

11 Billington-Greig, 'The Truth about White Slavery', p. 446.

12 Rebecca West, 'The White Slave Traffic Bill', *Clarion*, 22 November 1912, reprinted in Marcus (ed.), *The Young Rebecca*.

13 On Robins see John, *Staging a Life*.

14 Robins, *Where are You Going to . . .?*, p. 311. And see E. Slawson to R. Slate, 26 June 1914, in Thompson, *Dear Girl*, p. 226, on the deep impact the book had on Eva.

15 See Bristow, *Prostitution and Prejudice*. And see C.H. Norman, *The Freewoman*, 6 June 1912, p. 45. Philippa Levine suggests that the British authorities in the late nineteenth century were very relieved to find that the few English prostitutes in India were Jewish, and thus did not cast aspersions on the 'real' English (Levine, 'Venereal Disease, Prostitution and the Politics of Empire', p. 593).

16 Valverde, *The Age of Light, Soap and Water*, p. 14.

17 Valverde, *The Age of Light, Soap and Water*, p. 103.

18 Nina Boyle, *The Vote*, 15 June 1912.

19 Arthur Lee, quoted in *The Vote*, 7 September 1912.

20 See Katherine Vulliamy, 'Pass the Bill', *The Freewoman*, 13 June 1912, p. 75.

21 See Rebecca West, 'The White Slave Traffic Bill', p. 121; *The Shield*, August 1912.

22 Selective quoting of the second reading of the bill in *Common Cause*, 20 June 1912, and see Dora Marsden, *The Freewoman*, 11 July 1912.

23 *Common Cause*, 20 June 1912.

24 Sylvia Pankhurst, 'Protecting Women?', *Woman's Dreadnought*, 19 December 1914, p. 156.

25 Bristow, *Vice and Vigilance*, p. 193.

26 Christabel Pankhurst, *The Suffragette*, 7 August 1914, p. 301.

27 Public notice retained in the Fawcett Library. Thanks to David Doughan for drawing my attention to this.

28 Foucault, *The History of Sexuality Volume 1*, p. 18.

29 Ross, 'Fierce Questions and Taunts', p. 594.

30 Foucault, *The History of Sexuality Volume 1*, p. 118.

31 Elizabeth Sloan Chesser, *Woman and Womanhood*, 1912, quoted in Bland, ' "Guardians of the Race", or "Vampires upon the Nation's Health"?', in Whitelegg *et al*, *The Changing Experience of Women*, p. 376.

32 Jeffreys, *The Spinster and Her Enemies*.

33 See Spender, *There's Always been a Women's Movement This Century*.

34 Berry and Bishop, *Testament of a Generation*.

35 Winifred Holtby, 'Feminism Divided', 1926, reprinted in Berry and Bishop, *Testament of a Generation*.

36 Browne, 'The Sexual Variety and Variability among Women and

Their Bearing upon Social Reconstruction', 1915, reprinted in Row-botham, *A New World for Women.*

37 See Carby, '"White Women Listen!" Black Feminism and the Boundaries of Sisterhood', in Centre for Contemporary Cultural Studies (ed.), *The Empire Strikes Back*; Amos and Parmar, 'Challenging Imperial Feminism'; Spelman, *Inessential Woman*; Ramazanoglu, *Feminism and the Contradictions of Oppression*; Brah, 'Difference, Diversity and Differentiation', in Donald and Rattansi (eds.), *'Race', Culture and Difference.*

38 Gordon and DuBois, 'Seeking Ecstasy on the Battlefield', p. 51.

39 See Walkowitz, 'Male Vice and Feminist Virtue', p. 81; Gordon and DuBois, 'Seeking Ecstasy on the Battlefield', p. 43.

40 On Reclaim the Night demonstrations see *Spare Rib* 66, January 1978; *Spare Rib* 78, January 1979; *Spare Rib* 83, June 1979; Coote and Campbell, *Sweet Freedom*, p. 43.

41 On feminist analyses of the Yorkshire Ripper see Hollway, '"I Just Wanted to Kill a Woman." Why? The Ripper and Male Sexuality'; Bland, 'The Case of the Yorkshire Ripper', in Scraton and Gordon (eds.), *Causes for Concern*; Ward Jouve, *The Streetcleaner*; Smith, *Misogynies.*

42 See *Spare Rib* 66, January 1978.

43 See McLeod, *Women Working.*

44 Parmar, 'Rage and Desire: Confronting Pornography', in Chester and Dickey (eds), *Feminism and Censorship*; and see Eileen Fairweather, *Spare Rib* 83, June 1979.

45 See Norden, 'Campaign against Pornography'.

46 See FAC leaflet, Summer 1989, reprinted in *Feminist Review* 36, 1990.

47 Walkowitz, 'Male Vice and Feminist Virtue', p. 81.

48 See Wilson, 'Feminist Fundamentalism', in Segal and McIntosh (eds.), *Sex Exposed*, p. 27. For feminist analyses which look at pornography as representation, see Brown, 'A Feminist Interest in Pornography – Some Modest Proposals'; Coward, 'Sexual Violence and Sexuality'; Kuhn, *The Power of the Image*; Segal and McIntosh (eds) *Sex Exposed.*

49 See Onlywomen Press, *Love Your Enemy?.*

50 Pankhurst, *The Great Scourge and How to End It*, pp. 78–9.

51 Jeffreys, *Anticlimax*, p. 301, and see Jeffreys, *The Lesbian Heresy.*

52 On the celebration of racial difference see Rutherford (ed.), *Identity*, and Donald and Rattansi (eds.), *'Race', Culture and Difference.*

53 Southern Women's Writing Collection, 'Sex Resistance in Heterosexual Arrangements', in Leidhold and Raymond (eds.), *The Sexual Liberals and the Attack on Feminism*, p. 140.

54 And see Ardill and O'Sullivan, 'Upsetting an Apple-cart', for one account of lesbian policing of other lesbians over the issue of S/M.

55 Introduction to Snitow *et al* (eds.), *Desire*, p. 17.

56 See Jeffreys, *Anti-climax*; Campbell, 'Feminist Sexual Politics'.

57 See Shapiro, *Contraception*.

58 On sex education see Durham, *Sex and Politics*, Chapter 6, and Lees, *Sugar and Spice*, Chapter 5. One exception to the non-feminist material is Cousins, *Make It Happy*.

BIBLIOGRAPHY

UNPUBLISHED MANUSCRIPTS AND COLLECTIONS

Josephine Butler Collection, Fawcett Library, London.
Edward Carpenter Collection, Sheffield City Library, Sheffield.
Pearson Collection, Manuscripts Library, University College, London.
Sharpe Collection, Manuscripts Library, University College, London.
Elizabeth Wolstenholme Elmy Collection, British Library, London.

REPORTS AND PROCEEDINGS

Eugenics Education Society, *Annual Reports* 1909–1915, Eugenics Society, London.
Eugenics Education Society, *Council Minutes* 1907–1916, Eugenics Society, London.
London Council for the Promotion of Public Morality, *Annual Reports* 1901–1914, British Library, London.
Moral Reform Union, *Annual Reports* 1882–1893, British Library, London.
National Vigilance Association, *Executive Minutes*, unpublished, Fawcett Library.

NEWSPAPERS AND PERIODICALS

The Adult
British Medical Journal
Common Cause
Contemporary Review
Edinburgh Medical Journal
Englishwoman's Review
Eugenics Review
Fortnightly Review
Free Review
The Freewoman
Journal of the Personal Rights Association (later: *Personal Rights Journal*)
Journal of the Vigilance Association
Lancet
Modern Review

The New Freewoman
Nineteenth Century
Pall Mall Gazette
Popular Science Monthly
Sentinel
Shafts
The Shield
The Suffragette
Vigilance Record
The Vote
Votes for Women
Westminster Review
Woman's Dreadnought
Woman's Penny Paper
Woman's Signal

Primary Sources

Acton, William, *The Functions and Disorders of the Reproductive Organs*, London, John Churchill, 1857; 3rd edition, 1861; 5th edition, 1871; 6th edition, 1875.

Allbutt, H. Arthur, *The Wife's Handbook*, London, W.J. Ramsey, 1886.

Allbutt, Sir T.C. and Rolleston, H.R. (eds.), *A System of Medicine*, vol. 1 1896, vol. 8 1899, London, Macmillan and Co., second edition, 1905.

Allen, Grant, 'Plain Words on the Woman Question', *Fortnightly Review*, October 1889.

Atkinson, Mabel, *The Economic Foundations of the Women's Movement*, Fabian Tract No. 175, London, Fabian Society, 1914.

Aveling, Eleanor Marx and Aveling, Edward, *The Woman Question*, London, Swan Sonnenschein & Co., 1886.

Bachofen, J.J., *Myth, Religion and Mother Right*: Selections of Bachofen's writings including *Das-Mutter-recht*, 1861, London, Routledge & Kegan Paul, 1968.

Barash, Carol (ed.), *An Olive Schreiner Reader*, London, Pandora Press, 1987.

Barclay, James, 'The Suicide Scare', *Nineteenth Century and After*, vol. 60, December 1906.

Barnes, R. and Barnes, F., *A System of Obstetric Medicine and Surgery* vol. I, London, Small, Elder & Co., 1884.

Berkeley-Hill, O.A.R., 'The Declining Birth-Rate', *Lancet*, 8 July 1911.

Berry, Paul and Bishop, Alan (ed.), *Testament of a Generation: the Journalism of Vera Brittain and Winifred Holtby*, London, Virago, 1985.

Besant, Annie, *Theosophy and the Law of Population*, London, Theosophical Publication, 1901.

Besant, Annie, *An Autobiography*, London, T. Fisher Unwin Ltd., 1893, 2nd edition 1908.

Besant, Annie, 'The Economic Position of Women', *Our Corner*, vol. 10, 1887.

Besant, Annie, *Marriage as it was, as it is, and as it should be*, New York, Asa Butts, 1878.

Besant, Annie, *The Law of Population*, London, Freethought Publishing Co., 1877.

Billington-Greig, Teresa, 'The Truth about White Slavery', *Englishwoman's Review*, vol. 14, June 1913.

Billington-Greig, Teresa, *The Militant Suffrage Movement – Emancipation in a Hurry*, London, F. Palmer, 1911.

Black, Clementina, 'On Marriage: a Criticism', *Fortnightly Review*, vol. 47, 1890.

Black, Clementina, 'The Organization of Working Women', *Fortnightly Review*, vol. 46, 1889.

Blackwell, Dr Elizabeth, *Essays in Medical Sociology*, 2 vols., London, Ernest Bell, 1902.

Blackwell, Dr Elizabeth, 'Influence of Women in the Profession of Medicine', 1889, in Blackwell, Dr Elizabeth, *Essays in Medical Sociology*, vol. 2, London, Ernest Bell, 1902.

Blackwell, Dr Elizabeth, 'The Human Element in Relation to Sex', 1880, in Blackwell, Dr Elizabeth, *Essays in Medical Sociology*, vol. 1, London, Ernest Bell, 1902.

Blackwell, Dr Elizabeth, 'The Moral Education of the Young in Relation to Sex', 1878, in Blackwell, Dr Elizabeth, *Essays in Medical Sociology*, vol. 2, London, Ernest Bell, 1902.

Blackwell, Dr Elizabeth, *A Medical Address to the Benevolence of Malthus, Contrasted with the Corruption of Neo-Malthusianism*, London, Darks & Co., 1888.

Blackwell, Dr Elizabeth, *Purchase of Women: the Great Economic Blunder*, London, John Kensit, 1887.

Blackwell, Dr Elizabeth, *The Human Element in Sex: Being a Medical Enquiry into the Relation of Sexual Physiology to Christian Morals*, 1880, London, J. & A. Churchill, 4th edition 1884.

Blackwell, Dr Elizabeth, *Right and Wrong Methods with Dealing with the Social Evil*, Hastings, D. Williams, 1883.

Blackwell, Dr Elizabeth, *Counsel to Parents on the Moral Education of Their Children in Relation to Sex*, London, Bell & Sons, 1878, 8th edition 1913.

Blake, Matilda, 'The Lady and the Law', *Westminster Review*, vol. 137, 1892.

Blake, Matilda, 'Are Women Protected?', *Westminster Review*, vol. 137, 1892.

Blandford, Dr George Fielding, *Insanity and Its Treatment*, 1871, Edinburgh, Oliver and Boyd, 4th edition 1895.

Bloch, Iwan, *The Sexual Life of Our Time in Its Relation to Modern Civilisation*, London, Rebman Ltd, 1908.

Booth, J.B., *London Town*, London, T. Warner Laurie, 1929.

Braby, Maeve, *Modern Marriage and How to Bear It*, London, T. Warner Laurie, 1908.

Brooke, Emma, *A Superfluous Woman*, London, W. Heinemann, 1894.

Browne, Stella, 'Some Problems of Sex', *International Journal of Ethics*, 27 July 1917.

Browne, Stella, 'Woman and Birth-Control', in Paul, Eden and Paul, Cedar (eds.), *Population and Birth-Control: a Symposium*, New York, Critic and Guide Co., 1917.

Browne, Stella, 'The Sexual Variety and Variability among Women and Their Bearing upon Social Reconstruction', given to the British Society for the Study of Sex Psychology, 1915, reprinted in Rowbotham, Sheila, *A New World for Women: Stella Browne – Socialist Feminist*, London, Pluto Press, 1977.

Bulley, Louise, *A Talk on Questions of Sex. For Young Men and Girls of 18*, Seacombe, William Bros & Co., 1911.

Bunting, Lady Mary, 'The White Slave Traffic', *Contemporary Review*, CIII, 1913.

Caird, Mona, *The Morality of Marriage and Other Essays*, London, George Redway, 1897.

Caird, Mona, *The Daughters of Danaus*, London, Bliss, Sands & Foster, 1894.

Caird, Mona, 'Phases of Human Development', *Westminster Review*, vol. 141, 1894.

Caird, Mona, 'A Defence of the so-called "Wild Woman"', *Nineteenth Century*, vol. 31, 1892.

Caird, Mona, 'Ideal Marriage', *Westminster Review*, vol. 130, November 1888.

Caird, Mona, 'Marriage', *Westminster Review*, vol. 130, August 1888.

Cameron, Laura B., 'How We Marry', *Westminster Review*, vol. 145, 1896.

Campbell, Dr Harry, 'Eugenics from the Physician's Standpoint', *British Medical Journal*, 2 September 1913.

Campbell, Dr Harry, *Differences in the Nervous Organism of Man and Woman*, London, H.L. Lewis, 1891.

Carpenter, Edward, *My Days and Dreams*, London, George Allen & Unwin Ltd, 1916.

Carpenter, Edward, *The Intermediate Sex*, 1908, London, George Allen & Unwin Ltd, 1916.

Carpenter, Edward, *Love's Coming of Age*, London, Swan Sonnenschein, 1902, 5th edition 1906.

Carpenter, William, *Principles of Mental Physiology*, London, Kegan Paul, 1874, Trench & Co., 6th edition 1888.

Chant, Laura Ormiston, 'Woman and the Streets', in Marchant, James (ed.), *Public Morals*, London, Morgan and Scott, 1902.

Chant, Laura Ormiston, *Why We Attacked the Empire*, London, Horace Marshall & Son, 1895.

Chapman, Elizabeth, *Marriage Questions in Modern Fiction*, London, Bodley Head, 1897.

Chesser, Elizabeth Sloan, *From Girlhood to Womanhood*, Alliance of Honour, 1913; London, Cassell & Co., 1914.

Chesser, Elizabeth Sloan, *Woman, Marriage and Motherhood*, London, Cassell & Co., 1913.

Chesser, Elizabeth Sloan, *Perfect Health for Women and Children*, London, Methuen & Co., 1912.

Churchill, Winston, *My Early Life: a Roving Commission*, London, Thornton Butterworth, 1930.

Clapperton, Jane, *A Vision of the Future*, London, Swan Sonnenschein & Co., 1904.

Clapperton, Jane, *What do Women Want?*, London, Reynolds, *c.* 1900.

Clapperton, Jane, *Scientific Meliorism and the Evolution of Happiness*, London, Kegan Paul, Trench & Co., 1885.

Clare, Hope, 'Stagnant Virginity', *Free Review*, January 1897.

Clifford, William Kingdon, 'On the Scientific Basis of Morals', *Contemporary Review*, 1875, reprinted in Stephen, Leslie and Pollock, Sir Frederick (eds.), *Lectures and Essays by the Late William Kingdon Clifford*, 1885, London, Macmillan and Co., 1901.

Clouston, T.S., *Clinical Lectures on Mental Diseases*, London, J. & A. Churchill, 1883, 5th edition 1898.

Cobbe, Frances Power, 'Wife Torture in England', *Contemporary Review*, vol. 32, April 1878.

Cobbe, Frances Power, 'Celibacy v. Marriage', *Frazer's Magazine*, vol. 65, no. 336, February 1862.

Collet, Clara, 'Prospects of Marriage for Women', *The Nineteenth Century*, vol. 31, 1892.

Committee of Inquiry, *The State & Sexual Morality*, London, Allen & Unwin, 1920.

Cook, Lady, 'Virtue: what it is, and what it is not', *Modern Review*, vol. 1, October 1892.

Coote, William, *A Romance of Philanthropy*, London, National Vigilance Association, 1916.

Courtney, Janet, *An Oxford Portrait Gallery*, London, Chapman and Hall Ltd, 1931.

Crackanthorpe, Montague, 'Population and Progress', *Fortnightly Review*, vol. 80, December 1906.

Creighton, Louise, *The Social Disease and How to Fight It: a Rejoinder*, London, Longman, Green & Co., 1914.

Crichton-Browne, Sir James, 'Sex in Education', *Lancet*, 7 May 1892.

Cronwright-Schreiner, S.C. (ed.), *The Letters of Olive Schreiner 1876–1920*, Boston, Little, Brown & Co., 1924.

Darwin, Charles, *The Descent of Man and Selection in Relation to Sex*, London, John Murray, 1871, 1901.

Dawson, Oswald (ed.), *The Bar Sinister and Licit Love: the First Biennial Proceedings of the Legitimation League*, London, Reeves, 1895.

Dawson, Oswald, 'Legitimation and Licit Love', *Modern Review*, vol. 3, April 1894.

Delisle, Françoise, *Françoise*, London, Delisle Ltd, 1962.

Delisle, Françoise, *Friendship's Odyssey*, London, William Heinemann Ltd., 1946.

Dixie, Florence, *Gloriana or the Glorious Revolution of 1900*, London, Henry & Co., 1890.

Donkin, Bryan, 'Hysteria', in Tuke, Dr Hack (ed.), *A Dictionary of Psychological Medicine*, vol. 1, London, J. & A. Churchill, 1892.

Dowie, Ménie Muriel, *Gallia*, London, Methuen & Co., 1895.

Egerton, George, *Discords*, 1894, London, Virago, 1983.

Elderton, Ethel M., *Report of the English Birth Rate. Part 1, north of the Humber*, Cambridge, Eugenics Laboratory Memoirs, nos. 19 and 20, 1914.

Elderton, Ethel M. and Pearson, Karl, *A First Study of the Influence of Parental Alcoholism on the Physique and Ability of the Offspring*, London, Eugenics Laboratory Memoirs, no. 10, 1910.

Ellis, Havelock, *Studies in the Psychology of Sex Volume 2* (originally Volume 1): *Sexual Inversion*, 1897, Philadelphia, F.A. Davis Co., 3rd edition 1925.

Ellis, Havelock, 'Birth Control and Eugenics', *Eugenics Review*, vol. 9, April 1917.

Ellis, Havelock, *Studies in the Psychology of Sex Volume 6: Sex in Relation to Society*, Philadelphia, F.A. Davis Co., 1910, 1913.

Ellis, Havelock, *The Task of Social Hygiene*, London, Constable, 1912.

Ellis, Havelock, *The Problem of Race-Regeneration*, London, Cassell & Co. Ltd, 1911.

Ellis, Havelock, 'The Sterilization of the Unfit', *Eugenics Review*, vol. 1, October 1909.

Ellis, Havelock, *Studies in the Psychology of Sex Volume 3: Analysis of the Sex Impulse, Love and Pain*, Philadelphia, F.A. Davis Co., 1903.

Ellis, Havelock, *Man and Woman: a Study of Human Secondary Sex Characters*, London, Walter Scott, 1894, 6th edition 1926.

Ellis, Havelock, *The Criminal*, London, Contemporary Science Series, 1889.

Ellis, Havelock, *Woman and Marriage*, London, William Reeves, 1888.

Ellis, Mrs Havelock (Edith Lees), *The New Horizon in Love and Life*, London, A. & C. Black Ltd, 1921.

Ethelmer, Ellis, *Phases of Love: as it was, as it is, as it may be*, Congleton, Mrs Wolstenholme Elmy, 1897.

Ethelmer, Ellis, *Life to Woman*, Congleton, Mrs Wolstenholme Elmy, 1896.

Ethelmer, Ellis, *Baby Buds*, Congleton, Mrs Wolstenholme Elmy, 1895.

Ethelmer, Ellis, *The Human Flower*, Congleton, Mrs Wolstenholme Elmy, 1894.

Ethelmer, Ellis, *Woman Free*, Congleton, Women's Emancipation Union, 1893.

Ewart, C.T., 'Eugenics and Degeneracy', *Journal of Mental Science* 56, 1910.

The Fabian Women's Group, *Three Years' Work of the Women's Group*, London, LSE Library, *c.* 1911.

Fawcett, Millicent, 'The Emancipation of Women', *Fortnightly Review*, vol. 50, November 1891.

Féré, Charles, *The Evolution and Dissolution of the Sexual Instinct*, Paris, Charles Carrington, 1904.

Finot, Jean, *The Problem of the Sexes*, London, David Nutt, 1913.

Forel, August, *The Sexual Question: a Scientific, Psychological and Sociological Study*, 1906, London, Heinemann, 1922.

Fremantle, F.E., 'The Declining Birth-Rate', *Lancet*, 22 April 1911.

Galton, Francis, 'Restrictions in marriage', *Sociological Papers*, vol. 2, London, Macmillan and Co., 1906.

Galton, Francis, 'Studies in National Eugenics', *Sociological Papers*, vol. 2, London, Macmillan and Co., 1906.

Galton, Francis, *Inquiries into Human Faculty*, London, Macmillan, 1883.

Galton, Francis, *Hereditary Genius*, London, Macmillan, 1869.

Geddes, Patrick and Thomson, Arthur, *The Evolution of Sex*, London, Walter Scott, 1889.

Grand, Sarah, 'At What Age Should Girls Marry?', *The Young Woman* VII, 1898–9.

Grand, Sarah, 'Marriage Questions in Fiction: the Standpoint of á Typical Modern Woman', *Fortnightly Review*, vol. 63, January–June 1898.

Grand, Sarah, *The Beth Book*, 1897, Virago 1983.

Grand, Sarah, *The Heavenly Twins*, London, William Heinemann, 1893.

Grossmith, G. and Grossmith, W., *The Diary of a Nobody*, Bristol, J.W. Arrowsmith, 1892; London, Penguin, 1965.

Hamilton, Cicely, *Marriage as a Trade*, 1909, London, The Women's Press, 1981.

Hartley, Constance, *The Truth about Women*, London, Everleigh Nash, 1913.

Heape, Walter, *Sex Antagonism*, London, Constable & Co. Ltd, 1913.

Hemory, Gertrude, 'The Revolt of the Daughters – an Answer by One of Them', *Westminster Review*, vol. 141, 1894.

Hewitt, Emma, 'Woman's Duty', *Westminster Review*, vol. 152, 1899.

Higson, Jessie, *The Story of a Beginning*, London, SPCK, 1955.

How-Martyn, Edith and Breed, Mary, *The Birth Control Movement in England*, London, John Bale & Danielsson Ltd, 1930.

Huxley, T.H., *Evolution and Ethics*, London, Macmillan, 1893.

Ignota, 'Pioneers! O Pioneers!', *Westminster Review*, April 1906.

Ignota, 'The Awakening of Women', *Westminster Review*, July 1899.

Ignota, 'Judicial Sex Bias', *Westminster Review*, March 1898.

Johnson, Effie, 'Marriage or Free Love', *Westminster Review*, vol. 152, 1899.

Ker, Alice, *Motherhood: a Book for Every Woman*, London, John Heywood, 1891.

Knight, Mary, 'Woman v. the State', *Westminster Review*, July 1909.

Lane, J. Ernest, 'Racial Poisons 1: Venereal Disease', *Eugenics Review*, vol. 1, January 1910.

Leppington, Blanche, 'Debrutalisation of Man', *Contemporary Review*, vol. 67, May 1895.

Leslie, Dr Murray, 'Woman's Progress in Relation to Eugenics', *Eugenics Review*, vol. 2, January 1911.

Llewelyn Davies, Margaret (ed.), *Maternity: Letters from Working Women*, London, G. Bell & Sons Ltd, 1915; London, Virago, 1978.

Lombroso, C. and Ferrero, G., *The Female Offender*, London, T. Fisher Unwin, 1895.

M.A.B., 'Normal or Abnormal?', *Englishwoman's Review*, 14 December 1889.

McDougall, W., 'A Practicable Eugenic Suggestion', *Sociological Papers*, vol. 3, London, Macmillan and Co., 1907.

McLennan, J.F., *Studies in Ancient History*, London, Quaritch, 1876–7.

McPhee, Carol and FitzGerald, Ann (eds.), *The Non-Violent Militant:*

Selected Writings of Teresa Billington-Greig, London, Routledge & Kegan Paul, 1987.

Marchant, James, *Aids to Purity: Seven Personal Letters*, reprinted from 'Health and Strength', London, Health and Strength, 1909.

Marchant, James (ed.), *Public Morals*, London, Morgan & Scott, 1902.

Marcus, Jane (ed.), *The Young Rebecca: Selected Essays of Rebecca West 1911–17*, London, Macmillan, 1982.

Martin, Frances, 'The Glorified Spinster', *Macmillan's Magazine* 58, 1888.

Martindale, Louisa, *Under the Surface*, Brighton, Southern Publishing Co., 1908.

Matthews, Duncan J., *On Sterility in Women*, London, J. & A. Churchill, 1884.

Maudsley, Henry, *Pathology of Mind*, London, Macmillan and Co., 1879.

Maudsley, Henry, 'Sex in Mind and in Education', *Fortnightly Review*, 1874.

Maudsley, Henry, *Body and Mind*, London, Macmillan & Co., 1873.

Mearns, Rev. Andrew, *The Bitter Cry of Outcast London*, London, James Clarke & Co., 1883.

Mercier, Charles, *Textbook of Insanity*, London, Macmillan, 1902.

Mercier, Charles, 'Vice, Crime and Insanity', in Allbutt, T.C. and Rolleston, H.R. (eds.), *A System of Medicine*, vol. 8, London, Macmillan & Co., 1899.

Miller, George Noyes, *After the Strike of Sex, or Zugassent's Discovery*, London, William Reeves, 1896.

Miller, George Noyes, *The Strike of Sex: a Novel*, London, W.H. Reynold, 1891.

Minerva, 'Why Men do not Marry', *Woman's Penny Paper*, 28 June 1890.

Mjoen, Dr A., 'Legal Certificates of Health before Marriage', *Eugenics Review*, vol. 4, January 1913.

Mond, Frank (ed.), *The Burden of Woman*, London, New Age Press, 1908.

Mortimer, Geoffrey, *Chapters on Human Love*, London University Press, 1898.

Muller, Henrietta, 'What Woman is Fitted For', *Westminster Review*, January 1887.

Muller, Henrietta, 'The Future of Single Women', *Westminster Review*, January 1884.

Murray, Sir James A.H. (ed.), *A New English Dictionary on Historical Principles*, Oxford, Clarendon Press, 1884–1933.

National Council of Public Morals – National Birth-Rate Commission, *The Declining Birth-Rate*, London, Chapman & Hall, 1916.

Neville–Rolfe, Sybil, *Social Biology and Welfare*, London, Allen & Unwin, 1949.

Newman, W., *The Corruption Called Neo-Malthusianism*, with notes by Elizabeth Blackwell, London, Moral Reform Union, 1889.

Nichols, Mary Gove and Nichols, T.L., *Marriage: Its History, Character and Results*, New York, T.L. Nichols, 1854.

Nichols, T.L., *Esoteric Anthropology*, Malvern, T.L. Nichols, 1873.

Nichols, T.L., *Human Physiology: the Basis of Sanitary and Social Science*, London, Truber & Co., 1872.

Nordau, Max, *Degeneration*, translated from the 2nd edition, London, W. Heinemann, 1895.

Oppenheim, Annie I., *The Face and How to Read It*, London, T. Fisher Unwin, 1907.

Pankhurst, Christabel, *The Great Scourge and How to End It*, London, E. Pankhurst, 1913.

Pankhurst, Sylvia, *The Suffragette Movement*, 1931; London, Virago 1977.

Paul, Eden and Paul, Cedar (eds.) *Population and Birth-Control: a Symposium*, New York, Critic and Guide Co., 1917.

Pearson, Egon, *Karl Pearson: an Appreciation of Some Aspects of His Life and Work*, Cambridge University Press, 1938.

Pearson, Karl, *The Problem of Practical Eugenics*, London, Dulau & Co., 1909.

Pearson, Karl, *National Life from the Standpoint of Science*, London, Adam & Charles Black, 1901.

Pearson, Karl, *The Chances of Death and Other Studies in Evolution*, London, Edward Arnold, 1897.

Pearson, Karl, *The Ethic of Freethought*, London, Adam & Charles Black, 1888.

Pearson, Karl, '*The Positive Creed of Freethought*', being a lecture delivered at the South Place Institute on 15 April 1888, London, William Reeves, 1888.

Pearson, Karl, 'Variation in Man and Woman', *The Chances of Death and Other Studies in Evolution*, London, Edward Arnold, 1897.

Pember Reeves, Maud, *Round about a Pound a Week*, 1913; London, Virago, 1979.

Posoda, A., *Sociological Papers*, vol. 2. Sociological Society, 1906.

Quilter, Harry (ed.), *Is Marriage a Failure?*, London, Swan Sonnenschein & Co., 1888.

Re-Bartlett, Lucy, *Sex and Sanctity*, London, Longmans, Green & Co., 1912.

Re-Bartlett, Lucy, *The Coming Order*, London, Longmans, Green & Co., 1911.

Rentoul, Robert Reid, *Race Culture; or, Race Suicide? (A Plea for the Unborn)*, London, Walter Scott Publishing Co., 1906.

Rentoul, Robert Reid, *Proposed Sterilisation of Certain Mental and Physical Degenerates*, London, Walter Scott Publishing Co., 1903.

Rhondda, Viscountess, *This was My World*, London, Macmillan & Co., 1933.

Richardson, H.M., 'The Outcasts', *The Englishwoman*, vol. 3, no. 8, September 1909.

Ritchie, David, *Darwinism and Politics*, London, Swan Sonnenschein & Co., 1889.

Rive, Richard (ed.), *Olive Schreiner Letters: Vol. 1 1871–1899*, Oxford University Press, 1980.

Robins, Elizabeth, *Way Stations*, London, Hodder & Stoughton, 1913.

Robins, Elizabeth, *Where are You Going to . . .?*, London, Heinemann, 1913.

Romanes, George, 'The Mental Differences between Men and Women', *British Medical Journal*, 20 August 1887.

Saleeby, Caleb, *The Progress of Eugenics*, London, Cassell & Co. Ltd, 1914.

Saleeby, Caleb, *Woman and Womanhood: a Search for Principles*, London, Heinemann, 1912.

Saleeby, Caleb, *The Methods of Race Regeneration*, London, Cassell & Co. Ltd, 1911.

Scharlieb, Mary, *Womanhood and Race Regeneration*, London, Cassell & Co. Ltd, 1912.

Scharlieb, Mary, 'Adolescent Girlhood under Modern Conditions, with Special Reference to Motherhood', *Eugenics Review*, vol. 1, April 1909 – January 1910.

Schreiner, Olive, *From Man to Man*, London, T. Fisher Unwin Ltd, 1926; London, Virago, 1982.

Schreiner, Olive, *Woman and Labour*, London, T. Fisher Unwin, 1911.

Schreiner, Olive, 'The Buddhist Priest's Wife', 1892, reprinted in Barash, Carol, *An Olive Schreiner Reader*, London, Pandora Press, 1987.

Schreiner, Olive, *Dreams*, London, T. Fisher Unwin, 1890.

Schreiner, Olive, *The Story of an African Farm*, London, Chapman & Hall, 1883.

Shuster, E., *Eugenics*, London, Collins, 1913.

Sharp, Evelyn, *Unfinished Adventure*, London, John Lane, 1933.

Shaw, George Bernard, *The Quintessence of Ibsenism*, London, Constable & Co., 1926.

Simcox, Edith, 'The Capacity of Women', *Nineteenth Century*, vol. 22, 1887.

Snowden, Ethel, *The Feminist Movement*, London, Collins, 1911.

Sociological Society, *Sociological Papers*, vol. 2, London, Macmillan and Co., 1906.

Sociological Society, *Sociological Papers*, vol. 1, London, Macmillan and Co., 1905.

Spencer, Henry, 'The Comparative Psychology of Man', *Popular Science Monthly* 8, 1875–6.

Spencer, Herbert, *The Principles of Ethics*, vol. 2, London, Williams & Norgate, 1892, 1893.

Spender, Dale (ed.), *Time and Tide Wait for No Man*, London, Pandora Press, 1984.

Stead, W.T., *A Journalist on Journalism*, London, John Haddon and Co., 1892.

Stephen, Leslie and Pollock, Sir Frederick (eds.), *Lectures and Essays by the Late William Kingdon Clifford*, 1885, London, Macmillan, 1901.

Stockham, Alice B., *Karezza: Ethics of Marriage*, Chicago, 1896.

Stout, Edwin, 'W.T. Stead: a Character Sketch', in Stead, W.T., *A Journalist on Journalism*, London, John Haddon and Co., 1892.

Strachey, Ray, *Millicent Garrett Fawcett*, London, John Murray, 1931.

Strachey, Ray, *The Cause*, 1928, London, Virago, 1978.

Strahan, S.A.K., *Marriage and Disease*, London, Kegan Paul, Trench, Trubner & Co., 1892.

Stutfield, Hugh E.M., 'Tommyrotics', *Blackwood's Edinburgh Review*, vol. 157, June 1895.

Sweeney, John, *At Scotland Yard: being the Experience during 27 Years' Service of John Sweeney, Late Detective Inspector*, London, Grant Richards, 1904.

Swiney, Frances, *The Ancient Road or the Development of the Soul*, London, G. Bell & Sons Ltd, 1918.

Swiney, Frances, *Woman and the Natural Law*, 1906, London, C.W. Daniel, 1912.

Swiney, Frances, *The Awakening of Women or Women's Part in Evolution*, 1899, London, William Reeves, 1908.

Swiney, Frances, *The Bar of Isis*, London, Open Road Publishing Co., 1907.

Swiney, Frances, *The Cosmic Procession or the Feminine Principle in Evolution*, London, Ernest Bell, 1906.

Tait, Lawson, *Diseases of Women and Abdominal Surgery*, vol. 1, Leicester, Richardson & Co., 1889.

Talbot, Eugene, *Degeneracy: Its Cause, Signs and Results*, London, Walter Scott, 1898.

Taylor, J.W., 'The Diminishing Birth-Rate', *British Medical Journal*, 20 February 1904.

Taylor, Sir William, 'The Medical Profession in Relation to the Army', *Lancet*, 18 October 1902.

Thompson, William and Wheeler, Anna, *Appeal of one half of the Human Race,*

Women, against the pretensions of the other half, Men, to retain them in political and then in Civil and Domestic Slavery, 1825, London, Virago, 1983.

Tuke, Dr Hack (ed.), *A Dictionary of Psychological Medicine: Volume 1*, London, J. and A. Churchill, 1892.

Tweedie, Mrs Alec, 'Eugenics', *Eugenics Review*, vol. 9, January–June 1912.

Tylor, E.B., *Anthropology*, London, Macmillan, 1881.

Vickery, Alice, 'Response to Galton's "Studies in National Eugenics"', *Sociological Papers*, vol. 2, London, Macmillan and Co., 1906.

Wade, Willoughby F., 'Some Functional Disorders of Females', *Lancet*, 5 June 1886.

Wallace, Alfred, 'Human Selection', *Fortnightly Review*, vol. 48, 1890.

Ward, Lester F., *Pure Sociology*, New York, Macmillan and Co., 1903.

Webb, Beatrice, *My Apprenticeship*, London, Longmans, 1928.

Webb, Sidney, *The Decline in the Birth Rate*, London, Fabian Society, 1907.

West, Rebecca, 'The Freewoman', *Time and Tide*, 16 July 1926, reprinted in Spender, Dale (ed.), *Time and Tide Wait for No Man*, London, Pandora Press, 1984.

West, Rebecca, 'The White Slave Traffic Bill', *The Clarion*, 22 November 1912, reprinted in Marcus, Jane (ed.), *The Young Rebecca*, Macmillan, 1982.

Westermarck, Edward, *The History of Human Marriage*, London, Macmillan & Co., 1891.

Whetham, W.C.D., 'The Extinction of the Upper-classes', *Nineteenth Century and After*, vol. 66, 1909.

White, Arnold, *Efficiency and Empire*, London, Methuen, 1901.

White, Douglas, 'Eugenics and Venereal Disease', *Eugenics Review*, vol. 5, October 1913.

Wilson, Andrew, 'A Theory of Sex', *Lancet*, 26 September 1891.

Wolstenholme Elmy, Elizabeth, 'Suffrage', *Westminster Review*, vol. 148, October 1897.

Wolstenholme Elmy, Elizabeth, *Woman and the Law*, Congleton, Women's Emancipation Union, 1896.

Women's Co-operative Guild, *Working Women and Divorce: an Account of Evidence to the Royal Commission on Divorce and Matrimonial Causes*, London, David Nott, 1911.

Secondary Sources

Ackland, Valentine, *For Sylvia: an Honest Account*, London, Chatto and Windus, 1985.

Amos, Valerie and Parmar, Pratibha, 'Challenging Imperial Feminism', *Feminist Review* 17, 1984.

Ardill, Susan and O'Sullivan, Sue, 'Upsetting an Apple-cart', *Feminist Review* 23, 1986.

Auchmuty, Rosemary, *A World of Girls*, London, The Women's Press, 1992.

Bailey, Peter (ed.), *Music Hall: the Business of Pleasure*, Milton Keynes, Open University Press, 1986.

Banks, J.A. and Banks, Olive, *Feminism and Family Planning in Victorian England*, Liverpool University Press, 1964.

Banks, J.A. and Banks, Olive, 'The Bradlaugh-Besant Trial and the English Newspapers', *Population Studies*, 8 July 1954.

Banks, Olive, *Faces of Feminism*, Oxford, Martin Robertson, 1981.

Barker, David, 'How to Curb the Fertility of the Unfit: the Feeble-minded in Edwardian Britain', *Oxford Review of Education*, vol. 9, no. 3, 1983.

Barrett, Michelle *et al* (eds.), *Ideology and Cultural Production*, London, Croom Helm, 1979.

Bayley, David (ed.), *Police and Society*, London, Sage, 1977.

Beer, Gillian, ' "The Face of Nature": Anthropomorphic Elements in the Language of *The Origin of Species*', in Jordanova, Ludmilla (ed.), *Languages of Nature*, London, Free Association Books, 1986.

Beer, Gillian, *Darwin's Plots*, London, Routledge Kegan Paul, 1983.

Benn, Miriam, *Predicaments of Love*, London, Pluto Press, 1992.

Berkman, Joyce Avrech, *The Healing Imagination of Olive Schreiner*, Amherst, University of Massachusetts Press, 1989.

Biddis, Michael (ed.), *Images of the Race*, Leicester University Press, 1979.

Birken, Lawrence, *Consuming Desire: Sexual Science and the Emergence of a Culture of Abundance 1871–1914*, Ithaca and London, Cornell University Press, 1988.

Bland, Lucy, 'Banishing the Beast: English Feminism and Sexual Morality, 1885–1914', Ph.D thesis, University of Birmingham, 1993.

Bland, Lucy, 'Purifying the Public World: Feminist Vigilantes in Late Victorian England', *Women's History Review*, vol. 1, no. 3, 1992.

Bland, Lucy, 'Rational Sex or Spiritual Love? The Men and Women's Club of the 1880s', *Women's Studies International Forum*, vol. 13, nos. 1/2, 1990.

Bland, Lucy, 'The Married Woman, the "New Woman", and the Feminist: Sexual Politics of the 1890s', in Rendall, Jane (ed.), *Equal or Different: Women's Politics, 1800–1914*, Oxford, Blackwell, 1987.

Bland, Lucy, 'In the Name of Protection: the Policing of Women in the

First World War', in Smart, Carol and Brophy, Julia (eds.), *Women in Law*, London, Routledge and Kegan Paul, 1985.

Bland, Lucy, '"The Cleansing of the Portals of Life": the VD Campaign of the Early Twentieth Century', in Langan, Mary and Schwarz, Bill (eds.), *Crises in the British State, 1880–1930*, London, Hutchinson, 1985.

Bland, Lucy, 'The Case of the Yorkshire Ripper: Mad, Bad, Beast or Male?', in Scraton, Phil and Gordon, Paul (eds.), *Causes for Concern*, London, Penguin, 1984.

Bland, Lucy, '"Guardians of the Race", or "Vampires upon the Nation's Health"?: Female Sexuality and Its Regulation in Early Twentieth-Century Britain', in Whitelegg, Elizabeth *et al* (eds.), *The Changing Experience of Women*, Oxford, Martin Robertson, 1982.

Bland, Lucy, McCabe, Trisha and Mort, Frank, 'Sexuality and Reproduction: Three Official Instances', in Barrett, Michelle *et al* (eds.), *Ideology and Cultural Production*, London, Croom Helm, 1979.

Bordin, Ruth, *Women and Temperance*, Philadelphia, Temple University Press, 1981.

Boumelha, Penny, *Thomas Hardy and Women: Sexual Ideology and Narrative Form*, Brighton, Harvester Press, 1982.

Bowlby, Rachel, *Just Looking*, London, Methuen, 1985.

Brah, Avtar, 'Difference, Diversity and Differentiation', in Donald, J. and Rattansi, A. (eds.), *'Race', Culture and Difference*, London, Sage, 1992.

Branca, Patricia, *Silent Sisterhood: Middle-Class Women in the Victorian Home*, London, Croom Helm, 1975.

Brandon, Ruth, *The New Women and the Old Men*, London, Secker & Warburg, 1990.

Bristow, Edward, *Prostitution and Prejudice: the Jewish Fight against White Slavery, 1870–1939*, Oxford, Clarendon Press, 1982.

Bristow, Edward, *Vice and Vigilance*, Dublin, Gill & Macmillan, 1977.

Bristow, Joseph (ed.), *Sexual Sameness*, London, Routledge, 1992.

Britain, Ian, *Fabianism and Culture: a Study in British Socialism and the Arts, c. 1884–1918*, Cambridge University Press, 1982.

Broughton, Treva, 'Women's Autobiography: the Self at Stake?', *Prose Studies: History, Theory, Criticism*, vol. 14, September 1991.

Brown, Beverley, 'A Feminist Interest in Pornography – Some Modest Proposals', *M/F* 5 and 6, 1981.

Burchfield, R.W. (ed.), *The Oxford English Dictionary*, Oxford, Clarendon Press, 1989.

Burfield, Diana, 'Theosophy and Feminism: Some Explorations in Nineteenth-Century Biography', in Holden, Pat (ed.), *Women's Religious Experience*, London, Croom Helm, 1983.

Burman, Sandra, *Fit Work for Women*, London, Croom Helm, 1979.

Burton, Antoinette, 'The Feminist Quest for Identity: British Imperialist Suffragism and "Global Sisterhood", 1900–1915', *Journal of Women's History*, vol. 3, no. 2, 1991.

Burton, Antoinette, 'The White Woman's Burden: British Feminists and the Indian Woman, 1865–1915', *Women's Studies International Forum*, vol. 13, no. 4, 1990.

Caine, Barbara, *Destined to be Wives: the Sisters of Beatrice Webb*, Oxford, Clarendon Press, 1986.

Caine, Barbara, 'Beatrice Webb and the Woman Question', *History Workshop Journal*, 14, 1982.

Campbell, Beatrix, 'Feminist Sexual Politics', *Feminist Review* 5, 1980.

Carby, Hazel, '"White Women Listen!" Black Feminism and the Boundaries of Sisterhood', in Centre for Contemporary Cultural Studies (ed.), *The Empire Strikes Back*, London, Hutchinson, 1982.

Chamberlin, J. Edward and Gilman, Sander L. (eds.), *Degeneration: the Dark Side of Progress*, USA, Columbia University Press, 1985.

Chester, Gail and Dickey, Julienne (eds.), *Feminism and Censorship*, Dorset, Prism Press, 1988.

Chrisman, Laura, 'Allegory, Feminist Thought and the *Dreams* of Olive Schreiner', *Prose Studies: History, Theory, Criticism*, vol. 13, May 1990.

Clarke, John *et al*, *Ideologies of Welfare*, London, Hutchinson, 1987.

Clarke, Norma, 'Feminism and the Popular Novel of the 1890s: a Brief Consideration of a Forgotten Feminist Novelist', *Feminist Review* 20, 1965.

Coates, Chris *et al*, *Diggers and Dreamers*, Buckinghamshire, Communes Network, 1993.

Cohen, Deborah, 'Private Lives in Public Places: Marie Stopes, the Mothers' Clinics and the Practice of Contraception', *History Workshop Journal* 35, Spring 1993.

Cole, G.D.H. and Postgate, R., *The Common People, 1746–1946*, 1938, London, Routledge, 1992.

Collette, Christine, 'Socialism and Scandal: the Sexual Politics of the Early Labour Movement', *History Workshop Journal*, 23, 1987.

Collini, Stefan, *Public Moralists: Political Thought and Intellectual Life in Britain, 1850–1930*, Cambridge, Clarendon Press, 1991.

Collini, Stefan, *Liberalism and Sociology*, Cambridge University Press, 1979.

Cominos, Peter T., 'Late-Victorian Sexual Respectability and the Social System', *International Review of Social History* 8, 1963.

Conway, Jill, 'Stereotypes of *Femininity* in a Theory of Sexual Evolution', in

Vicinus, Martha (ed.), *Suffer and be Still*, USA, Indiana University Press, 1976.

Coote, Anna and Campbell, Beatrix, *Sweet Freedom: Struggle for Women's Liberation*, Oxford, Blackwell, 1982.

Cott, Nancy, 'Passionlessness: an Interpretation of Victorian Sexual Ideology, 1790–1850', *Signs* 4, 1979.

Cousins, Jane, *Make It Happy*, London, Virago, 1978.

Coveney, L. *et al*, *The Sexuality Papers: Male Sexuality and the Social Control of Women*, London, Hutchinson, 1984.

Coward, Rosalind, *Patriarchal Precedents: Sexuality and Social Relations*, London, Routledge and Kegan Paul, 1983.

Coward, Rosalind, 'Sexual Violence and Sexuality', *Feminist Review* 11, 1982.

Davidoff, Leonore, *The Best Circles*, London, Croom Helm, 1982.

Davidoff, Leonore and Hall, Catherine, *Family Fortunes: Men and Women of the English Middle Class, 1790–1850*, London, Hutchinson, 1987.

Davin, Anna, 'Imperialism and Motherhood', *History Workshop Journal* 5, 1978.

Davis, Tracy C., *Actresses as Working Women*, London, Routledge, 1991.

Delamont, Sara and Duffin, Lorna (eds.), *Nineteenth-Century Woman*, London, Croom Helm, 1978.

Dixon, Joy, '"Spiritual Androgynes": Women and Men in the Theosophical Society in England, 1880–1920', unpublished paper, 1988.

Donald, James and Rattansi, Ali (eds.), *'Race', Culture and Difference*, London, Sage, 1992.

Donzelot, Jacques, *The Policing of Families*, London, Hutchinson, 1979.

Doughan, David and Sanchez, Denise (eds.) *Feminist Periodicals 1855–1984*, Sussex, Harvester Press, 1987.

Duberman, Martin *et al* (eds.), *Hidden from History: Reclaiming the Gay and Lesbian Past*, London, Penguin, 1991.

Duffin, Lorna, 'Prisoners of Progress: Women and Evolution', in Delamont, Sara and Duffin, Lorna, *The Nineteenth-Century Woman*, London, Croom Helm, 1978.

Durant, John R., 'Scientific Naturalism and Social Reform in the Thought of Alfred Russel Wallace', *British Journal for the History of Science*, vol. 12, no. 40, 1979.

Durham, Martin, 'USA: Abortion and Politics of Morality', *Parliamentary Affairs*, vol. 47, no. 2, April 1994.

Durham, Martin, *Sex and Politics: the Family and Morality in the Thatcher Years*, London, Macmillan, 1991.

Dyhouse, Carol, *Feminism and the Family in England, 1880–1939*, Oxford, Blackwell, 1989.

Dyhouse, Carol, *Girls Growing Up in Late Victorian and Edwardian England*, London, Routledge and Kegan Paul, 1981.

Dyhouse, Carol, 'Social Darwinistic Ideas and the Development of Women's Education in England, 1880–1920', *History of Education*, vol. 5, no. 1, 1976.

Elston, Mary-Ann, 'Women and Anti-Vivisection in Victorian England, 1870–1900', in Rupke, N.A. (ed.), *Vivisection in Historical Perspective*, London, Croom Helm, 1987.

Epstein, Deborah, '"Neither Pairs nor Odd": Female Community in Late Nineteenth-Century London', *Signs* 15, 1990.

Faderman, Lillian, *Odd Girls and Twilight Lovers: a History of Lesbian Life in Twentieth-Century America*, London, Penguin, 1992.

Faderman, Lillian, *Surpassing the Love of Men*, London, Junction Books, 1981.

Farrall, Lyndsay, *The Origins and Growth of the English Eugenics Movement, 1865–1915*, New York and London, Garland Publishing Inc., 1985.

Farrall, Lyndsay, 'Controversy and Conflict in Science: a Case Study – the English Biometric School and Mendel's Laws', *Social Studies of Science*, 1975.

Fee, Elizabeth, 'Nineteenth-Century Craniology: the Study of the Female Skull', *Bulletin of History of Medicine* 53, 1979.

Feminist Anthology Collective, *No Turning Back*, London, The Women's Press, 1981.

First, Ruth and Scott, Ann, *Olive Schreiner: a Biography*, London, André Deutsch, 1980.

Fleming, G.H., *Victorian 'Sex Goddess': Lady Colin Campbell and the Sensational Divorce Case of 1886*, Oxford University Press, 1990.

Foot, Paul, *Immigrants and Race in British Politics*, London, Penguin, 1965.

Forrest, D.W., *Francis Galton*, London, Elek, 1974.

Forster, Margaret, *Significant Sisters*, London, Penguin, 1984.

Foucault, Michel, *The History of Sexuality Vol. 1: an Introduction*, London, Allen Lane, 1979.

Foucault, Michel, *Birth of the Clinic*, London, Tavistock Publications, 1973.

Freeden, Michael, *The New Liberalism: an Ideology of Social Reform*, Oxford, Clarendon Press, 1978.

Froggart, P. and Nevin, N.C., 'The "Law of Ancestral Heredity" in the Mendelian-Ancestrian Controversy in England, 1889–1906', *Journal of Medical Genetics*, vol. 8, 1971.

Fryer, Peter, *The Birth Controllers*, London, Secker & Warburg, 1965.

Garner, Les, *A Brave and Beautiful Spirit: Dora Marsden 1882–1961*, Aldershot, Avebury, 1990.

Garnett, Jane and Matthew, Colin (eds.), *Revival and Religions since 1700: Essays for John Walsh*, London, Hambleton Press, 1993.

Gay, Peter, *Education of the Senses: the Bourgeois Experience Victoria to Freud Vol. 1*, New York, Oxford University Press, 1984.

Gilbert, Bentley B., *The Evolution of National Insurance*, London, Michael Joseph, 1966.

Gilbert, Sandra M. and Gubar, Susan, *No Man's Land: the Place of the Woman Writer in the Twentieth Century Vol. 2: Sexchanges*, New Haven and London, Yale University Press, 1989.

Gilman, Sander L., 'Black Bodies, White Bodies: towards an Iconography of Female Sexuality in Late Nineteenth-Century Art, Medicine and Literature', *Critical Inquiry* 12, Autumn 1985.

Glendinning, Victoria, *Rebecca West: a Life*, London, Weidenfeld & Nicolson, 1987.

Goldberg, D. (ed.), *The Anatomy of Racism*, Minneapolis, University of Minnesota Press, 1990.

Gordon, Linda, 'Why Nineteenth-Century Feminists did not Support "Birth Control" and Twentieth-Century Feminists do', in Thorne, Barrie and Yalom, Marilyn (eds.), *Rethinking the Family: Some Feminist Questions*, New York and London, Longman, 1982.

Gordon, Linda, *Woman's Body, Woman's Right*, London, Penguin, 1977.

Gordon, Linda and DuBois, Ellen, 'Seeking Ecstasy on the Battlefield: Danger and Pleasure in Nineteenth-Century Feminist Thought', *Feminist Review* 13, 1983.

Gorham, Deborah, '"The Maiden Tribute of Modern Babylon" Re-examined', *Victorian Studies*, Spring 1978.

Gould, Stephen Jay, *The Mismeasure of Man*, London, Penguin, 1981.

Gould, Stephen Jay, *The Panda's Thumb*, London, Penguin, 1980.

Greenway, Judy, 'Sex, Politics and Housework', in Coates, Chris *et al*, *Diggers and Dreamers*, Buckinghamshire, Communes Network, 1993.

Greenway, Judy, 'Uneasy Bedfellows: Free Love, Feminism and Anarchism in the Late Nineteenth and Early Twentieth Century', unpublished paper, 1992.

de Groot, Joanna, '"Sex" and "Race": the Construction of Language and Image in the Nineteenth Century', in Mendus, Susan and Rendall, Jane (eds.), *Sexuality and Subordination*, London, Routledge, 1989.

Hall, Catherine, *White, Male and Middle Class: Explorations in Feminism and History*, London, Polity Press, 1992.

Hall, Lesley, *Hidden Anxieties: Male Sexuality, 1900–1950*, London, Polity Press, 1991.

Hall, Ruth, *Marie Stopes*, London, Virago, 1978.

Hammerton, A. James, *Cruelty and Companionship: Conflict in Nineteenth-Century Married Life*, London and New York, Routledge, 1992.

Hardy, Dennis, *Alternative Communities in Nineteenth-Century England*, London, Longman, 1979.

Harris, Kevin, *Sexual Ideology and Religion: the Representation of Women in the Bible*, Brighton, Wheatsheaf, 1984.

Harrison, Brian, 'State Intervention and Moral Reform in Nineteenth-Century England', in Hollis, Patricia (ed.), *Pressure from Without*, London, Edward Arnold, 1974.

Harrison, K., 'No Means No – That's Final', *New Law Review*, vol. 142, no. 6526, 1991.

Hartman, Mary S., *Victorian Murderesses*, London, Robson Books, 1985.

Hennegan, Alison, Introduction to Hall, Radclyffe, *The Well of Loneliness*, 1928, London, Virago, 1982.

Heyck, T.W., *The Transformation of Intellectual Life in Victorian England*, London, Croom Helm, 1982.

Holden, Pat (ed.), *Women's Religious Experience*, London, Croom Helm, 1983.

Hollis, Patricia, *Ladies Elect: Women in English Local Government 1865–1914*, Oxford, Clarendon Press, 1987.

Hollis, Patricia, *Pressure from Without*, London, Edward Arnold, 1974.

Hollway, Wendy, '"I just wanted to kill a woman." Why? The Ripper and Male Sexuality', *Feminist Review* 9, 1981.

Holton, Sandra Stanley, 'The Suffragist and the "Average Woman"', *Women's History Review*, vol. 1, no. 1, 1992.

Humphries, Stephen, *A Secret World of Sex*, London, Sidgwick & Jackson, 1988.

Hynes, Samuel, *The Edwardian Turn of Mind*, London, Oxford University Press, 1968.

Iacovetta, F. and Valverde, Mariana (eds.), *Expanding Boundaries: New Essays in Women's History*, Canada, University of Toronto Press, 1992.

Irvine, John *et al* (eds.), *Demystifying Social Statistics*, London, Pluto Press, 1979.

Jackson, Margaret, *The Real Facts of Life: Feminism and the Politics of Sexuality*, c. *1850–1940*, London, Taylor and Francis, 1994.

Jackson, Margaret, 'Sexology and the Social Construction of Male Sexuality (Havelock Ellis)', in Covency, L. *et al*, *The Sexuality Papers: Male Sexuality and the Social Control of Women*, London, Hutchinson, 1984.

Jacobus, Mary *et al*, *Body/Politics*, London, Routledge, 1990.

Jalland, Pat, *Women, Marriage and Politics, 1860–1914*, Oxford, Clarendon Press, 1986.

Jeffreys, Sheila, *The Lesbian Heresy*, London, The Women's Press, 1994.

Jeffreys, Sheila, *Anti-climax*, London, The Women's Press, 1990.

Jeffreys, Sheila, *The Spinster and Her Enemies: Feminism and Sexuality, 1880–1930*, London, Pandora Press, 1985.

John, Angela V., *Staging a Life: a Biography of Elizabeth Robins 1862–1952*, London, Routledge, 1995.

Jones, Greta, *Social Darwinism and English Thought: the Interaction between Biological and Social Theory*, Sussex, Harvester Press, 1980.

Jordanova, Ludmilla, *Sexual Visions*, London, Harvester Wheatsheaf, 1989.

Jordanova, Ludmilla (ed.), *Languages of Nature*, London, Free Association Books, 1986.

Jordanova, Ludmilla, ' "Natural Facts": an Historical Perspective on Science and Sexuality', in MacCormick, Carol and Strathern, Marilyn (eds.), *Nature, Culture and Gender*, Cambridge University Press, 1980.

Kabbani, Rana, *Europe's Myths of Orient*, London, Pandora Press, 1986.

Kapp, Yvonne, *Eleanor Marx: the Crowded Years 1884–1898*, London, Virago, 1979.

Katz, Jonathan, 'The Invention of Heterosexuality', *Social Review*, part 21, no. 1, February 1990.

Kazama, Maki, 'Seeking after the New Morality: *The Freewoman*, a radical feminist journal, November 1911 – October 1912', unpublished MA dissertation, York University, 1988.

Kent, Susan Kingsley, *Sex and Suffrage in Britain, 1860–1914*, USA, Princeton University Press, 1987.

Kersley, Gillian, *Darling Madame: Sarah Grand and Devoted Friend*, London, Virago, 1983.

Kevles, Daniel J., *In the Name of Eugenics*, London, Pelican, 1986.

Knight, Patricia, 'Women and Abortion in Victorian and Edwardian England', *History Workshop Journal* 4, 1977.

Krebs, Paula, 'Interpreting South Africa to Britain: Olive Schreiner, Africans and Boers', Societies of southern Africa in the Nineteenth and Twentieth Centuries seminar, Institute of Commonwealth Studies, 1994.

Kuhn, Annette, *The Power of the Image*, London, Routledge and Kegan Paul, 1985.

Lanchester, Elsa, *Elsa Lanchester Herself*, London, Michael Joseph, 1983.

Langan, Mary and Schwarz, Bill (eds.), *Crises in the British State, 1880–1930*, London, Hutchinson, 1985.

Laqueur, Thomas, *Making Sex*, Cambridge, Massachusetts and London, Harvard University Press, 1990.

Leathard, Audrey, *The Fight for Family Planning*, London, Macmillan, 1980.

Ledbetter, Rosanna, *A History of the Malthusian League 1877–1927*, Columbus, Ohio State Press, 1976.

Lees, Sue, *Sugar and Spice*, London, Penguin, 1993.

Legg, L.G. Wickham (ed.), *Dictionary of National Biography, 1931–49*, Oxford University Press, 1949.

Leidhold, Dorchen and Raymond, Janice (eds.), *The Sexual Liberals and the Attack on Feminism*, Oxford, Pergamon Press, 1990.

Levine, Philippa, 'Venereal disease, Prostitution and the Politics of the Empire: the Case of British India', *Journal of the History of Sexuality*, vol. 4, no. 4, 1994.

Levine, Philippa, '"Walking the Streets in a Way No Decent Woman Should": Women Police in World War I', *Journal of Modern History* 66, March 1994.

Levine, Philippa, *Feminist Lives in Victorian England*, Oxford, Basil Blackwell, 1990.

Levine, Philippa, '"So Few Prizes and So Many Blanks": Marriage and Feminism in Late Nineteenth-Century England', *Journal of British Studies* 28, April 1989.

Levine, Philippa, *Victorian Feminism*, London, Hutchinson, 1987.

Lewis, Jane (ed.), *Labour and Love: Women's Experiences of Home and Family, 1850–1940*, Oxford, Blackwell, 1986.

Lewis, Jane, *The Politics of Motherhood*, London, Croom Helm, 1980.

London Feminist History Group, *The Sexual Dynamics of History*, London, Pluto Press, 1983.

Lorimer, Douglas, *Colour, Class and the Victorians*, Leicester University Press, 1978.

Love, Rosaleen, 'Alice in Eugenics Land: Feminism and Eugenics in the Scientific Careers of Alice Lee and Ethel Elderton', *Annals of Science* 36, 1979.

Luker, Kristine, *Abortion and the Politics of Motherhood*, USA, University of California Press, 1984.

MacCormick, Carol and Strathern, Marilyn (eds.), *Nature, Culture and Gender*, Cambridge University Press, 1980.

McHugh, Paul, *Prostitution and Victorian Social Reform*, London, Croom Helm, 1980.

McKenzie, D., 'Sociobiologists in Competition: the Biometrician–Mendelian Debate', in Webster, Charles (ed.), *Biology, Medicine and Society, 1840–1940*, Cambridge University Press, 1981.

MacKenzie, Norman and Mackenzie, Jeanne (eds.), *The Diary of Beatrice Webb Vol. 1 1873–1892*, London, Virago, 1982.

MacKenzie, Norman and MacKenzie, Jeanne, *The First Fabians*, London, Quartet, 1979.

McLaren, Angus, *A History of Contraception. From Antiquity to the Present Day*, Oxford, Blackwell, 1990.

McLaren, Angus, *Birth Control in Nineteenth-Century England: a Social and Intellectual History*, London, Croom Helm, 1978.

McLeod, Eileen, *Women Working: Prostitution Now*, London, Croom Helm, 1982.

Mahood, Linda, *The Magdalenes: Prostitution in the Nineteenth Century*, London and New York, Routledge, 1990.

Malmgreen, Gail (ed.), *Religion in the Lives of English Women 1760–1930*, London, Croom Helm, 1986.

Manvell, Roger, *The Trial of Annie Besant and Charles Bradlaugh*, London, Elek/Pemberton, 1976.

Marcus, Steven, *The Other Victorians: a Study of Sexuality and Pornography in Mid-Nineteenth-Century England*, 1964, London, Weidenfeld & Nicolson, 1966.

Mazumdar, Pauline, 'The Eugenists and the Residuum: the Problem of the Urban Poor', *Bulletin of Medicine*, vol. 54, no. 2, 1980.

Mendus, Susan and Rendall, Jane (eds.), *Sexuality and Subordination*, London, Routledge, 1989.

Mitchell, Juliet and Oakley, Ann (eds.), *The Rights and Wrongs of Women*, London, Penguin, 1976.

Morantz, Regina Markell, 'Feminism, Professionalism and Germs: the Thoughts of Mary Putnam Jacobi and Elizabeth Blackwell', *American Quarterly*, vol. 34, 1982.

Mort, Frank, *Dangerous Sexualities: Medico-Moral Politics in England since 1830*, London, Routledge and Kegan Paul, 1987.

Moscucci, Ornella, *The Science of Women: Gynaecology and Gender in England, 1800–1929*, Cambridge University Press, 1990.

Moscucci, Ornella, 'The Science of Women: British Gynaecology 1849–1890', D.Phil, Oxford, 1984.

Mosedale, Susan Sleeth, 'Science Corrupted: Victorian Biologists Consider "The Woman Question"', *Journal of the History of Biology*, vol. II, no. 1, Spring 1978.

Mosse, George L., *Nationalism and Sexuality*, USA, University of Wisconsin Press, 1985.

Munday, Felicity, 'Women's Attitudes to Womanhood and Marriage in the Periodical Press, 1885–95', MA dissertation, University of Warwick, 1970.

Nead, Lynda, *The Female Nude*, London, Routledge, 1992.

Nead, Lynda, *Myths of Sexuality: Representations of Women in Victorian Britain*, Oxford, Basil Blackwell, 1988.

Newsome, Stella, *The Women's Freedom League, 1907–1957*, London, Women's Freedom League, *c.* 1960.

Newton, Esther, 'The Mythic Mannish Lesbian: Radclyffe Hall and the New Woman', in Duberman, Martin *et al* (eds.), *Hidden from History: Reclaiming the Gay and Lesbian Past*, London, Penguin, 1991.

Nield Chew, Doris, *The Life and Writings of Ada Nield Chew*, London, Virago, 1982.

Nord, Deborah Epstein, '"Neither Pairs Nor Odd": Female Community in Late Nineteenth-Century London', *Signs* 15, 1990.

Norden, Barbara, 'Campaign against Pornography', *Feminist Review* 35, 1990.

Oakley, Ann, 'Wisewomen and Medicine Men', in Mitchell, Juliet and Oakley, Ann (eds.), *The Rights and Wrongs of Women*, London, Penguin, 1976.

Oldfield, Sybil, *Spinsters of This Parish*, London, Virago, 1984.

Olroyd, D.R., *Darwinian Impacts: an Introduction to the Darwinian Revolution*, Milton Keynes, Open University Press, 1980.

Onlywomen Press, *Love Your Enemy? Debate between Heterosexual Feminism and Political Lesbianism*, Onlywomen Press, 1981.

Owen, Alex, *The Darkened Room: Women, Power and Spiritualism in Late Victorian England*, London, Virago, 1989.

Parmar, Pratibha, 'Rage and Desire: Confronting Pornography', in Chester, Gail and Dickey, Julienne (eds.), *Feminism and Censorship*, Dorset, Prism Press, 1988.

Parry, Noel and Parry, Jose, *The Rise of the Medical Profession*, London, Croom Helm, 1976.

Pearson, Michael, *The Age of Consent*, London, David and Charles, 1972.

Peel, J.D.Y., *Herbert Spencer: the Evolution of a Sociologist*, London, Heinemann, 1971.

Pennybacker, Susan, '"It was not what she said, but the way in which she said it": the London County Council and the Music Halls', in Bailey, Peter (ed.), *Music Hall: the Business of Pleasure*, Milton Keynes, Open University Press, 1986.

Petchesky, Rosalind Pollock, *Abortion and Women's Choice*, London, Verso, 1986.

Peterson, M. Jeanne, 'Dr Acton's Enemy: Medicine, Sex and Society in Victorian England', *Victorian Studies*, Summer 1986.

Peterson, M. Jeanne, *The Medical Profession in Mid-Victorian London*, USA, University of California, 1978.

Pfeffer, Naomi, *The Stork and the Syringe*, London, Polity, 1993.

Pierson, Stanley, *Marxism and the Origins of British Socialism*, Ithaca and London, Cornell University Press, 1973.

Poovey, Mary, *Uneven Developments: the Ideological Work of Gender in Mid-Victorian England*, London, Virago, 1989.

Prebble, John, *The Highland Clearances*, Harmondsworth, Penguin in association with Secker & Warburg, 1969.

Prochaska, F.K., *Women and Philanthropy in Nineteenth-Century England*, Oxford, Clarendon Press, 1980.

Ramazanoglu, Caroline, *Feminism and the Contradictions of Oppression*, London, Routledge, 1989.

Rendall, Jane (ed.), *Equal or Different: Women's Politics, 1800–1914*, Oxford, Blackwell, 1987.

Rendall, Jane, *The Origins of Modern Feminism*, London, Macmillan, 1985.

Richardson, Ruth, *Death, Dissection and the Destitute*, London, Routledge and Kegan Paul, 1988.

Riley, Denise, *Am I That Name? Feminism and the Category of 'Woman' in History*, London, Macmillan, 1988.

Robinson, Paul, *The Modernisation of Sex*, London, Elek, 1976.

Rolley, Katrina, 'Cutting a Dash: the Dress of Radclyffe Hall and Una Troubridge', *Feminist Review* 35, 1990.

Roper, Michael and Tosh, John (eds.), *Manful Assertions: Masculinities in Britain since 1800*, London and New York, Routledge, 1991.

Rose, June, *Marie Stopes and the Sexual Revolution*, London, Faber & Faber, 1992.

Rose, Nikolas, *The Psychological Complex: Psychology, Politics and Society in England, 1869–1939*, London, Routledge and Kegan Paul, 1985.

Rosen, Ruth, *The Lost Sisterhood*, Baltimore and London, Johns Hopkins University Press, 1982.

Ross, Ellen, 'Fierce Questions and Taunts: Married Life in Working-Class London 1870–1914', *Feminist Studies*, vol. 8, no. 3, Fall 1982.

Rover, Constance, *Love, Morals and the Feminists*, London, Routledge and Kegan Paul, 1970.

Rowbotham, Sheila, *A New World for Women: Stella Browne – a Socialist Feminist*, London, Pluto Press, 1977.

Rowbotham, Sheila and Weeks, Jeffrey, *Socialism and the New Life: the Personal and Sexual Politics of Edward Carpenter and Havelock Ellis*, London, Pluto Press, 1977.

Royle, Edward, *Radicals, Secularists and Republicans*, Manchester University Press, 1980.

Rubinstein, David, *A Different World for Women: the Life of Millicent Garrett Fawcett*, London, Harvester Wheatsheaf, 1991.

Rubinstein, David, *Before the Suffragettes: Women's Emancipation in the 1890s*, Brighton, Harvester Press, 1986.

Rupke, N.A. (ed.), *Vivisection in Historical Perspective*, London, Croom Helm, 1897.

Russett, Cynthia Eagle, *Sexual Science: the Victorian Construction of Womanhood*, London, Harvard University Press, 1989.

Rutherford, Jonathan (ed.), *Identity: Community, Culture and Difference*, London, Lawrence and Wishart, 1990.

Ryan, Patricia, 'The Ideology of Feminism in Britain, 1900–1920', unpublished MSc, University of Wales, 1978.

Sahli, Nancy Ann, 'Elizabeth Blackwell, MD (1821–1910): a Biography', unpublished PhD, University of Pennsylvania, 1974.

Said, Edward, *Culture and Imperialism*, London, Vintage, 1994.

St John Stevas, Norman, *Obscenity and the Law*, London, Secker & Warburg, 1956.

Samuel, Raphael, 'The Discovery of Puritanism, 1820–1914: a Preliminary Sketch', in Garnett, Jane and Matthew, Colin (eds.), *Revival and Religion since 1700: Essays for John Walsh*, London, Hambleton Press, 1993.

Savage, Gail, '"The Wilful Communication of a Loathsome Sore": Marital Conflict and Venereal Disease in Victorian England', *Victorian Studies*, Autumn 1990.

Schenk, Faith and Parker, A.S., 'The Activities of the Eugenics Society', *Eugenics Review*, vol. 68, September 1968.

Schonfield, Zuzanna, *The Precariously Privileged*, Oxford University Press, 1987.

Scraton, Phil and Gordon, Paul (eds.), *Causes for Concern*, London, Penguin, 1984.

Searle, G.R., *Eugenics and Politics in Britain, 1900–1914*, Leyden, Noordhoff International, 1976.

Searle, G.R., *The Quest for National Efficiency*, Oxford, Blackwell, 1971.

Sebestyen, Amanda, 'Women against the Demon Drink', *Spare Rib*, no. 100, 1980.

Segal, Lynne and McIntosh, Mary (eds.), *Sex Exposed*, London, Virago, 1992.

Semmel, Bernard, *Imperialism and Social Reform, 1895–1914*, London, Allan & Unwin, 1960.

Sennett, Richard, *The Fall of the Public Man*, Cambridge University Press, 1973.

Shanley, Mary Lyndon, *Feminism, Marriage and the Law in Victorian England, 1850–1895*, London, I.B. Tauris, 1989.

Shapiro, Rose, *Contraception*, London, Virago, 1987.

Shiman, Lillian, '"Changes are Dangerous": Women and Temperance in Victorian England', in Malmgreen, Gail (ed.), *Religion in the Lives of English Women, 1760–1930*, London, Croom Helm, 1986.

Showalter, Elaine, *Sexual Anarchy: Gender and Culture at the Fin de Siècle*, London, Bloomsbury, 1991.

Showalter, Elaine, *The Female Malady: Women, Madness and English Culture, 1830–1930*, London, Virago, 1987.

Showalter, Elaine, 'Syphilis, Sexuality and the Fiction of the *Fin de Siècle*', in Yeazell, Ruth (ed.), *Sex, Politics and Science in the Nineteenth-Century Novel*, Baltimore, Johns Hopkins University Press, 1986.

Showalter, Elaine, *A Literature of Their Own: British Women Novelists from Brontë to Lessing*, London, Virago, 1979.

Shuttleworth, Sally, 'Female Circulation: Medical Discourse and Popular Advertising in the Mid-Victorian Era', in Jacobus, Mary *et al*, *Body/Politics*, London, Routledge, 1990.

Siegel, Sandra, 'Literature: the Representation of "Decadence" ', in Chamberlin, J. and Gilman, Sander (eds.), *Degeneration: the Dark Side of Progress*, USA, Columbia University Press, 1985.

Simmons, Harvey, 'Explaining Social Policy: the English Mental Deficiency Act of 1913', *Journal of Social History*, vol. 11, no. 3, 1978.

Smart, Carol and Brophy, Julia (eds.), *Women in Law*, London, Routledge and Kegan Paul, 1985.

Smith, F.B., 'Sexuality in Britain, 1800–1900: Some Suggested Revisions', in Vicinus, Martha (ed.), *A Widening Sphere: Changing Roles of Victorian Women*, USA, Indiana University Press, 1977.

Smith, F.B., 'Labouchère's Amendment to the Criminal Law Amendment Bill', *Historical Studies*, 67, 1976.

Smith, Joan, *Misogynies*, London, Faber and Faber, 1989.

Smith, W. Sylvester, *The London Heretics, 1870–1914*, London, Constable, 1967.

Smith-Rosenburg, Carroll, 'A Richer and Gentler Sex', *Social Research*, vol. 53, no. 2, Summer 1986.

Smith-Rosenburg, Carroll, *Disorderly Conduct: Visions of Gender in Victorian America*, Oxford University Press, 1985.

Snitow, Ann *et al* (eds.), *Desire: the Politics of Sexuality*, London, Virago, 1984.

Soloway, Richard Allan, *Birth Control and the Population Question in England, 1877–1930*, Chapel Hill and London, University of North Carolina Press, 1982.

Southern Women's Writing Collective, 'Sex Resistance in Heterosexual Arrangements', in Leidhold, Dorchen and Raymond, Janice (eds.), *The Sexual Liberals and the Attack on Feminism*, Oxford, Pergamon Press, 1990.

Spelman, Elizabeth, *Inessential Woman*, London, The Women's Press, 1988.

Spender, Dale, *There's Always been a Women's Movement This Century*, London, Pandora, 1983.

Stallybrass, Peter and White, Allon, *The Politics and Poetics of Transgression*, London, Methuen, 1986.

Stanley, Liz, *The Auto/biographical I*, Manchester University Press, 1992.

Stanley, Liz (ed.), *The Diaries of Hannah Cullwick*, London, Virago, 1984.

Stearns, Carol Z. and Stearns, Peter N., 'Victorian Sexuality: Can Historians do Better?' *Journal of Social History*, vol. 18, no. 4, 1985.

Stedman Jones, Gareth, *Outcast London: a Study in the Relationship between Classes in Victorian Society*, London, Penguin, 1976.

Stedman Jones, Gareth, 'Working-Class Culture and Working-Class Politics in London, 1870–1900', *Journal of Social History*, Summer, 1974.

Steedman, Carolyn, *Childhood, Culture and Class in Britain: Mary Macmillan 1860–1931*, London, Virago, 1990.

Stepan, Nancy, 'Race and Gender: the Role of Analogy in Science', in Goldberg, D. (ed.), *The Anatomy of Racism*, Minneapolis, University of Minnesota Press, 1990.

Stepan, Nancy, 'Biological Degeneration: Race and Proper Places', in Chamberlin, J. and Gilman, Sander (eds.), *Degeneration: the Dark Side of Progress*, USA, Columbia University Press, 1985.

Stepan, Nancy, *The Idea of Race in Science: Great Britain 1800–1960*, London, Macmillan, 1982.

Stokes, John, *In the Nineties*, London, Harvester Wheatsheaf, 1989.

Storch, Robert, 'Police Control of Street Prostitution in Victorian London', in Bayley, David (ed.), *Police and Society*, London, Sage, 1977.

Sulloway, Frank J., *Freud, Biologist of the Mind*, London, Fontana, 1980.

Summerfield, Penny, 'The Effingham Arms and the Empire: Deliberate Selection in the Evolution of Music Hall in London', in Yeo, Eileen and Yeo, Stephen (eds.), *Popular Culture and Class Conflict 1590–1914*, Sussex, Harvester Press, 1981.

Summers, Anne, 'The Correspondence of Havelock Ellis', *History Workshop Journal*, 32, 1991.

Summers, Anne, *Angels and Citizens: British Women as Military Nurses, 1854–1914*, London, Routledge and Kegan Paul, 1988.

Summers, Anne, 'A Home from Home – Women's Philanthropic Work in the Nineteenth Century', in Burman, Sandra, *Fit Work for Women*, London, Croom Helm, 1979.

Symondson, A. (ed.), *The Victorian Crisis in Faith*, London, SPCK, 1970.

Tagg, John, 'Power and Photography: a Means of Surveillance', *Screen Education*, no. 36, Autumn 1980.

Taylor, Anne, *Annie Besant: a Biography*, Oxford University Press, 1992.

Thomas, Keith, 'The Double Standard', *Journal of the History of Ideas* 20, 1959.

Thompson, Tierl (ed.), *Dear Girl: the Diaries and Letters of Two Working Women, 1897–1917*, London, The Women's Press, 1987.

Thomson, Mathew P., 'The Problem of Mental Deficiency in England and Wales, *c.* 1913–1946', unpublished D.Phil, Oxford University, 1992.

Thorne, Barrie and Yalom, Marilyn (eds.), *Rethinking the Family: Some Feminist Questions*, New York and London, Longman, 1982.

Tickner, Lisa, *The Spectacle of Women: Imagery of the Suffrage Campaign 1907–1918*, London, Chatto & Windus, 1987.

Tomalin, Claire, *The Invisible Woman: the Story of Nelly Ternan and Charles Dickens*, London, Penguin, 1991.

Tomalin, Claire, *The Life and Death of Mary Wollstonecraft*, London, Penguin, 1977.

Tosh, John, 'Domesticity and Manliness in the Victorian Middle Class', in Roper, Michael and Tosh, John (eds.), *Manful Assertions: Masculinities in Britain since 1800*, London and New York, Routledge, 1991.

Trudgill, Eric, *Madonnas and Magdalens*, London, Heinemann, 1976.

Turnbull, Annemarie, '"So Extremely Like Parliament": the Work of the Women Members of the London School Board, 1870–1904', in the London Feminist History Group, *The Sexual Dynamics of History*, London, Pluto Press, 1983.

Turner, E.S., *Roads to Ruin: the Shocking History of Social Reform*, London, Michael Joseph, 1950.

Valverde, Mariana, 'The Concept of "Race" in First-Wave Feminist, Sexual and Reproductive Politics', in Iacovetta, F. and Valverde, Mariana (eds.), *Expanding Boundaries: New Essays in Women's History*, Canada, University of Toronto Press, 1992.

Valverde, Mariana, *The Age of Light, Soap and Water: Moral Reform in Canada, 1885–1925*, Ontario, McLelland and Stewart Inc., 1991.

Valverde, Mariana, '"The Love of Finery": Fashion and the Fallen Woman in Nineteenth-Century Social Discourse', *Victorian Studies*, Winter 1989.

Valverde, Mariana, 'A Passion for Purity', *Women's Review of Books*, vol. V, no. 4, January 1988.

VanArsdel, Rosemary T., 'Florence Fenwick Miller, 1854–1935: a Life of Many Choices', unpublished manuscript, London, Fawcett Library, 1990.

Vicinus, Martha, 'Distance and Desire: English Boarding School Friendships, 1870–1920', in Duberman, Martin *et al* (eds.), *Hidden from History: Reclaiming the Gay and Lesbian Past*, London, Penguin, 1991.

Vicinus, Martha, *Independent Women: Work and Community for Single Women 1850–1920*, London, Virago, 1985.

Vicinus, Martha, '"One Life to Stand beside Me": Emotional Conflicts in

First-Generation College Women in England', *Feminist Studies*, vol. 8, no. 3, Fall 1982.

Vicinus, Martha (ed.), *A Widening Sphere: Changing Roles of Victorian Women*, London, Methuen & Co. Ltd, 1980.

Vicinus, Martha (ed.), *Suffer and be Still*, USA, Indiana University Press, 1976.

Walker, Pamela J., '"I live but not yet I for Christ liveth in me": Men and Masculinity in the Salvation Army, 1865–90', in Roper, Michael and Tosh, John (eds.), *Manful Assertions: Masculinities in Britain since 1800*, London and New York, Routledge, 1991.

Walkowitz, Judith, *City of Dreadful Delight: Narratives of Sexual Danger in Late Victorian London*, London, Virago, 1992.

Walkowitz, Judith, 'Science, Feminism and Romance: the Men and Women's Club, 1885–1889', *History Workshop Journal*, 21, 1986.

Walkowitz, Judith, 'Male Vice and Female Virtue: Feminism and the Politics of Prostitution in Nineteenth-Century Britain', in Snitow, Ann *et al* (eds.), *Desire: the Politics of Sexuality*, London, Virago, 1984.

Walkowitz, Judith, 'Jack the Ripper and the Myth of Male Violence', *Feminist Studies*, vol. 8, no. 3, Fall 1982.

Walkowitz, Judith, 'Male Vice and Female Virtue: Feminism and the Politics of Prostitution in Nineteenth-Century Britain', *History Workshop Journal*, 13, 1982.

Walkowitz, Judith, *Prostitution and Victorian Society*, Cambridge University Press, 1980.

Ward Jouve, Nicole, *The Streetcleaner*, London, Marion Boyars, 1986.

Ware, Vron, *Beyond the Pale: White Women, Racism and History*, London, Verso, 1992.

Watts, Ruth, 'Knowledge is Power – Unitarians, Gender and Education in the Eighteenth and Nineteenth Centuries', *Gender and Education*, vol. 1, no. 1, 1989.

Webster, Charles (ed.), *Biology, Medicine and Sociology, 1840–1940*, Cambridge University Press, 1981.

Weeks, Jeffrey, *Sexuality and Its Discontents*, London, Routledge and Kegan Paul, 1985.

Weeks, Jeffrey, *Sex, Politics and Society: the Regulation of Sexuality since 1800*, London and New York, Longman, 1981.

Weeks, Jeffrey, *Coming Out*, London, Quartet Books, 1977.

Whitbread, Helena (ed.), *I Know My Own Heart: the Diaries of Anne Lister 1791–1840*, London, Virago, 1988.

Whitelegg, Elizabeth *et al*, *The Changing Experience of Women*, Oxford, Martin Robertson, 1982.

Williams, Claire, 'The Destiny of the Race: Women and Eugenics in Late Victorian and Edwardian England', unpublished MA, University of Essex, 1980.

Williams, Raymond, *Keywords: a Vocabulary of Culture and Society*, London, Fontana, 1976.

Wilson, Elizabeth, 'Feminist Fundamentalism', in Segal, Lynne and McIntosh, Mary (eds.), *Sex Exposed*, London, Virago, 1992.

Wilson, Elizabeth, *The Sphinx in the City*, London, Virago, 1991.

Wilson, Robin, 'Imperialism in Crisis: the "Irish Dimension"', in Langan, Mary and Schwarz, Bill (eds.), *Crises in the British State, 1880–1930*, London, Hutchinson, 1985.

Wiltshire, David, *The Social and Political Thought of Herbert Spencer*, Oxford University Press, 1978.

Wittinger, Catherine, *Annie Besant and Progressive Messianism, 1847–1933*, Lewiston/Queeston, The Edwin Mellen Press, 1988.

Yeazell, Ruth (ed.), *Sex, Politics and Science in the Nineteenth-Century Novel*, Baltimore, Johns Hopkins University Press, 1986.

Yeo, Eileen and Yeo, Stephen (eds.), *Popular Culture and Class Conflict 1590–1914*, Sussex, Harvester Press, 1981.

Young, Robert, 'The Impact of Darwin on Conventional Thought', in Symondson, A. (ed.), *The Victorian Crisis in Faith*, London, SPCK, 1970.

Young, Robert, 'Malthus and the Evolutionists', *Past and Present*, no. 43, May 1969.

INDEX

Scharlieb, Mary, 232, 289
Schreiner, Olive, 4, 6, 8, 14–16, 20–
    21, 25, 32, 35, 40, 44–6, 119,
    126, 265–6
self-control, sexual, 283–6
separate spheres, xviii, 50
sex and language, 273–7
sex education, 59, 125, 139–43, 182,
    306, 314
sexology, 54, 256–65, 278–80, 290–
    96, 307
sexual
  abuse, 252–3
  assault, 253–6
  relations, inter-racial, 62–3
  violence, 252–6, 309–10
sexuality, female, 49, 258–61, 286–7
  and religion, 62
  and reproduction, 271–3
  medical constructions of, 54–70
  reproductive physiology, 63–7
sexuality, male
  medical constructions of, 54–8
sexuality, 'primitive', 57
Sharpe, Loetitia, 18–19, 33–4, 37,
    39, 42, 67, 214
Sharpe, Maria, 7–8, 10, 14–45, 52,
    151, 166, 173–82, 197
Showalter, Elaine, xviii, 118
Simcox, Edith, 50
Simmons, Minna, 170
Sinclair, Upton, 281
Slate, Ruth, 170
Slawson, Eva, 170
Smith-Rosenberg, Carroll, 258, 289
Social Democratic Federation, 159,
    161
social purity movement, 52, 95–123
sociology, 48–9
Somerset, Isabel, 96, 109
Spencer, Herbert, 89, 225

spinsterhood, 61–3, 161–4, 168,
    170–71, 178, 257, 281–3
Stead, W. T., xiv–xv, 8–9, 119, 153,
    156, 297–8, 301
  'The Maiden Tribute of Modern
    Babylon', xv, xvi, xvii, 7–9,
    23, 58–60, 100
sterilization, 239–40
Stockham, Alice B., 284
Sullivan, James, 159–60
Swiney, Frances, 217–22, 230, 233,
    246

Tait, Lawson, 56, 65–6
Tasker, Amy, 292–3
temperance, 98, 110–11, 114
theosophy, 167–8
Thicknesse, Ralph, 8–9, 32, 34, 38,
    140
Thompson, Tierl, 170
Thompson, William, 132

Valverde, Mariana, 301
venereal disease, 146–9, 183, 185,
    236–7, 243–6
Vicinus, Martha, 162, 261
Vickery, Alice, 202, 203, 207–9,
    212–13, 219–20, 233
Vigilance Association (Personal
    Rights Association), 100–101
Vigilance Record, 95, 103, 105–6
virginity, 178

Wade, Willoughby, 56
Walkowitz, Judith, xix, 112, 118,
    119, 175
Walters, Mrs, 14–15
Ward, Lester, 220
Ware, Vron, 62
Watson, Edith, 253, 285
Wells, Ida B., 31, 62